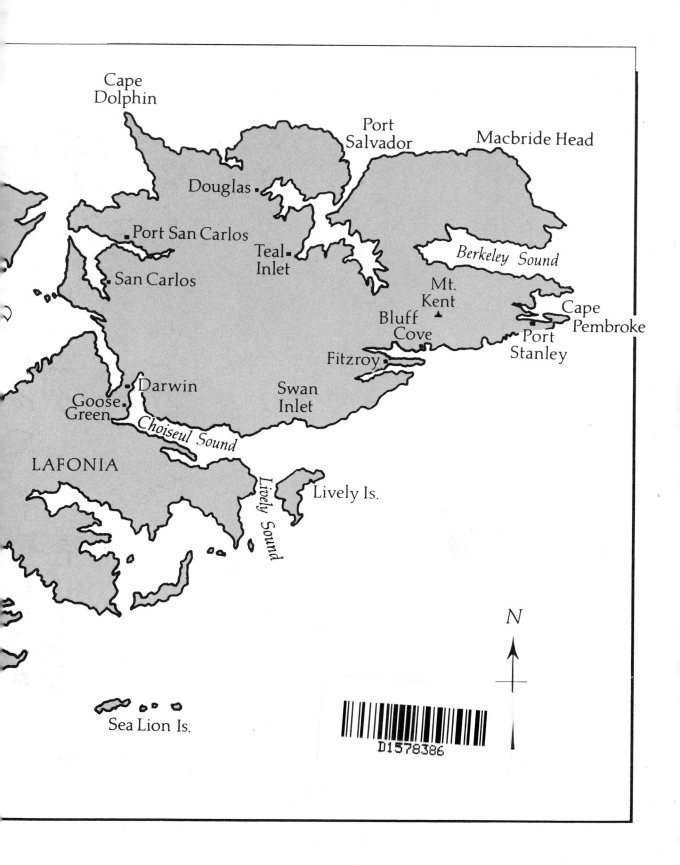

Cape
Dolphin

Port
Salvador

Macbride Head

Douglas .

Port San Carlos .

Teal .
Inlet

Berkeley Sound

San Carlos .

Mt.
Kent
▲

Cape
Pembroke

Bluff
Cove

Port
Stanley

Fitzroy .

Darwin .

Swan
Inlet

Goose .
Green

Choiseul Sound

LAFONIA

Lively Sound

Lively Is.

N

Sea Lion Is.

D1578386

The
Royal Navy
and the
**Falklands
War**

The Royal Navy
and the
Falklands
War

David Brown

Head of the Naval Historical Branch

Leo Cooper

London

First published 1987 by Leo Cooper Ltd.

Leo Cooper is an independent imprint of
the Heinemann Group of Publishers,
10 Upper Grosvenor Street, London W1X 9PA.

LONDON MELBOURNE JOHANNESBURG AUCKLAND

ISBN 0–85052–0592

Designed by Brooke Calverley

Printed by Redwood Burn Limited
Trowbridge, Wiltshire

Contents

Introduction

This book was conceived as a tribute to all those who took part in and contributed to the success of Operation 'Corporate', in particular those of the naval services – the Royal Navy, Royal Fleet Auxiliary, Royal Marine Auxiliary Service, the Merchant Navy, the Queen Alexandra's Royal Naval Nursing Service and the Royal Marines, as well as all the men of the Army and Royal Air Force who found themselves attached to naval and Marines units. Behind the men 'at the sharp end', there were the legions of the staffs and organizations which kept the ships at sea and maintained the Commando Brigade on the far shore – condemned in time of peace as the excessive 'tail', in war they showed that they were none too numerous. As might have been expected, British industry provided wholehearted and unstinted support, rising to a new challenge every day, as it seemed, during the two and a half months of active hostilities. With the parts played by the other Services and their contributors, teeth and tail were united to form the body corporate which succeeded in restoring British rule in the Falkland Islands and South Georgia.

Although many might feel that their contribution is not fully reflected in the following pages, only in one area is this intentional. For reasons which they well know, the doings of the submariners must remain discreetly unreported for the time being and it must suffice to say that all those who served in the South Atlantic are in the debt of the men of the six submarines which provided the advanced guard and then the first line of defence against the Argentine Navy. That the Fleet did not venture forth after the example of the *General Belgrano* does not detract from the dangers and discomforts of long patrols, often in shallow and inadequately charted waters, right up to the time of the Argentine Government's acceptance that the campaign was over.

I am grateful for the ready assistance and guidance of many officers and men of the Royal Navy and Royal Marines who took part in the various aspects of the campaign. Without their help it would not have been possible to piece together, and in some instances reconcile, the various accounts, semi-official, private and published, British and Argentine, which have been used to compile this narrative. I am also indebted to Admiral Sir Peter Stanford KCB MVO, the Vice Chief of the Naval Staff from 1982 to 1984, and to Mr Alistair Jaffray CB, the Deputy Under-Secretary of State for the Royal Navy until 1984, for their permission and encouragement to undertake this work.

David Brown
June, 1984

Although what follows is published by permission of the Ministry of Defence, any opinions which may be expressed are my own and do not represent those of the Ministry, the Navy Department or the Naval Service as a whole.

DB
September, 1986

Maps

View over Two Sisters of the final battlefields,
Wireless Ridge to the left, running down to Navy
Point, and the tangled summits of Mount
Tumbledown to the right, overlooking Port Stanley
(via Captain S.H.G. Johnston RN)

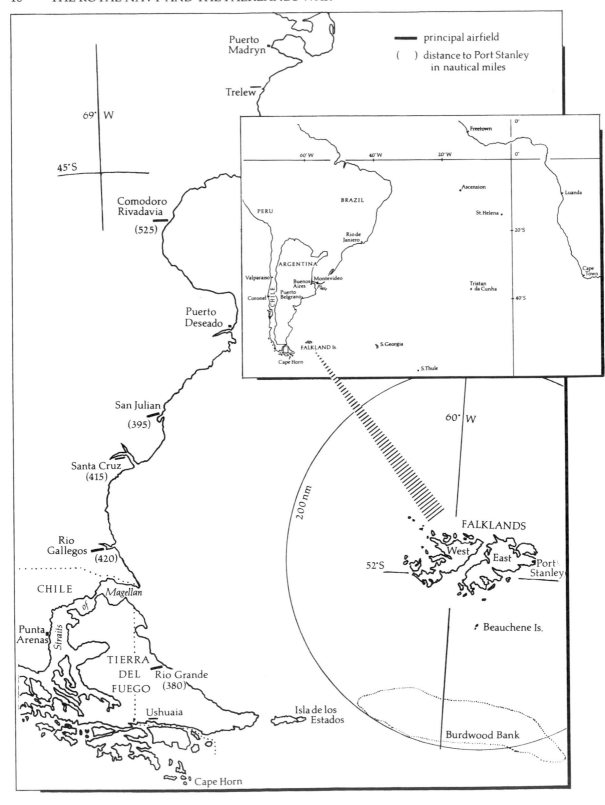

principal airfield

( ) distance to Port Stanley in nautical miles

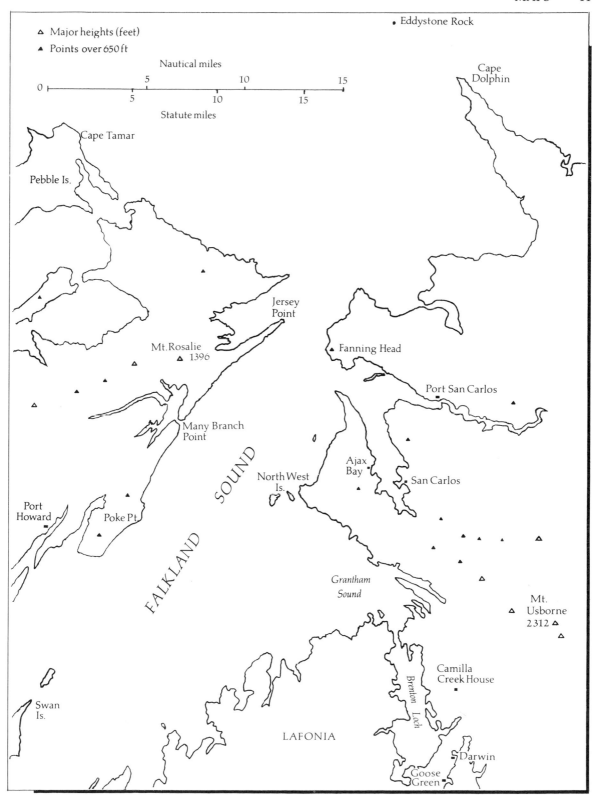

• Eddystone Rock

△ Major heights (feet)
▲ Points over 650 ft

Nautical miles

0   5   10   15

5   10   15

Statute miles

Cape Dolphin

Cape Tamar

Pebble Is.

Jersey Point

Mt. Rosalie
△ 1396

Fanning Head

Port San Carlos

Many Branch Point

FALKLAND SOUND

North West Is.

Ajax Bay

San Carlos

Port Howard

Poke Pt

Grantham Sound

Mt. Usborne
2312 △

Camilla Creek House

Swan Is.

Brenton Loch

LAFONIA

Darwin

Goose Green

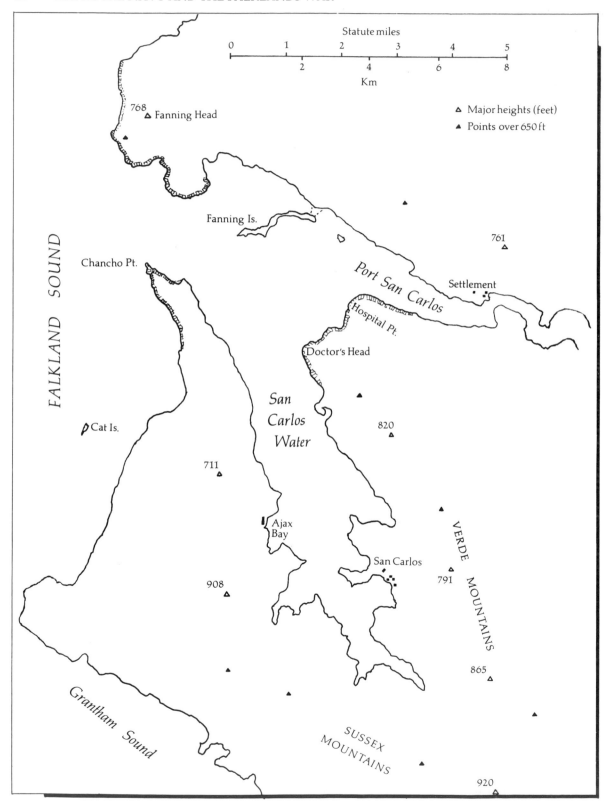

Statute miles

0   1   2   3   4   5

2   4   6   8

Km

△ Major heights (feet)

▲ Points over 650 ft

768 △ Fanning Head

FALKLAND SOUND

Fanning Is.

Port San Carlos

761 △

Settlement

Chancho Pt.

Hospital Pt.

Doctor's Head

San Carlos Water

Cat Is.

820 △

711 △

Ajax Bay

San Carlos

VERDE MOUNTAINS

791 △

908 △

865 △

Grantham Sound

SUSSEX MOUNTAINS

920 △

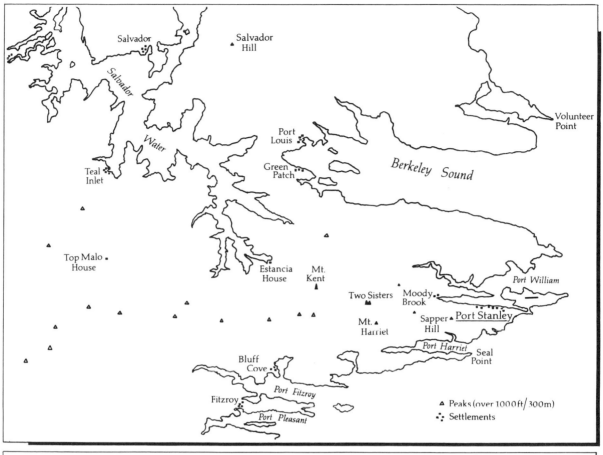

Peaks (over 1000 ft / 300 m) ▲
Settlements ⦂·

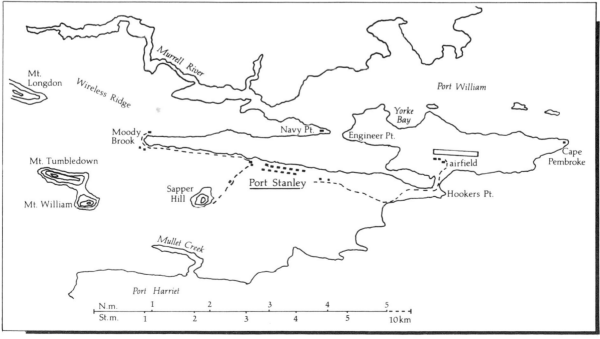

Glossary

AAC   Army Air Corps (British)

Aden   30mm aircraft cannon (British)

AEW   Airborne Early Warning (radar)

Agave   French multi-purpose airborne radar fitted in Super Etendard – associated with AM.39 Exocet missile

AIM-9   Sidewinder air-to-air missile, carried by Sea Harrier (-9G and -9L) and A-4Q Skyhawk (-9B)

AOA   Amphibious Operating Area – the land and sea area in the vicinity of the landing beaches and the amphibious shipping anchorage: in practice, San Carlos Water and Port San Carlos and the surrounding hills, together with the northern part of the Falkland Sound outside San Carlos Water. Became the Transport Area from 1 June, 1982

ARA   *Armada Republica Argentina*: Navy of the Argentine Republic

AS.12   Air-to-surface missile carried by RN Wasp helicopters (see Appendix I)

ASW   Anti-Submarine Warfare

Avcat   High flash-point kerosene-based aviation fuel used by RN carrier-based turbine-engined aircraft

Avgas   Low flash-point aviation gasoline (petrol)

BAM   *Base Aerea Militar*: Military (ie Air Force) Air Base, eg
    Dr Mariano Moreno (Buenos Aires)
    Comodoro Rivadavia
    Condor (Goose Green)
    El Palomar (Buenos Aires)
    Malvinas (Port Stanley)
    Mendoza
    Reconquista (Santa Fe Province)
    Rio Gallegos
    Tandil

BAN   *Base Aerea Naval*: Naval Air Base, eg
    Bahia Blanca ('Comandante Espora')
    Calderon (or Borbon) (Pebble Is.)
    Rio Grande ('Almirante Quijada')
    Trelew ('Almirante Zar')   Ushuaia

BAS   British Antarctic Survey – a scientific research organization funded by the British Government to conduct research in the Antarctic and Falkland Islands Dependencies

Bergen   Royal Marines Arctic back-pack

Blowpipe   man-portable, shoulder-launched surface-to-air missile used by British and Argentine ground forces

BMA   Brigade Maintenance Area (British); the military logistic support area, including workshops and medical facilities as well as ammunition, stores, fuel and provisions dumps

CAP   Combat Air Patrol: originally a defensive fighter mission but subsequently extended to any air-to-air fighter mission

Carl Gustav   84mm recoilless anti-tank weapon (Swedish-built, used by Royal Marines)

Casevac   *Casualty Evac*uation (usually by helicopter)

CdoFAS   *Comando de la Fuerza Aerea Sur*: Southern Air Command – the Argentine Air Force operational control headquarters based at Comodoro Rivadavia

Chaff   Metallic foil, launched by ships or released from aircraft to form radar reflecting clouds to distract or confuse missile homing heads or human operators

COMAW   Commodore, Amphibious Warfare (British)

'Corporate'   The overall code-name bestowed upon the operation to recover the Falkland Islands. Individual operations within the framework of 'Corporate' received separate names

Dracone   'Sausage-shaped' flexible towed bulk fuel container; buoyancy provided by the contents, which have a lower specific gravity than water

Dieso   Diesel-type light oil fuel burned by RN steam and turbine-engined ships and also usable by Wasp helicopters

ECM Electronic Counter Measures – active anti-radio/radar techniques and tactics, particularly 'jamming' of transmissions

Elta Israeli electronics firm: an Elta target-indicating radar was installed at Goose Green to support the Argentine Air Force 20mm AA guns

Elint Electronic Intelligence – the gathering of data by ESM (qv) techniques

ESM Electronic Support Measures – passive techniques and tactics, particularly the interception of radio and radar transmissions

Exocet Surface-to-surface (MM.38) and air-to-surface (AM.39) homing missile; (see Appendix I)

FAA *Fuerza Aerea Argentina*: Argentine Air Force

FCO Foreign and Commonwealth Office (British)

FFO Furnace Fuel Oil – a heavy fuel oil burned by a few older steam ships (eg HMS *Hermes* and SS *Queen Elizabeth II*)

FIMEZ Falkland Islands Maritime Exclusion Zone: a 200-mile radius zone centred on 51–40' South 59–30' West (2 miles south-east of the entrance to Port Howard), announced by the British Government on 7 April, 1982, and effective from 0400 GMT (midnight local) on 12 April

FOB Forward Operating Base (helicopters)

GPMG 7.62mm General-Purpose Machine Gun (belt-fed), used by infantry on bipod or tripod mount, in ships and helicopters on a pintle mount

GR3 Harrier GR3 – the short form used to differentiate between the Sea Harrier and the RAF Harrier (see SHAR)

ICRC International Commission of the Red Cross

IFF Identification Friend or Foe – an ultra-high frequency radio interrogator and transponder system used in association with warning radars to differentiate between known friendly and hostile or unidentified contacts

Landing Craft
and Ships for details see Appendices I, II, IV

LCU Landing Craft, Utility (British)

LCVP Landing Craft, Vehicles and Personnel

LPD Landing Platform, Dock (British)

LSL Landing Ship, Logistic (British)

LST Landing Ship, Tank (Argentine)

Lepus High-candlepower flare for illumination of surface targets, released by Sea Harriers

LGB Laser-guided bomb – a 1,000lb (454 kg) aircraft bomb with a nose attachment featuring a laser seeker, guidance unit and control fins. The seeker picks up reflected 'beams' from an object illuminated by a laser target-marker and the guidance unit converts the input to command signals to home the bomb (US Air Force code-name 'Paveway') on to the source of the reflection

LMG Light Machine Gun – the 1938 Bren Gun re-chambered and re-barrelled to fire 7.62mm ammunition

'Lola' Logistic Loitering Area – the holding area east of the TEZ (qv) used by RFAs and STUFT supporting but not in company with the Carrier Battle Group

LVT Landing Vehicle, Tracked – an amphibious armoured personnel carrier used by the Argentine Marine Corps

Marisat Maritime Satellite communications system – used by auxiliary and merchant vessels

Mexeflote Motorised pontoon platform, operated by Royal Corps of Transport and carried to the operational area on the sides of some LSLs

Milan Wire-guided anti-tank missile (of Franco-German origin) in service with the Royal Marines and British Army; used with success for engaging bunkers

Mile A nautical mile is equal to one degree of latitude at the Equator and, unlike the equivalents which follow, is a natural unit of measurement of distance, used universally for sea navigation and very widely for air navigation

= 6,080 feet
= 1.1515 statute miles
= 1.7371 versts
= 1.8532 kilometres

NGS Naval Gunfire Support – bombardment of shore targets by warships, not necessarily in direct tactical support of military operations

Omega Very-low-frequency automatic world-wide commercial navigation system, used by shipping and aircraft (including some Argentine Air Force tactical squadrons)

'Paraquet' Code-name given to operation to recover South Georgia: reputedly intended to be 'Paraquat' (a commercial weed-killer), the meaningless corruption originating from a typist's error

PNG Passive Night Goggles – image-intensifying night vision aids used by specially-trained RN Sea King Mark 4 pilots for low-level overland flying, specifically for landing and extracting Special Forces reconnaissance teams

R.530 French air-to-air missile (radar or infra-red homing) carried by Dassault Mirage IIIEA interceptor

Rapier Trailer-mounted surface-to-air missile system operated by Royal Artillery and RAF Regiment batteries

RAS	Replenishment at Sea (pronounced 'Razz') – transfer of liquid [RAS(L)] or solid [RAS(S)] stores between ships underway (see also 'Vertrep')
RFA	Royal Fleet Auxiliary – merchant-manned fleet of Ministry of Defence-owned support vessels (and landing ships) operated on behalf of the Royal Navy
RMAS	Royal Maritime Auxiliary Service (formerly Port Auxiliary Service – PAS) – broadly, the counterpart of the RFA for inshore and harbour support tasks, but also with responsibility for ocean salvage
RNSTS	Royal Navy Supply and Transport Service – the civilian supply and issuing organization responsible for the timely provision of all non-fuel stores to the Fleet (the personnel embark in RFAs and, during 'Corporate', STUFT)
Roland	Tracked-vehicle-mounted surface-to-air missile (French) deployed by Argentine Army at Port Stanley
'Rosario'	The code-name for the Argentine invasion of the Falkland Islands
SA–7	Soviet 'Strela' (NATO code-name 'Grail') man-portable shoulder-launched surface-to-air missile (infra-red homing) – supplied to Argentine forces by Peru in May, 1982
Seacat	Short-range surface-to-air missile (RN and Argentine Navy)
Sea Dart	Medium-range surface-to-air missile (RN and Argentine Navy)
Sea Skua	Short-range air-to-surface (RN helicopters)
Seaslug	Medium-range surface-to-air missile (RN)
Sea Wolf	Short-range surface-to-air missile (RN) (for details of these naval missiles, see Appendix I)
Shafrir	Israeli-built air-to-air missile (infra-red homing) supplied with Dagger fighters – reputedly a development of the Sidewinder AIM–9B
SHAR	Sea Harrier – the abbreviated form used on 'State Boards' and in signals was generally adopted as a nickname for the fighter.
Shrike	(AGM–45A) US-supplied air-to-surface 'anti-radiation' missile (homes on radar transmissions) – used by RAF Vulcans
Sidewinder	see AIM–9
'Sixty-Six'	'Bazooka'-type 66mm anti-tank rocket with disposable launcher used, in the absence of tanks, by Royal Marines as a personal close-support weapon (M72)
Ski Jump	An inclined ramp at the forward end of the flight deck of a carrier, for flying off fixed-wing short take-off aircraft. The Sea Harrier accelerates extremely rapidly but, even when heavily loaded, requires a short deck run to reach true flying speed; this is, however, not long enough when less than the full length of the flight deck is available. The invention, by Lieutenant-Commander J. W. Taylor RN, of the ski jump provided, in effect, a 'runway in the sky', the aircraft leaving the ramp on an upward curve, with neither sufficient upward thrust from the 21,500lb-trust Pegasus engine nor sufficient forward speed for wing-borne flight, but sufficient height (and time) for the aircraft to accelerate to 'flying speed', usually reached about 400 yards ahead of the carrier.
Skyguard	Anti-aircraft radar fire control system – used by Argentine Air Force and Army in association with 35mm Oerlikon AA guns
SS.11	Wire-guided anti-tank missile (launched by AAC and Commando Brigade Air Squadron Scout helicopters)
Stinger	Man-portable shoulder-launched surface-to-air missile (infra-red homing) – US-supplied, used only by British Special Forces
STOVL	Short Take-off, Vertical Landing – the preferred mode of operation of the Sea Harrier, which has insufficient power to get airborne vertically when carrying a full fuel and weapons load (see 'Ski Jump')
STUFT	Ships Taken up from Trade – requisitioned or chartered merchant vessels, commanded and manned by Merchant Navy crews (except for the minesweeping trawlers), accompanied by Naval Parties.
'Sutton'	The code-name for the British invasion of East Falkland
TA	Transport Area – the amphibious phase of the recovery of East Falkland came to a close with the break-out of the RM Commandos and Parachute Regiment battalions and the AOA was renamed, with effect from 1 June, 1982
Task Force	A 'family tree' organization for the conduct of operations. The 'Task Force' embraced all formations allocated to the operation; the 'Task Groups' were the largest self-contained subordinate commands and detached 'Task Units' for specific missions, during which certain roles could be further delegated to 'Task Elements'. All were numbered in a sequence which took as a basic 'root' the identity of the next most senior command. Thus, TE 317.8.2.3 was a ship on the screen (TU 317.8.2) of the Carrier Battle Group (TG 317.8), under the direct orders of Commander-in-Chief Fleet (Commander, TF 317)

TEZ — Total Exclusion Zone: geographically the same area as the FIMEZ (qv), the TEZ was announced by the British Government on 28 April, 1982, and was enforced from 1100 GMT (dawn, local) on 1 May; from that time, any ship or aircraft, military or civilian, engaged in support of the Argentine occupation of the Falkland Islands, or present in the TEZ without the authority of the British Government (and therefore presumed to be supporting the Argentine presence) would be liable to attack

TPS-43 — (properly AN/TPS-43) Air-portable long-range air warning and control radar system – deployed to Port Stanley by Argentine Air Force

'Trala' — 'Tug, Repair and Logistics Area' – a mobile haven for RFAs and STUFT, located to the east of the TEZ (earlier known as 'Lola' (qv))

Vertrep — Vertical Replenishment – the transfer of stores by helicopter. The removal of the need for alongside transfers by jackstay (US Navy Hi-line), for all but the heaviest and most awkward loads gives the ships freedom of manoeuvre and a greater degree of flexibility to the task group commander

VT Fuze — Variable Time Fuze – a proximity fuze which uses radar principles to initiate the detonation of a shell or bomb at a lethal distance from an air target or at a set height above a surface target. Conventional fuzes rely upon contact or pre-set mechanical or chemical time delays

VYCA2 — *Grupo 2 de Vigilancia y Control Aereo* – the Argentine Air Force air defence warning, control and co-ordination organization installed at Port Stanley

Prologue

BATTLE GROUP DEPLOYMENT, 1914

On the blustery late-spring evening of 1 November, 1914, off the coast of Chile, a Royal Navy cruiser squadron ill-advisedly accepted battle with a much superior German squadron. Two large armoured cruisers were sunk with all hands – some 1,600 men and their admiral. Two ships, the light cruiser HMS *Glasgow* and the weak auxiliary cruiser *Otranto*, escaped in the gathering dusk off Coronel.

Not until 6 November did a full report of the disaster reach the British Admiralty, cabled from the most southerly telegraph station in the world, at the Chilean town of Punta Arenas, on the Straits of Magellan. With a clear idea of the threat which the German ships posed and the force needed to deal with them, Admiral Fisher, the First Sea Lord, moved swiftly and decisively, ordering the battlecruisers HMS *Invincible* and *Inflexible* to detach from the Grand Fleet in Scottish waters for service in the South Atlantic. They sailed from Devonport on 11 November with full coal bunkers, provisions for three months and stores and ammunition for the ships already in the South Atlantic. It was a feat which was not to be bettered 68 years later.

Twenty-five days after leaving Plymouth Sound, Vice Admiral Sir Doveton Sturdee joined the rest of his force in Port William, the sheltered inlet outside Port Stanley at the eastern extremity of the Falkland Islands, unaware that his opposite number, Vice Admiral Count Maximilian von Spee, with five cruisers, was less than 250 miles away, heading for the same destination. The next morning, 8 December, the German squadron was seen approaching: scarcely any of Sturdee's ships were ready for sea, but von Spee retired when the strength of the Royal Navy's squadron was realized and, too late, recognized the distinctive tripod masts as the two battlecruisers reached the open sea.

With the *Glasgow* leading, the British ships – the *Invincible*, *Inflexible* and four cruisers – chased the fleeing enemy through the calm south Atlantic for two hours until, at midday, the battlecruisers were close enough to open fire, at a range of eight miles. Von Spee, knowing that he could neither out-run nor out-fight his big opponents, deliberately sacrificed his own chances of escape by turning his flagship, the *Scharnhorst*, and

The battlecruiser *Invincible*, Admiral Sturdee's flagship, as she appeared at the time of the first Battle of the Falklands, in December 1914 *(via author)*

her sister-ship, the *Gneisenau*, to draw fire from his three light cruisers, the *Leipzig*, *Nürnberg* and *Dresden*, which made off to the south, pursued by HMS *Glasgow* and two larger cruisers, the *Cornwall* and *Kent*.

Three hours after the 'split', the *Scharnhorst*, shattered by 12in shells, foundered while driving at the battlecruisers for a torpedo attack – not one of her 700-odd men survived. The *Gneisenau* then became the sole target for the *Invincible*, *Inflexible* and the *Carnarvon*, a slow ship which had only just caught up. The German armoured cruiser was brought to a dead stop after an hour's pounding and when her guns fell silent at last the British ships ceased fire, rescuing 187 of her officers and men after she sank.

Two of the three light cruisers had been bought only brief survival. The *Glasgow* took the *Leipzig* under fire at long range, an hour and a half after the German ships had been ordered to detach, and continued to engage this ship after the *Cornwall* came up in support. The *Kent* took a further two hours to run down the supposedly faster *Nürnberg*, but then closed the range rapidly, disregarding the many hits which the German ship scored, and fought her to a standstill in under an hour, then watched as she sank slowly, flooding through opened seacocks.

The *Leipzig*'s end was more protracted, for her opponents continued to fight at long range until her guns ran out of ammunition, four hours after the *Glasgow* had first opened fire. 1,400 rounds of 6in and nearly 900 rounds of 4in had been needed to finish the *Leipzig*, whereas the *Kent* had fired only 634 6in shells at the *Nürnberg*. In both instances the British ships moved in quickly to pick up survivors, but the shellfire and the chill water had taken a tragic toll and of the combined crews of about 580 men, only twenty-five survived.

The German shooting had been accurate until the guns had been smothered by the sheer weight of hits. The *Invincible* had attracted most of the *Scharnhorst*'s and *Gneisenau*'s fire, sustaining twenty-two hits compared with three on the *Inflexible*, but neither of the battlecruisers had suffered serious damage. The *Leipzig* had managed to hit the *Cornwall* with eighteen shells but landed only two on the distant *Glasgow*; *Kent*'s decision to close the *Nürnberg* resulted in her having to accept thirty-eight hits – although the light 105mm shells did not affect her ability to steam or fight, the *Kent* lost four men dead and twelve wounded, out of the British total of six dead and twenty wounded. The German Navy's losses – some 1,900 men – in this seven-hour battle were nearly double those of both sides in the twelve-week war of 1982.

HMS *Kent* avenged her sister-ship, HMS *Monmouth*, on 8 December 1914, sinking the *Nurnberg* in a 90-minute duel. In the months after the battle, the *Kent*, operating from secluded bays in Chilean Tierra del Fuego, took a prominent part in the hunt for the escaped *Dresden* and, on 14 March 1915 in company with the *Glasgow*, brought her to bay at Mas a Fuera, Juan Fernandez *(via author)*

The victory off the Falklands was less than complete. Although von Spee's two colliers had been found and sunk by two British ships attempting to catch up with the battle, the cruiser *Dresden* had escaped. Only the *Glasgow* was fast enough to overhaul her, but Captain J. D. Luce RN was preoccupied with the *Leipzig* and did not break off even after the *Cornwall* had caught up and was obviously hitting the latter hard. This 'failure', for which Admiral Sturdee was to be blamed by the First Sea Lord, led to the continued deployment of up to six Royal Navy cruisers in South American waters until mid-March 1915. The solitary German ship remained one step ahead of her pursuers, hiding in isolated inlets, until she was finally tracked down by the *Kent* and *Glasgow* at Juan Fernandez, short of fuel and with her machinery badly in need of overhaul. The British cruisers opened fire, but the *Dresden* scuttled herself to avoid further waste of life.

PART I

A Convenient Station
near Cape Horn

The Falkland Islands lie not far from one of the world's great ocean turning points – 'focal areas of trade' in strategic jargon – but one which did not see a great deal of traffic until the nineteenth century. A Spanish expedition was the first to round the South American mainland, in 1520, reaching the Pacific through the straits named after its Portuguese leader, Magellan. The peculiarities of the Spanish colonial system, whereby the wealth of Chile and Peru were exploited by way of the Isthmus of Panama and communication between the River Plate and Peru was permitted only by the overland route, across the Andes, led to the neglect of the Straits of Magellan by Spanish navigators. English seamen sought out the rich Spanish trade off the west coast of South America and Drake's voyage in 1578 was followed in the year of the Armada by Cavendish. The latter died during a second attempt but one of his companions, John Davis, better known as an Arctic explorer discovered the Falklands on 14 August, 1592.

The next English adventurer, Sir John Hawkins, also sighted the Falklands, early in 1594, and then passed into the Pacific through the Straits. Later in the decade the Dutch sought an alternative route to the East Indies and this took van Noort through the Straits in 1599; one of his ships, unable to make headway against the prevailing wind, turned back and was blown within sight of the most westerly group of the Falklands' islets, the Jasons, which were known as the 'Sebaldines', after the commander of the Dutch ship, Sebald de Waerdt.

Not until 1616 was the southernmost point of the continent rounded, by Willem Schouten, who named the headland and the island after his native town of Hoorn. Cape Horn, as it became generally known, soon gained a reputation for its ferocious weather and seas and while the Straits of Magellan were more sheltered, they were navigationally 'challenging', with a prevailing wind facing the westbound voyager and an inhospitable coastline with equally inhospitable natives. The English turned their attention elsewhere when the wars with Spain ended and the Dutch East India Company, a bureaucratic organization, objected strongly to sailors arriving in their Spice Islands by any other than the approved route, from the west, so that there were few, if any, passages around the Horn or through the Straits until the later years of the seventeenth century, when the lure of Spanish gold called again.

The predators were the buccaneers, a polyglot assortment of bandits who had started in a small way in the West Indies but quickly grew in strength and daring until they were able to undertake profitable raids on the major Spanish towns which served as trans-shipment entrepots between the Pacific and Atlantic. In 1683 an expedition left the Caribbean to pillage 'at source'. Pausing only to seize a better ship which, after embarking more than enough West African maidens, they renamed the 'Bachelors' Delight', they set off for the Straits of Magellan, to raid the coastal towns of Chile. Before reaching the Straits, they were blown eastwards to sight again the Falklands, early in 1684.*

Six years later, by which time Britain and Spain were again at war, a privateer named John Strong made the first recorded landing on the Falklands, on 27 January, 1690. The channel between the two main islands he named Falkland's Sound, in honour of the Viscount who had been Treasurer of the Navy at the date of his departure (but who was now in the Tower, under suspicion of misusing the funds of the Navy).

The wars, which lasted from 1689 to 1714 with only a short break, saw passages around South America become almost popular. The buccaneers, dignified by 'Letters of Marque' into privateers, passed into the Pacific and ships of the newly-founded French South American Company voyaged in both directions. These produced a rash of fresh sightings of the Falklands: in 1708, Captain Poree, of St Malo, was twice blown out to the islands by gales but failed to realize that his two sightings were of the same group. Later in that year, another British privateer, Woodes Rogers, sighted the islands and went on to the Pacific where he rescued the unfortunate Alexander Selkirk (the original for Robinson Crusoe), who had been marooned by his captain in 1704 on Juan Fernandez, the isolated group of islands 400 miles west of Valparaiso, where the *Dresden* was to meet her end 210 years later.

By 1721 the islands to the east of the Straits were known by a bewildering variety of names – 'Hawkins' Land', 'The Sebaldines', the 'Anican Islands', 'The Coast of the Assumption', 'Les Iles Nouvelles' (which, by 1716, they were not) and 'Belgia Austral', the last being a hopeful bid by a Dutch explorer in 1721. The term 'Falklands' Isles' was used but not until later did it become common in British usage. This coincided with the first statement of strategic interest in the Falklands, made by Commodore Anson on his return from his 1739–44 round-the-world raiding cruise. Anson never saw the islands, but his squadron suffered great hardship in

---

* This voyage, led by William Cowley, with William Dampier as one of the Mates, contributed to English literature; the poet Coleridge passed over the dusky maidens, however, preferring (and exaggerating) the misadventures which befell after the shooting of an albatross by one of the crew.

reaching the Straits of Magellan and he recognized

> the prodigious import a convenient station might prove, situated so far to the southward, and so near Cape Horn . . . This, even in time of peace, might be of great consequence to this station, and in time of war, would make us masters of those seas.

This appeared in 1748 and two years later the Admiralty ordered the preparation of an expedition to settle a garrison. The Spanish learned of the plan and, after a personal appeal from the Ambassador to King George II, the project was abandoned for the time being.

The Spanish were convinced that the islands belonged to them by virtue of the 1494 Treaty of Tordesillas – a papal arbitration which shared the undiscovered world between Spain and Portugal without reference to any other nation: that the islands had not yet been sighted by a Spanish ship was immaterial, the islands lay to the west of the line of demarcation, 370 leagues to the west of the Cape Verde Islands. In 1763 a Spanish vessel, albeit one from the Viceroyalty of Peru, at last visited the islands. The Spanish 'parliament' at Madrid, the *Cortes*, declined an offer by the ship's owner to claim, colonize and govern them in the name of Spain, mainly because he had been assisted in his exploration by a Jesuit 'cosmographer' and the Spanish authorities wished to give the Society of Jesus no opportunity to extend their influence.

In the same year a French Colonel of Infantry, Louis de Bougainville, persuaded the Ministry of Marine to allow him, at his own expense, to equip and command an expedition to colonize the islands on behalf of the French India Company. Leaving St Malo in September, 1763, his two ships arrived in Berkeley Sound on 3 February, 1764, and landed two ex-Canadian families and volunteers from the ships as settlers. A fort was built and guns landed to defend the settlement, which was named Port Louis, before de Bougainville and his ships departed in early April.

The British Government might have been prepared to give way gracefully to Spain, but it was not ready to stand by while the French installed themselves in a position commanding the approaches to the Pacific. Commodore the Hon John Byron, with the frigate *Dolphin* and the sloop *Tamer*, sighted the Falklands on 13 January, 1765, and after a brief examination of suitable locations raised the Union Flag on Saunders Island and claimed the islands for Great Britain on 23 January. This was regarded as quite sufficient and the two ships left four days later.

A British garrison did not arrive until January, 1766, when the frigate *Jason*, the bomb-ketch *Carcass* and the transport *Experiment* landed twenty-five Marines, four 12pdr guns and a 'portable blockhouse' which had been carried out in kit form, at Port Egmont, Saunders Island. The *Jason* remained to survey the islands but did not discover the French settlement at Port Louis until 4 December. Courteously, each side demanded that the other should leave the islands but there the matter ended and the *Jason* left for England in January, 1767.

Unbeknown to the two local commanders, the days of the French settlement were already numbered. In September, 1766, Louis XV acknowledged the Spanish claims to sovereignty over the islands. Charles III was under no obligation to pay compensation for the restoration of what he regarded as his own lands, but he handsomely reimbursed de Bougainville, who formally handed over Port Louis to a Spanish garrison on 1 April, 1767. The French name given by the settlers, 'Les Isles Malouines', was simply hispanicized into 'Las Islas Maluinas', but Port Louis became 'La Soledad' – solitude – and was regarded as aptly named by the Spanish soldiery sentenced to serve there.

The new occupants suspected, but did not know of for certain, the existence of a British settlement. It was confirmed when the French colonists returned to Europe in the autumn of 1767 but the Captain-General of Buenos Aires was not informed until the summer of 1768 and it was not until November, 1769, that a Royal Navy sloop and a Spanish survey schooner met, to their mutual surprise. Again the formal letters of protest were courteous, as were the exchanges of visits, but the Spanish Governor, who had invented yet another name for the group – 'Las Islas Magellan' – did place a time limit of six months on the British presence, from 30 November, 1769. Even if one of the British sloops had left immediately on receipt of this warning, the passage time to England and back to the Falklands would have been too great to permit reinforcement before the end of May, 1770.

The Spanish force actually appeared on 4 June, 1770. After a few days of preliminaries and a brief exchange of fire between the five Spanish ships (with 126 guns and 1,500 seamen and soldiers) and the British sloop and blockhouse (eighteen guns and about 120 seamen and Marines), the latter surrendered on 10 June. The terms were quite favourable and included a signature by the Spanish for all items which could not be carried away in the sloop *Favourite*, which left on 11 July. The news of the bloodless expulsion of the garrison reached Britain before her return, in late September.

The Spanish, in informing the British Government, excused the action by stating that the colonial authorities at Buenos Aires had acted on their own initiative, without the *Cortes'* knowledge. This was untrue and the justification for the act was based on a wilful misinterpretation of a treaty which was not relevant – a diplomatic device which was to be repeated 212 years later under similar circumstances. It is probable that the British Government of the day would have let the matter rest, but public opinion was against concession and so the Fleet was mobilized in August, 1770. Sixteen ships of the line and ten frigates were commissioned out of reserve: one of the former category was the new 64-gun Third Rate *Raisonnable*, whose captain signed on his 12-year-old nephew as his servant. The lad later served aboard the *Carcass* and the *Dolphin*, commanded by the George Farmer who had been the Falklands naval commander in

June, 1770, but he was never to see the islands for himself in the course of his illustrious career, which ended at Trafalgar.

When it became apparent that France was unwilling to go to war over the Falklands, Charles III of Spain backed down and agreed in January, 1771, to restore Port Egmont, though reserving right of sovereignty over the islands. This future point of contention was not pressed by the British Government, although the Opposition recognized it as containing 'the genuine seeds of perpetual hostility and war' – a slight exaggeration, but nonetheless prophetic.

The frigate *Juno*, with two other vessels, took out a garrison to Port Egmont and, after mustering the items on the 1770 inventory, formally took possession on 16 September, 1771. The sloop *Hound* remained as guardship until April, 1773, when she left without relief, the Admiralty having sent out in her stead a prefabricated 'shallop' named *Penguin*. The garrison was reduced to twenty-five Marines and the fifty-man crew of the small craft but even this minor presence, sufficient to uphold the principle of possession without unduly annoying the Spanish, was a target for Government economies and in April, 1774, the storeship *Endeavour* arrived to embark the garrison, guns, stores and the sound timbers of the *Penguin*. Watched by a North American sealing ship, the *Endeavour* sailed on 22 May, 1774, leaving fixed over the door a lead plaque which restated the British claim to sovereignty:

> Be it known to all nations that Falklands Islands, with this fort, the store-houses, wharfs, harbours, bays and creeks thereunto belonging are the sole right and property of His Most Sacred Majesty King George the Third, King of Great Britain, France and Ireland, Defender of the Faith, etc., in witness whereof this plate is set up, and His Britannic Majesty's Colours left flying as a mark of possession by SW Clayton, Commanding Officer at Falklands Islands.
>
> AD 1774

The Spanish garrison remained at Soledad throughout the Royal Navy's occupation of Port Egmont and thereafter, a convict settlement being established towards the end of the century. On 25 May, 1810, the prominent citizens of the city of Buenos Aires expelled the Viceroy of La Plata and declared that they would rule the huge provincial empire, which included modern Uruguay, Paraguay and Bolivia, as well as the settled northern provinces of Argentina, on behalf of Ferdinand VII of Spain, until such time as the mother country was cleared of the French.

The Viceroy retired to Montevideo, where loyal forces rallied to him, including the Soledad garrison. The abandonment of the 'Maluinas' was sanctioned by the *Cortes*, sitting under British protection at Cadiz, on the understanding that the islands were to be re-occupied when circumstances permitted. They never did.

The Plate colonists' declared loyalty to the Spanish Crown did not survive the attempts by the Viceroy to put down what he saw as a revolt and after capturing Montevideo in June, 1814, they turned to assist Chile in her struggle against the Viceroy of Peru. On 9 July, 1816, a representative assembly met in Buenos Aires and declared that the 'United Provinces of the Rio de la Plata' were completely independent of Spain, to whose former colonies they fell heir. This imperial mantle was already a little ragged – Paraguay had gone its own way in 1811, Uruguay was seized by the Portuguese and added to Brazil in 1816 and in the north the province of Alto Peru saw almost continuous fighting between Spanish loyalists and various groups of rebels up to 1825, when Spain gave up and the local patriots opted for complete autonomy, calling their country Bolivia. Those provinces left within the union actively resented Buenos Aires' assumption of leadership and internal disputes went on for thirty-five years after the declaration of independence.

For nine years the Falklands remained unclaimed. They were frequented by American sealers who enjoyed the freedom from any authority and came to regard it as their right. The first visit by a United Provinces' warship occurred in March, 1820, when the *Mercuria*, bound for Chile with Government stores, was carried there by a gale. The captain, an American, sold the ship to a shipwrecked French Navy crew, who dropped off him and his men and the stores at Rio de Janeiro.

On 1 November, 1820, the *Heroina*, commanded by another American, Daniel Jewitt, arrived intentionally in Berkeley Sound to take possession of the islands on behalf of the Provinces, much to the surprise of the resident sealers, who were generally unimpressed by the dilapidated state of the warship and her near-mutinous crew. After Jewitt's departure, the sealers returned to their activities and were not inconvenienced again for several years.

The United Provinces granted a lease of land at Soledad, with fishery and grazing rights, to Louis Vernet in 1823. Vernet, whose origins are uncertain but who was at the time a naturalized citizen of La Plata Province, established a profitable settlement in 1826 and two years later his grant was extended to twenty years, with exclusive fishery rights, including those for the seal industry. At the same time a convict settlement was opened on a government reserve at San Carlos, on Falkland Sound.

The American sealers had scant regard for any law or authority which infringed their 'right' to work where they wished and, to deal with them, Vernet was appointed as the United Provinces' Governor on the islands. Britain, which had not stirred when Buenos Aires had claimed the islands in 1820, protested immediately but took no further action; relations between Vernet and the Royal Navy were amicable, Captain Robert Fitzroy and HMS *Beagle* being cordially welcomed when the ship called early in 1830.

After repeated warnings, Vernet arrested two American sealers for poaching in July, 1831, and personally took one of them, the *Harriet*, to Buenos Aires. At the latter port was the USS *Lexington*, whose captain, Silas Duncan, demanded that Vernet be handed over to the United States for trial as a pirate or, failing that, the United Provinces Government should arrest and try him. Duncan did not wait for a reply, but sailed forthwith for the Falklands, where he arrived at Port Soledad on 20 December, 1831, flying the French flag. He invited Vernet's principal agents on board, arrested them and then hoisted the US ensign before landing an armed party. This force spiked the settlement's guns, seized all personal weapons and blew up the magazine and then went on to sack the defenceless place. Several leading settlers were taken on board the *Lexington*, seven of them in irons and treated as pirates, and the ship returned to the Plate, anchoring in Uruguayan waters off Montevideo. Duncan held his prisoners only until the United Provinces acknowledged that the men had been supervising the fisheries with official approval, put them ashore and then sailed off. The Buenos Aires Government was incensed and lodged a claim for compensation with the US Government. The latter did not reply officially until 1884, when the Argentine claim for damages for abuse of its citizens was dismissed as groundless.

News of the incident reached England in the spring of 1832 and appeared to confirm an earlier rumour that the United States were contemplating the establishment of a naval base to protect the sealers' interests. The Commander-in-Chief, South America Station, was accordingly instructed, 'in the name of His Britannic Majesty, to exercise the rights of sovereignty' over the Falklands. In November, he sent Captain Richard Onslow, with the sloop *Clio* and the frigate *Tyne*, and they arrived at Port Egmont on 20 December, a year to the day after *Lexington*'s visitation.

Vernet was still in Buenos Aires and the acting-Governorship devolved upon the commander of the San Carlos penal settlement, Major Juan Mestivier. By an unfortunate but unrelated coincidence, Mestivier was murdered by one of the convicts soon after the British warships' arrival at Saunders Island – a century after his death, he was to become a legendary leader of the resistance to the invader! His successor, Lieutenant Pinedo of the colony's schooner, the *Sarandi*, was unable to offer any resistance to the *Clio* when she put into Berkeley Sound on 2 January, 1833, and left under strong protest, refusing to haul down his country's flag. Delayed by bad weather, Pinedo was obliged to watch the raising of the Union Jack on 3 January, when Captain Onslow formally took possession of the Falklands.

The British Government ignored the United Provinces' protests. It also ignored the re-acquired possession, leaving Vernet's agents in charge and free to administer the settlement as before, the only mark of change of ownership being orders to the storekeeper to raise the Union Jack on Sundays and whenever ships arrived.

In August, 1833, a small group of gauchos and freed Indian convicts murdered the storekeeper and three of Vernet's other employees. Law and order was not restored until January, 1834, when the frigate HMS

Tyne arrived, sought out by an English sealer. The *Tyne*'s First Lieutenant and a small party of seamen and Marines were left to govern and rebuild the colony and to conduct a survey of the islands. Successive naval Governors, supported by half-yearly warship visits and survey vessels, built up the livestock and human population and by 1841 the Admiralty was confident enough to recommend the development of the Falklands as a permanent colony.

In August, 1841, Lieutenant Richard Moody, Royal Engineers, was appointed Lieutenant-Governor and he arrived at Port Louis on 22 January, 1842. More than a year passed before, on 23 January, 1843, Letters Patent established 'Her Majesty's Settlements in the Falkland Islands and their Dependencies', raising Moody to the status of full Governor and Commander-in-Chief. The addition of the position of Admiral of the Islands, in September, 1843, gave him civil maritime jurisdiction over the surrounding waters. The Argentine Government again protested over the formal adoption of the colony, but again the protest was rejected. National pride, rather than practical considerations, may have been at the back of the protest, for it is reputed that, five years earlier, the dictator Juan Manuel Rosas had offered to relinquish the Argentine claim on the Falklands if Buenos Aires' debt to a London merchant bank could be written off. The offer was not accepted.

The capital was moved from Port Louis to Stanley, on the inner harbour of Port William, in July, 1845. The growth of the settlement was slow and mistakes were made in attempting to stimulate the economy, full advantage being taken by unscrupulous outsiders and those settlers who could not foresee the consequence of their greed. By 1852 sheep farming had been introduced and four years later the Falkland Islands Company was incorporated by Royal Charter, to manage and develop large tracts of land. West Falkland was not colonized until 1867 but within two years all the land had been leased to sheep-farming settlers and the flocks expanded rapidly.

For a few years the Falklands, and Port Stanley in particular, derived a greater income from transient shipping than from their pastoral industry. The discovery of gold in California and, later, Australia, led to a dramatic increase in the volume of shipping traffic around the Horn. With no mainland harbour facilities south of the River Plate, Port Stanley was the only service station on the long run between Montevideo and Valparaiso and ships could obtain fresh water, fresh vegetables and meat and, at high cost, repairs. With the South Atlantic weather, there was no shortage of custom for the repairers and the wreckers, the latter benefiting not only from the genuine casualties but also from the dishonest owners or masters defrauding insurance companies and nervous crews unwilling to face Cape Horn in ill-found vessels.

The boom years were from 1850 to 1870. Thereafter, the appearance of the steam ship in greater numbers, inherently safer as it was able to choose its route, and with new requirements, primarily coal instead of provisions, led to the eclipse of Port Stanley. The failure on the part of the British Government to provide a coal depot in the Falklands, even when the desirability was obvious, was directly responsible for the decline of a profitable industry. The Chilean Governor of Punta Arenas, at the western end of the Straits of Magellan, showed greater foresight and his community, as isolated and in a more desolate spot even than Port Stanley, prospered accordingly.

The success of Punta Arenas and Chilean colonization aroused Argentine pride and from 1880 there were disputes over the ownership of the Straits, Tierra del Fuego and Patagonia. A compromise settlement in 1881 recognized Chilean sovereignty over the Straits and Argentina got eastern Patagonia and, thereby, international recognition of her claim to the continental mainland opposite the Falklands. In 1884 and 1885 the Argentine Government added 'contiguity' to its claims to the Falklands and added the Falklands to a semi-official map of Argentina, as a possession. The British Government answered politely but firmly – the question would not be re-opened. Although not satisfied, the Argentine Government maintained a dignified position: it would continue to regard the Falklands as an integral part of Argentina and maintain an attitude of protest – no resort to force or other coercion was even hinted.

This was as well, for in 1879, again as an economy measure, the small Marines garrison was withdrawn and defence was provided by deterrence only, in the form of the Royal Navy's South American Squadron. The removal of the garrison was, in a way, beneficial, for the islands' Government had had to contribute to its upkeep and the elimination of this expenditure allowed the settlement to become independent of the British Treasury in 1881, when local income at last exceeded expenditure.

In the same year the Montevideo-based South American Squadron paid a visit to Port Stanley that was remarkable in that, for the first time, members of the Royal Family were aboard to see the islands. The sons of the Prince of Wales, Prince Albert Victor and Prince George (later King George V) were midshipmen in HMS *Bacchante*, which arrived on 24 January but left within 24 hours, before the Princes could go ashore, having been summoned urgently to the Cape of Good Hope.

The Falklands at last became a full Colony on 29 February, 1892, by virtue of an Order-in-Council. A week earlier, the first purpose-built Anglican Church on the islands had been consecrated as Christ Church Cathedral, a suitable seat for the diocese of the Falklands, which included the whole of South America and which had been established in 1869. The temporal celebration in no way overshadowed the spiritual occasion, for news of the new colonial status did not reach Port Stanley until April, when the contract mail steamer arrived.

The monthly steamer was the only regular form of communication between the Falklands and the outside world for thirty years, from 1880 until 1910. London was linked by telegraph with Montevideo during the 1870s and the line was extended to Punta Arenas a few years later. In 1897 a report recommending the development of naval facilities at Port Stanley suggested the linking of the islands to Punta Arenas but this was not approved by the British Treasury.

The 1897 report estimated that the provision of stores depot, coaling facilities, fixed defences and a 600-foot drydock, capable of accommodating battleships, would cost just over half a million pounds. Only reduced repair facilities and a small stores depot were approved and begun in May, 1899, on Navy Point, opposite the town. As usual in Falklands construction projects, lack of labour delayed the work, which had progressed little when a fresh round of 'cuts' brought even this to a halt, in August, 1903. The South American Station was disbanded at the same time and its area of responsibility absorbed into the South Atlantic Station, with its base at Freetown, over 5,000 miles from the Falklands, but even this arrangement lasted only for thirteen months. From September, 1904, until 23 January, 1913, the only Royal Navy representation in South American waters was by ships of a cruiser squadron normally to be found on training duties in the West Indies. Annual visits to South America and the Falklands were made whenever possible, but there was a notable failure in 1910, when no ship could be spared to attend the Chilean or Argentine centenary independence celebrations.

Despite the 1881 boundary settlement, relations between Chile and Argentine deteriorated during the closing years of the century, until both countries were almost ready to go to war over the disputed southern sector. Both sides agreed to British arbitration and in December, 1902, after a lengthy survey, King Edward VII awarded most of Patagonia to Argentina, together with the eastern half of Tierra del Fuego, while Chile retained both shores of the Straits of Magellan, with undisputed access to the Atlantic. The islands to the south of Tierra del Fuego were also awarded to Chile: three of these – Lennox, Picton and Nueva – off the eastern entrance to the Beagle Channel became a renewed source of friction, initially in 1915, when the Chileans were accused of fortifying them, and more seriously sixty years later, when offshore economic zones were being claimed.

South Georgia, the nearby island groups and part of the Antarctic mainland, became the Falkland Islands Dependencies in 1906. Argentina had no grounds for objection to this declaration but, in 1908, she resumed her protests over the Falklands themselves. The occasion was the Postal Union Convention, at which the right of colonies to issue stamps was among the topics. The Argentine delegation asserted that the Falklands had no such right and entered a reservation when the Convention was ratified. Two years later the Falklands appeared on an official map of Argentina as an Argentine possession. The Government was not ready to offend Britain further, however, and the 1914 official census did not include the islands – that had to wait until 1947.

The Falklands obtained a day-to-day link with the outside world in August, 1910, when a 5-kilowatt wireless-telegraphy station, paid for from the colony's own funds, was opened. With a range of 400 miles, it could just reach Punta Arenas, at the end of a cable from London, and twice as far as the wireless set in the new cruiser HMS *Glasgow*, which arrived at Port Stanley on 23 January, 1913, to re-establish the South-East Coast of America Station, after a break of nearly ten years. Her commanding officer, Captain John Luce RN, remained the Senior Officer on the Station until the arrival of Admiral Sir Christopher Cradock in October, 1914, and thereafter took part in the battles off Coronel and the Falklands and in the final act of the campaign, the sinking of the *Dresden* at Juan Fernandez.

The Falklands were undefended until mid-November, 1914, when two small field guns and some Marines were landed from the old battleship *Canopus*, and the only fuel stocks were those carried in Admiralty colliers. During the war shore oil fuel tanks were constructed, a stores depot erected and stocked, a more powerful wireless station built, and, as important, a cable laid to Maldonado, in Uruguay. Warships, mainly old cruisers, were frequent visitors to Port Stanley, where they rested and replenished between patrols. One of these, HMS *Lancaster*, sister-ship of the *Monmouth* sunk at Coronel and the *Kent* and *Cornwall* at the Falklands, landed and installed two of her 6in guns in 1916 in a battery on Sapper Hill, behind Port Stanley: the guns were 'given' to the Falklands' Government after the First World War and were still in place, though unusable, in 1982.

With the end of the war in 1918 the islands resumed their quiet life. The South America Station, as it was now titled, remained in being, but with fewer ships, until 1927, when Britain's economic situation led to a 'rationalization' in which the length of the North and South American Atlantic seaboards came under the Commander-in-Chief, America and West Indies Station. The Falklands naval establishments were closed, the wireless station being handed over to the Governor, and the cable to Uruguay was taken up.

Anglo-Argentine relations between the World Wars were generally good, although the rise of fascism in Italy and, later, Spain struck an answering chord in Argentina, so many of whose inhabitants derived from those countries. The growing influence of the Pan-American movement was not welcomed in Buenos Aires, mainly due to resentment of United States' leadership of a largely Spanish-speaking community: the United States had, in 1927, been principally the cause of a very rapid decline in Argentine prosperity as the result of a protectionist ban on the import of Argentine beef and cattle.

The next round in the Falklands dispute was started, unwittingly, by Britain, which issued a set of commemorative stamps to mark the centenary of the re-occupation of the Falklands. The Argentine authorities retaliated by refusing to issue visas to British passport-holders born in the Falklands – the latter, it was announced, were Argentine subjects. This annoyance was suspended in 1935, but was resumed the next year, the Argentine postal authorities simultaneously issuing a 1-peso stamp for the 'Malvinas'. The British Government ignored the pinpricks as best as it could and avoided unnecessary controversy, even to the extent of dropping the question of a direct mail service between Argentina and the islands. The Argentine Government, in its turn, elected not to submit its case to the International Court of Justice or to the League of Nations, of which Argentina was a staunch member, and limited itself, internationally, to reservations and declarations at inappropriate conventions and conferences. Rather to everyone's surprise, one such declaration, at the 1938 Postal Union Convention, added South Georgia and sundry Antarctic Dependencies to the Argentine list.

On the outbreak of the Second World War, in September, 1939, the Port Stanley wireless station was taken over by the Admiralty. The light cruiser HMS *Ajax* was in the Plate, where her commanding officer, Captain H. H. Harwood RN, learned of a 'concentration of German merchant vessels' off the Patagonian coast. Believing that this presaged an invasion by German nationals resident in Argentina, the *Ajax* sailed for Port Stanley, where she arrived on 12 September, 1939. The scanty defences of the island were put in order and a floatplane base was established at Chartres, in West Falkland, before the *Ajax* went north to patrol off the Plate, to intercept German merchant ships attempting to leave the neutral ports for Europe.

Royal Navy reinforcements began to reach the South Atlantic from mid-September and Harwood was appointed as Commodore, South Atlantic Division, on the 17th. To *Ajax* were added the heavy cruisers *Exeter* and *Cumberland* and two destroyers; the last were too short-ranged for such detached service and were recalled at the end of the month, but not before HMS *Hotspur* had been the first ship of her type to visit Port Stanley, escorting a ship bringing British reservists from Montevideo to reinforce the Falkland Islands Defence Force. The New Zealand-manned HMS *Achilles* joined in place of the destroyers in October, 1939.

The four cruisers refuelled and made good defects at Port Stanley at regular intervals between their patrols, which extended as far north as Rio. Harwood was still worried about the German reservists in Patagonia and he ensured that *Cumberland* and *Exeter* were off the Falklands together on 8 December, to guard against an attempted anniversary raid twenty-five years after the destruction of Admiral Graf von Spee's squadron. The day passed without incident and on the 9th the *Exeter* headed north to join the *Ajax* and *Achilles*: four days later the three cruisers found and fought the pocket battleship *Graf Spee* in the approaches to the Plate.

The *Cumberland* raised steam and left Port Stanley as soon as news of the engagement began to arrive and she reached Montevideo, where the German ship had taken refuge, thirty-four hours after leaving the Falklands, about 1,000 miles away. The *Graf Spee* was scuttled by her crew off the Uruguayan port on 17 December and the Germans crossed the Plate to be interned in Argentina. HMS *Exeter* had been badly damaged in the action and could not seek refuge in a neutral port, for fear of internment, so she limped back to Port Stanley for temporary repairs, arriving as the *Graf Spee* blew herself up. The *Achilles* and *Ajax* followed a few days later and on Christmas Eve the *Cumberland* and her sister-ship *Dorsetshire* reached Port Stanley. This Christmas, 1939, gathering of warships was the most powerful seen since 1914 and was not to be repeated until 1982.

The warships returned to their patrols from 29 December and on 21 January, 1940, the *Exeter* was ready to begin her passage to the United Kingdom. With the threat from warship raiders lifted, Armed Merchant Cruisers – converted liners – began to take the place of some of the 'regular' warships, the *Alcantara* and *Queen of Bermuda* beginning patrols from Port Stanley in February and March, 1940. The stores depot was restocked and the oil fuel tanks filled once again, the first Royal Fleet Auxiliary tanker to offload being the *Olwen*. The shore defences were not improved but after it was discovered that a raider had laid mines off the Cape of Good Hope, two auxiliary minesweepers were allocated to Port Stanley, the whaler *Roydur* and the trawler *William Scoresby*, which arrived in May and June, 1940, respectively. The naval presence ashore was sufficiently permanent to require a 'base depot ship' and in May, 1940, the name '*Pursuivant*' was selected; the formal commissioning did not occur until 5 March, 1941.

The South American Division's area of operations was, in fact, a quiet backwater for two years after the Battle of the Plate, with just a few auxiliary cruisers to show the flag and protect Allied interests in this unthreatened corner. This changed briefly in January, 1942, following a report that the Japanese intended to capture the Falklands and hand them over to the Argentine Government. It is difficult to believe that the Admiralty could have taken a threat from Japan seriously, but the light cruiser HMS *Birmingham* joined the auxiliary cruiser *Asturias* and in early January the pair ostentatiously cruised off the Patagonian ports while an elaborate communications 'spoof' suggested that two imaginary warships (named *Invincible* and *Inflexible*!) were on their way south to reinforce the Falklands.

The excitement died down in early February, but in the autumn a British infantry battalion arrived as a garrison for the Falklands, apparently to deter any Argentine attempt to take advantage of Britain's preoccupations elsewhere. The Government in Buenos Aires, still claiming sovereignty over the Falklands and Dependencies, continued to observe the strict neutrality which it had declared at the outbreak of war. There was nevertheless strong sympathy for the Axis cause in the German-trained Army and in a vociferous section of the Press. The coup which brought members of this clique to power in June, 1943, altered the pattern of Anglo-Argentine relations, substituting low-level confrontation for the gentlemanly difference of opinion which had never been allowed to become open argument.

Driven by rabid nationalism, the Junta's ambition for expansion could only be realized in one direction, southwards, towards Antarctica and the offshore islands. Most of the land and the islands opposite Argentina had already been claimed by Britain early in the century, but, unlike the Falklands and South Georgia, there had not been the 'continuous use and possession' which is one of the basic principles of sovereignty in law, and Argentina, who together with Chile claimed overlapping sectors in the Antarctic ocean and continent, sought to stake her claim by occupation. This took the form of visits by survey teams during the Antarctic summer; these teams left marks claiming possession, which were subsequently collected by the trawler HMS *William Scoresby* and formal protests made to Argentina. The Admiralty responded to the encroachments by establishing the Falkland Islands Dependencies Survey in 1944 and setting up bases on islands off the Graham Land peninsula.

An Inter-American Conference opened at Chapultepec, Mexico, on 21 February, 1945. Argentina did not attend, despite invitation, and was not associated with the declaration renewing pledges of mutual assistance and purpose until it was made plain that the main current 'purpose' was agreement to join the United Nations Organization. The pro-Axis Junta in Buenos Aires was in a difficult position: membership of the Inter-American treaty was a pre-requisite for UN membership, but to join the former, Argentina would have to declare war on the remaining Axis powers. Faced with exclusion from what was clearly to be the most important post-war international forum, the Junta gave way with ill grace and declared war against Germany and Japan on 27 March, 1945. A month later, on 30 April, Argentina was admitted to the founding conference of the UN, at San Francisco. The war was not yet over, reconstruction of the shattered occupied countries and rehabilitation of their oppressed peoples had urgently to be discussed, but considerable persuasion was needed to keep the Argentine delegation from putting the Falklands on the agenda!

Although Argentina was to take no steps which in any way shortened the war, the Junta did at least promise that no Nazi war criminals would be given sanctuary. With a large and vociferous German community, Argentina had difficulty in honouring this promise – as the Israeli 'snatch' of Adolf Eichmann in 1960 showed – but two U-boats which arrived in the Plate after epic voyages from Europe, *U.530* on 10 July and *U.977* on 17 August, were turned over to the Allies. To part with such modern vessels must have come hard to the Navy, whose fleet had been up-to-date in 1939 but was obsolete six years later, having been cut off from the huge technological advances made by the Allies and Axis and from the new equipment – radar, sonar, improved communications and fire control and weapons – which had been shared with co-belligerents. Annual post-war cruises in North American and European waters by the training cruiser *La Argentina* made the Navy fully aware of the gap but lack of money caused by internal policies and the lack of interest shown by Army-dominated regimes meant that the Navy had to make do with second-hand ships, aircraft and equipment until well into the 1970s.

An internal power struggle in Argentina saw the emergence, early in 1946, of Colonel Juan Peron as the elected President of the Republic. Minister of War and latterly Vice-President in the military governments of the preceding three years, he was the leader of a clique of 'young colonels' and the favourite of the trades unions and city mobs, whom he had wooed when serving as Minister of Labour. An attempt by certain factions of the Army to oust him in October, 1945, had been thwarted by a vast 'popular demonstration' which paved the way for his supporters' landslide victories in elections held in February, 1946.

Under Peron, who was to remain in power until 1955, the campaign for the 'return' of the Falklands increased in breadth and stridency, led by the Press, whose hysterical nationalism bordered on xenophobia, and found support across the political spectrum. Despite this unity, Peron was not inclined to military adventure and declined to take Argentina's case to the International Court of Justice, or even to the United Nations, despite continuous rumours that he was about to do so.

The propaganda campaign began in earnest early in 1947, when the Argentine Ministry of Foreign Affairs announced the establishment of a committee to gather records which would confirm the country's 'irrevocable rights' to the Falklands and South Georgia. The State schools introduced a highly emotive course of teaching on this aspect of Argentine history and the Government published a census with the Falklands' population included as a district of Patagonia: the numbers did not tally with the Colony's own annual count of its inhabitants. Later in the year, the Argentine delegation at an international civil aviation conference complained of the erection in the Falklands of a meteorological reporting station, which was of international benefit.

Between January and March, 1947, the Argentine Navy's annual expedition to the Antarctic set up the first permanent base on British-claimed territory, in the Melchior Islands, off Graham Land. The Chilean Navy, which was also in the hunt, established a base in Discovery Bay, South Shetlands, in March, 1947. The cruiser HMS *Nigeria* was sent to the Falklands from South Africa to support the Governor while the British Government protested to the two South American states. As usual, the protests were rejected but Britain took no action to expel the intruders.

The most significant political event in the Western Hemisphere in 1947 was the signature in Rio de Janeiro of an Inter-American Treaty of Reciprocal Assistance. The signatories of the pact, generally known as the Rio Treaty, agreed to regard an attack on one American nation as an attack on all (this formula was also used as the basis for the North Atlantic Treaty, signed two years later). Britain ratified the treaty on behalf of her mainland and island colonies but Argentina refused to sign. Driven by an ideology whose main working components were nationalism and jealousy of what he saw as North American hegemony, Peron held back; not until 1951 did Argentina join the Treaty and even then the main reason for the President's change of heart was that only by doing so could he obtain weapons from the USA.

The Organization of American States was founded at Bogota in 1948. In his opening speech, in March, the Argentine delegate's main topic was the restoration of the Falklands. This marked the beginning of the new season of intensified external and internal propaganda. An Argentine naval base had been officially established on Deception Island, in the South Shetlands, at the end of January. In Patagonia, British-owned sheep farms were expropriated 'for defence purposes, in the name of the people'; the people concerned all appeared to be friends of the Minister of Marine.

It was rather unfortunate that the British Government should have chosen this moment to close the Falklands naval establishment. The decision to transfer part of the wireless station to the Falklands Government and to decommission HMS *Pursuivant* was announced in the spring of 1948 and the base actually closed on 26 May. This money-saving measure was taken by Peron to indicate infirmity of resolve and, after a few months' preparation, a movement dedicated to the restoration of the Falklands was formed, rejoicing in the name of 'The Flame of the Argentine Spirit'. The Press and 'Rent-a-Mob' demonstrations whipped up public excitement and in October the Argentine Navy assembled the largest 'Antarctic Task Force' ever: for the first time most of the major warships of the active fleet were included.

The threat to the Falklands was obvious and in November, after the Task Force had sailed for exercises, the British Foreign Secretary, Mr Ernest Bevin, gave his Argentine opposite number the clearest possible warning that any invasion of the Falklands would be met with the appropriate armed force. The potentially explosive situation in the South Atlantic was defused by a British proposal that, to avoid the risk of any incident, the number of ships deployed south of 60° South latitude should be limited. Argentina and Chile agreed to this and from the end of 1948 the Royal Navy provided only one sloop to support the British Antarctic Survey (the Colonial Office successor to the Admiralty's Falkland Islands Dependencies Survey) ships: the South American states' surveys were undertaken by their navies and thus their contingents were larger, though lightly armed.

Mr Bevin had established a principle of deterrence which was to stand for over thirty years; although individual Argentinians, or groups, made a nuisance of themselves on the Falklands and there were periodic demonstrations outside the British Embassy in Buenos Aires to 'condemn British occupation', their Government took no active steps to further its ambitions. The annual campaigns of claim and counter-claim in Antarctica continued, however, obliging the Royal Navy to deploy two sloops or frigates to the Falklands each season and, from 1954, to maintain a small Royal Marines garrison on Deception Island.

The Antarctic question was shelved, for the time being, in 1958, 'International Geophysical Year'. The various nations involved in this area cooperated well and, in December, 1959, signed a thirty-year agreement to suspend territorial claims and to prohibit all military activity south of 60° South. From 1957 the Royal Navy had reduced its presence to a single ship – HMS *Protector* which, like her successor, HMS *Endurance*, enjoyed two summers each year, refitting in Britain during the northern summer and spending the southern summer surveying and supporting the British Antarctic Survey.

In the meantime Peron had been ousted. After the death of his popular wife, Eva, in 1952, he lost his touch and with it the support of the unions and the Army, whose conflicting interests had been held together only by the Perons' team effort. A declaration that Argentina would send troops to fight in Korea if requested by the United Nations had to be retracted when massive demonstrations in the industrial centres showed the unions' disagreement. The 'welfare dictatorship' had ruined the Argentine economy and Peron's efforts to restore it offended almost all sections of society, culminating in his excommunication when he acted against the Catholic Church. But his gravest offence, which was directly responsible for his downfall, was to insult his entire nation by granting an American oil company exploitation rights in large tracts of Argentina. National pride was outraged and Peron fled to Paraguay.

This strong trait of nationalism was to dog subsequent Governments, Junta and democrats in turn, as they came to the realization that foreign involvement was essential to the country's industrial development, whatever the promises the incoming Generals or politicians may have made to the people before assuming power. The Peronista-dominated unions would accept a siege economy to secure loans from the International Monetary Fund, but would not accept that North American expertise was necessary to exploit the oil resources needed to repay the loan. Thus, in 1962, Argentina became virtually self-sufficient for oil fuel but in the next year a President was elected on a manifesto whose main theme was the termination of foreign oil contracts, a promise which was honoured immediately, to the economic detriment of Argentina.

In the same year, 1963, there was an obvious increase in the agitation for the 'return' of the Falklands, with the introduction of 'Malvinas Day', a national holiday. The advent of a nationalist administration was clearly a major influence on the timing of the claim, but it is probable that the Argentinians had been watching closely the British Government's decolonization programme. By 1963 many African colonies were independent states in their own rights and the timetable for most of the Caribbean and West Indies islands had been published and it must have been apparent to the Argentine Government and people that the Falklands were not on the list. What does not appear to have been apparent to Argentina was the common principle that independence was granted to those territories whose people actually wanted to end dependence. The Falkland Islanders, as they were to make plain during the two decades which followed, did not want any more independence than they already possessed in their democratic island legislature and certainly did not want to exchange the rule of their appointed Governor for the uncertainties and volatility of Buenos Aires government.

Argentina took the matter to the United Nations in 1964 and in December, 1965, the General Assembly passed a Resolution which invited Britain and Argentina to negotiate to find a peaceful solution: the Resolution drew both sides' attention to the 'provisions and objectives' of the UN Charter, the 1960 Resolution on decolonization and the interests of the population of the Falklands. During the years of on-off negotiation which followed, successive Argentine Governments refused to accept the principle of self-determination and the islanders refused to accept Argentina.

The first incident for many years occurred in September, 1964, when an Argentinian civil pilot landed a Cessna on Stanley Racecourse, stuck an Argentine flag in the turf, handed a leaflet to a surprised local and took off again. The British Government protested, the Argentine Government apologized. HMS *Protector* landed a platoon (about thirty-two men) of Royal Marines as a token garrison in 1965 but this was reduced to one officer and five Marines when she left at the end of the 1965/66 'season'.

An extreme right-wing group – the '*Movimiento Nueva Argentina*' – took advantage of what they thought to be the complete withdrawal of the Royal Marines and on 28 September, 1966, hijacked an Aerolineas Argentinas DC-4 airliner, whose pilots were forced to land on Stanley Racecourse, a feat which required considerable skill. The eighteen members of '*Operacion Condor*' then held the five crew, the Governor of Tierra del Fuego and his nineteen innocent fellow-passengers and some over-curious islanders hostage, giving up only after two days to the Royal Marines and the local Falkland Islands Defence Force volunteers.

Simultaneously, there were anti-British demonstrations in many Argentine cities, the British Consulate in Rosario was ransacked and shots were fired at the villa in which the Duke of Edinburgh was staying during an unofficial visit in connection with Argentina's 150th anniversary of independence. The Argentine Government did little about these mainland events, but it did not take kindly to the kidnapping of a very senior official and apologies for the DC-4 incident were tendered in Buenos Aires and London. This did not stop the Foreign Minister, Nicanor Costa Mendez, from making capital out of the event to renew claims at the United Nations. The hijackers were handed over to the naval transport *Bahia Buen Suceso* (of which more will be heard) on 2 October and were taken to Ushuaia, where they remained in naval custody until they were tried and imprisoned in June, 1967, on charges ranging from piracy to conspiracy against the state.

The British Government had ordered the frigate HMS *Puma* to the Falklands but the Argentine apologies were accepted, so that three weeks later the frigate was taking part in the Argentine Navy's annual major fleet exercise. The Royal Marine garrison was quietly restored to platoon strength and a naval hovercraft unit was later added, to provide mobility.

Relations between Britain and Argentina were surprisingly good during the next eight years. Talks on sovereignty were effectively ruled out by the islanders' vehement refusal to consider any form of alternative to British rule. In 1971 the two Governments even reached agreement on a variety of issues which had hitherto restricted the islands' development due to the sovereignty dispute. The Falklanders were at last free to move in Argentina, under cover of a document which got round the need for the disputed passport, while remaining exempt from Argentine military service; their children were given favoured status, with reserved school places and scholarships in Argentia (where all schoolchildren were taught that '*las Malvinas son Argentinas*'). There were exemptions from duties and taxes on both sides and postal and telephone rates were standardized on those of the country of origin. Most important of all, for day-to-day relations, air and sea services between Argentina and the Falklands were instituted, the first of the twice-monthly amphibian flights between Comodoro Rivadavia and Stanley Harbour arriving on 2 February, 1972.

The amphibian was suitable only for summer operations and in May, 1972, the Argentine authorities were given permission to build a 'temporary' airstrip on the Cape Pembroke peninsula, about two miles to the west of Port Stanley. The airfield came into operation in the following November.

The improvement in relations benefited the Argentine Navy, which was able to obtain ships and weapons not only from Britain but also in the United States. From Britain was ordered the first guided-missile destroyer to enter service in South America, the Type 42 *Hercules*, and technical assistance was given to the building of a second, the *Santissima Trinidad*, in an Argentine shipyard. The United States sold five old destroyers (completed in 1944 and 1945) between 1971 and 1973 and also supplied two equally old but modernized submarines, the *Santa Fe* and *Santiago del Estero*. Two brand-new submarines, *San Luis* and *Salta*, had been ordered in Germany in 1969 and, delivered in prefabricated sec-

Sisters under different flags – the *Santissima Trinidad* outboard of HMS *Newcastle* at Portsmouth in August 1981, during the Argentine Type 42's visit to the United Kingdom for weapons systems tuning *(J.H. Sparkes)*

tions, were completed in Argentina in 1974.

The other major units in the fleet were two 6in cruisers, the *General Belgrano* and *Nueve de Julio* ('9 July'), completed for the US Navy in 1938 and transferred to Argentina at rock-bottom prices in 1951. A more recent acquisition was the British-built aircraft carrier *Veintecinco de Mayo* ('25 May'); built in 1945 as HMS *Venerable*, she had been transferred to the Royal Netherlands Navy in 1948 as the *Karel Doorman*. Twenty years later she suffered a severe boiler-room fire while under refit and was sold to Argentina, replacement machinery being purchased from Britain, where it had lain in the uncompleted carrier *Leviathan* since 1945. Restored to operational service again, she was delivered to the Argentine Navy in the autumn of 1969.

The Argentine naval air arm received second-hand US Navy aircraft in a re-equipment programme in the late 1960s. Besides Lockheed P-2 Neptunes for long-range reconnaissance from shore bases and Grumman S-2 Trackers for ship-borne anti-submarine patrols and reconnaissance, the Navy began to operate a more up-to-date attack aircraft, the Douglas A-4 Skyhawk: the model was the original US service version, the A-4B (A4D-2 until 1962), redesignated A-4Q for export to Argentina. A lightweight aircraft, suitable for operations from the *25 de Mayo*'s short steam catapult and small flight deck, the Skyhawk could carry a respectable load of conventional free-fall bombs or, as an interceptor, two Sidewinder air-to-air missiles, at up to 600 mph. A small number of Sikorsky SH-3 Sea King anti-submarine helicopters was also purchased. The only brand-new aircraft in the new front-line inventory, they were similar in appearance to the Royal Navy's Westland-built Sea Kings but lacked the latter's many improvements.

The Air Force was also supplied with A-4B Skyhawks and later received A-4Cs, with a limited bad-weather attack capability and two additional underwing hardpoints for fuel or ordnance. The US Government attempted from 1967 to curb Latin and South American expenditure on sophisticated weaponry and was not prepared to supply more advanced fighter aircraft, while Britain's politically-stultified aviation industry had little to offer but reworked out-of-date aircraft such as the dozen Canberra light bombers supplied to the *Fuerza Aerea Argentina* in 1970. Argentina therefore turned to France to buy the Mach 2.0 Dassault Mirage fighter which had become very popular among smaller air forces after its success in Israeli service in the 1967 'Six Days' War'; ten single-seat Mirage IIIEA interceptors and two IIIDA two-seat trainers entered service in 1972.

The armed forces' modest improvement programme came to an end in 1973, even before the world's economy was hit by the post-'Yom Kippur War' oil crisis; so too, unfortunately, did the improvement in Argentina's general external relations. In March the first elections since the 1965 coup were won by the *Peronistas*, the new President gaining a wide majority while the party provided no fewer than twenty of the twenty-two provincial Governors. President Campora lost no time in inviting the geriatric Juan Peron to return from exile and the man who had escaped to Paraguay in disgrace in 1952 flew home on 20 June, 1973. So huge a crowd turned out to welcome home their one-time idol that it was decided to divert the aircraft to the nearby military airfield. Peron was thus deprived of an enthusiastic demonstration in which thirty-five people died! Peron and his third wife, 'Isabelita', were elected President and Vice President in September, 1973, on a frankly nationalistic manifesto, whereas on past performance a socialist régime might have been expected. The quiet improvement in Anglo-Argentine relations over the Falklands came to an abrupt halt as the Buenos Aires negotiators demanded that sovereignty should be the main item for discussion, while London avoided the issue.

In 1974 Argentina took the matter to the UN again and the General Assembly passed a Resolution calling on both parties to accelerate their attempts to find a solution to the sovereignty question. The Falklands islanders did not object to further talks but would not take part, thereby rendering negotiations pointless. Peron died in July, 1974, his wife taking over as President. This, and internal problems, distracted attention from the Falklands for a few months, but in December, 1974, a Peronista newspaper began a campaign demanding the invasion of the Falklands. The Government publicly dissociated itself from the idea, but in April, 1975, following inflammatory remarks in the Press by the Minister for Foreign Affairs, the British Ambassador delivered a second clear warning that any attack on the Falklands would be met with force.

In July, 1975, the British Government proposed a cooperative development of resources in the area; this was rejected by the Argentinians as it effectively avoided the sovereignty question. Failing in this, the British Government commissioned an economic survey, under the leadership of Lord Shackleton. The announcement of the survey, in October, 1975, angered all parties in Argentina and the timing of the team's arrival in Port Stanley, on the 143rd anniversary of Captain Onslow's repossession, was extremely tactless.

The immediate result, apart from the fury of certain sectors of the Press, was the mutual withdrawal of Ambassadors, at Argentine suggestion. The Foreign Minister, Arauz Castex, gave prophetic warning of the likely result of what his country saw as British intransigence, that there might be 'only one course open to Argentina irrespective of what Government might be in power.' Talks between the two countries were resumed in February, 1976, in New York, and during the course of these it was yet again impressed upon the Argentine Ministry for Foreign Affairs that the Falklands would be defended with force, if need be.

On 17 February, while the talks were in progress, the Argentine destroyer *Almirante Storni* intercepted and fired on the British Antarctic Survey research ship *Shackleton*. The incident took place some eighty miles south of the Falklands, not far from the area where the main action of the 1914 Battle of the Falklands began, in waters claimed by the Argentine as hers, by virtue of their being within 200 miles of the continental shelf. The *Shackleton* was not hit and managed to prevent her larger and faster assailant from putting a boarding party aboard. The affair had been entirely an Argentine Navy enterprise, in planning and execution, and the Government, through the delegation in New York, promised that the research ship would be allowed to complete her programme without further interference.

The Royal Navy's Ice Patrol Ship, HMS *Endurance*, was at this time on her final deployment, the decision having been taken in 1974 that, as part of the general reduction in the British Forces' 'out-of-area' capability, her task was not essential. The *Shackleton* incident resulted in her retention for a further season, a process which was repeated year by year thereafter, but only at the insistence of the Foreign and Commonwealth Office, for the Ministry of Defence could maintain her only at the expense of other commitments.

On 24 March, 1976, after three years of elected government, which had been accompanied by economic disaster and ever-increasing factional terrorism, the armed forces seized power in a bloodless coup. The Junta, led by General Videla, appointed a monetarist Minister of Finance who managed to bring the country's external balance of payments into credit by the end of the year. The 'economic miracle' lasted for a few years, persuading the international money-lending community that a sort of stability had been achieved in Argentina, so that vast sums were loaned to the country, where they were, all too often, ill-invested.

Internally, the Junta ruled a far from stable country. Determined to eliminate terrorism, it struck back ruthlessly and, within a year of its coming to power, Amnesty International estimated that up to 6,000 opponents of the régime were in prison and a further 2,000 had 'disappeared'; not included among the '*desaparecidos*' were forty-six detainees who had been shot out of hand in August, 1976, in retaliation for the murder of a retired Army officer. The new President of the United States, Jimmy Carter, so disapproved of these violations of human rights that he suspended certain categories of military aid. Touchy as ever, the Junta, on 28 February, 1977, rejected all US military aid and continued to eliminate internal opposition as it saw fit.

As a gesture against outside interference in Argentine affairs, the refusal of supplies may have been acceptable to the nation and to the Army, but it greatly affected the efficiency of the Navy and the Air Force, both armed to a major extent with second-hand United States equipment. It was, as so often in this corner of the world, ill-timed, for Argentina was about to wish upon herself yet another confrontation with her nearest neighbour.

The dispute about the three islands in the eastern approaches to the Beagle Channel dated back to 1915. Although there were minor incidents from time to time, not until the late 1960s, when offshore oil exploitation in such waters had become a practical and economic proposition and the recognition of sea-bed frontiers gave title to the resources, did real trouble arise between Argentina and Chile. Unable to settle the matter bilaterally, the two countries agreed, in July, 1971, to the appointment of a Court of Arbitration, to be composed of five judges who had formerly served the International Court of Justice and whose decision would be sanctioned by the British Government – a tribute to the fairness of the 1902 settlement. The Court, all of whose members had to be acceptable to both Governments, began its deliberations when Senora Peron was in power and delivered them after she had been ousted. Her Majesty the Queen herself ratified and announced publicly the unanimous judgement, on 2 May, 1977: to the profound shock of Argentina, the five judges had upheld the Chilean claim to sovereignty, confirming the British arbitration of seventy-five years before.

In 1902 Argentina had accepted what was undoubtedly a disappointment with quiet dignity. The 1977 rulers were of different stock and like petulant children they prepared to take by force what they had been denied by reasoned argument.

During the southern winter of 1977 Argentina sought to improve her forces, buying abroad where this was possible. In the short term, as far as the Navy was concerned, this led to the arming of three ex-American destroyers with four French-built MM.38 Exocet missiles apiece. Off-the-shelf material was not immediately available and orders were placed for other ships and equipment for delivery in 1978.

Perhaps as a diversionary exercise, for the Beagle Channel was the more important at the time, the Argentine Government applied pressure off the Falklands. This action took the form of harassment of Eastern Bloc fishing vessels, seven Russians and two Bulgarian craft being arrested for fishing in 'Argentine' waters off the Falklands; one of the Bulgarian vessels tried to escape and was hit by gunfire, a crew-member being wounded. These incidents, in September and October, 1977, were seen by the British Government as hard-line preliminaries to a round of Anglo-Argentine talks scheduled for December, not as a possible smoke-screen and distraction for local consumption, to draw attention from the impending real crisis with Chile. Late in November, 1977, it was therefore decided to deploy a small task group to the South Atlantic, 'to respond flexibly to limited acts of aggression'.* The force, which comprised the nuclear-propelled submarine *Dreadnought* off the Falklands, with two general-purpose frigates and an oiler on the latitude of the Plate, could hardly be termed a deterrent, for it was intended that the Argentine Government should remain unaware of its presence, which was maintained until the talks ended in mid-December.

Less than a month later, on 11 January, 1978, the Argentine Fleet sailed in force from its main base at Puerto Belgrano and a fortnight later, while it was still at sea, exercising, the Argentine Government informed Chile and Britain that it was not going to accept the International Court of Justice's ruling on the Beagle Channel question. War in the South Atlantic was suddenly very close and for a month both sides concentrated their forces and violated each other's airspace over the southern provinces, until the two Presidents, Videla of Argentina and Pinochet of Chile, met and agreed to establish a bilateral commission to reach a solution. A deadline of 2 November, 1978, was set.

In this breathing space Argentina continued to re-arm. The Navy bought two 1,170-ton corvettes, the *Drummond* and *Guerrico*, from France; originally ordered by South Africa, they had been embargoed while building and were finally delivered in October, 1978, each armed with four Exocets. Somewhat surprisingly, in view of the past Argentine sympathy towards nazism, Israel became a prime supplier of weapons. Four 'Dabur'-class patrol craft were delivered and Gabriel surface-to-surface missiles were ordered for a pair of fast attack craft being built in Germany. More important, twenty-six surplus fighter-bombers were purchased from Israel: these were copies of the French Dassault Mirage 5, built between the 1967 and 1973 Arab-Israeli wars when supplies of the French-built example were embargoed. The Argentine Air Force already had sixteen Dassault Mirage IIIEA interceptors in service and ordered four more from France. At about the same time, the Argentine Navy, seeking to replace the Douglas A-4Q Skyhawks which had been the stan-

---

* Franks Report (1983), para 65. This Report is the basis for much of the detail of events recorded in this Chapter.

dard carrier fighter-bomber since the mid-60s, ordered fourteen Dassault Super Etendards. This was the only conventional (catapult and arrester wire) shipboard aircraft in production in the West, outside the United States, and although unremarkable in general performance it was designed for the carriage of the air-launched version of the Exocet, the AM.39. Consideration had been given to the British Sea Harrier, but no equivalent air-to-surface missile was available with this aircraft, which was also considered to lack the necessary radius of action but was otherwise ideal for the small carrier *25 de Mayo*, whose catapult and arrester gear would be on the limits when operating the 12-tonne Super Etendard.

No real progress was made with Britain over the Falklands during 1978, but the Argentine public's attention was riveted to the staging of the World Cup in their country and even the commonplace terrorism in Argentina abated. The national team won the Cup and the country benefited from some useful external propaganda.

The deadline of 2 November for settlement of the Beagle Channel dispute passed without agreement and again the two countries squared up to one another. After seven weeks of heightening tension and deployments, the opposing Governments agreed, mainly as the result of US encouragement, to examine the possibility of mediation by the Vatican. This was offered by a papal emissary, on condition that the two sides used no force and accepted the Pope's arbitration; this was solemnly agreed by Argentina and Chile on 8 January, 1979.

1979 and 1980 passed relatively quietly, by South American standards. Britain and Argentina resumed exploratory talks on co-operation in the development of off-shore resources. The British Foreign Secretary, Lord Carrington, favoured 'leaseback' – transfer of sovereignty to Argentina but continued British administration – as a solution to the dispute, but held to the principle that the islanders must be respected as the actual inhabitants. The latter liked none of the Foreign and Commonwealth Office's suggestions and decided that the British delegation at the talks due in February, 1981, should propose a 'freeze' in the sovereignty dispute.

Yet again, the timing was unfortunate. The Argentine economy, hitherto buoyed up by high beef and grain prices, was beginning to feel the drag of the massive borrowing from abroad during 1980 and by the end of the year its condition was critical. In February, 1981, the peso had to be devalued and the crisis deepened. Under such circumstances, it was natural that the Argentine Government, under the outgoing President Videla, was looking for some success and as the Pope's only suggestion to date on the Beagle Channel dispute had been the establishment of a 'demilitarized zone of peace', on 12 December, 1980, the Falklands appeared to be the major hope.

Under the circumstances, it was not surprising that the Argentine delegation totally rejected the idea of a freeze on sovereignty discussions, but in the round of talks in February, 1981, there was a 'narrowing of the issues' which led the Foreign and Commonwealth Office to believe that the islanders might be prepared to countenance preliminary discussions on sovereignty. This possibility faded when, in October, the newly-elected Falkland Islands Legislative Council proved to be more anti-Argentine than its predecessor.

The Argentine Government had scarcely had time to consider the implications of the February talks before the Chilean dispute emerged again: the Vatican, after two years' consideration, confirmed Chile's title to the disputed islands. President Videla, as one of his last acts before retiring on 29 March, 1981, formally rejected the Pope's judgement. A number of incidents along the border led to its closure in late April, only for it to be re-opened a fortnight later after the Pope had appealed to the two Governments for restraint.

During the Argentine winter of 1981 four unconnected items occurred which appear to have given heart to the new President and his Junta, consisting of the three Service chiefs. In April President Reagan asked the US Congress to lift its ban on the supply of arms to Argentina, apparently on the basis of a supposed improvement in the human rights situation: Congress did not agree. In June the British Secretary of State for Defence announced major reductions in the Royal Navy which included the ending of the regular South Atlantic deployments – HMS *Endurance's* 1981–82 season would be her last, in spite of appeals from the Foreign Secretary and protests from the House of Commons and the Falkland Islands. In September the Foreign Secretary met the Argentine Minister for Foreign Affairs in New York and told him that the British Government could not force the islanders to accept unwelcome terms, although it 'would continue to do their best to persuade the Islanders of the benefits of an accommodation'; this was taken by the Argentine Press, at least, as an admission that the British Government agreed that the status of the Falklands could not be maintained. Finally, in October, some of the islanders, who had always insisted that they wished to remain British, were denied full British citizenship by the Nationality Act. In some Argentine eyes the Falkland Islands had been virtually abandoned.

In December, 1981, President Videla resigned; he had been unable to cope with the financial problems, which were now almost completely out of hand. In his place the Commander-in-Chief of the Army, General Leopoldo Galtieri, was appointed President, while retaining his place on the Junta; even the Commander-in-Chief had to make promises to win the support of the Army councils which kept the Junta in power and it was widely rumoured that Galtieri's main undertaking was that the 'Malvinas' should be recovered. Certainly, the lecturer in military history at the Argentine Army Staff College, Dr Juan Carlos Murguizur, states that he learnt of the intention to invade in the month that Galtieri came to power and believed that the latter's confidence that Britain would not go to war over the Falklands had been confirmed by 'the positive response which had been received from the highest political level in the USA'.*

From late January, 1982, up to the opening of the next round of talks on 26 February, the Argentine Press reflected the impatience of the new President, with speculation that should Britain continue to be unco-operative there would be justification for the use of force in seizing the Falklands. The Ministry of Foreign Affairs, now under Nicanor Costa Mendez once more, formally notified the British Government that Argentina wanted a commission, with a life of one year, to examine and recommend on the subject of sovereignty and that the outcome of the negotiations should be recognition of Argentine sovereignty over the Falklands and Dependencies.

The entire Junta was supporting the official line, but there was evidence that the Navy, under Admiral Jorge Anaya, was orchestrating the Press campaign and was actually in favour of an invasion. The *Endurance*, visiting the naval base at Ushuaia in January, 1982, encountered a very chilly reception, but was then, in February, permitted to follow this up with a maintenance period at Mar del Plata, where the usual warm hospitality was enjoyed.

The February talks in New York saw acceptance of the Argentine demand for a short-life commission to consider and recommend a solution to the sovereignty dispute. It was agreed that no full statement would be issued until both Governments had been consulted and that a joint *communiqué* should be issued on 1 March, giving no information other than that both sides were resolved to find a solution and that an Argentine procedural proposal was under consideration. But on the same day the Ministry of Foreign Affairs in Buenos Aires published a fuller and slanted version, in which the aim of the proposed discussions was the early transfer to Argentina of sovereignty, and which ended with a veiled threat of other means to achieve the end.

The British Minister in charge of the New York delegation, Mr Richard Luce, who was the grandson of Captain Luce of the *Glasgow*, protested to his Argentine opposite number but neither he nor Dr Costa Mendez apologized or accepted responsibility, although both denied any intention to apply pressure by threats. These were the last pre-war exchanges on the subject of the Falklands, the islands which had always been on the front page of Argentine newspapers but the back page of British atlases.

---

* 'The South Atlantic Conflict', *International Defence Review*, No 2/83.

PART II

Scrap at South Georgia

The bleak, mountainous island of South Georgia, 700 miles to the east of Port Stanley, had had only one period of real usefulness since it had been discovered by Captain James Cook in 1775. For half a century, from 1904, it had been a centre of shore whaling activity, but the decline in the industry from the 1950s, as pelagic (open ocean) whaling using factory ships became the most efficient means of exploiting the dwindling stocks, led to the abandonment of the Grytviken and Leith stations. The only human inhabitants were the transient population of scientists of the British Antarctic Survey, a party about thirty-strong, whose leader, the Base Commander, was the official representative of the Governor of the Falkland Islands.

The firm of Christian Salvesen, based at Leith, the port of Edinburgh, had been one of the most important in the Antarctic whaling industry and was still the manager of the Crown leases for the South Georgia whaling stations. In 1978, Constantino Davidoff, a Buenos Aires scrap metal dealer, signed a contract with Salvesens giving him an option on the derelict machinery. The option was taken up two years later and in December, 1981, Davidoff visited Leith Harbour, South Georgia, to inspect the whaling station. Unfortunately his letter informing the British Embassy in Buenos Aires of his visit arrived after he had sailed and when he reached South Georgia, on 20 December, he did not seek entry permission at Grytviken as he was required to do, but landed at Leith.

There may have been some excuse for Davidoff, but there was none for the captain of the ship which took him there, the Argentine Navy ice-breaker *Almirante Irizar*, who was well aware of the need for diplomatic clearance. The Argentine Navy had used Davidoff's visit as an opportunity for deliberate provocation and although the dealer apologised for the problems caused, the Argentine Ministry of Foreign Affairs had already rejected a formal British protest, having first denied all knowledge of the visit. At the time of the denial, 6 January, 1982, it is quite likely that the Ministry did not have a full knowledge of the facts, for the Navy appears to have acted on its own initiative.

Davidoff expressed his anxiety that his activity should not cause further difficulties and asked for full instructions on entry procedures. He also offered to transport supplies to the British Antarctic Survey (BAS) team and to make available the services of a medical team with the scrap party. The British Embassy was notified on 9 March that forty-one workmen were to leave on the 11th, aboard the Argentine Navy transport *Bahia Buen Suceso*, and that they would be working at Leith for about four months; Salvesens were also informed by Davidoff, who had asked for, and been given, an extension of the contract until March, 1984 – hardly the action of a man party to a plan to provoke the British again.

The Argentine Navy again took advantage of the opportunity thus offered. The use of the naval transport was not exceptional. The Navy was responsible for sea traffic in Antarctic regions so that little could be read into the use of a naval vessel for commercial purposes, but this did place the blame for what was to follow on the Navy and its Commander-in-Chief, Anaya. On 19 March the *Bahia Buen Suceso* went direct to Leith Harbour, landed the workmen and Service personnel who raised the Argentine flag and defaced the notice which warned against unauthorised landings. The Argentine *chargé d'affaires* in London may personally have been speaking in good faith when, on 22 March, he explained to the Foreign and Commonwealth Office that Davidoff was responsible for the action, that the ship had no Service personnel or weapons on board and that the Argentine Government did not intend to manufacture a crisis, but this was a tissue of lies, with the possible exception of the degree of Government involvement. Anaya was intent on scoring points and would do so whatever the diplomatic cost.

HMS *Endurance* sailed from Port Stanley on 20 March with her own Royal Marine detachment of twelve men, commanded by Lieutenant Keith Mills, supplemented by an NCO and eight Marines from the Falklands garrison. The *Bahia Buen Suceso* sailed from Leith next day, leaving the workmen behind, and the *Endurance* arrived at Grytviken on the 23rd. The British Government was anxious not to escalate what appeared to be a minor incident and the *Endurance* was ordered not to take any action against the workmen, although she did use her Wasp helicopters to keep them under observation.

Diplomatic exchanges were completely fruitless, the Argentine Ministry of Foreign Affairs being given no freedom to manoeuvre, thanks to the Navy's machinations. Costa Mendez told the British Ambassador in Buenos Aires that he would see if Davidoff could be persuaded to remove his men, but that the threat implicit in the *Endurance*'s presence was unacceptable in certain quarters, naming Admiral Anaya. On 24 March the Argentine Navy sailed a corvette to take up station between South Georgia and the Falklands for the purpose of intercepting HMS *Endurance* should she succeed in taking off the Argentinians at Leith. The latter received more direct support on the next day with the arrival of the naval transport *Bahia Paraiso*; a modern ship designed to support Antarctic expeditions, she had embarked two helicopters, an Army Puma troop-carrier as well as her own smaller Alouette.

The *Bahia Paraiso* left Leith on 26 March and took up a station fifteen miles to the north of South Georgia, where she remained. On the same day units of the Argentine Navy sailed for exercises with the Uruguayan Navy in the Plate estuary. The exercise, which in itself was unusual for the time of year, as this was traditionally the Argentine Navy's period of least efficiency due to the conscription cycle, was given out as being for anti-submarine training and the Argentine Navy contribution included the carrier *25 de Mayo*, the Type 42 guided missile destroyers *Hercules* and *Santissima Trinidad* (only recently returned from missile firing trials off Britain), two corvettes, *Drummond* and *Granville*, and the amphibious landing ship *Cabo San Antonio*, an unlikely participant in an anti-submarine warfare exercise. The sailing and the identities of the ships was reported in the Argentine Press, but what was not reported was the presence of a marine infantry battalion in the landing ship and a naval 'Commando' aboard the destroyer *Santissima Trinidad*. The Press itself did not know that, after months of planning, the Navy and marines had conducted a dress rehearsal for an invasion on 19 March, or, more importantly, that after much vacillation the Junta had taken its crucial decision to invade the Falklands on 26 March.* The target date was 1 April – the amphibious force would meet bad weather which would cause the timetable to be set back by twenty-four hours.

In previous assessments of the risk of Argentine action against the Falklands and the Dependencies, it had been assumed by the British that there would be a progressive build-up of tension and incidents which would give sufficient warning time to enable the Government to take whatever steps, diplomatic or military, it considered necessary to protect British sovereign territory. On at least two occasions in the past Argentine Governments had also been given direct warnings that Britain would meet force with force and these had been immediately effective. Now, in March, 1982, the tension existed but the pattern of incidents had not followed the expected one of interrupted communications with the Falklands, harassment of British shipping, occupation of uninhabited dependent islands and so forth.† The direct threat to the Falklands does not appear to have been recognized, even after Costa Mendez, in replying to the British Government on 28 March, linked the South Georgia affair to the United Kingdom's 'persistent lack of recognition . . . of the titles of sovereignty which my country has over the Malvinas, South Georgia and South Sandwich Islands', and warned that crises such as the present one would recur as long as the sovereignty dispute remained unsolved.

* Report of Rattenbach Commission, *Siete Dias*, 1983.

† Franks Report, p. 67.

On 29 March the Prime Minister and Foreign Secretary decided that a nuclear-powered Fleet submarine should be sent to support the *Endurance*. The Navy had already ordered the Royal Fleet Auxiliary (RFA) stores ship *Fort Austin* to the South Atlantic to replenish the *Endurance*, whose stores and provisions would last only three more weeks, and she left Gibraltar on the same day. This was not the Navy's first initiative, for two days earlier, another RFA, the tanker *Appleleaf*, bound from Curacao to the UK with a full load of fuel, had been ordered to divert to Gibraltar to embark general naval stores and then sail south to support the *Endurance* and *Fort Austin*. The logistics line, so crucial to the subsequent campaign, was thus opened even before the first shots were fired. No combatant units were deployed as yet, but the Commander-in-Chief, Fleet, Admiral Sir John Fieldhouse, ordered Rear Admiral J. F. Woodward, the Flag Officer, First Flotilla, then at Gibraltar exercising with sixteen destroyers and frigates, to prepare plans for the detachment of a task group to the South Atlantic.

On 31 March intelligence was received in London that the Falklands were to be invaded on 2 April and that evening the Prime Minister conferred with the Secretary of State for Defence, Mr John Nott, two junior Foreign Office Ministers and the First Sea Lord, Admiral of the Fleet Sir Henry Leach, representing the Chief of the Defence Staff, Admiral of the Fleet Sir Terence Lewin, who was out of the country. Admiral Leach was instructed to prepare the force which he had advised would be required to retake the islands 'without commitment to a final decision as to whether or not it should sail'. A message was sent to President Reagan, informing him of the intended invasion and requesting that he use his influence to deter General Galtieri from authorizing the landing – Britain could not acquiesce in any occupation but would not escalate the dispute or initiate hostilities. The Governor of the Falklands, Mr Rex Hunt, and the British Ambassador at Buenos Aires were informed of the indications of invasion.*

The *Endurance*, which was still watching the activities of the Argentinians at Leith, was ordered to leave Grytviken and return to Port Stanley, but before sailing Captain Barker landed Lieutenant Mills and his twenty-one Marines to protect the BAS personnel and maintain the watch on Leith. The tiny force, armed with machine-guns, 'bazooka'-type 66mm anti-tank rockets and an 84mm Carl Gustav rocket launcher, took up positions on King Edward Point, a flat peninsula to seaward of Grytviken. Next morning, 1 April, a four-man team was sent to establish an observation post to keep Leith under surveillance, but the team was withdrawn when the Governor of the Falklands' radio warning of imminent invasion was overheard.

President Reagan telephoned General Galtieri late on 1 April, but the

* Franks (para 63).

latter at first refused to accept a call and later, when he did agree to speak, he did so in terms which made it apparent that Argentina was determined on invasion, accepting all that war might entail. Beset by domestic, economic and social problems, the Junta had made the oft-repeated and invariably wrong decision to divert the masses by offering glory in a foreign adventure and could not now turn back without losing face among their own 'peer group' of Service officers.

The message informing the Prime Minister of the Argentine attitude was sent at 0245 on 2 April (10.45pm on the 1st in Port Stanley) and its arrival followed soon after the receipt of intelligence that the invasion had actually been ordered. Admiral Leach was on hand to advise the members of the Cabinet that a balanced naval force, built around two aircraft carriers and with an amphibious assault component, could be sailed in five days for operations in the South Atlantic. At 0330 the first signal was sent to bring the Fleet in Home ports to short notice for sea and Rear Admiral Woodward was soon afterwards ordered to send a group south from the Gibraltar area. Before dawn Royal Navy and Royal Marines personnel were being recalled from their Easter leave, which had only just begun. The Royal Navy was moving to a war footing three hours before the first shots were fired in the Falklands.

Chapter Two

Operacion ROSARIO

On 30 March the annual rotation of the Falklands Royal Marines garrison began with the arrival of Major M. J. Norman RM and his forty-two men aboard the research ship *John Biscoe*. Under normal circumstances the outgoing garrison, commanded by Major G. R. N. Noott, would have handed over and left on the next day, but the Governor, Mr Rex Hunt, asked for its retention and so there were nearly twice as many Marines at Port Stanley as usual; the detachment of nine of the 'old' party to South Georgia was almost compensated by the presence of Lieutenant C. Todhunter RN and nine naval ratings, left behind by the *Endurance* to continue a survey task.

From 31 March the garrison established observation posts at Pembroke Lighthouse, overlooking the entrance to Port William, and on Sapper Hill, which commanded a view of the coastline to the south of Port Stanley and from which the *Gneisenau* and *Nürnberg* had first been seen on 8 December, 1914. During the hours of darkness the naval party manned the Falkland Islands Company coaster *Forrest* and maintained a radar watch from Port William. Major Norman assumed command on 1 April and that morning he and Major Noott were told by the Governor of the probable invasion on the 2nd.

The Royal Marines were too few to prevent landings but were deployed to hold up the progress of the invasion sufficiently to force the Argentine commander to negotiate. The airfield runway was obstructed with vehicles and a section of Marines was positioned to cover the area against a helicopter landing, with a machine gun in the sand dunes overlooking the most accessible beach. Another section, with two machine guns, covered the narrow isthmus joining the airfield peninsula to that on which Port Stanley stands and two more sections were stationed to the west in support. A landing to the south of the town, in Port Harriet or Mullet Creek, was considered to be less probable and just one section on the ridge behind Stanley was added to the observation post on Sapper Hill. The *Forrest* again patrolled in Port William and No 5 Section, with six Marines led by Corporal S. C. York, was installed on Navy Point, the western side of the narrow entrance to Port Stanley.

General view from Cape Pembroke, looking east towards Port Stanley and the hinterland where the battles of June 1982 took place. The nearer inlet on the right-hand edge is Yorke Bay, where the main Argentine landings were made on 2 April, and beyond that is the opening of the Murrell River, overlooked by Mount Longdon. In the far distance, the bulk of Mount Kent looks down on the distinctive towers of Two Sisters, almost in line with Stanley Harbour, with Mount Harriet and, nearer to the camera, Mount Tumbledown and Mount William (MoD)

The Argentine Navy, which was mounting the landings with token Army participation, was taking no chances and was indulging in considerable 'overkill'. The main assault force was the 2nd Marine Infantry Battalion, which was to be landed from the Landing Ship (Tank) *Cabo San Antonio*, together with one platoon of soldiers of the Army's 25th Infantry Regiment. Two more platoons of this regiment were embarked in the icebreaker *Almirante Irizar*, which was carrying two Coastguard helicopters. The submarine *Santa Fe* was to land a party of swimmers and a seventy-strong naval 'Special Forces' group was aboard the Type 42 destroyer *Santissima Trinidad*. In all, there were over 1,000 troops immediately available to deal with the eighty-five Royal Marine and Navy defenders of Port Stanley. The latter's heaviest weapons were a few Carl Gustav and 66mm rocket launchers: besides their own heavy weapons and the 30mm cannon in the nineteen armoured amphibious landing vehicles (LVTs), the Argentine invaders could call upon the destroyers *Santissima Trinidad* and *Hercules* and the corvettes *Drummond* and *Granville* for gunfire support if required. The naval transport *Isla de los Estados*, carrying stores and provisions, made up the force, which was commanded by *Contralmirante de Infanteria Marina* (Rear Admiral of Marines) Carlos Busser. In distant support, 550 miles to the north, *Contralmirante* Gualter Allara was at sea in the carrier, screened by five old ex-US Navy destroyers and accompanied by the oiler *Punta Medanos*.

The *Forrest*, on radar watch in Port William, began sending reports of shipping to the east as early as 2.30am on 2 April and these were soon confirmed by the Marine observation post at Cape Pembroke Lighthouse. The first Argentine troops were, however, already ashore and had been for several hours. The *Santissima Trinidad* had anchored off Mullet Creek, five miles to the south of Port Stanley, well before midnight and launched inflatables which landed the naval 'Commando'. These troops split into two parties, one of which was to capture Government

House while the other neutralized the Royal Marines' barracks at Moody Brook, at the western end of Port Stanley harbour, and moved off at 1.00am. Like the other forces detailed for the invasion, they were ordered to use the minimum force – the Junta wanted a bloodless occupation.

The next Argentinians ashore were the frogmen from the *Santa Fe*, to secure the beach at Yorke Bay, to the north of the airfield, at 3.30am. Having ensured that there were no obstacles or sentries, some of the swimmers pushed on to occupy the eastern point of the Port Stanley narrows, 200 yards from where Corporal York had set up his observation post.

The Royal Navy section had meanwhile been employed on 'internal security'. Led by Colour Sergeant J. Noone RM, and accompanied by the Chief Secretary as the representative of the civil power, they had rounded up the thirty Argentine nationals resident in Port Stanley by 4.00am, placing them in protective custody. Most were servicemen and civil servants representing various official Argentine organizations and the senior officer was *Vice-Comodoro* (the Argentine Air Force equivalent of a Lieutenant-Colonel) Hector Gilobert, who represented the state airline.

The first firing was heard by the defenders at 6.05am, as the Argentine Special Forces attacked the empty Moody Brook camp with small arms fire and grenades. Ten minutes later Government House came under attack, the Argentinians opening fire without warning. The attack was repulsed, with the loss of the officer leading the enemy group, Marine *Capitan de Corbeta* (Lieutenant-Commander) P. E. Giachino – the first man to be killed in the war. The two sides settled down to an exchange of fire which lasted for the next three hours, the Royal Marines silencing snipers and winkling out three Argentine marines who had gone to ground in a hayloft.

Government House, Port Stanley, the target of the Argentine commandos and the headquarters of the defending forces *(MoD)*

As the fight for Government House began, the *Cabo San Antonio* began disgorging her LVTs at Yorke Bay. The Royal Marines on the airfield and at the isthmus by Hookers Point had been pulled back to meet the threat from the south of Stanley after the attack on Moody Brook had been heard. The Argentine Army platoon occupied the airport buildings while the marine infantry forced on up the road to the town, three miles to the west, in their amphibious armoured carriers. The first check was met some way to the east of Port Stanley, when the LVTs ran into Lieutenant C. W. Trollope's blocking position. The column was brought to a halt by hitting the leading vehicle with a Carl Gustav on the front and a 66 rocket on the passenger compartment. None of the occupants of this vehicle emerged, but the Royal Marines were obliged to fall back as the Argentine troops emerged from the other fifteen LVTs and opened fire. The Army platoon was ordered up from the airfield to reinforce the marines but the offer of assistance by the *Drummond*, to provide gunfire support with her 100mm main armament, was not taken up.

Only one of the outlying Royal Marines sections managed to fight its way into the Government House perimeter to reinforce the small garrison. The others were gradually pinned down by the increasing number of Argentine troops, who were being landed on the airfield by the Lynx helicopters of the two Type 42 destroyers and the *Almirante Irizar*'s Puma, as well as direct from the *Cabo San Antonio*, beached in Yorke Bay. The obstructions on the airfield were removed – they were intended only to prevent an air-landed assault – and at 8.30am the first Argentine Air Force C-130 Hercules landed, bringing more men of the Army's 25th Infantry Regiment.

By now it was apparent to Major Norman that the Argentinians were ashore in overwhelming numbers. He accordingly advised the Governor that while a determined resistance could be made, it would be relatively brief; the success of a breakout, in daylight and in singularly open country, was problematical. Mr Hunt, who had been determined from the outset to spare the town from any fighting which might injure the civil population or damage property, decided to ask for terms, using *Vice-Comodoro* Gilobert as an intermediary. *Contralmirante* Busser came to Government House at 9.15am and, after terms had been arranged, the Governor formally surrendered himself and the garrison.

Despite coming under heavy fire from small arms and light artillery, none of the defenders had been hit and the islanders had also escaped without injury. The Argentines lost three dead, including the Special Forces leader, and seventeen wounded.

The Marines and naval personnel at Government House were disarmed and Majors Norman and Noott went off under escort to collect the fighting sections which had been cut off. They did not mention Corporal York's No 4 Section, isolated on Navy Point: the six men had not been engaged and were given permission to go to ground before Busser had arrived at Government House – now they could not be contacted and they made their way off the Point undetected.* Lieutenant Todhunter RN of the survey party changed into plain clothes and, while the Argentine troops were taking possession, calmly collected his survey notes and packed them with the personal possessions which he was allowed to take out of the island.

The invaders were already beginning to recover from the battle, enjoying themselves for the benefit of their own emotional media, running up the blue and white Argentine flag on every pole in sight and forcing Royal Marines to lie prone for the cameramen. The captured British servicemen were then allowed to collect personal items (but no uniform) from Moody Brook and were flown out to Comodoro Rivadavia that evening, the Marines and sailors in a C-130 and the Governor, certain officials, their families and three Marines' wives in a more comfortable Fokker F.28 Fellowship airliner. In forty days the Marines would be back in East Falkland, bringing with them the flag which they had lowered outside Government House and which they would raise again, after an absence of seventy-five days. In the meantime, the group of Britons was flown from southern Argentina to Montevideo and from there to RAF Brize Norton, in Oxfordshire, where they arrived on 5 April.

The aggressors were consolidating throughout the remainder of 2 April. The two infantry platoons aboard the *Almirante Irizar* were taken by helicopter to Goose Green and Darwin, on the isthmus which joins Lafonia to East Falkland, and where the Air Force intended to establish a base for operations by Pucara light attack aircraft of III Air Brigade (whose usual headquarters was at Reconquista, where the sub-tropical climate was in marked contrast to the late autumn in the Falklands). A reinforced company of infantry was taken around by sea to Fox Bay, on West Falkland, to establish a presence on that island.

The *Cabo San Antonio* and *Almirante Irizar* off-loaded motor transport, AA batteries, artillery, provisions and ammunition, as well as the personnel, among whom were included about seventy Air Force personnel who were to operate the airfield. Only seven C-130s were available, but these were supplemented by Lockheed Electras, Fokker F.27 Friendships and F.28s, which were to bring in the vast majority of the 13,000 Argentinians who would serve, at one time or another, in the islands. A very early arrival was Group 2, Air Warning and Control (*VYCA Grupo 2*): on standby since mid-March and warned for the Falklands on 29 March, *VYCA 2* was flown in on the afternoon of 2 April to set up its excellent Westinghouse AN/TPS-43 radar system on Sapper Hill, behind Port Stanley. By 6 April it was operational and, able to provide good radar cover out to a distance of 240 miles, it formed the heart of a co-ordinated

* Members of the newly-arrived Naval Party 8901 contingent, they lacked the local knowledge needed to remain at large in the open country of East Falkland and were captured by a patrol four days later and returned to Britain on 20 April with the South Georgia garrison.

air defence system which included seventy automatic AA guns (Army 35mm, Air Force 35mm and 20mm, Marines 30mm), seven Tigercat missile launchers (the land-based variant of the British Seacat) and a single French-built Roland anti-aircraft missile system.

The news of the invasion began to reach London at about midday on 2 April, 8.00am Falklands time. The Port Stanley broadcasting station kept up a commentary on the Argentines' progress and relayed messages right up to the moment of the surrender. The broadcast was intercepted by the South Georgia garrison, HMS *Endurance*, and the research ship *Bransfield*, which was between South Georgia and Ascension. The news was announced in Britain during the afternoon and was greeted with a sense of shock and national affront. Most people were not entirely certain where the Falklands were, nor why the Argentinians – a nation associated mainly with corned beef (although Fray Bentos is actually a town in Uruguay) and Grand Prix drivers – should want them. Nevertheless, by midsummer, few families had not been touched by the war which was to follow the invasion and all were given ample opportunity to catch up and keep up with events, thanks to the media.

Chapter Three

The Defence of Grytviken

Lieutenant Keith Mills and his garrison at King Edward Point heard the news of the landings near Port Stanley at 0600 on 2 April. In a howling Force 10 gale, they began to prepare defensive positions, laid wire on the beach and laid explosives on the wooden jetty. Caches of rations and ammunition were hidden behind Grytviken so that the Marines could continue to fight from the mountains if they were forced out of their first position. The BAS personnel in the local area were sent back to take shelter in Grytviken church, only the Base Commander, Mr S. Martin, remaining to control the radio link with the small teams in various camps in isolated areas of South Georgia.

The preparations were interrupted by the arrival in Cumberland Bay of the *Bahia Paraiso*, but she was unable to do more than carry out a brief reconnaissance as the weather was too bad for any attempt at a landing, by helicopter or boat. In the early evening the Argentine ship contacted the garrison by radio, telling it to expect an important message on the following forenoon. Lieutenant Mills passed this information to HMS *Endurance*, which had turned back from the Falklands late on 1 April and was now steaming at her best speed of about 12 knots to support the Grytviken Marines.

The 'important message' was passed by VHF radio at 1030 on 3 April and was, predictably, an invitation to follow the example of the Governor and surrender. Lieutenant Mills, to ensure that the isolated bases, HMS *Endurance* and the *Bransfield* were aware of what was going on, repeated the message back to the *Bahia Paraiso* on HF (high-frequency) radio which could be intercepted at very much greater range than his low-powered VHF transmitter which, he told the Argentine ship, was unserviceable. The other side was displeased by this procedure and insisted that the Marines should go down to the beach to surrender. This exchange made it obvious that the Argentinians knew of the presence of a garrison and Lieutenant Mills' reply to the call for surrender left them in no doubt that any landing would be resisted.*

* Contrary to Scheina's allegation (*USNI Proceedings*, June, 1982), the *Guerrico* did not contact the Marines and there was no radioed denial of a British military presence.

The corvette *Guerrico*, which had brought out seventy-nine marine infantrymen who had been transferred to the *Bahia Paraiso* early that morning, now entered the cove and the transport's Alouette made a reconnaissance flight over the British Marines. Lieutenant Mills, assuming that the corvette was going to send a boat inshore with a demand for surrender, went down to the jetty to dissuade the Argentine commander from landing troops. This hope disappeared with the arrival of the Puma, which disgorged a score of marines about fifty yards from the jetty. One of these troops aimed his rifle at Lieutenant Mills, who withdrew quickly, reaching the defensive position before the Argentinians opened fire.

The Puma returned very soon with a second load of marines but this time it was received by accurate machine-gun and rifle fire from the defenders. Hit in the hydraulic and oil systems, the helicopter limped across the cove trailing black smoke and crash-landed on a small plateau above the steep shore opposite King Edward Point. The Alouette had also come too close and it too was hit, though not seriously: the naval pilot landed beside the crashed Puma to check his own damage and to see what assistance he could give. The Army helicopter's cabin had been hit by at least thirty bullets and the marines had suffered heavy casualties, with several dead and seriously wounded. One of the Alouette's crew and the Puma's engineer set up a machine gun and opened fire on the Marines across the cove, but this was the only contribution made by the second 'wave'. The Alouette pilot, after establishing that his aircraft was flyable, returned to the *Bahia Paraiso* with one of the wounded and then began a shuttle, carrying forty marines, two on each trip, to land them on the far side of the cove. The *Guerrico*, which had left the cove and was lying about a mile from the entrance, took no hand in the fighting while the Alouette was thus engaged.*

It was at about this juncture that outside observers arrived on the scene. The *Endurance*, whose curtailed passage to the Falklands had resulted in her disappearing off the *Bahia Paraiso*'s plot, had been listening-in to the exchanges between Lieutenant Mills and the Argentine transport and as soon as she was sufficiently close Captain Nick Barker launched one of his two Wasp helicopters, flown by Lieutenant-Commander Tony Ellerbeck. The range was too great for the Wasp to carry its AS.12 missiles and the mission was intended to provide 'real-time' information for the *Endurance* until she could close the range for her armed helicopter. Lieutenant-Commander Ellerbeck landed the Wasp behind a ridge overlooking Grytviken and watched the final stages of the battle.

The *Guerrico* returned to King Edward Cove to lend its firepower to the

* E. Villarino, 'Exocet' (*Siete Dias* 'Special Project', Buenos Aires, 1983); this publication by a leading Argentine weekly news review recounts the combat activities of the various Argentine naval aviation units in some detail, most of which tally very closely with British reports of the same incidents.

attack. For a relatively small ship (1,170 tons), this was quite formidable: as well as four Exocet surface-to-surface missiles, which could not be used against the Marines but were a major threat to the *Endurance*, she was armed with an automatic 100mm gun (3.9in) forward, a modern version of the 40mm Bofors anti-aircraft gun aft and a 20mm AA gun on each beam. Against this, the Marines had only a Carl Gustav and a few 66mm anti-tank rocket launchers, the former with an effective range of 500 yards and the latter about 300 yards. *Guerrico* opened up with the 40mm as she entered the cove, closing to point-blank range. Under accurate and heavy fire, Lieutenant Mills waited until the corvette was well inside, so that she had little room to manoeuvre, and only then replied.

The commanding officer of the *Guerrico*, in his eagerness, had underestimated his opponents badly. The first Carl Gustav round, fired by Marine D. Combes, hit the water short of the ship but went on to explode under the waterline amidships, the 10lb shell causing internal damage and flooding. The upper decks were raked with small-arms and machine-gun fire and, as she turned to make for open water again, at least three 2lb '66' rockets hit her on and around the 100mm turret. The corvette, with over 1,000 rifle-calibre bullet holes in her, drew out of range and then, at a distance of about 3,500 yards, attempted to engage with her 100mm gun. This would have been the sensible procedure at the outset, but now it was not successful, for the '66' hits had damaged the gun elevation gear and it was only with considerable difficulty that the *Guerrico* managed to get the 30lb shells near the defenders' positions.

More inconvenience, and the only casualty, was caused by the fire of the Argentine marines who had landed near the jetty and across the cove. After about twenty minutes, however, all firing ceased, including that from the corvette. Virtual stalemate had been reached for the present – the Argentine troops who had been landed had no immediate hope of resupply or reinforcements and had lost, for all practical purposes, their heavy support. The Marines were probably better off for ammunition and rations and had one section of the enemy pinned down, but they were completely cut off, for some of the Argentinians on the far side of the cove had now moved around through Grytviken and were on the only track leading from King Edward Point. Lieutenant Mills had not been ordered to defend his position to the last man, his task had been to oblige the Argentine authorities to use force to seize South Georgia: this had been achieved, at disproportionate material cost to the aggressors, and now his main concern was for his men, who would inevitably sustain casualties if the defence was maintained until nightfall, still over four hours away.

With considerable courage the young lieutenant rose and walked towards the Argentine marines near the jetty. They soon ceased fire and an officer came forward to negotiate. Lieutenant Mills obtained a guarantee of good treatment after pointing out that neither side held an advantage, and that this particular officer's group was at a distinct disadvantage, and he wished to minimize casualties on both sides. The Marines left their positions, laid down their weapons on the beach, defused the explosives on the jetty and were taken off to the *Bahia Paraiso*, where their captors treated them with considerable respect and attended to Corporal Peters' wounded arm. The BAS personnel from Grytviken were also taken to the transport and confined with the Marines, but the outlying parties and two young women filming for a television wildlife series were overlooked.

Lieutenant-Commander Ellerbeck had watched the final stages of the defence of King Edward Point from his ridge and returned to the *Endurance*. Painted red, with an armament of only two old 20mm Oerlikon AA guns and the Wasps' wire-guided missiles, the patrol ship was hardly the ideal offensive unit, but Captain Barker had to be dissuaded from attempting to intercept either the Argentine tanker which was believed to be supporting the operation or the *Bahia Paraiso*, which sailed as soon as she could on the evening of 3 April. The *Endurance* closed South Georgia as the *Bahia Paraiso* and *Guerrico* left and remained until the 5th, hiding among the icebergs by day and lying up in isolated inlets by night while her helicopters watched the score of Argentine marines left behind as occupants and guards for the scrap metal workers.

With stocks running low, the *Endurance* headed northwards to rendezvous with RFA *Fort Austin*, now nine days out from Gibraltar.

HMS *Endurance* underway at slow speed 'in her natural habitat', off a South Georgia glacier, with one of her Wasp helicopters on deck and the other crossing her bows in a climbing turn. Captain Nick Barker's extensive knowledge of the inlets along the rugged coast enabled him to hide his highly visible ship during a large part of the three weeks it took to deploy a force to recapture the island *(MoD)*

RFA *Resource* sailed from Rosyth shortly after midnight on 6 April, after 88 hours of non-stop embarkation and stowage of stores, which she subsequently dispensed in the TEZ and San Carlos Water during the height of the fighting *(MoD)*

Pilot's view of HMS *Hermes'* flight deck, with two 846 Squadron Sea King 4s approaching to land *(MoD)*

HMS *Antrim* underway at slow speed in Cumberland Bay on 25 April, after the Argentine surrender *(MoD)*

Chapter Four

The Task Force Prepares

The Argentine invasion, although it took the public, Press and Parliament almost completely by surprise, did not find the Royal Navy and Ministers altogether unprepared. The Commander-in-Chief's staff at Fleet headquarters, at Northwood, had been taking precautionary measures since 29 March, when it first became apparent that diplomacy might fail to find a solution. In Whitehall, the Navy Department* had not long since conducted a procedural exercise which had covered many aspects of the swift mobilization of the Fleet and its deployment, so that not only the key permanent staff, but also the 'augmentees' who would be called in to reinforce them, were well acquainted with the necessary routine.

The order on 1 April to bring the carriers to 48 hours notice for sea began the process. HMS *Hermes* and *Invincible* had been involved in major exercises in February and early March, the former acting as an assault ship with 40 Commando RM, twenty-nine helicopters and five Sea Harriers embarked, and the latter as an anti-submarine carrier with a standard load of nine ASW Sea King Mk 5 helicopters and five Sea Harriers. Both were now at Portsmouth, the *Hermes* in the second week of a six-week 'Dockyard Assisted Maintenance Period' with most of her major systems opened or dismantled for maintenance and the *Invincible* with her ship's company on leave, but otherwise more obviously ready for sea. Also at Portsmouth were the two assault ships, *Fearless* and *Intrepid*; the *Fearless* had also taken part in the annual amphibious exercise off North Norway, supporting 42 Commando, but she had reverted to her normal role as the officer cadets' and midshipmen's training ship. HMS *Intrepid* had actually paid off, her ship's company had dispersed to new jobs and she was being de-stored in preparation for reserve or, possibly, disposal. Already in reserve was the RFA *Stromness*, a fast stores replenishment ship which was also to play a major part in the forthcoming campaign.

While the Dockyard, the Fleet Maintenance Group and the ships' staff

---

* The old and respected term 'Admiralty' lapsed on 1 April, 1964, when the Royal Navy's operational and administrative headquarters ceased to be an independent department of state and became one of the constituent Departments of the Ministry of Defence.

hurriedly buttoned up first the *Hermes* and then the *Fearless*, rectifying all known defects, the Naval Stores and Transport organization began the colossal task of preparing the ships not just for sea but also for a long deployment. Food – fresh, tinned, dried, frozen – clothing of all types, thousands of individual stores and spares items for the different classes of ship and versions of equipment, ammunition and ordnance in larger quantities than had been known since the end of the Second World War and fuel of three main types ('Dieso' for the gas turbines of the most modern ships and the boilers of the Type 12 and 'Leander'-class frigates, 'FFO' for the older steam-driven ships and 'Avcat' for the aircraft) all had to be loaded, not only into the ships before sailing but also into their accompanying replenishment RFAs and the ships which would keep the RFAs topped up. The Supply Officers of the individual ships assisted by making up their 'shopping lists' – in itself a complex task – and the stores arrived from all the various depots, by rail, by the Ministry of Defence's own transport fleet and by commercial vehicles. Particularly urgent items were flown to nearby airfields and were then delivered by helicopter to the Dockyards or direct to the ships.

Storing HMS *Hermes* for the South Atlantic while work over the side continues – an old-fashioned 'humping' party passes boxes on the starboard forward gangway, side-by-side with a mobile conveyor belt *(MoD)*

To clear the mountains of stores which rapidly built up all available Service manpower was called in to work around the clock: at Portsmouth, the RN Display Team, the Field Gun Crew and the tenants of the Detention Quarters, as well as personnel from nearby naval establishments, worked alongside the ships' parties and the Dockyard Stores men who would normally have undertaken the job. As the jetties were cleared of stores, so the debris mounted – discarded transit crates, packing cases and boxes – and such was the preoccupation with loading that clearing-up could not begin for a fortnight.

The Dockyard at Gibraltar, run down over the years and scheduled since July, 1981, for closure, could not provide the range or quantity of material required to stock the seven ships which were to form the first 'wave'. Rear Admiral Woodward, flying his flag in the 'County'-class guided-missile destroyer *Antrim*, took what he could but then had to pair off his ships with those which were not allocated to the force, the outbound vessels taking provisions, ammunition, spares and, in at least one instance, personnel on board. With five different types, most of the transfers were between dissimilar ships, the 'Leanders' *Ariadne*, *Euryalus*, *Aurora* and *Dido* serving, respectively, the *Antrim* and her sister-ship *Glamorgan* and the Type 42s *Coventry* and *Glasgow*; the Type 21 frigate *Active* supplied the *Sheffield*, while her sister, HMS *Arrow* took what the *Euryalus* and *Dido* could spare after they had looked after the destroyers. Only the two Type 22s, *Battleaxe* and *Brilliant*, were evenly matched, to provide the latter with everything that could be spared or, if necessary, detached.

The transfer was made more straightforward by the number of helicopters available. Every ship had an embarked flight – a Wasp in each of the 'Leanders', a Wessex in the 'Counties' and a Lynx in the others (two in the case of the Type 22s) – and the helicopter support ship RFA *Engadine* was on hand with her Sea Kings. There was even a spare deck capable of operating the big helicopters if need be, on the accompanying fast tanker RFA *Tidespring*.

The destroyers and frigates stored throughout the day, heading away from Gibraltar. There were three more frigates in the base, *Plymouth*, her sister-ship *Yarmouth* and the Type 22 *Broadsword*, all of which had been taking part in the now-abandoned exercise. The first was due to begin an Assisted Maintenance Period which would take several weeks and a number of families were due to fly to Gibraltar to join their husbands: the *Plymouth* was ordered to join Admiral Woodward's group and sailed on the 2nd with RFA *Appleleaf*, leaving the *Broadsword* with a list of those to be contacted and told not to come. The *Broadsword* and *Yarmouth* remained at Gibraltar to make final preparations before sailing for the Indian Ocean, where they were to relieve the patrol at the entrance to the Persian Gulf. HMS *Sheffield* had been returning from the patrol when she joined the exercise and was then despatched to the South Atlantic, in the wake of the RFA *Fort Austin*, which had been one of her support ships: the other, the tanker *Brambleleaf*, was detached from the Indian Ocean to join the Falklands operation by way of the Cape of Good Hope.

The whereabouts of the submarines was exercising the media. The nuclear-powered Fleet submarine *Spartan* had embarked stores and torpedoes at Gibraltar and had sailed on 1 April and the *Splendid* sailed from Faslane on the same day. The Press was not told of these deployments, but correspondents learned that the *Superb* had sailed from Gibraltar and came to the wrong conclusion: in fact, she was returning to Faslane, although that was not made public for several days after her arrival. In the meantime, HMS *Conqueror* had left Faslane on 4 April, also bound for the South Atlantic.

Storing continued on Saturday, 3 April in the Dockyards. The Prime Minister, in the House of Commons, announced the formation of the 'task force' which was to be despatched to recover the islands. The force now included 3 Commando Brigade RM, which comprised 40, 42, and 45 Commandos RM, the Commando Logistics Regiment RM and No 29 [Commando] Regiment, Royal Artillery. To these were added the 3rd Battalion of the Parachute Regiment and a dozen Rapier surface-to-air missile launchers of 'T' Battery, 12 Air Defence Regiment, RA. Even though almost all the available amphibious assault shipping would eventually be deployed, this would not be able to carry the 3,000 Marines and soldiers and personal weapons, let alone the tens of thousands of tons of vehicles, heavy weapons, spare equipment and, above all, rations and ammunition. Moving the men was relatively simple, the material was not: the seventy Volvo over-snow vehicles came down from Arbroath to the south coast by rail during the weekend, as did 3 Commando Brigade's reserve ammunition, but not all units could find rail transport and the roads to Portsmouth, the Royal Corps of Transport marine base at Marchwood, on Southampton Water, and Devonport were the scenes of activity not seen since the end of the Second World War. A deadline had been set for the sailing of the force and as, for various reasons, this could not be missed, the ships were not all 'combat-loaded' to be able to supply the troops with material in the right order in the early stages of the landings.

The ships immediately to hand were the *Fearless*, which would serve as the headquarters ship of Commodore M. C. Clapp, the Commodore, Amphibious Warfare,* and Brigadier J. H. A. Thompson OBE, commanding the reinforced 3 Commando Brigade, and four Landing Ships (Logistics) (LSLs) *Sir Geraint* and *Sir Galahad* at Devonport and *Sir Lancelot* and *Sir Percivale* at Marchwood: all these LSLs were manned by the RFA, with British officers and mainly Chinese ratings. The *Intrepid* was now being recommissioned, with her former crew who were haled back from leave and new jobs. *Sir Tristram* was in Belize and would catch up during the passage south but the sixth LSL, *Sir Bedivere*, was at Vancouver and would be unlikely to take part in the early stages of the amphibious operation. It was decided, therefore, to bring the RFA *Stromness* back into service to serve as an assault platform in the initial stages and then in her stores support role.

There was still insufficient troop and military transport lift capacity and so, on 3 April, the necessary Statutory Instruments were signed to permit the Navy Department to take ships up from trade. Almost the first to be

---

* 'Commodore' in the Royal Navy is a title and not a rank and denotes an appointment held by a senior Captain. Commodore Clapp – 'COMAW' – was one of eight such officers in 1982 and the only one with a sea-going job.

'STUFT' was the P&O flagship *Canberra*, homeward-bound with a load of passengers on a cruise, who were to be replaced by two Commandos and 3 Para. Much of their heavy equipment and ammunition, as well as eight light tanks of the Blues and Royals, would go in the 'Ro-Ro' (roll-on/roll-off) ferry *Elk*.

Additional logistics support was also needed and nine British Petroleum tankers of the 'British River' class were taken up. Two of these, *British Tay* and *British Tamar*, had already undertaken trials to evaluate their suitability as 'Convoy Escort Oilers', but for the time being their main task was to supply the RFAs in the forward areas. Liaison teams from the RFA were provided for these ships to enable them to work with the practised auxiliaries and the Navy.

The helicopters began to embark in the big ships on 3 April. The anti-submarine Sea Kings of 826 and 820 Squadrons went to the *Hermes* and *Invincible*, respectively, and were joined in the former by the 'Commando' Sea King Mark 4s of 846 Squadron. The ASW squadrons would fly all round the clock and were relatively well-off for aircrew, 826 Squadron, for example, having fifteen full crews (each consisting of two pilots, an Observer and a sonar operator) for nine aircraft. The assault helicopter squadron, which would have twelve aircraft when brought up to full strength, had a much smaller surplus of experienced pilots and no spare cabin crewmen.

The Sea Harrier squadrons had begun to arrive on 2 April, eight Sea Harriers being flown on to the *Hermes* as she lay in the dockyard. Three more arrived on Sunday the 4th, while *Invincible*'s complement of eight flew in on the same day. As originally formed, the two squadrons, 800 in *Hermes* and 801 in *Invincible*, had only five aircraft each, but by absorbing the 'headquarters' training squadron (899), calling forward reserve aircraft and impressing a trials aircraft from the experimental establishment at Boscombe Down, a total of twenty fighters was put together. Maintenance crews were found for the enlarged squadrons, but such was the shortage of pilots that, in spite of the attachment of seven fully-navalized Royal Air Force pilots, two pilots who were still undergoing operational flying training were also taken along, to complete the course en route.

From the very outset of planning Ascension Island had been intended for a most important role. Roughly halfway between the United Kingdom and the Falklands, it could provide a forward anchorage and, thanks to the 10,000-foot runway built by the US Government, a major logistics base for receipt and despatch of men and material by sea and air; the first air support movements – four Lockheed Hercules from RAF Lyneham – took off on 2 April. The Wideawake airfield was operated by Pan American Airways, whose US Air Force contract allowed for 285 aircraft movements per year, in support of Ascension's very mixed working community, which included the US National Aeronautics and Space Agency (NASA), the BBC and the Cable & Wireless communications

The backbone of the stores 'air bridge' between the United Kingdom and Ascension was provided by the Lockheed Hercules medium transport aircraft of the RAF's Lyneham Transport Wing. The majority of the 13,000 hours flown by the four squadrons of the Wing were accumulated on the northern sector, but the longest sorties flown were by the probe-fitted aircraft flown by No 47 Squadron RAF between Ascension and the ships off the Falklands (*MoD*)

company. A hundred years before, the Admiralty had built a sizeable base, with accommodation, workshops and even a hospital, but this had not been used after the First World War and, even at its height, the base had never boasted more than a small stone jetty for use by ships' boats and lighters. The anchorage off the jetty is subject to a long, heavy and uncomfortable swell, as are ships, which must lie between a quarter and a half mile offshore. In such unfavourable circumstances, helicopters were to play an essential part in ship-to-ship and ship-to-shore movements.

As early as 1 April, five naval Wessex 5 transport helicopters had been prepared for airlift from RNAS Yeovilton to Ascension, two for embarkation in RFA *Tidespring* and the others for local stores delivery duties. The first pair were flown out on 4 April in a civilian Short Belfast freighter of the Stansted-based TAC HeavyLift Ltd (which had bought the RAF's inventory of this aircraft when the type had been retired on grounds of economy in 1976) and reassembled by the Naval Aircraft Servicing Unit, Ascension, otherwise known as Naval Party 1222. These aircraft were operational by the time that the next two were delivered, on 6 April.

The 'Wessi' had been preceded, on the 3rd, by three Lynxes which arrived complete with air and ground crews and a full range of stores, by courtesy of the RAF Hercules of the Lyneham Transport Wing. The Lynxes, manned by the 815 Squadron Trials Flight and the Flights of HMS *Newcastle* and *Minerva*, were modified to fire the Sea Skua air-to-surface missile – which had not yet been formally accepted into service – and were intended for RFA *Fort Austin*. They embarked on 6 April, so that when the otherwise unarmed stores ship left Ascension to support the *Endurance* she had a powerful, if untried, defensive capability.

The first surface ship to leave the United Kingdom for the South Atlantic sailed quietly from Portland on Sunday, 4 April. The Royal Maritime Auxiliary Service ocean-going tug *Typhoon* was certainly not the most glamorous unit to deploy but she was an essential part of the supporting forces, as she would demonstrate at South Georgia. It was soon appreci-

ated that more tugs would be needed and three United Towing Company vessels were requisitioned – the *Irishman*, *Salvageman* and *Yorkshireman*.

Under the full glare of publicity, the aircraft carriers sailed on Monday, 5 April, *Invincible* passing vast crowds watching from the walls of Portsmouth and on Southsea seafront half an hour ahead of the *Hermes*. All concerned in their despatch in such a short time deserved the applause, but particular credit must go to the Dockyard staff at Portsmouth: few of those waving goodbye to the ships or watching the drama on television could have imagined, for example, that only 24 hours earlier the *Hermes'* island was festooned with scaffolding or that storing of both ships had continued until the last gangway had been moved away. The eleven Sea Harriers and eighteen Sea Kings on *Hermes'* deck were there not only for the usual ceremonial purposes but also to permit the hangar to be used as a sorting office for the vast quantity of extra stores, which even included 200 tons of ammunition for the Marines. The *Invincible* had fewer of her aircraft ranged, but among her deck cargo were anonymous crates which contained extra Sea Dart missiles, for herself and for the three Type 42 destroyers, 2,000 miles closer to Ascension.

Four hours before the carriers began to get under way at Portsmouth, the Type 21 frigates *Alacrity* and *Antelope* left Devonport and during the

Left 5 May: The *Hermes* sails from Portsmouth half an hour after the *Invincible*, her hangar so crammed with stores and ammunition that most of her aircraft have to be parked on deck. The last (in Royal Navy service) of a line of highly-successful 'Fleet carriers', this old ship fully demonstrated the soundness of an earlier British design philosophy *(MoD)*

Above The first ship to sail from the United Kingdom, and one of the last to return (on 24 September), was the RMAS tug *Typhoon*, here seen in South Georgia waters *(MoD)*

6 April: the Landing Ship (Logistic) *Sir Galahad* leaves Devonport for the last time, her midships deck loaded with stores and vehicles and with three Gazelle helicopters of 3 Commando Brigade Air Squadron on her flight deck. Devonport was the last UK port of call for four of the ships lost 'down South' – the *Antelope*, which sailed with the *Sir Galahad*, the *Ardent*, which left on 19 April, and the *Atlantic Conveyor (MoD)*

day met the LSLs *Sir Geraint* and *Sir Galahad* from the same port and *Sir Lancelot* and *Sir Percivale* from the Solent. The LSLs were carrying up to 400 Marines, Army, Naval and RAF personnel apiece, as well as the stores, weapons and ammunition, and the 3 Commando Brigade Air Squadron, with its three Scout and nine Gazelle helicopters. Two RFA tankers left on the 5th, the *Olmeda* from Devonport to accompany the carriers and the *Pearleaf* from Portsmouth to join the LSL group. The former had embarked two more anti-submarine Sea Kings, of 824 Flight, embarked and aboard the 'AEFS' (Ammunition, Explosives, Food and Stores ship) RFA *Resource* was a Wessex 5 for 'Vertrep' duties – vertical replenishment of stores. The *Resource* had been at Rosyth when the Fleet had been brought to short notice and had worked round the clock to load with a full cargo of war supplies, picking up the last items at Portland shortly before midnight on the 5th.

HMS *Broadsword* and *Yarmouth* left Gibraltar on the same day, heading east for the Suez Canal. Some twelve hours after their departure it was decided that their presence was more urgently required in the south and they were ordered to return to Gibraltar and prepare for deployment to the South Atlantic. Of the eleven destroyers and frigates now at sea for 'Corporate', only the *Yarmouth*, the oldest of all, would come through unscathed.

The last sailings of what may be regarded as the 'first wave' were on 6 and 7 April. The *Fearless*, having put ashore her 'young gentlemen' to return to Dartmouth as late as the 5th, sailed from Portsmouth on the next day, carrying vehicles and heavy equipment for 3 Commando Brigade, three more Scout helicopters of the Brigade Air Squadron and another three Sea King 4s of 846 Squadron. Commodore Clapp and his staff were aboard when she sailed and Brigadier Thompson and his staff joined by helicopter off Portland. On the next day the *Stromness* left Portsmouth just after dark. Although her sailing was twenty-four hours after the time called for on 3 April, her departure, fully stored and with military rations for 7,500 men for a month and 358 Royal Marines aboard, was a magnificent achievement, bearing in mind that on 2 April she was in dock, completely destored prior to disposal and with only a care and maintenance crew on board.

The departure of the United Kingdom component of the task force marked only a change of task, not tempo, as far as the Dockyards and Naval Stores and Transport organization were concerned. Rather more time was available to prepare the next small group of warships and RFAs to leave, but there was a steady stream of 'STUFT' to equip with replenishment gear, radio gear compatible with that in the Fleet, commercial satellite communications equipment, additional fuel tanks, fresh water production plants, extra accommodation and facilities for operating helicopters. Portsmouth Dockyard led the way on the conversions, with as many as five merchant ships at a time being fitted out and with at least one in hand from 8 April until 21 May; altogether, twenty-five tankers, freighters, tugs, and short-sea ferries were modified and, in the case of the tankers, loaded, at this one yard up to mid-June. This was, of course, in addition to the normal warship work, which now involved the incorporation of new or modified equipment shown to be necessary as the results of experience 'down south' as well as routine maintenance. The Dockyard workshops prefabricated most of the steelwork for the various installations, which were designed by the Navy's own architects, the Royal Corps of Naval Constructors, whose centenary year this was.

Devonport Dockyard undertook fewer STUFT conversions but some of these were among the most well-known ships as they included the four aircraft transports, beginning with the ill-fated *Atlantic Conveyor* and continuing with the *Atlantic Causeway*, *Contender Bezant* and *Astronomer*. Much of the dockyard's additional work consisted of accelerated turn-rounds for the frigates which would be required for later 'Corporate' deployment. HMS *Minerva* entered Plymouth Sound on 2 April flying her paying-off pennant in anticipation of a long refit but left five weeks later after a comprehensive maintenance period and the *Battleaxe*'s programmed fifteen-week docking period was cut to ten weeks. The departure of so many ships for operations outside the NATO area meant that those that were left had to have a higher rate of availability, which led to further work for Devonport as some frigates were run on beyond intended maintenance periods.

Making up for the shortage of ships fell largely to Chatham Dockyard's lot. Sentenced to closure by the 1981 Review, Chatham was the home of the 'Standby Squadron', the very small reserve of frigates awaiting disposal. On 13 April the *Falmouth* (a sister-ship of the *Yarmouth*) was ordered to be brought forward off the Sales List and was commissioned just nine days later. Four more frigates were surveyed but such was the shortage of naval personnel in some categories that it was not until 26 May that the decision was made to bring forward HMS *Berwick*, *Zulu*, *Tartar* and *Gurkha*, the first two to be prepared for service by Chatham and the second pair at Rosyth. Although no STUFT conversions were undertaken at Chatham, the workshops joined the prefabrication programme, sending metalwork to Portsmouth and Devonport.

In normal times the Royal Navy's mine countermeasures ships are based on the Forth and when it was decided that a number of trawlers should be taken up as minesweepers, they were taken in hand at Rosyth Dockyard for the installation of communications gear and other essential equipment. Commissioned with all-naval crews from three 'Ton'-class minesweepers, *Farnella*, *Junella*, *Cordella* and *Northella*, later joined by the *Pict*, were the only STUFT to wear the White Ensign and operated as the 11th Mine Counter Measures Squadron. Two North Sea oil industry support vessels, the *Wimpey Seahorse* and *British Enterprise III*, were modified at Rosyth, the former as a mooring vessel for laying the mooring buoys and cables which would be needed at South Georgia and the Falklands themselves, and the latter as a 'despatch vessel' to ply between Ascension and the forward areas with passengers and urgent stores too heavy or awkward to be air-dropped. Rosyth also despatched the two Offshore Patrol Vessels HMS *Leeds Castle* and *Dumbarton Castle* for use as despatch vessels and the Post Office cable ship *Iris* was converted for the same purpose at Devonport.

The 'Ellas', as the five auxiliary minesweepers became known, went from Rosyth to Portland to be fitted with their replenishment gear and the deck fittings for the sweeping equipment. Portland's main task was that of working-up warships and auxiliaries, but a Fleet Maintenance Group was in attendance for running repairs. The FMG now became heavily involved in the material preparation of not only warships but also RFAs and STUFT, completing the fitting-out of the new RFA tanker *Bayleaf*, modifying the STUFT tanker *British Esk* for the supply of Dieso fuel and installing a Service radio and power supplies in her swimming pool and building and testing fresh water plant for the two 'Castles', among other tasks, most of which were more appropriate to a Dockyard than to a 'Naval Base'.

Portland continued to be responsible for working ships up as fighting units and evaluating new tactics at sea. Flag Officer Sea Training's staff provided detachments to accompany southbound ships as far as Ascension, the first such team being made up of damage control experts who left with HMS *Fearless*. After the departure of the first wave virtually all warships spent a few days at Portland, exercising every aspect of their organizations – 'sea riders' even flew out to Gibraltar to work up HMS *Ambuscade* on passage to Ascension, so that she might not miss the gruelling but necessary experience. Particular attention was devoted to air defence exercises, the opposition being provided by the Fleet Requirements and Air Direction Unit, a civilian-manned 'squadron' based at Yeovilton. Using Canberras and Hunters, FRADU simulated Super Etendard/Exocet attacks as well as more conventional massed low-level attacks in the Portland exercise areas and also for the benefit of the Surface Weapons Establishments, which were busy devising improvements to the various defensive missile systems throughout the campaign. The 'resident work-up tanker' for most of the period was RFA *Grey Rover* and she too was fully occupied, for many of the chartered merchant ships conducted their replenishment trials and training with her off Portland.

The work of the Dockyards and the uniformed maintenance organization was supplemented by shipbuilding industry contractors, working to naval Constructors' designs and with Dockyard supervision. The first conversions were, in fact, those of the liner *Canberra* and the ferry *Elk*, carried out at Southampton by Vosper Ship Repairers; the *Canberra* arrived from a cruise on 7 April (the day after the *Elk* had been put in hand) and sailed on the 9th with 40 and 42 RM Commandos and 3 Para on board, amid emotional scenes.* In the intervening two days two helicopter decks had been added, at the expense of upper deck fittings and bulwarks, and the 'standard' replenishment and communications kits added to turn her into a 'Landing Platform Luxury (Large)'. Vospers also converted the second LPL(L) – the *Queen Elizabeth 2*, the water tanker *Fort Toronto*, the *Europic Ferry* and, towards the end of the campaign, the large passenger ferry *Rangatira*. Elsewhere, the Ro-Ro ferry *Norland* was partly modified at Hull, where industrial action delayed her sailing by twenty-four hours on 20 April (the only such blot on an otherwise clean record of co-operation between the Navy Department, employers and the unions), and had her helicopter deck added at Portsmouth.

Like Chatham, Gibraltar Dockyard was also promised with closure. Its value was underlined at the very outset of the operation by its support to Rear Admiral Woodward's force of destroyers and frigates and the three RFAs, *Fort Austin*, *Appleleaf* and *Tidespring*, and then the storing of *Broadsword* and *Yarmouth*, which sailed south on 8 April. This depleted the already low stocks to such an extent that the Type 21 frigate *Ambuscade* carried a cargo of extra ammunition when she left Devonport on 9 April for Gibraltar, where she was to be stationed as Guardship. Four days later the RMAS ammunition transport *Throsk*, which had been in reserve at the beginning of April, left with a cargo of medical and aviation stores, a replenishment 'kit' and other gear. This load was intended for a specific ship, the P&O liner *Uganda* which, when taken up on 10 April, was on an educational cruise in the Mediterranean. The school parties were put ashore in Naples and the ship proceeded to Gibraltar, where she was converted for use as a hospital ship, with full surgical facilities and ward accommodation for 300 patients, tended by naval medical personnel who included Queen Alexandra's Royal Naval Nursing Service sisters. A helicopter deck capable of operating a Sea King was built on aft, for receiving casualties, necessitating very heavy reinforcement of the deck below and using up most of the dockyard's stock of steel plate and beams.

The *Uganda* was declared to the Red Cross as a hospital ship and was marked with the appropriate markings on her repainted white hull. In keeping with her strictly non-combatant role, she was not fitted with cryptographic machines nor did she carry ciphers or codes. To support the *Uganda* by evacuating casualties from the combat area to her operating area, the three survey ships HMS *Hydra*, *Hecla* and *Herald* were fitted out as 'Ambulance Ships', the *Hecla* at Gibraltar and the others at Portsmouth. Like the *Uganda*, they bore red crosses on a white hull and were declared to the International Committee of the Red Cross. Their Wasp helicopters were also painted with red crosses and exchanged their red

---

* Legend has it that the Marines persuaded the Paras to occupy the lower accommodation decks by telling them that less ship movement would be felt, compared with on the more luxurious accommodation on the decks above, which the wily Commandos occupied.

flashing anti-collision lights for blue 'ambulance' lights. Thus equipped, the four Red Cross vessels sailed, the *Uganda* from Gibraltar on 21 April, preceded by HMS *Hecla* on the 20th and the other two 'H's from Portsmouth on the 24th.

No further hospital ship declarations were made by the Ministry of Defence, but the presence of a special surgical team in the *Canberra* was reported in the Press, certain sections of which seem to have believed that when she disembarked her troops she would serve as a hospital ship. No such misunderstanding could be entertained for the *Hermes* and *Fearless*, both of which had additional surgical teams embarked. One result of this departure of large numbers of medical personnel was the suspension of professional nursing training at the RN Hospitals at Haslar and Stonehouse as the instructing staff either went to sea or took the places of the ward staff who had done so.

The welfare of the families of the men overseas is at any time a major concern of the Navy's shore organization, but the arrangements were now enlarged to deal with the vastly greater numbers. Those left behind in the various establishments did their best to sustain the morale of anxious wives by organizing social activities and keeping families informed as much as was possible, a task which grew more difficult as the numbers of ships involved and the casualties grew.

To ensure that, in the worst case, families learned of casualties first and that care was immediately available, the Naval Casualty Reporting System was set up early in April. Under the administration of the Commander-in-Chief, Naval Home Command, Admiral Sir James Eberle, reporting cells were manned around the clock and individual shore establishments throughout the country were given the responsibility for the unhappy task of notifying the next-of-kin of the casualties; this could be done quickly when the family lived in married quarters, but up to twenty-four hours could be spent tracing others who could not be found immediately at the expected address. The system was intended to avoid unnecessary distress, usually caused by outside interference, almost invariably involving the media.

It has been said, with some justification, that the Royal Navy lacked rapport with the media, the Army's good relations with the Press in Northern Ireland being held up as an example of what can be achieved. At least some of this misunderstanding, which took the form of, at best, mistrust on the Navy's part, was due to the nature of the Navy's work, the most impressive area of which is found well away from land or international airport terminals, so that achievement is reported late or not at all, except through Ministry of Defence Press Releases. The few newspapers which employ capable defence correspondents are trusted to a greater extent, but they are a tiny remnant of the informed and responsible community which reported on naval affairs up to the First World War – before the Official Secrets Acts, which were intended originally to discourage spies but now have the effect of suppressing politically undesirable discussion.

It was widely supposed that the Navy intended to take no journalists other than those employed by the Defence Public Relations organization and that those who were embarked immediately before the carriers sailed were included on the Prime Minister's insistence. Be that as it may, sixteen writers, two photographers, two radio reporters and three television reporters supported by four technicians did go to sea, eleven with the carrier group and sixteen with the amphibious ships. A very few of this number were experienced war correspondents who had an inkling of what to expect and went prepared for the conditions.

Chapter Five

Passage South

Once clear of Spithead, HMS *Hermes* embarked her twelfth Sea Harrier and, like the *Invincible*, began a steady shuttle with her helicopters to the various Naval Air Stations – Lee-on-Solent, Portland, Yeovilton and Culdrose – to which last-minute stores items and modification kits were being delivered. Their progress down-Channel, in company with their attendant RFAs, was quite leisurely so that when, on 6 April, the *Invincible*'s Engineering Department noticed that the starboard main gear box coupling was making suspicious noises, the dockyard equipment needed to change the unit could be flown to Culdrose, on the Lizard Peninsula, and then brought on board by helicopter.

The gear box change was the first of a number of engineering problems which would normally have been undertaken in a dockyard but which had to be accomplished at sea by the ships' staffs. It also showed the need for a repair facility in the forward area, to provide material and technical assistance and advice. The Royal Navy had had no repair ship since the decommissioning of HMS *Triumph* in 1972 and so a North Sea support vessel, the *Stena Seaspread*, was chartered (involving a change of registry from Swedish to British) and fitted out at Portsmouth between 12 and 16 April to carry a Fleet Maintenance Group with workshops, spares and basic materials, much of which had to be stowed in standard containers welded to the upper deck at Portsmouth. After practising an Olympus main engine change in HMS *Nottingham* – an evolution never intended to be carried out away from a dockyard – the FMG embarked and the *Stena Seaspread* sailed on 16 April, the day the carriers arrived at Ascension.

The eleven days on passage were fully employed in exercises and drills for all on board and in preparing the ships and aircraft for war. The times taken to bring the ships to 'Action Stations' were reduced by frequent practice until most could achieve a fully-closed-up state in about four minutes. Such a state could not be sustained indefinitely and an intermediate state, with just enough men closed up to fight all systems and steam the ship in 'Defence Watches', was adopted. Everyone became accustomed to doing their work encumbered by protective clothing and survival kit – anti-flash gear, gas-mask case, lifejacket and 'once-only survival 'suit', a lightweight waterproof cover-all intended to protect survivors in the water from exposure.

Inevitably, the carriers' main concern was working up their aircrew. While the command evolved tactics to deal with the Exocet, conventional air attack and ships, the individual pilots practised interceptions by day and night, air combat manoeuvres, the post-Vietnam name for 'dogfighting', and delivering the assorted weapons which the Sea Harrier could carry. In fact, few of these had actually been fired or released by the Sea Harrier and the 'clearances' for safe carriage and delivery were obtained by *Invincible*'s 801 Squadron for the 2in rocket projectile, the 'Lepus' flare and the 1,000lb air-burst bomb. 801 also fired the first live Sidewinder missile to be launched by a front-line Sea Harrier squadron: this, like the cluster-bomb release by 800 Squadron, was seen in one of the earliest television reports to reach the United Kingdom.

The anti-submarine and Commando helicopter crews also flew intensively. Live depth-charges and homing torpedoes were dropped and rear-cabin machine-guns were fired, while the 'dippers' practised their intricate pattern of 'jumps' to box-in imaginary fast submarines and the 'junglies' rehearsed assault troop drills. The latter, the Sea King 4s of 846 Squadron, also had to train in the use of a new piece of equipment which was to give the squadron a true night operating capability. The ASW squadrons had had such a capability since the introduction in 1961 of the Wessex 1, whose accurate and reliable auto-pilot could be trusted to bring the helicopter into the hover, in the desired position, even on the darkest, nastiest night; radar had been added to produce the Wessex 3* in 1967 and the Sea King, in its ASW versions, further refined the all-weather system. The Sea King 4 had neither the auto-pilot nor the radar, which would not have been of any great use for overland operations and would have reduced the available cargo volume and weight, and the pilots' visual judgement was in any case the best available for terrain clearance and selection of approach. Hitherto, for night operations, only flares dropped by the helicopters or lights laid by ground parties had been available; it was envisaged that in the Falklands there would be a requirement for more covert operations and passive night-viewing goggles were provided for a proportion of the pilots of 846 Squadron. Using 'image intensification' techniques, the goggles amplified whatever natural light was available to provide a view which may not have been 'as clear as day' but was certainly sufficient for most night operations below cloud or clear of mist. No opportunity for practice with the 'PNG' was found before the ships sailed and the selected pilots of 846 Squadron had therefore to learn how to make the most of the cumbersome goggles while flying at night from the *Hermes*.

* The Flights embarked in *Glamorgan* and *Antrim* were still equipped with the Wessex 3 as the guided-missile destroyers' hangar and difficult access design could not cope with the larger Sea King.

As well as the existing and specially-procured equipment, there was a large measure of self-help and improvisation throughout the task force, aided by the civilians who were accompanying the ships as manufacturers' technical representatives. Prominent among the latter were the Ferranti experts who accompanied the Sea Harrier squadrons to tune the fighters' radar and computer system, writing new programmes to improve the performance and flexibility of the latter. A Squadron modification, devised by 800 Squadron's engineers, gave the Sea Harrier a simple self-protection against radar-controlled missiles or guns: small bundles of 'chaff' (once known as 'Window') were stowed in the air-brake recess under the rear fuselage. A pilot, warned by his passive radar warning receiver that a radar was locked on to his aircraft, could dispense a cloud of metallized plastic foil to confuse or distract the fire-control radar, simply by opening the air-brake briefly. Helicopters, which had no difficulty in dispensing the bundles by hand through open doors or windows, were supplied with chaff as the situation required.

As the ships became more efficient and the carriers began to exercise against one another, two major areas of weakness were recognized. It was likely that the Argentine Air Force and naval air arm would both employ a low-level approach for strike missions, to take advantage of the gap 'under the radar', where the earth's surface curves down and away from the straight line of the radar's 'pulses'. Even the high-mounted antennae on the bigger ships could not look down sufficiently to detect a low-flying aircraft much outside twenty-five miles. Between 1951 and 1978 the Royal Navy had been able to cope with the low-flyer by putting a high-powered radar into an aircraft to look down and extend the radar horizon. These Airborne Early Warning (AEW) aircraft had been able to direct fighters to intercept incoming strikes at long range, well clear of the Fleet's missile and gun defences and before hostile aircraft could launch anti-ship missiles. The withdrawal of the fixed-wing strike carrier HMS *Ark Royal* meant the end of AEW in British naval service and although the RAF was operating a few old Shackleton aircraft equipped with AEW radar (and was expecting the AEW Nimrod to enter service later in 1982), these would not be able to provide any service to the task groups in the South Atlantic. Admiral Woodward would have to rely upon a distant barrier of radar picket ships which would themselves be exposed to sudden attack while providing a small extension to the warning time available to the 'High Value Units'. The other hope for early warning was the interception of the strike aircraft's radar transmissions by the ships' warning receivers; against this had to be weighed the universal knowledge of the need for 'radar silence'. The Argentine Forces were as aware as the Royal Navy that even a brief burst of radar would be detected and would therefore minimize its use.

The other problem concerned close-in defence against low-flying aircraft and sea-skimmers like Exocet. Area anti-aircraft weapons such as the Sea Dart in the *Invincible* and the Type 42 destroyers and the Seaslug in the two 'Counties' were effective against high- and medium-level targets but less so against wave-top targets; the 20-year-old Seacat was widely fitted, in most frigates, the amphibious assault ships and *Hermes*, but it was relatively slow, was ineffective against Exocet and only one missile could be controlled per mounting. The only missile system which was likely to be able to deal with the short-range enemy was the Sea Wolf. Matched with a tracking system which could follow a 4.5in shell in flight, Sea Wolf was the only genuine anti-missile missile in service at sea anywhere in the world but was fitted in only two of the ships now on their way south, the Type 22 frigates *Broadsword* and *Brilliant*. The gun had given way to the missile as an anti-aircraft weapon (although the 4.5 in in its automatic single-barrelled Mark 8 and semi-automatic twin Mark 6 versions was exercised against medium-level targets in training) and was regarded primarily as an anti-surface weapon, the 4.5in for bombardment of shore targets and the venerable automatic light-calibre automatic guns, the 40mm Bofors and 20mm Oerlikon, for use in stopping craft too small to be worth a 4.5in shell or an Exocet. The Bofors and Oerlikons were fitted in all destroyers and frigates, two of the former in ships with no other gun armament and two of the latter in ships with a 4.5in. Effective in the hands of the fathers of the men now manning identical guns, they were now too few to be sure of any ship having the firepower to defend herself against a determined attack. No supplementary weapons of similar power could be provided within the time available and so all ships, from the converted trawlers, through the RFAs to the carriers, contrived to draw, borrow or 'half-hitch' as many General-Purpose Machine Guns (GPMG) or Light Machine Guns (LMG – an updated version of the well-known Bren Gun) which were then fixed to improvised mountings around the upper deck.

The aircraft were 'camouflaged' during the passage to Ascension. Initially, this took the form of painting over all the white and yellow markings – the white individual numbers were repainted black, the blue of the national roundel markings was extended to meet the red centre circle and warning markings were largely obliterated. Shortly before arrival at Ascension, it was decided to paint out the white undersides of the Sea Harriers with the dark grey used on the upper surfaces: the *Hermes'* aircraft were all completed, but the *Invincible* ran out of grey paint and had to await the delivery of additional supplies to complete the last three aircraft.

Chapter Six

The Advance Guard

Admiral Woodward shifted his flag from the *Antrim* to *Glamorgan* on 4 April, to enable the former to prepare for detached service. The destroyers and frigates paired off for training and pooling of tactical ideas during the first days, progressing to more complex exercises which included the rapid detaching of 'surface attack groups' for simulated Exocet strikes. The *Antrim, Glamorgan, Brilliant* and *Arrow* each had four of the twenty-two-mile range MM.38 version of this weapon and their helicopters were worked-up in the necessary scouting and targeting to enable the missiles to be fired over the radar horizon. The Lynx helicopters aboard the Type 42 destroyers and Type 21 and 22 frigates already had, or (in some cases) were about to be given, a powerful weapon of their own, the Sea Skua guided missile with a range of several miles and the punch of a 6in shell; the Sea Skua had not yet been fully cleared for normal service but conditions were no longer normal and it was accordingly issued.

All the ships had managed to embark more than the 'book' allowance of ammunition and provisions, which were stowed in every available corner. At the same time non-essential items – trophies and Battle Honours boards were obvious examples – were landed at Gibraltar and now ships were making their own arrangements for minimizing or containing damage by removing as many inflammable fittings as possible and positioning damage control gear in more accessible stations. A much-increased interest in first-aid was noted and all warships and RFAs, throughout the task force, trained teams of non-medical personnel to deal with injuries and wounds. Above all, the ships' companies were repeatedly drilled until they knew their ships and systems thoroughly, against the day they would have to face real emergencies. Of the eight warships in Admiral Woodward's vanguard, all the escorts but *Arrow* would indeed sustain serious damage through enemy action and the training would pay off.

RFA *Fort Austin* was to have sailed from Ascension as soon as she had embarked the three Sea Skua-fitted Lynxes but she did not leave until 9 April, by which time she had also embarked a surgical team, flown out from Britain in an RAF VC-10 transport. The delay gave an opportunity to send warships in support of the *Fort Austin* and on 7 April Captain Brian Young of the *Antrim* was ordered 'to proceed with despatch', with HMS *Plymouth* and RFA *Tidespring* in company, to Ascension. The oiler first topped up the six ships remaining with Admiral Woodward and then pressed on to join the destroyer and the frigate.

The three ships crossed the Equator in company on 8 April. The *Antrim* and *Tidespring* paid their respects and were duly visited by King Neptune, his Queen, the Barber and the Bears. This grisly Court was unable to find the *Plymouth*, due to smart evasive action by Captain David Pentreath, but the group was sighted and overflown by a 'Bear' which had nothing to do with sailors' traditional ritual. The Russians were taking an interest in current affairs and the big Tupolev Tu 20 Bear maritime reconnaissance aircraft became a familiar sight, flying regular 'snooping' sorties from their base at Luanda, in Angola, some 1,500 miles due east of Ascension.

The '*Antrim* Group' arrived at Ascension on 10 April, a day after the *Fort Austin* had sailed, and themselves left on the following day, having embarked awaiting stores, 'M' Company of 42 RM Commando, the Royal Marines of No 2 Special Boat Section, troopers of 'D' Squadron, 22 SAS Regiment – all flown out by the RAF's Hercules and VC-10s – and air and ground crews of 845 Naval Air Squadron with the two Wessex 5s which were to provide the air transport force, operating from the *Tidespring*. A few hours after they departed, Admiral Woodward reached Ascension with his other ships, joined on passage by RFA *Appleleaf*.

The *Antrim* Group overhauled the *Fort Austin* on 13 April and refuelled her before pressing on together to meet HMS *Endurance* on the following day. As the missile destroyer and frigate passed close to the small red and white patrol vessel, their crews spontaneously cheered, providing a moving experience for the lonely and, by now, under-fed *Endurance* men. They were not to be left alone again and, as a refuelling point was improvised, provisions and stores were 'RAS-ed' from the *Fort Austin*. The improvised fuel rig served well for the subsequent RAS with the *Tidespring*, to top up the *Endurance*'s diesel tanks, and she was then ready to turn back to return to South Georgia, accompanied by the *Antrim*, *Plymouth* and *Tidespring*.

The *Fort Austin* parted company and headed northwards for a rendezvous with the second south-bound group of warships. This comprised the Type 42 destroyers, *Glasgow*, *Sheffield* and *Coventry*, the Type 21 frigate *Arrow*, all led by Captain John Coward, commanding the Type 22 *Brilliant*. These ships had arrived at Ascension on 11 April, with the *Glamorgan* and *Appleleaf*, and left, after three days of hard work embarking yet more stores and ammunition, on the 14th. The *Appleleaf* followed the *Brilliant* Group, which was ordered to proceed at 25 knots to a position about 1,200 miles south of Ascension, providing a very distant screen for the carriers and cover for the *Antrim* Group.

This last was now on its way to recapture South Georgia. The plan had been worked out and approved by Commander-in-Chief, Fleet, during the preceding week, but Government approval for the operation was dependent upon the state of the negotiations being undertaken by the American Secretary of State, Mr Alexander Haig. South Georgia was not regarded by the British as being negotiable, the Argentines having no sustainable claim on the islands, but the Prime Minister held her hand until 20 April, when the Cabinet gave the go-ahead for the recapture of the island and Captain Young of HMS *Antrim* was ordered to 'Execute Operation "Paraquet"'. By this time, his little force was already inside the South Georgia Maritime Exclusion Zone, replenishing from the *Tidespring* so as to begin operations fully fuelled.

The *Plymouth* closes to refuel from the *Tidespring* before the Royal Navy closes in on South Georgia for the final assault *(MoD)*

The nuclear-powered Fleet submarines had already arrived in the Maritime Exclusion Zone around the Falklands. The Argentine Government had been warned that from midnight (Buenos Aires time) on 12/13 April their warships or merchant ships navigated within 200 miles of the Falklands only at their own risk. The Argentine reaction was to withdraw whatever larger surface warships as were in the area, to publicize 'blockade-running' by fast light craft from the mainland and to run in a few merchant ships of the state shipping line. These last were observed but were allowed to pass: to sink a civilian vessel without warning was unthinkable and the alternative – surfacing to give the crew orders to abandon ship – would have compromised the submarine's position. For the time being, therefore, the *Spartan, Splendid* and *Conqueror* watched and reported the invaders' activities, including the laying of a minefield off Cape Pembroke in mid-April.

The minefield was intended to deter close-range bombardment of the airfield and any attempt at a repetition of the Argentine Navy's landing operation. Coastal defences consisted of mobile batteries of 105mm pack howitzers manned by the Argentine Army and Marines; these could be moved with ease in the Port Stanley area, where there were a few miles of metalled road and some good tracks, but for the more distant districts, only seaborne or airborne transport could be used. Two captured coasters, the *Forrest* and *Monsunnen*, the naval transport *Isla de los Estados* and the oil-rig support vessel *Yehuin* plied between Port Stanley and the out-lying garrisons, and there was eventually a helicopter force of eleven Bell UH-1 'Hueys', six Pumas and four CH-47 Chinooks, provided by the Army, Coastguard and Air Force.

The Army theatre commander decided that, in the short term at least, the more important targets would have to rely primarily on guns and surface-to-air missiles for anti-aircraft defence. The quantity of pierced steel planking which could be delivered by sea was limited and Airfield Construction Group 1 was ordered to extend the dispersal area to enable transport aircraft to be unloaded to reinforce and resupply the garrison, instead of using the planking to lengthen the 4,100-foot (1,250-metre) tarmac runway to permit the operation of Mirages and Daggers. The provision of facilities for jet interceptors and strike aircraft would also have had to include adequate fuel stocks, storage for which did not exist.

The AA defences provided were quite formidable, particularly as the likely attack aircraft would have to overfly the targets at low level to deliver their weapons accurately. The Army and Air Force brought in a total of fourteen twin 35mm Oerlikon automatic cannon, with five Skyguard radar control systems which could search for and track targets in virtually any weather. The Air Force also flew in fifteen twin 20mm Rheinmetall cannon with Israeli Elta radar systems. The Marine Battalion had landed with twelve single-barrelled 30mm Hispano guns and three triple launchers for Tigercat missiles. The Army also had four of these launchers, which fired a missile virtually identical to the Royal Navy's Seacat. Probably the most effective system was, however, the Army's one and only operational Roland: French-made, this missile had a slant range of about seven miles and a ceiling of about 15,000 feet and was controlled by a very accurate radar system.

This miscellany of generally effective weapons and systems produced in five different countries and operated by three separate Services was used to defend the Port Stanley airfield, the town itself and the garrison headquarters at Moody Brook and the airstrip at Goose Green, on the narrow isthmus joining Lafonia to East Falkland, where the Air Force had deployed a squadron of 'our own unspeakable IA-58 Pucara'.* The weapons' control centres and search radars were tied in to a centralized Anti-Aircraft Operations Centre which was formed around *VYCA 2*,

* *Aeroespacio*, May/June, 1983, p. 52. The 500-metre strip was renamed *Baso Aerea Malvinas 'Condor'*.

which was responsible for control and reporting of all aircraft in the Falklands area. *VYCA 2*'s settling-in and work-up had been upset on about 10 April, when the TPS-43 radar antenna had been blown over in a gale, and it was not resumed until the 13th, when the unit was moved from its exposed position on Sapper Hill to a site on the south-west edge of the town of Stanley, where it would not only be safer from the elements but would also enjoy the sanctuary of the town, which, it was rightly believed, would not be deliberately attacked by the British. A dummy antenna and vehicles were erected on the original Sapper Hill site and certainly served to confuse the British intelligence gatherers and analysts for several weeks.

Intelligence on the Argentine garrison's strength and activities came, as might be expected, from a wide variety of sources. The Argentine media gave useful details in its enthusiasm to tell the masses of the glorious liberation and show pictures of the island, many of the airfield area, where the piles of newly-arrived equipment could be seen and identified. Islanders repatriated at their own request because they had no desire to be 'liberated' brought eye-witness accounts and notes, many of which told of poor morale in some units and deprivation among the young conscript soldiers, many of whom had been hastily recalled after the invasion shortly after completing their statutory period of military service, and an outline of the order of battle and main locations of the Army's 10th Brigade and the Air Force's Malvinas Command was gradually patched together. Until the arrival of the carrier task group, with its Sea Harrier tactical reconnaissance fighters, direction-finder-equipped ships and the special forces reconnaissance teams, the British analysts had to work largely on the basis of 'What would we do if we had what we know the Argentinians have got?' – a method which invariably results in surprises for both sides.

Chapter Seven

Halfway House

Admiral Woodward left Ascension with HMS *Glamorgan* on 14 April and on the next day met the *Hermes* and transferred his flag to the carrier. She was now in company with HMS *Alacrity*, *Broadsword* and *Yarmouth*, the latter pair having left Gibraltar, after storing and ammunitioning, on 8 April and joined the *Hermes* off the Canaries. The *Invincible*, which was putting the final touches to the coupling change, was well astern but that afternoon completed the job and carried out a full-power trial to prove that she could again reach 28 knots. The tanker *Olmeda* had been detached to the north to find and transfer personnel and stores to HMS *Fearless*, but instead surprised the *Antelope*, shepherding the five LSLs, first by the appearance of her Sea King in mid-ocean and then by the equally unexpected arrival of the RFA herself over the horizon.

A few minutes before midday on 16 April HMS *Hermes* anchored off Ascension Island, the first of the arrivals from Britain. Admiral Woodward flew north in a Sea King to visit the *Fearless* for talks with Commodore Clapp (COMAW), returning as the *Invincible* anchored, in the late afternoon. The ships were fully employed in storing from the airfield dumps and one another even before they arrived off the island, the heavy lift capacity of the Sea Kings aboard the two carriers being fully utilized to distribute the pre-loaded cargo nets. On the 16th, 220 'Vertrep' sorties were flown, by all types of helicopter, and the total of over 300 movements made Wideawake the busiest 'airport' in the world on that day and exceeded Ascension's normal annual quota.

The Navy, having its own attendant 'filling stations', made no demands upon the local American-owned and -supplied aviation fuel stocks, but the Royal Air Force transport aircraft were entirely dependent upon the co-operation of the Pan American authorities who ran the airfield and its support facilities for refuelling. During the stores build-up, the daily arrivals generally comprised six C-130 Hercules, three RAF VC.10s and two or three chartered civilian aircraft, Belfasts or Boeing 707s, all from the United Kingdom. The quantity of fuel required by these aircraft for the 4,000-mile return flight was considerable and its delivery to the aircraft was complicated by the limited number of fuel bowsers

The Ascension 'Air Head': five RAF Lockheed Hercules share the Wideawake hardstanding with (left) a Nimrod, a camouflaged Victor tanker and (centre-right) a USAF Lockheed C-141 Starlifter transport. The nearest Hercules is one of the 'resident' flight of extended-range aircraft, fitted for in-flight refuelling, which flew the first of their 19 long missions to drop supplies to the ships on 16 May *(MoD)*

available and the distance between the airfield and the bulk fuel storage 'farm'. The latter was, in turn, fed from a resident American oil tanker lying offshore. Usually the farm was topped up weekly but as long-range aircraft movements increased, the frequency had to be stepped up until the transfer of fuel ashore was virtually continuous. The dependence on bowsers was much reduced by the installation, by the Royal Engineers, of a temporary pipeline between the farm and the aircraft hardstandings.

The small group of naval personnel (Naval Party 1222) who had arrived on 6 April as the nucleus of the Support Unit was soon joined by a unique Naval Supply and Transport Service team, whose expertise in the routine of receipt and despatch of all manner of stores was as welcome as its fork-lift trucks. Working parties of any available Service personnel, irrespective of their trade, were pressed into assisting the civilian experts, sorting stores as they arrived direct from the United Kingdom or by helicopter or lighter from the ships and arranging the packages into 'lanes' according to their destination, ready for loading into helicopter cargo nets. These nets were usually needed in greater quantities than seemed to be available and the conscripted working parties were therefore landed from some ships to assist with loading and unloading ashore, to ensure a fast turn-around.

Responsible for the flow of stores through the island, for the accommodation, welfare and discipline of all British personnel based on or passing through Ascension and for the maintenance of smooth working relations with the usual residents was a naval officer, Captain Bob McQueen, the Commander, British Forces Support Unit. Bedevilled by shortage of suitable lodgings for the various groups for which he was responsible, his main task was complicated by the insistence on the part of some authorities at home on sending what he regarded as unnecessarily large specialist contingents. When protests failed to check the inflow, he simply 'deported' unwanted personnel, some so quickly that they flew out on the same aircraft that they had arrived in. The deployment of a permanent force of RAF tankers, maritime patrol aircraft and long-range transports, which began at the same time as the arrival of the carriers, resulted in a vast influx of Air Force personnel, followed in the first half of

May by another wave as the RAF took responsibility for the air and ground defence of the island. The strength of NP1222 reached a peak of 120 men at one time but was more usually between eighty and ninety. The Army contingent was about half that size while there were, at the height of Operation 'Corporate', some 800 RAF personnel on Ascension. A few permanent buildings and acres of tented camps provided over-crowded and makeshift housing, supplemented in early May by the hiring of a prefabricated modular camp which was flown in from the United States and erected to provide air-conditioned quarters for the long-range aircraft crews.

The addition of an extra 1,000 residents to the population of Ascension imposed a strain on the local resources. Water was in short supply, although this could be made good while large warships were present, and the scale of commodities which could be purchased in the township was inadequate for both the residents' and the Servicemen's needs. Despite the occasional tantrum by some visitor or resident unaware of the other side's rights or problems and the need to impose restrictions on public communications (which hit the Pan Am employees hardest as they were no longer permitted to telephone the USA at will) Captain McQueen and his staff managed to attract the support and hold the good-will of the American population and their St Helenian employees. The importance of the locals' contribution should not be underestimated, for they provided the essential services upon which the Ascension link de-pended and they did so efficiently and without complaint.

The Amphibious Force began to arrive at Ascension on 17 April, HMS *Fearless*, RFA *Stromness* and the five LSLs anchoring during the day. Heli-copter transfers continued throughout the day, the main emphasis being on off-loading stores from the carriers and their escorts to the new ar-rivals. The *Hermes*, for example, transferred 200 tons of Royal Marines' ammunition and A Company, 40 RM Commando to the *Sir Tristram*.

The most important event of the day was, however, the arrival of Admiral Sir John Fieldhouse, the Commander-in-Chief, Fleet, and Com-mander, Task Force 317, who flew in with a score of staff officers, includ-ing his Land Forces Deputy, Major-General Jeremy Moore, to confer with Admiral Woodward, Commodore Clapp, Brigadier Julian Thompson (commanding 3 Commando Brigade) and their staff officers. The plans which had been worked out by the various staffs were discussed and inte-grated t the meeting aboard the *Hermes* and it was decided that, after a period of blockade and 'precursor' operations to reconnoitre the islands and inflict attrition on Argentine forces, an assault would be mounted by 3 Commando Brigade on the west coast of East Falkland, in San Carlos Water, before 24 May, the date being dictated by the advance of winter, with the expectation of bad weather, and the need to get the troops ashore before prolonged retention aboard ship affected their morale and physical fitness.* The assault would be delivered when air superiority had been established by the Sea Harriers.

Admiral Fieldhouse and his retinue flew back to Britain on the same day, leaving Rear Admiral Woodward twenty-four hours to make his final preparations before sailing with the 'Carrier Battle Group' – Task Group 317.8. Commodore Clapp was to remain at Ascension until the ships of the Amphibious Group (TG 317.0) had assembled and all the units of 3 Commando Brigade (TG 317.1) had arrived and been given some training ashore and afloat.

18 April: the *Invincible* off Ascension, shortly before she sailed to catch up with the main body, which had sailed during the forenoon *(MoD)*

RFAs *Sir Percivale* and *Sir Geraint*, their stern doors wide open, re-stow their cargoes off Ascension *(MoD)*

In the late forenoon of 18 April, the *Hermes, Broadsword, Glamorgan, Yarmouth* and *Alacrity*, with RFAs *Olmeda* and *Resource*, got under way. The occasion was marked by the first submarine 'scare' – subsequent analysis suggested that what appeared to be the feather of a periscope was in fact a whale 'blowing', but the excitement was real enough, with frigates and helicopters establishing contact with a solid, manoeuvring target. HMS *Invincible* was delayed, awaiting urgently-required stores, and did not sail until later on the 18th but caught up the main group with ease.

* West Falkland was favoured in some quarters as a suitable initial base area, but as well as being closer to the mainland airfields, it would have meant a second, probably opposed, over-water assault to reach East Falkland. Salvador Inlet, on the north coast, was too narrow and easily obstructed and supporting warships would have to lie unprotected off shore. As far as the author can ascertain, Lafonia was never considered as a serious suggestion and was certainly not warmly advocated by the Navy, as has been alleged elsewhere.

The stores airlift to Ascension was halted, except for some very high priority items, from 17 April until early on the 21st. The Hercules and VC.10s continued to arrive, but now they were ferrying out the RAF personnel and equipment to support the deployment of Nimrod maritime reconnaissance aircraft, Victor air-to-air tankers and Vulcan bombers. The first Nimrods had flown into Ascension on 5 April and these had been employed on patrols around the island and the approaching British ships, the latter particularly appreciating the mail drops provided. The arrival of the first six Victors on 18 April added a new dimension to the capability of the land-based air component although, initially, they could only refuel one another. There was, however, an urgent programme in hand to restore the Vulcans' receiving capability and to provide the necessary probes and 'plumbing' for Nimrod Mark 2 and Hercules aircraft, to enable them to operate as far south as the Falklands.

While awaiting the remainder of the amphibious group, the LSLs and *Fearless* re-stowed their military loads and redistributed them where necessary, so that the equipment could be landed in the order in which it would be needed on the 'far shore'. The *Hermes* had disembarked four of her nine Sea King 4s and these were available, with the three aboard the *Fearless*, for Vertrep and troop drills. The Commando Brigade Air Squadron Gazelles flew ashore from the LSLs and were modified by the Naval Aircraft Servicing Unit at Wideawake to carry a pair of 7-round rocket pods apiece, for use in a 'gun-ship' role in support of the troop-carrying assault helicopters.

The *Canberra* and *Elk* arrived on 20 April, having refuelled at Freetown en route. The tug *Salvageman* also anchored off Ascension, having made the passage direct but not without incident, for she had suffered a fire in her galley. While the Marines and Paras went ashore by day for tactical training and weapon firing – the latter on ranges improvised by Captain McQueen's all-purpose team – the *Fearless'* artificers and mechanics set to work to modify the *Elk*, cutting down her high upper-deck bulwarks to provide a clear area for helicopter operations, clearing a covered space forward which gave hangar accommodation for three Sea Kings and fitting a pair of 40mm Bofors guns. (Exactly how these guns came to be allocated to the *Elk* is not entirely clear, for they were to come to be regarded as highly desirable weapons and not all of the LSLs were equipped with the two guns intended – *Sir Percivale* had only the port fo'c'sle Bofors mounted.) The *Fearless* technicians next turned to the *Salvageman*'s galley and re-wired that and thereafter were available to provide first-aid to other STUFT as they arrived. The requisitioned tankers *British Tay* and *British Tamar* reached Ascension on 22 and 25 April, respectively, the latter with the tug *Irishman*, and the small RFA oiler *Blue Rover* on the 26th. The tankers spent little time at anchor, waiting only to embark mail and the inevitable stores before heading south. The tugs left for a holding position to the north-east of South

Georgia and the Hospital Ship *Uganda*, which called on 28 April, left on the next day for her station. Two more frigates, the *Argonaut* and the *Ardent*, arrived with the RFAs *Regent* and *Plumleaf* on the 29th, followed soon after by the Forward Repair Ship *Stena Seaspread*. The four ships needed to complete the Amphibious Group, the landing ship *Intrepid*, the Aircraft Transport *Atlantic Conveyor* and the ferries *Norland* and *Europic Ferry*, the first ear-marked to carry 2nd Battalion, the Parachute Regiment, and the latter to carry the Paras' ammunition, stores and support units, had not left Home Waters until 25 and 26 April. The sixth LSL, *Sir Bedivere*, which had been at Vancouver when the Falklands were invaded, returned to Marchwood on the 25th, loaded and re-stored and set off for Ascension just two days later.

The Russians continued to take an interest in activities at Ascension, Bears appearing at intervals to fly past the anchorage at a respectful distance, and a spy trawler arrived on 2 May, remaining until after the fighting was over to monitor the air and sea movements and, presumably, the signals traffic. The Argentine merchant marine also put in an appearance: the Nimrods sighted and reported the *Rio de La Plata* as the freighter approached and passed within four miles of the island on 25 April. No action was taken, other than to order the only frigate, HMS *Antelope*, to ensure that the freighter did not turn back once it had gone over the horizon, escorting the ship out to a distance of 100 miles.

The *Rio de La Plata*'s unchecked progress raised the question of the local defence of the British base: the 1,000 men ashore were not fighting men and there was no long-range air warning radar on air defence, so that Ascension seemed vulnerable to a 'suicide'-type sea- or airborne sabotage raid which could inflict severe damage upon the whole enterprise. In late April, therefore, it was decided that the Royal Air Force should assume the air and ground defence roles and on 6 May No 3 Wing, RAF Regiment, was flown in as the airfield garrison, later to be joined by No 15 Squadron of the Regiment. Four days later, on the 10th, a Marconi air-portable surveillance radar station was operational on the highest point of the island and the existence of a 200-mile radius Terminal Control Area was announced internationally: all aircraft wishing to pass through the Ascension TCA would henceforth be obliged to notify Wideawake or risk interception.

The fighters which would enforce the TCA had already arrived from the United Kingdom. Within a week of the carriers' departure, it had been announced that 'the number of Harriers is to be doubled' and that the RAF would contribute a squadron of twelve such aircraft. The balance was provided by forming 809 Squadron at Yeovilton on 12 April, with only a couple of aircraft at first but increasing to eight during the next fortnight. The Sea Harriers were obtained from the remnant of 899 Squadron left behind to continue pilot training, from Maintenance Units and direct from the Hawker-Siddeley (British Aerospace) factory at Dunsfold, whence one was delivered weeks ahead of schedule. Out of thirty-four Sea Harriers ordered for the Royal Navy, one was still under construction, one had been lost in an accident a year before the war and twenty-eight were now in front-line squadrons: indeed, by the end of April, only four were left in the United Kingdom, two to be used for trials to clear new equipment and the other pair for pilot training.

The Harrier GR3s of No 1 Squadron RAF required modifiction and their pilots needed familiarization with shipboard techniques and procedures before they could embark for operations. Although the Harrier had been landed aboard ships over the years, this was a demonstration of potential rather than of an operational capability and for sustained flying from a ski-jump-equipped carrier some undercarriage strengthening was required, in addition to the cutting of drain holes to get rid of rain and salt water and the masking of existing holes and crevices to prevent the ingress of moisture. (The Sea Harrier, designed with exposure to the corrosive effects of seawater in mind, already had such minor refinements and many of its major airframe and engine components were made from non-corroding material.) Clearance to use certain naval weapons, such as the 2in rocket pod (the RAF used a 2.67in – 68mm – weapon), had to be obtained, but the requirement that the Harriers should be capable of a secondary air-to-air combat role, as well as their usual purely ground-attack role, meant that they had to be modified to fire the Sidewinder missile, a modification which involved the installation of control units and extensive wiring in the fuselage and wings. More wiring and a bulged aerial panel under the nose were needed for a radar 'transponder', a device triggered by a ship's radar pulses to provide a larger 'blip' which could be more readily picked out of weather and sea clutter on the radar screen.

While the ten Harriers earmarked for initial embarkation were being modified, the pilots went to Yeovilton to practice take-offs from the ski-jump and landings on the 'dummy deck' at the airfield, in between air combat manoeuvring training sorties. The naval pilots of 809 Squadron, among whom were a high proportion of very experienced Lieutenant-Commanders who had begun their flying training up to twenty years previously, were ready to deploy by the end of April and on the 30th the eight Sea Harriers began their long flight to Ascension. With air-to-air refuelling from RAF Victors, the aircraft were airborne for over nine hours, with just one refuelling stop on the ground. Eight Harriers of No 1 Squadron followed between 3 and 5 May, theirs being a non-stop flight – the longest attempted up to that date by a single-seat single-engined RAF aircraft.

The ship that was to take the fighters south was the *Atlantic Conveyor*, a Cunard container ship with a stern ramp giving access to two large vehicle decks. Taken up after the departure of the carriers, she was fitted out at Devonport between 16 and 24 April to carry Sea Harriers and operate helicopters. No overhead protection for the aircraft was possible, but the wide flat container deck's edges were lined with three tiers of containers and 'portakabins' (the latter providing additional accommodation and workshop space) to make a sheltered pen for twenty-four helicopters and fighters. Fuel cells were installed in adapted containers and provision made for refuelling the aircraft on deck, providing liquid oxygen for the Sea Harriers and fresh water for washing down all aircraft. The *Atlantic Conveyor* was also to be the aircraft repair ship with a team of technicians from the Navy's Mobile Aircraft Repair, Transport and Salvage Unit – a much-respected organization of which cynics said that its primary role was the creation of weekend traffic jams in Southern England, the 52-foot 'Queen Mary' aircraft transport being ideal for this purpose.

Although the Sea Harriers and Harrier GR3s were to join the ship at Ascension, to save their unnecessary exposure to salt-laden air on passage, the *Atlantic Conveyor*'s other aircraft, six Wessex 5 of 848 Naval Air Squadron and five CH-47C Chinooks of No 18 Squadron RAF, were embarked for the whole of the voyage from Devonport. 848 Squadron had formed as recently as 19 April and on the same day two aircraft had embarked on the departing RFA *Regent*. The *Atlantic Conveyor* loaded stores, aircraft ordnance and spares, ammunition, rations and an entire tented camp for 4,500 men, complete with 'the usual offices', before embarking her helicopters and conducting Sea Harrier flying trials immediately prior to her departure on 25 April. Sailing in company with the *Europic Ferry*, which was carrying military equipment and personnel, she broke the journey to Ascension to refuel in Sierra Leone and arrived at Ascension on 5 May, the same day as HMS *Intrepid*, which had left home

25 April: Lt Cdr Tim Gedge, the Commanding Officer of 809 Squadron, makes the first trial approach to the *Atlantic Conveyor* a few hours before the STUFT Aircraft Transport leaves Plymouth. Standard 40-ft (12 m) containers, two- and three-deep, provide some shelter for the two RAF Chinooks parked on deck and the lower tier is used for office and workshop accommodation *(MoD)*

waters a day later with the RFA oiler *Bayleaf*. The re-commissioning, re-storing and overhaul of the assault ship *Intrepid* was one of the major support achievements of the campaign and was completed by Portsmouth Dockyard and the Portland Naval Base in just twenty-two days.

The ferry *Norland* was to have left with the *Intrepid* on 26 April, but the strike at Hull delayed her programme by twenty-four hours and the fitting of her helicopter pad was not completed until that day; she did not arrive at Ascension until 7 May, the last of the essential units needed for the reinforced 3 Commando Brigade's lift. Three of the five main units of the Brigade – 40 and 42 RM Commandos and 3 Para – had already reached Ascension by sea and now the others, 45 RM Commando and 2 Para, were flown out to join their ships, RFA *Stromness* and the *Norland*. A new Company was also raised and flown out to join the *Canberra*: 'Juliet' Company, 42 RM Commando, was made up of the Marines of the two Falklands Naval Parties who had been repatriated and returned to Britain on 5 April, given leave and then re-equipped.

Even before the Amphibious Group was complete, the first contingent left Ascension for the Falklands area – the five slow LSLs, still escorted by HMS *Antelope*. The eight Sea Harriers of 809 Squadron and six Harrier GR3s of No 1 Squadron landed aboard the *Atlantic Conveyor* on 6 May, after one of the Chinooks had been flown off to assist with the Ascension stores lift; most of the ship's load of victualling and general naval stores, as well as NAAFI supplies, were vertrepped to RFA *Stromness* – fortunately, as events were to prove. Special weather-proof plastic bags had been manufactured for the aircraft parked on the *Atlantic Conveyor* and these were fitted once all were embarked.

HMS *Argonaut* sailed from Ascension with the *Ardent*, *Regent* and *Plumleaf* on 6 May, to join the Carrier Group. The main body of the Amphibious Group sailed on 7 May, as the *Norland* arrived. The large ferry remained just long enough to work up 2 Para in amphibious landing drills, took on board stores and left to catch up with the assault force.

The anchorage was almost quiet again, after nearly a month of hectic activity, during which over fifty warships, RFAs and STUFT had arrived, stored and exercised and then left for what had been since 25 April a 'hot' war. Yet to come were another nine destroyers and frigates, the five minesweeping trawlers and the patrol vessels HMS *Leeds Castle* and *Dumbarton Castle*, which would be based at Ascension to serve as Guardships and to ferry stores to the combat groups from the airhead. Another twenty-one requisitioned ships would pass through and the biggest of all would pass by, out of sight, to reach the forward areas before the end of the fighting. Most of the Royal Fleet Auxiliary was already south of Ascension and only five more Blue Ensign ships were yet to call, but two of these were among the most remarkable, having been in the Pacific when called to join the 'Corporate' forces.

The LSL *Sir Bedivere* had reached Marchwood on 25 April, sailed again

HMS *Dumbarton Castle* refuels alongside the *Alvega*. At 57,000 tons deadweight the largest tanker to be taken up from trade, the *Alvega* was employed as a fuel depot at Ascension from mid-May (*MoD*)

on 27th and reached Ascension on 9 May to load stores and embark the bomb disposal experts of the Navy's No 3 Fleet Clearance Diving Team, the RAF Explosive Ordnance Demolitions Team and 11 Field Regiment, Royal Engineers. The other RFA from the Pacific was the fast Fleet re-plenishment oiler *Tidepool* (*Tidespring*'s sister-ship), which had been on passage for delivery to the Chilean Navy, which was to buy her, but was summoned back on 16 April, to the delight of her crew. She came back through the Panama Canal, loaded with fuel at Curacao and stopped off Ascension only long enough to embark necessities before pressing on at her best speed to join the Amphibious Group, 1,000 miles south of the island, on 11 May. On the previous day, a Nimrod of No 206 Squadron RAF was able to give a few hours' support to the Group, using its newly-acquired in-flight refuelling capability for the first time.

The importance of Ascension as the Task Force's forward supply base in no way diminished as the shipping traffic slackened off. The ships which left the United Kingdom in May were generally better stored and equipped than their predecessors, which had left in such a hurry, so that there was less need for re-stowing and redistribution on arrival at Ascension. However, every ship heading south was used to take parcels, boxes and packing crates down to the combat zone, Naval Party 1222 ensuring that each vessel carried a full cargo by the expedient of holding her mail until the last load, which was often flown out after she had sailed. The *Leeds Castle* began her supply runs in mid-May, followed a week later by the requisitioned cable-vessel *Iris*, carrying urgent freight and personnel forward. Also in May, RAF Hercules of No 47 Squadron started a series of flights which must rank as one of the most outstanding achievements in the history of the Air Force. Refuelled by Victor tankers, they undertook twenty-five-hour missions to drop supplies and even personnel to ships within the Exclusion Zone, at a distance of over 3,300 miles from Ascension. These return trips, which were equivalent to a Hercules taking off from London to drop five tons of supplies near New York and then flying back, took place almost daily, sometimes in appalling weather, and required two full crews per aircraft. Only the most urgent stores went forward by this means; the material flown to Ascension and taken forward by sea kept the Task Force at sea, but 47 Squadron's loads enabled individual ships to fight, float and fly their aircraft.

Santa Fe alongside the jetty at Grytviken: the superficial damage caused to the conning tower casing by the *Endurance* Flight Wasps' AS.12 missiles can just be seen *(MoD)*

Two of the 'Ellas' – *Junella* (left) and *Farnella* – in lumpy seas while on passage to South Georgia *(MoD)*

Recovery after an eventful CAP –
an 800 Squadron Sea Harrier lands
on board the *Hermes* minus a
Sidewinder but with the plugs in
the Aden cannon ports. On 21
May, five of the squadron's pilots
accounted for six Argentine jets,
four of which were shot down by
the missiles and two by 30mm
shells; a sixth pilot missed a
Mirage with a Sidewinder – only
he and Lt-Cdr Neil Thomas did
not use guns in these combats
(MoD)

Sunset brings respite to San Carlos
Water – the *Broadsword* patrols
the northern end of the assault ship
anchorage, seen from a machine-
gun position on board the
Intrepid *(MoD)*

PART III

Chapter One

The Recapture of South Georgia

Cabinet approval for the recapture of South Georgia by the group of ships under the command of *Antrim*'s Captain Brian Young was given in the evening of 20 April, when the ships were well within the 200-mile zone declared by both the British and Argentine Governments. The exact strength of the occupation force was not known, but it did not appear that any attempt had been made to move outside the Grytviken and Leith settlements; certainly, none of the outlying BAS camps had been troubled by the invaders.

The plan for Operation 'Paraquet' called for the landing of Special Forces – Special Air Service and Special Boat Section – reconnaissance teams to observe Grytviken and Leith, prior to any assault. At dawn on 21 April, therefore, HMS *Antrim* launched her Wessex 3 to reconnoitre a landing site chosen by the SAS on the Fortuna Glacier, ten miles west of Leith. Lieutenant-Commander Ian Stanley, the Flight's commanding officer, reported that, despite a high wind and driving rain, a landing was possible and returned to the *Antrim*, thirty miles off the coast, to refuel and embark four SAS troopers. The Wessex 3 then took off, and the two 845 Squadron Wessex 5 assault helicopters from RFA *Tidespring* landed in turn on *Antrim* to pick up the remainder of the party and then the three aircraft set off in formation, led by the radar-equipped Wessex 3.

The first attempt failed, the helicopters running into thick low cloud and driving rain over the coast and snow storms inland. A couple of hours later, in the early afternoon, they tried again and, in spite of low cloud and snow squalls, with turbulence and sudden sharp changes in wind direction adding to the problems caused by the lack of visual references as the white snow merged with the white cloud, the helicopters landed their score of troops and the latters' gear on the glacier. All three aircraft returned safely.

Nobody had a comfortable night. The ships were battered by a Force 10 storm, with gusts of wind up to 70 knots and heavy seas which, besides inflicting other damage, put one of the *Antrim*'s Seacat launchers out of action. The storm eased at daylight on the 22nd, but the SAS party on the glacier reported by radio that their position was untenable. As the troops

'Humphrey', *Antrim*'s Wessex 3 (XP142) seen in 'warpaint' as Lt-Cdr Ian Stanley holds off from the ship in Cumberland Bay, South Georgia *(MoD)*

were unable to make their own way out, the three Wessex were sent in again, although the weather was worse even than it had been on the previous day. Lieutenant-Commander Stanley left the Wessex 5s at the coast and made three attempts to climb to the glacier but was driven back by low cloud, snow squalls and the wind, which varied between 10 and 70 knots, producing violent turbulence and heavy downdraughts from the surrounding mountains. Baffled, all three helicopters returned to their ships to refuel, taking off again as soon as this was complete to make a fresh attempt.

The weather had improved by the time that Lieutenant-Commander Stanley's formation reached the coast and all three 'Wessi' managed to climb the glacier and land beside the stranded SAS men. Before all the men and their gear could be loaded, the visibility began to lower again as the strengthening wind whipped up loose snow. One of the Wessex 5s, having embarked its 'stick', decided to take off but when transitioning from the hover to forward flight the pilot appears to have become disorientated by the sudden loss of outside visual 'cues' in the white-out which reduced visibility to a few yards. The helicopter touched the ground and skidded for fifty yards, ending up on its side. The crew and passengers extricated themselves and were picked up by the other Wessex 5 and the Wessex 3, which then took off without mishap and headed down the glacier, the assault helicopter following the well-instrumented anti-submarine aircraft.

On the way down, the Wessex 3 crossed a small ridge on the glacier but the Wessex 5 was seen to pull up suddenly, possibly to avoid the crest of the ridge, which it struck, then skidded and fell on its side. There could be no question of the Wessex 3, overloaded with ten passengers as well as its own crew, remaining to attempt a further rescue and so it returned to HMS *Antrim* to disembark the troops and prepare for another sortie. First aid kits and blankets for the expected exposure victims were loaded and Lieutenant-Commander Stanley took off on his third trip to the glacier. Although he managed to establish radio contact with the stranded helicopter crew and troops, the weather foiled two attempts to climb the glacier and he had to go back to the ship to await another slight clearance. This came within an hour and the Wessex crew managed to find a way to the survivors, none of whom was seriously injured, in spite of some of them being involved in both accidents, and retrieved them all without further incident. The helicopter landed on the *Antrim* about an hour before sunset – the rescue had been a very close-run thing, for it is unlikely that the stranded men would have survived a night on the Fortuna Glacier.

Ian Stanley and his crew were not yet finished with rescuing SAS parties. Before dawn on the next morning, 23 April, they were again airborne, this time looking for a missing 'Gemini' inflatable boat. During the night the *Antrim*, fully darkened, had entered Stromness Bay, on which

Leith Harbour is situated, to lower the SAS' Boat Troop Geminis, which would land reconnaissance parties. The outboard motors in three of the five craft refused to start and the following morning radio contact could be made with only one of those which had got away. The other Gemini's engine had given up the ghost while it was making its way inshore and the craft drifted until found eight miles away by the persistent Wessex 3 which had spent a nervous hour before dawn searching Stromness Bay, without alerting the Argentine troops.

HMS *Endurance*, with the SBS on board, was operating independently to the south-east of Grytviken. Having ascertained from a party of three BAS members and two Anglia Television documentary makers (Lucinda Buxton and Anne Price) that the Argentinians had not been seen so far from the main base, Captain Barker landed No 2 SBS in Cumberland Bay East to keep a watch on Grytviken. The Marines' Gemini engines appear to have been more reliable than their SAS counterparts, but on the 23rd the SBS reported that wind-blown glacier ice was puncturing the inflatables' skins and they had to be taken off by the *Endurance* during the following morning.

Captain Young's squadron was increased by the arrival of RFA *Brambleleaf* on 22 April. The oiler was the only 'Corporate' ship to join via the Cape of Good Hope, having been summoned from the Mombasa area. She encountered very severe weather shortly before reaching the South Georgia area and sustained considerable damage to her bows, causing some seawater flooding of her oil tanks. The damage required repair and it was decided that she should pump over as much as possible of her cargo to the *Tidespring* and then return to the United Kingdom. The pumpover began late on the 22nd and continued into the next day, the two tankers being covered by HMS *Plymouth*.

The transfer of oil fuel was interrupted by the detection of an Argentine Air Force C-130 Hercules on a reconnaissance flight. The aircraft, which was over 1,250 miles from its base, closed to within eight miles of the three ships, thirty miles north-east of the northern tip of South Georgia, but did not detect the *Antrim* or *Endurance*. At about the same time, Captain Young was alerted to the possible presence of the submarine

In the South Georgia Exclusion Zone – the *Plymouth*'s port Oerlikon crew at Action Stations. In the background is the RFA *Brambleleaf*, which would soon exchange her aviation fuel with the *Tidespring* and return to the UK, and the *Antrim* is on the frigate's port quarter, visible between the two whip aerial masts *(MoD)*

Santa Fe in the area and he therefore ordered all of his ships, with the exception of the *Endurance*, to clear out of the 200-mile zone. The Ice Patrol Ship, remained in South Georgia waters, relying upon ice floes and Captain Nick Barker's cunning and local knowledge to escape detection and attack.

Endurance was only partly successful. The enemy were aware that she was in the area and on 24 April, while she was recovering the SBS and their Geminis from Hound Bay, the crew of the 'Red Iceberg'* were horrified to see an Argentine Air Force Boeing 707 approaching. The 20mm AA guns were manned and the ship's upper deck lined with sailors and Special Forces troops, the former armed with the standard SLR (rifles) and the latter with the wide variety of very personal weapons which the SAS in particular affect. The 707 made two passes at about 3,000 feet but would not approach closer than two to three miles, somewhat to the disappointment of some of the marksmen. What was not known at the time was that the *Endurance* was also sighted and approached by the *Santa Fe*, against which she was completely defenceless. Fortunately, and for reasons unknown, the submarine commander did not attack.

At this stage, Operation 'Paraquet' was not going to plan, through no fault of Captain Young. The Leith and Stromness reconnaissance had not only failed, it had also cost the squadron its most effective assault transport (the two Wessex 5s). The *Endurance*, which was to have been used as the main assault ship, landing troops by means of Geminis, her own boats and helicopters, was to the south-east of Grytviken while the troops, a company of 42 RM Commando, were in the *Tidespring* over 200 miles away. An American newspaper had announced the presence of a British force off South Georgia as early as 20 April. This had been taken up by the world's Press and by the close of the 24th the Argentine Air Force had been able to confirm the reports.

Captain Young received a welcome reinforcement on 24 April. As soon as the loss of the two Wessex 5s was known to Admiral Woodward (on the 22nd), the *Brilliant* was detached from the advanced screen to join the *Antrim*; although her two Lynxes lacked the load-lifting capability of the larger assault helicopters, they were more versatile and were genuine all-weather aircraft. The *Brilliant*, which had made a fast passage in bad weather, refuelled from the *Tidespring* and then entered the Exclusion Zone with the other two warships, leaving the oiler outside.

The Argentine submarine had left Mar del Plata several days previously with reinforcements for the South Georgia garrison. The decision to use her for this purpose was taken without the prior knowledge of the Fleet Commander, *Contralmirante* J. J. Lombardo, who could undoubtedly have found a better use for this long-range submarine. The *Santa Fe* put into Grytviken on 24 April, unloaded supplies and twenty marines,

---

* A nickname coined by Cindy Buxton and Annie Price and used in the former's splendid book, *Survival – South Atlantic*, published in 1983 by Granada.

and sailed before dawn on the 25th to cover the entrances to Stromness and Cumberland Bay. A few minutes before 0900 the submarine was on the surface five miles off the entrance to Cumberland Bay, preparing to dive, when a helicopter was sighted half a mile away. *Capitan de Corbeta* Hugo Bicain cancelled the order to dive, deciding to remain on the surface, where he would be immune to the helicopter's homing torpedoes. It was the wrong decision – the *Antrim*'s ubiquitous Wessex was armed with depth-charges!

Lieutenant-Commander Stanley had taken off at 0810 for an antisubmarine search in the approaches to Cumberland Bay; at the same time, one of the *Brilliant*'s Lynxes had been launched, armed with a homing torpedo, to search along the north-east coast. *Plymouth* Flight's single Wasp was standing by on deck, ready for a follow-up strike with AS.12 missiles. Visibility below the 400-foot cloud-base was between 1,000 and 2,000 yards but the helicopters maintained radar silence to avoid detection by possible warning receivers. Not until the Wessex 3 had searched Cumberland Bay was the observer permitted to make a single sweep with the radar: Lieutenant Christopher Parry almost immediately saw a tiny 'blip' off the coast and the helicopter turned to investigate. At three-quarters of a mile the *Santa Fe* appeared out of the mist and the first British naval aircraft attack on a submarine at sea since April, 1945, was delivered. The weapon was essentially the same Mark 11 depth-charge, in service since 1943, and as on many previous occasions it was most effective, one of the two dropped exploding close to the port side of the submarine and causing sufficient internal damage to prevent the submarine from diving, as well as starting leaks in external fuel tanks.

Bicain turned to run for the relative safety of Cumberland Bay and King Edward's Cove but was harassed the whole way, first by the Wessex, which used a door-mounted General-Purpose Machine Gun (GPMG) to keep the heads down on the *Santa Fe*'s bridge, then by the *Brilliant*'s Lynx, which made a hopeful but unsuccessful attack with a homing torpedo and then added its GPMG fire. The *Plymouth*'s Wasp was scrambled on receipt of the Wessex's first sighting report and was homed to the scene by Lieutenant Parry, only to be beaten to a firing position by the first of *Endurance*'s helicopters, flown off ten minutes later but from nearer at hand. Lieutenant D. W. Wells, aiming the AS12 missiles, scored a hit with the first, the 56lb warhead exploding inside the submarine's large fin, but missed short with the next; so close was the *Endurance*, Lieutenant-Commander Ellerbeck was able to return, reload and get back to the *Santa Fe* just before *Plymouth* Flight could fire. Again one hit and one miss resulted, the AS12 flying through an empty space in a fibreglass section of the fin to explode on contact with the water. The *Plymouth* aimer fired only one missile and claimed a hit on the waterline; with a 50-mile flight back to the frigate to re-arm this would be the Wasp's only strike.

Endurance Flight, on the other hand, had just begun. By 1000 her second Wasp was on its way, flown by Lieutenant T. S. Finding, who encountered machine-gun fire from the garrison positions on King Edward Point, where Lieutenant Mills had held out on 3 April. The helicopter was untouched and Leading Aircrewman R. Nadin scored another hit on the empty fibreglass portion of the fin, which was by now looking rather ragged. As he flew out, still untouched, Lieutenant Finding warned the inbound crew of the ground fire, which included anti-tank rockets and rifle-fire by now. Tony Ellerbeck's third attack, delivered as the submarine was between King Edward Point and the BAS pier at Grytviken, at the head of the cove, was even more strongly opposed, with at least one machine-gun now in action on the *Santa Fe*. Again the Wasp escaped damage, although two approaches were made before the crew was satisfied with the firing position, and Lieutenant Wells scored his third and most damaging hit: the missile struck the periscope standards, wrecking these and adjacent pumps and wounding an Argentine seaman manning a machine-gun. At 1100, two hours after she had first come under attack, the *Santa Fe* ran alongside the pier, listing and apparently on fire.

Within an hour Captain Young had decided to mount the assault on Grytviken as soon as possible. The intended landing force, 'Mike' Company, 42 RM Commando, was 200 miles away, aboard the *Tidespring*, although the Second-in-Command of 42 Commando, Major Guy Sheridan, was aboard the *Antrim* with elements of the Company, a mortar and a reconnaissance section, the ten Marines of the ship's detachment and the SAS and SBS troops – some seventy-five assorted but highly-trained and very well armed infantry in all. There were, in addition, two naval gunfire support parties, Royal Artillery teams which would direct the ships' bombardment of Argentine positions before and during the assault. Major Sheridan held his 'Orders Group' to brief all participants at 1345, just an hour before the first 'wave' was due to land.

The first men ashore were an NGS team, which was landed by *Endurance*'s Wasp, again flown by Lieutenant-Commander Ellerbeck. Their approach was covered by HMS *Plymouth*, which fired a dozen 4.5in shells at the intended landing site, ceasing fire as the Wasp touched down at 1420. The spotting officer almost immediately called for gunfire against Argentine troops on Brown Mountain, between the landing site and Grytviken and the frigate obliged with forty rounds of 4.5in during the next twenty minutes, firing at a rate of sixteen rounds per gun per minute in short bursts. The first wave of the assault proper was landed by *Antrim*'s Wessex and *Brilliant*'s two Lynxes at Hesteletten, about two and a half miles from Grytviken, on the southern side of King Edward's Cove. As the remainder of the landing force was ferried ashore in the three helicopters, subsequently joined by Ellerbeck's Wasp, the *Antrim* and *Plymouth* fired when called upon to do so, engaging a possible Argen-

25 April: the *Plymouth* firing on Brown Mountain to cover the assault force's advance on Grytviken. The frigate has just finished a turn to come into the *Antrim*'s wake and the smoke of the opening salvo is still on her quarter *(MoD)*

tine gun position along the shore and the area where the wreckage of the Puma shot down on 3 April still lay, and finally the track to Grytviken itself, firing a total of 235 high-explosive shells.

The troops stormed Grytviken, running through a minefield without hurt, to the amazement of the demoralized defenders, who outnumbered the Marines and SAS troopers. A white flag was run up alongside the Argentine flag at Grytviken at 1705, just as *Plymouth* Flight and *Endurance*'s other Wasp were about to take off to land Marines from the latter ship, which had been standing by as a mobile reserve all afternoon. They were to provide a blocking party between Grytviken and Stromness to prevent the Argentines from withdrawing. Major Sheridan requested the *Antrim* and *Plymouth*, which had remained 'around the corner' from the main Argentine position on King Edward Point, to show themselves, but three large white flags appeared over the Point a few minutes before the destroyer arrived in view, followed by the frigate. The *Endurance* Flight Commander, who had landed an NGS spotting team for HMS *Antrim* after troop lifts, made his final trip to take Major Sheridan across to King Edward Point to accept the Argentine surrender from the local commander, *Capitan de Corbeta* Lagos. Lieutenant-Commander Ellerbeck had enjoyed, appropriately, the rare privilege of witnessing the beginning and end of the Argentine occupation.

The day's activities were not yet over. Captain Pentreath of the *Plymouth* was ordered to take his own ship and the *Endurance* into Stromness Bay to persuade the Argentine forces there to surrender. Captain Barker contacted the commander of the small detachment of marines, *Capitan de Corbeta* Alfredo Astiz, on a commercial radio frequency as dusk fell. Astiz agreed that the scrap metal workers at Husvik should surrender forthwith but initially declared that he and his men would fight on. He soon recognized the impossibility of his position, however, and, after he had attempted to persuade Captain Barker to land on the football pitch at Leith to accept the surrender in person, agreed to walk out to meet troops who would be landed on the foreshore early the following morning. Only later did Nick Barker learn why Astiz had been so anxious for him to fly ashore – the helicopter landing 'H' concealed a sizeable charge of explosive which was to be used to greet the Wasp as it touched down!

As early as 1730 GMT on the 25th Captain Young had signalled: 'Be pleased to inform Her Majesty that the White Ensign flies alongside the Union Flag at Grytviken.' He could be justifiably proud of his achievement, for South Georgia had been retaken without any loss of life – indeed, the only casualties were the *Santa Fe* crewman and a British soldier who had sprained his ankle – in an opportunistic and improvised assault. *Capitans de Corbeta* Bicain and Lagos signed a formal surrender aboard the *Antrim* that evening and on the following morning Astiz signed the Leith surrender document aboard the *Plymouth*, in the presence of Captain Pentreath and the still outraged Captain Barker.

The Argentine Air Force let it be known that a reconnaissance aircraft attempted to contact the South Georgia forces on 26 April but had departed when it received no reply to radio calls. It would appear that more positive action was intended and that the Argentine authorities were not certain of the surrender before the following day. According to a 1985 Spanish account,* a strike of three II Air Brigade Canberras, led by a Boeing 707 'shepherd', took off from the naval air base at Rio Grande, in Tierra del Fuego, on the 26th to attack British ships off Grytviken. One of the bombers had to turn back when its wingtip external tanks would not jettison – with 1,150 miles to fly in each direction, the extra drag of empty tanks was unacceptable – leaving the formation south of the Falklands. The 707 and the two Canberras reached the South Georgia area and were told by a shadowing KC-130 tanker that there were ships present. Low cloud and generally bad weather prevented the bombers from finding targets and they therefore returned to base. The ships detected by the KC-130 cannot be identified, but it is likely that they were any or all of HMS *Brilliant* and the two RFA tankers. As the latter were virtually defenceless, the British forces had reason to be thankful for South Georgia's inhospitable climate.

The White Ensign was now secure over South Georgia, but there was much to do to tidy up the mess made during the twenty-two days that the blue and white flag had flapped. The Argentine marines and sailors were searched and their particulars noted – a task which occupied the whole day as there were 137 of them. They were then confined in Shackleton House, at Grytviken, until they could be embarked in the *Tidespring*. The sailor who had been wounded in the final Wasp AS.12 attack was operated on by HMS *Antrim*'s surgical team, assisted by the Argentine naval surgeon from the *Santa Fe*. Unfortunately, the sailor's foot had to be amputated but the man, the only casualty of the assault operation, recovered well.

More tragic was the death of one of the *Santa Fe*'s petty officers on 27 April. The submarine was being moved from its position blocking the

* Mafe Huertas & Romero Briasco, *Falklands – Witness of Battles* Federico Domenech, Valencia (1985).

only useable pier, a small party of Argentine key personnel being supervised by Royal Navy submariners gathered from the four warships and guarded by Royal Marines. The Marines were particularly instructed to prevent any attempt to scuttle the boat and the Argentine personnel were given to understand that any such action would result in the culprit being shot. As the submarine was being moved, it lurched and, under orders from his Argentine superior on the bridge, Petty Officer Felix Artuso began to operate a 'forbidden' control which it was mistakenly believed would flood the boat: he ignored shouted warnings and was shot by the sentry, who could think of no other means of stopping him. An inquiry was held by Captain Young, and Bicain, who attended the proceedings, joined in exonerating the much-distressed Marine. Once in its new position, the *Santa Fe* was immobilized by explosive charges, which loosened her rudder. Slow flooding finished the job and the submarine settled on the bottom with only her battered fin showing.

The Argentine defenders had mined and booby-trapped most of the buildings on King Edward Point and at Leith, Astiz' talent for inventive nastiness being particularly evident at the latter. The prisoners were invited to dismantle the more dangerous booby-traps and indicate the positions of the anti-personnel mines, but the work of clearance went on for many days after their departure, HMS *Endurance*'s personnel undertaking much of this hazardous task.

The fifty-one scrap workers and their two local overseers were accommodated aboard the *Endurance* until 30 April, when they were transferred to the *Tidespring*, together with the Argentine Navy prisoners. (The exception was Astiz who, it now transpired, was an even more unpleasant individual than was already recognized and was wanted by the Swedish and French Governments for questioning in connection with crimes he had committed during Argentina's anti-terrorist 'dirty war'. While his men lived in cramped discomfort aboard the oiler, Astiz was held under close arrest in a more comfortable cabin aboard HMS *Antrim*.) Captain Barker then went off to retrieve the two remaining outlying BAS parties, one of which, on Bird Island, insisted on bringing two ducks. All the BAS personnel and the two intrepid TV photographers embarked in the *Antrim* and she and RFA *Tidespring* sailed for Ascension on 2 May. The *Plymouth* and *Brilliant* had already sailed, on 28 April, so that HMS *Endurance* was once again alone off South Georgia, although this time she had the Marines of Mike Company ashore to support.

An editor in Fleet Street thought to add to the numbers, instructing his correspondent afloat to proceed to South Georgia within twenty-four hours, to interview the 'OC Troops': the correspondent was at the time aboard *Canberra* off Ascension, unable to go ashore even there. News of the message provoked widespread mirth in the Task Force and the Navy Department, but it was a sorry reflection on the ignorance of the news-hungry staff.

Chapter Two

The Carriers Close In

It will be recalled that the Carrier Group sailed from Ascension a week before the capture of South Georgia. From the time of departure the carriers maintained a continuous screen of three Sea Kings airborne for anti-submarine protection, a screen which was maintained day and night, interrupted only when storms and mountainous seas made submarine attacks as well as flying impossible. The twenty Sea King 5s were to fly a total of 2,253 sorties during 'Corporate', each sortie averaging more than three hours in length.

The carriers' Sea King 5s flew over 2,250 hours during the operation and, with only two lost, enjoyed the lowest attrition rate of any shipborne aircraft. By far the majority of missions were spent on the anti-submarine screen, three aircraft being maintained on station day and night in all but the most extreme weather. Here a Sea King 5 of 820 Squadron, its sonar body trailing below, proceeds to a fresh 'dip' *(MoD)*

The ships themselves went into a routine of 'Defence Watches' on 19 April, with teams closed up for immediate action in the operations rooms, at weapons and in damage control headquarters. Although more relaxed than 'Action Stations', it was still a tiring routine, particularly in cold and heavy weather, and not until 9 July was HMS *Yarmouth* finally able to relax to a normal peacetime routine, her eighty days constituting a somewhat uncomfortable record. From 23 April all ships changed from keeping local time (by then about two hours behind Greenwich) to GMT, or 'Z' time,* which was used off the Falklands, at Ascension and at North-wood. This removed any possible ambiguity which may have arisen over

* 'Z' derived from 'zone', ie the Greenwich Time Zone; by international convention each time zone is distinguished by a letter

signal origination, aircraft movements, intelligence of enemy movements, and so forth and the ships' companies, used to time zone changes and fixed routines, settled down without difficulty to getting up four hours before daybreak and turning in not long after nightfall. There were to be advantages besides those for the command, for the early hour of rising meant that most personnel were fully awake and fed when dawn, the traditional hour for surprise attack, came and, furthermore, had had two hours to carry out ship's tasks which could not be done when the threat of attack existed after daybreak.

Damage control practices and first-aid lectures were accompanied by steps to reduce casualties. Many formica panels were stripped out and mirrors were either removed or covered with lattices of masking tape to minimize casualties and damage from splinters. Personnel were not permitted to sleep below the waterline – a precaution which applied more to the already overcrowded large ships than to the frigates and destroyers and was, naturally, a cause of great personal inconvenience over such a long period in unpleasant weather conditions. On the other hand, many officers and men became rejuvenated overnight by the disappearance of their beards when 'Shave Off' became the order of the day, to ensure the fit of anti-gas respirators. As the ships moved out of the tropics, some turned down the heating between decks, not to conserve energy but to acclimatize everyone in preparation for the sudden arrival in the southern autumn.

Inevitably ships developed defects during the passage. Both the *Yarmouth* and *Alacrity* dropped out with machinery defects and had to catch up after completing repairs, while other ships were able to keep up with the force as their technicians replaced or repaired the faulty items. Weather, too, took its toll, with moisture reaching sensitive electrics in the weapons systems and the sheer weight of waves damaging light structures and fittings. Such 'fair wear and tear' is expected and the task force was prepared for it, but few individuals had any experience of extended sustained operations so far from a main base and the achievement of the ships' technical departments in keeping *all* the ships moving and fighting or, in the case of the RFAs, replenishing, surpassed all expectations. Not until early June was the first ship withdrawn for reasons other than action damage.

The RFAs *Olmeda* and *Resource* were with the carrier group and *Appleleaf* was with the advanced group led by HMS *Brilliant*. All the warships refuelled frequently and would embark stores and provisions from *Resource* at longer intervals. The availability of fuel was always a major concern of the command, but it was never a source of anxiety, thanks to the thorough planning and skilful improvisation of the headquarters Shipping and Transport organization. *Olmeda*, the main supplier to the thirsty carriers, would herself be replenished by the *Appleleaf* and *Brambleleaf* and when the latter had to return with storm damage and contaminated fuel, the first of the STUFT tankers to arrive, the *British Esk*, was sent forward to pump-over her cargo and was followed by the other 'British Rivers' in steady succession. The stores RFAs were no less critical to the success of the operation: the *Fort Austin*, whose commanding officer was the Senior RFA Officer Afloat, Commodore S. C. Dunlop, was 1,000 miles astern of the carrier group after her rendezvous with the *Endurance* and would not catch up until the carriers were in the Exclusion Zone. The *Resource*'s sister-ship *Regent* was supporting the Amphibious Group, as was the *Stromness*, which was carrying some stores in addition to a Marine Commando. To resupply, or 'consolidate', these dry-stores ships, the Navy Department chartered first the *Saxonia* and then the *Geestport*, to carry forward fresh and frozen provisions and the usual range of 'Naval and Victualling Stores'. The ammunition requirements of *Fort Austin* and *Fort Grange*, which left Devonport in mid-May after completion of a long refit, were met by the freighter *Lycaon*, which actually reached the South Atlantic before the *Fort Grange*.

Admiral Woodward's carrier group was not yet at the point of this huge projectile aimed at the Argentine occupiers of the Falklands, but it was the first known to have been sighted by the enemy. At about noon, local time, on 21 April a high-flying aircraft was detected heading towards the group and a pair of Sea Harriers of HMS *Hermes*' 800 Squadron was launched to investigate. The leader, Lieutenant Simon Hargreaves, reported sighting a Boeing 707 which, on close inspection, proved to be not a civil airliner but an Argentine Air Force transport sent out to locate British naval units. This mission, and the others which followed, was an indication of the flexibility which might be expected of the *Fuerza Aerea Argentina*, and also of the skill and nerve of its aircrew: to fly 2,300 nautical miles (4,200km) from the nearest point of Argentina in an unarmed aircraft, equipped only with a non-military cloud-and-collision warning radar, to seek, and find, a well-armed and alert naval task force was a worthy exploit and one which gave the British command much food for thought. The 707 was shepherded away and allowed to return to El Palomar with photographs of the Sea Harrier and a somewhat misleading report of the position and strength of the carrier group, which had been glimpsed through broken cloud from six miles up (38,000 feet).

The shadower, or one of the other two Argentine Air Force 707s, was back after midnight on 21/22 April. The *Invincible* was now the 'duty carrier' and Lieutenant B. D. Haigh of 801 Squadron made the Sea Harrier's first 'live' night interception. The 707's track was so far displaced from the carrier group that it is doubtful whether a worthwhile report was brought back by this aircraft. It reappeared in the late afternoon and three more of 801's pilots, Lieutenant-Commanders J. E. Eyton-Jones and G. J. M. W. Broadwater and Flight Lieutenant P. C. Barton RAF, were given the opportunity for a close look at the opposition.

The possibility that these shadowers were homing an Argentine Navy surface group or submarine to intercept the carriers was not overlooked and was dealt with by a deep search by a supporting Nimrod from Ascension and a late afternoon 'clearance search' by Sea Harriers to ensure that no surface units had reached a position for making a dusk attack. During the night the carrier group was overflown by RAF Victor tankers supporting a Victor undertaking a surface search to the west of South Georgia, in support of 'Paraquet': this aircraft, of 55 Squadron RAF, flew approximately 7,700 miles (nearly a third of the circumference of the Earth), supported by three tankers, on what was, to date, the RAF's longest operational flight.

The progress of the South Georgia operations was followed closely, and, following the débâcle on Fortuna Glacier, Admiral Woodward ordered HMS *Brilliant* to detach from the advanced group to reinforce Captain Young's squadron. Captain J. F. T. G. 'Sam' Salt RN, commanding HMS *Sheffield*, was deputed to lead Task Unit 317.8.2, now consisting of three Type 42s and a Type 21.

In the early afternoon of the 23rd the Sea Harriers were again scrambled to investigate a contact approaching from the west. For variety, this turned out to be not the Argentine 707, but a Douglas DC-10. On closer inspection it proved to belong to the Brazilian national airline, VARIG, and, after flying in loose formation for a short while, the fighters broke away and returned to the *Invincible*. Formal regrets for any alarm that may have been caused to passengers were expressed and the Brazilian Press showed an understanding of the need for the check. The Argentine shadower duly arrived in the early evening, in the middle of a RAS with the *Olmeda*, and was again escorted away.

Two hours later, after nightfall, the first British serviceman to be lost in Operation 'Corporate' was killed in a helicopter crash. Petty Officer B. Casey was flying as aircrewman in one of the five 846 Squadron Sea King 4s still embarked in the *Hermes* when the aircraft crashed into the sea near the ship. The pilot was quickly rescued, but there was no sign of Petty Officer Casey, although HMS *Yarmouth* and the two RFAs and their helicopters searched until an hour after dawn the following morning. The search was hampered after midnight by a sudden deterioration in the

23 April: An 801 Squadron Sea Harrier formates on an Argentine Air Force Boeing 707 over the South Atlantic. The implications of the white-painted Sidewinder were not lost on the *FAA* – the Royal Navy was already carrying 'warhead missiles' *(FAA via J.C. D'Odorico)*

weather, giving the first rough seas encountered since leaving Ascension.

The wind and sea moderated during 24 April and the Sea Harriers of 800 Squadron were able to launch and intercept the mid-afternoon 707, which was turned back eighty miles away from the carrier group. This was the second 707 incident of the day, for HMS *Endurance*, 1,100 miles to the south-south-west, had earlier been approached by another aircraft of this type. Events in the South Georgia area were now reaching a critical stage and the main force was within 1,000 miles of Argentina. Although the Argentine Air Force had little strike capability at such a distance, near-continuous shadowing of the carriers was possible, so that the Royal Navy was denied surprise in the direction or timing of its initial approach, while the Argentine Navy was being provided with all the targeting information it needed, should it wish to take the offensive. After very careful consideration, the British Government gave warning, late on the 24th, that any Argentine aircraft, military or civil, engaged in surveillance of British warships would in future be regarded as hostile and was liable to be shot down.

On 25 April, as the defenders of Grytviken were breaking out the white flags, the carriers met up with the *Sheffield* group, less than 1,000 miles due north of South Georgia and 1,500 miles from Port Stanley. Admiral Woodward now had four guided missile destroyers (*Glamorgan*, *Sheffield*, *Coventry* and *Glasgow*), three frigates (*Broadsword*, *Arrow* and *Alacrity*) and RFA *Appleleaf* in company with his two carriers; sixty miles astern a fourth frigate, the *Yarmouth*, with the *Resource* and *Olwen*, was catching up after the unavailing search on the night of the 23rd/24th. The Admiral now exercised the concentrated air defence organization, pitting one carrier against the rest of the force to practise raid reporting and allocation of defensive systems while identifying and correcting weaknesses. This was only partly achieved during the next three days, for the weather again worsened and stayed bad with few short intermissions. The gales and heavy seas curtailed flying from the carriers and completely prevented any replenishment on 27 April. On this day the Carrier Battle Group (as Admiral Woodward's group was now known) advanced only 150 miles during the twenty-four hours.

The Argentine Government, and the merchant shipping of the rest of the world, had been warned that from dawn on 30 April (1100Z, or 7.00am local) the Maritime Exclusion Zone was to be replaced by a Total Exclusion Zone, in which all ships and aircraft, naval, military or civil, in any way supporting the illegal occupation of the Falkland Islands were liable to attack if found within a 200-mile radius of a point taken as the centre of the islands and located in the Falkland Sound. The British Government's declaration had been made on the 28th, on the assumption that the carriers would be in position when the TEZ became effective, but the delay caused by the storm upset this timetable and Admiral

Woodward was hard-pressed to reduce the period of postponement of enforcement of the TEZ to only twenty-four hours.

Fortunately the weather improved somewhat on 28 April, allowing another air defence exercise. The 707 made its first appearance since 24 April, possibly hoping that the weather would keep the Sea Harriers on deck. If so, then it was disappointed, for *Hermes* launched a Combat Air Patrol (CAP) which was held at a range of over 100 miles in the direction of the snooper. The 707 made no attempt to approach closer and thus no interception was made.

HMS *Brilliant* and *Plymouth* joined from South Georgia on the afternoon of 29 April, ferrying the Special Forces (D Squadron SAS and No2 SBS) to the carriers for their next deployment. The *Plymouth* was to have returned to South Georgia after RAS but Captain Pentreath obtained Admiral Woodward's consent to his remaining for the first day's operations in the TEZ. It was at about this time that the BBC World Service began to anticipate events in its reports, a habit which was to lead to increasing irritation both at sea and in Whitehall. On this occasion a report that Special Forces were already ashore on the Falklands and disguised as sheep was greeted with amusement and jokes about wellington boots.

The last major replenishment of all ships before entering the TEZ began in the late afternoon of 29 April, when the Carrier Battle Group was some 500 miles east of Port Stanley. Fog descended at dusk and lasted most of the night. A 707 was detected approaching from the east at about midnight but the Sea Harriers were held on deck on this occasion and the shadower, unaware of the bad visibility at sea level, turned away before closing within 100 miles. This was the last occasion on which the transport jet was to bother the carriers, but it would continue to monitor the southward progress of the groups which were to follow, as will be related.

As the big RAS came to an end in the forenoon of 30 April, a Sea Harrier CAP investigated a radar contact which proved to be a large Argentine factory trawler, the *Narwal*. As the vessel appeared to be conforming to the movements of the group, it aroused suspicion that it was a spy ship and its progress was plotted thereafter, so that it could be dealt with if and when the suspicion was confirmed.

RFA *Appleleaf* was detached at noon to replenish from the *British Esk*, having pumped over her remaining aviation fuel to the *Olmeda*. Although her main role was that of a Support Oiler, supplying the Replenishment Oilers, a large part of her actual task was to be replenishing warships, to which she supplied fuel on eighty-one occasions in the sixty-five days up to the end of the fighting.

In the late evening of 30 April Admiral Woodward and his twelve warships and two RFAs turned to the west and began their run into the Exclusion Zone.

Chapter Three ————————————————————

The Argentine Preparations

The build-up of the Argentine defences at the key points in the Falklands has already been described. One more airfield was taken over as a temporary base, the Navy occupying Pebble Island, which became BAN (Naval Air Base) Borbon, a somewhat grandiose title for a couple of short and narrow grass strips from which four Beech T-34C Turbo-Mentor armed trainers and a detachment of up to six Air Force Pucaras were to fly coastal reconnaissance sorties. The Turbo-Mentors belonged to the 4th Naval Attack Squadron and the base was supported by U.K.-built Short Skyvan light transport aircraft belonging to the *Prefectura Maritima*, the Argentine Coast Guard service, which also based Puma helicopters and some patrol boats in the Falklands. On 25 April the only jet combat aircraft to operate from Port Stanley arrived: like the Turbo-Mentors, the three Macchi MB.339A advanced trainers belonged to a shore-based naval air unit, the 1st Naval Attack Squadron, which could provide a useful tactical-reconnaissance and light attack force under favourable circumstances.

The main defences of the islands against a British attempt at repossession were, however, the Argentine Navy and Air Force. In combination, they alone could inflict such attrition on the Royal Navy that landings would have to be abandoned, before or after they had been attempted. The Argentine submarine force was small – just three seaworthy boats before the loss of the *Santa Fe* – to maintain more than one vessel continuously on patrol for any length of time, and although the modern, German-built *San Luis* and *Salta* were fast and very quiet, their torpedo armament was still unreliable. The surface fleet, with no other role but that of attack, possessed only five up-to-date ships – the two Type 42 destroyers and the three Type A.69 corvettes, and six old ships – four Exocet-armed ex-US Navy destroyers, the cruiser *General Belgrano* and a potential trump card, the carrier *25 de Mayo*. With eight or nine A-4Q Skyhawks of the 3rd Naval Attack Squadron, six S-2E Tracker antisubmarine patrol aircraft and four Sea King ASW helicopters, she could search and strike out to a radius of about 300 miles and provide a measure of A/S defence for herself and her screen, the most important elements of

Super Etendards of the French Navy demonstrate the 'buddy' flight-refuelling system. This was not used by the Argentine Navy's 'SUE' unit, which preferred to employ the Argentine Air Force's KC-130 (Hercules) as tankers *(MoD)*

which would be the two Type 42 destroyers.

The Super Etendards could not operate from the carrier, which would require modification to launch and recover them. The French Government had embargoed all spares and technical assistance, so that the five aircraft and the one AM-39 Exocet per aircraft already delivered represented the entire inventory. The missiles had not yet been matched to the aircraft when the Junta ordered the invasion and the French technicians were ordered not to assist the Argentinians in setting the system to work. There have, however, been reports that Israeli specialists had no compunctions about involving themselves in a system which they had not been hired to service and thus in a war that was none of their concern. Certainly by mid-April the Super Etendard/Exocet combination was a going concern in Argentine Navy service and the first pair of aircraft deployed from their home air station at Espora, near Puerto Belgrano, to BAN Rio Grande on 19 April and a second pair followed before the end of the month. The fifth aircraft remained at Espora as a source of spares. The squadron worked up at Rio Grande in the radar-silent tactics that would be used, co-operating with the two remaining serviceable SP-2H Neptunes, which would shadow the British task group and provide up-to-date targeting information.

Anti-shipping strike was the naval pilots' primary role, but the Air Force's tactical units were completely unaccustomed to long over-water missions and had no experience of attacks on fast-moving targets. The A-4Cs of IV Air Brigade, the A-4Bs of V Air Brigade and the Daggers of VI Air Brigade all came from inland bases (IV Brigade's, at Mendoza, was only 150 miles from the Pacific) and the pilots had to be instructed in ship recognition and low-level over-water strike tactics by the naval strike pilots. The form of attack was dictated by the limited choice of weapons available to the Argentine Air Force. In the absence of a guided or stand-off weapon, the most effective ordnance for use against shipping would be 500lb (227kg) or 1,000lb (454kg) bombs; unguided high-velocity rockets were available but lacked the warhead weight to inflict lethal damage and these appear to have been used by only one Air Force strike. Low-level bombing gave the best chance of hits, for the bombs would be released at very short range, just before the aircraft passed over the target (or, if retarding tails were fitted, as it passed over). Traditional dive-bombing, as well as being less accurate, would put the attacking aircraft into the ideal bit of the sky and at the right height for defensive missile systems and radar-predicted gun systems. The Air Force pilots had to learn to fly at less than 30 feet, in formation, and to stay out of one another's way while pressing an attack on a target which could move its own length while they were covering the last mile, probably under fire.

The Skyhawk pilots were fortunate that their aircraft had recently been fitted with a modern long-range navigation aid which could receive the 'Omega' navigation system's radio signals to give very accurate positions. The Israeli-built Daggers, intended originally for quite short-range missions in generally clear weather, had no such aids: the Argentine Air Force requisitioned ten Learjets and one Hawker-Siddeley HS.125 business jets and their crews and used these to lead Dagger strikes to the Falklands. Once these 'pathfinders' had turned back, the fighter pilots were on their own, with map, compass, airspeed indicator and stop-watch to get them home. The business jets, which carried an Air Force pilot or navigator on operational sorties, were formed into the 'Phoenix Squadron' and carried out diversionary 'spoof' missions to distract attention from the strikes. Five Air Force Learjet 35A light transports were already fitted with cameras and would undertake high-level photographic reconnaissance missions in clear weather.

There was little precedent for the sheer distance the single-seat single-engined strike aircraft would have to fly – between 380 nautical miles (700km) and 420 miles (775km) from the mainland airfields to the Port Stanley area. Only the United States Air Force tactical fighters operating against North Vietnam from Thailand, between 1967 and 1973, had regularly flown such long-range missions, but their 25–30-ton Phantoms and Thunderchiefs had huge internal fuel capacity and were supported by a fleet of fast tanker aircraft. The Argentine Air Force had just two Lockheed KC-130H Hercules tankers to top up its strike aircraft, but only the three dozen Skyhawks (and the Navy's Super Etendards) were equipped with the receiving gear. With the standard load of 1,140 gallons (5,170 litres = 9,000lb) of fuel and either three 500lb or two 1,000lb bombs, the A-4Bs and Cs could just reach East Falkland, flying the last 40–50 miles at low level, below the radar horizon but at a height at which their 1950s-technology engine was consuming a ton of fuel every quarter of an hour. The Argentine Navy A-4Qs (essentially similar to the A-4BS) delivered one such unrefuelled strike but so short of fuel were the survivors on return that they too used the KC-130s thereafter.

The more numerous Daggers and Mirages had no provision for in-

A IV Brigade A-4C, on its way to the Falklands with a single 1,000lb (454 kg) bomb, prods at the basket of the flight-refuelling drogue to top up prior to descending through the solid cloud cover in search of targets. The dark brown and 'sand' colour scheme was more appropriate to the high plains area over which the Brigade usually operated than to the oversea and drab island colours of the Falklands environment *(FAA via J.C. D'Odorico)*

flight refuelling and were entirely dependent upon what they could lift from their own base. The Mirage IIIEA interceptors, which would fly high-level fighter patrols, carried only 484 gallons internally (2,200 litres = 3,900lb) but could carry two enormous 375-gallon (1,700 litres) 'jugs' under their wings: with 9,900lb of fuel, the Mirage could spend about 10 minutes to the east of the Falkland Sound, carrying three air-to-air missiles, one Matra R.530 radar-homing and two Matra R.550 Magic infra-red homing missiles. The Dagger could also be used for fighter patrols, carrying two Israeli-designed Shafrir infra-red missiles. A much simplified variant of the Mirage, lacking a radar and other electronics, the Dagger had an additional 110-gallon (500 litres) internal tank and could carry 860 gallons externally in three 1,300-litre tanks, for a total of 10,650lb of fuel. In the attack role, the centre-line tank gave way to a pair of 1,000lb bombs: the loss of tankage was in part compensated for by the removal of the missiles and their pylons and the drag which they caused. The bomb-armed Daggers delivered only one attack to the east of the Falkland Sound area, which marked the prudent limit of their range. The Mirage and Dagger were, on paper, Mach 2.0 fighters but configured for long range they were unable to attain Mach 1.0 due to the drag of the tanks*: the apparent speed advantage over the subsonic Sea Harrier was thus

* The 'supersonic' pinion tanks could be used only for local defensive missions as they contained only 110 gallons (500 litres) each.

reduced by practical considerations, although it remained sufficient to disengage from combat without recourse to the thirsty afterburner, which could not be used if the aircraft was to return to the mainland safely.

The bulk fuel requirement of the fighters, bombers and reconnaissance aircraft operating from the southern bases was assured by the stationing of a requisitioned oil tanker, with 15,000 tons of fuel embarked, off the Patagonian coast.

The Air Force A-4s, Daggers and Mirages deployed to the airfields in Patagonia and Tierra del Fuego during the second half of April. It has been stated that the Southern Air Command had eighty-two combat aircraft at its disposal at the end of April, 1982. In fact this figure included tanker and reconnaissance aircraft and there were only sixty-five fighters and strike aircraft, as well as the four Super Etendards and eight A-4Q Skyhawks of the Argentine Navy based at Rio Grande. The Air Force contribution was as follows:*

Comodoro
 Rivadavia 4 Mirages of VIII Air Brigade
 San Julian 9 A-4Cs of IV Air Brigade
      10 Daggers of VI Air Brigade

Rio Gallegos 22 A-4Bs of V Air Brigade
      4 Mirages of VIII Air Brigade

Rio Grande 9 Daggers of VI Air Brigade

 Trelew 7 Canberras (which staged through the forward airfields to refuel before missions)

The tanker and transport C-130 Hercules aircraft were based at Comodoro Rivadavia, although they too staged through the southerly airfields for some missions, and the small maritime reconnaissance element, consisting initially of a pair of old SP-2H Neptunes, was at the naval airfield at Rio Grande.

Well-trained and highly-motivated, if lacking in experience, the Argentine Air Force seems to have been confident that it could play its full role in what was to be its first real war.

* Ruben O. Moro, *La Guerra Inaudita*, Editorial Pleamar, Buenos Aires, 1986.

Chapter Four

The First Strike

As the Carrier Battle Group headed towards the TEZ on the evening of 30 April, eleven Victor tankers and two Vulcan bombers took off in a stream from Ascension, the last aircraft leaving the runway shortly after midnight (GMT). The leading Vulcan soon dropped out, leaving the stand-by, flown by Flight-Lieutenant M. Withers RAF, to undertake the first British bombing mission of the war and the longest such mission ever flown by any air force up to that date. The Vulcan, laden with nearly ten tons of bombs, required five refuellings from the Victors during the seven-hour flight south, the Victors accompanying the bomber being topped up by their fellows.* Well to the north-north-east of Port Stanley, Flight-Lieutenant Withers let down to 300 feet above sea level to make a run-in underneath the radar lobe of the TPS-43 radar. The Vulcan's own bombing radar was not switched on until within sixty miles of the target, to avoid warning the Argentine defenders, and Flight-Lieutenant Withers began the climb to the bombing altitude of 10,000 feet at about fifty miles, when the *VYCA 2* crew on duty could have been expected to detect the big aircraft.

As it happened, although an alert radar operator in the carrier group almost certainly detected the Vulcan over 200 miles to the north-west before it began its final let-down, the Argentinians on watch at the TPS-43 site did not, and not until it was within ten miles of its target, the runway, was it picked up by an army 'Skyguard' fire-control radar which was promptly jammed. The load of twenty-one 1,000lb bombs was released in a five-second 'string' which resulted in a line of hits about 1,000 yards long, at an oblique angle of about 35° to the runway.† The first bomb of the pattern hit the runway not quite halfway along from the eastern end, which was the touch-down end most of the time due to the prevailing westerly wind, and blocking the left-hand side with its crater and debris.

---

* Due to a sequence of technical difficulties, the last Victor deliberately transferred so much fuel to the Vulcan that it was unable to return to Ascension without topping up from a twelfth (reserve) tanker.

† The established tactic for an attack on a 'long thin' target such as a runway (or a submarine).

The remaining bombs 'walked' across the prepared shoulder to the south of the runway, over the main airfield access road, behind the hangars and control tower, and then off into the boondocks.

The bombs were released at 0746,* about three hours before dawn, and the Vulcan immediately turned away to the east and began its climb to return to Ascension. Only then did the Argentine AA guns open fire, when the aircraft was far out of range. The coded signal announcing a successful attack was sent to Northwood and was intercepted by HMS *Hermes*, whose Sea Harrier pilots would be the next to attack. Flight-Lieutenant Withers and his weary crew refuelled once on the return trip and landed back at Ascension at about 1545, having flown 7,860 miles. The mission was a magnificent achievement by all who flew it – the

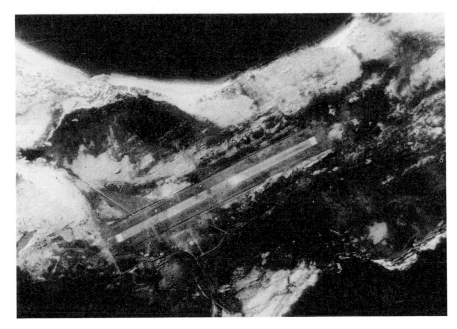

The photograph taken by a Sea Harrier which confirmed the Vulcan's 1,000lb hit on the Port Stanley runway and the superficial scars caused by the 800 Squadron bombs (two dark patches to the left – east – of the crater) *(MoD)*

twelve Victor crews and the Vulcan crew who crowned it with success with the hit on the runway.

Meanwhile, shortly before dawn, the *Invincible* launched the first Sea Harrier Combat Air Patrol, while the *Hermes* prepared to fly off all twelve of her Sea Harriers for strikes on Port Stanley airfield and the Pucara base at Goose Green. At about 1045 the two 801 Squadron fighters closed Port Stanley at 8,000 feet and were greeted with AA fire. After taking photographs of the damaged runway, the CAP withdrew and climbed up to patrol height.

The Sea Harriers of 800 Squadron took off from the *Hermes* between 1048 and 1058 and took departure for East Falkland as soon as the last was airborne, flying at very low level. The twelve aircraft were to attack in

* All times quoted are GMT (three hours ahead of the local time kept by the Argentinians), unless indicated as local time – indicated by 'am' or 'pm'.

three formations, two at Port Stanley and the other at Goose Green, the force splitting before it crossed the coast to the north of Berkeley Sound. Four Sea Harriers, carrying between them nine air-burst 1,000lb bombs and three delayed-action 1,000-pounders, split off from the Port Stanley strike and 'jinked' to deliver a 'flak suppression' attack, pulling up well out of AA gun and missile range to toss the bombs at the known defensive positions; the delayed-action bombs would keep the enemy on their toes for a few hours afterwards. Seconds after the radar-fused air-burst bombs had exploded around the airfield, at 1100, Lieutenant-Commander A. D. Auld, the CO of 800 Squadron, led in his five aircraft to drop three 1,000lb parachute-retarded bombs on the runway threshold and the contents of twelve cluster-bomb containers on the airfield buildings, hardstandings and parked aircraft. They were greeted by 35mm and 20mm gunfire, Tigercats and at least one Roland missile, but the high speed and terrain-hugging approach, with the cluster-bomb Sea Harriers climbing to just 200 feet only long enough to release their load in a proper swathe, defeated all but one of the gunners, and he only managed to obtain one 20mm hit on the rear end of the last aircraft to attack, that flown by Flight-Lieutenant D. H. S. Morgan RAF.

Minutes later Lieutenant-Commander R. V. Frederiksen attacked Goose Green with two 'cluster-bombers' and a Sea Harrier carrying three retarded bombs. His strike had flown down the Falkland Sound at wave-top height, past Fanning Head and Chancho Point enclosing San Carlos Water and Ajax Bay, and then turning to the south-east to climb up over the peat of Lafonia for a surprise attack on the Pucaras at Goose Green. The AA defences were caught unawares and the only ground fire was a last-minute burst by a machine gun.

The attacks had inflicted some damage and casualties at both targets. Most of the Pucaras had been dispersed to Goose Green on 29 April, but a couple were slightly damaged at Port Stanley, in among the dummies which the Argentine Air Force base personnel had erected. A Falklands Government Islander light transport and the Governor's own Cessna light plane were badly damaged. At Goose Green one spread of cluster bombs had hit a dispersal, as *Teniente* Antonio Jukic was taxiing for take-off; the Pucara received a direct hit and Jukic and six III Air Brigade

ground crew were killed. Retarded bombs hit the runways at both targets, but at Port Stanley they did not penetrate the macadam surface before exploding and the superficial damage was easily repaired, while at Goose Green the craters in the beaten earth strip were readily filled in and compacted.

On the other side the inevitable ground-to-air overclaims began. Two Sea Harriers were stated to have been shot down over Port Stanley by the AA guns, one by the marine-manned Tigercats and one by the Army Roland. Less excusable was a wretched propaganda concoction to account for poor Jukic's death—he had been killed in making a single-handed attack which had set HMS *Hermes* on fire. The tale caught on quickly in the Argentine popular Press, which persisted in the fiction long after it was obvious that the carrier was intact. As late as the beginning of 1983 an Army Staff College lecturer was still writing of this attack as fact and drawing the conclusion that the Pucara was an ideal torpedo-attack aircraft.*

Lieutenant-Commander A. R. W. Ogilvie's four flak suppressors began their recovery at 1141 and the last of the Goose Green aircraft touched down at 1155. The BBC television reporter assured the world that he had 'counted them all back'. Within an hour the first 800 Squadron CAP was airborne, Sidewinder missiles on launcher shoes fitted to the underwing bomb pylons. Flight-Lieutenant Morgan's damaged Sea Harrier was ready for action by mid-afternoon, patches applied to the holes in the vertical fin.

801 Squadron was maintaining a standing CAP, with two aircraft on station over Port Stanley and two more at immediate readiness on deck, and at 1130, as the strike aircraft were returning to the *Hermes*, the *Invincible*'s fighter controller directed them towards a pair of contacts inbound from the mainland. The Sea Harriers, at 15,000 feet, gained contact with their Blue Fox radars over West Falkland, about 130 miles west of the carriers, and soon afterwards sighted two Mirages high above them,

* Dr J. C. Murguizur, *International Defence Review*, No 2/83.

1 May: The Rheinmetall 20mm AA guns of the *FAA*-manned 'Fierro' Battery sited around Port Stanley airport claimed to have destroyed three and damaged two Sea Harriers of the first strike; a fourth Sea Harrier was believed to have been destroyed by a Marine Corps Tigercat missile. This cheerful gun's crew was located near Hooker's Point *(FAA via J. C. D'Odorico)*

approaching head-on. The Mirages dived towards the CAP, the first firing a single Matra R.530 radar-homing missile at a range of four miles; the second dived below the Sea Harriers, pulled up and fired at two miles. The naval fighters, taken at a severe disadvantage, opened their air brakes to release the chaff to break the radar lock and then took evasive action on the missiles, the first of which missed by 200 yards and the second by less than thirty. The Mirages shot through, diving at supersonic speed, and escaped. This slashing attack, under close radar control from *VYCA 2* at Port Stanley, had come very close to success and if the tactics were to be repeated then the Sea Harriers would have few chances of inflicting casualties on the Argentine fighters.

It was now about an hour after daybreak and Admiral Woodward detached five of his ships from the screen. While the *Glamorgan*, *Alacrity* and *Arrow* headed towards the Falklands, the *Brilliant* took the *Yarmouth* off to the north-west, to hunt for a submarine which was believed to be on patrol to the north-east of East Falkland.* The former group was protected by the CAP, which now had a pair of fighters from each squadron available, one controlled by the *Invincible* and the other by *Glamorgan*. The anti-submarine group would be less likely to attract the enemy's attention, being well out of sight of land, but could readily be covered by the CAP if necessary.

Once on their way, the *Brilliant* and *Yarmouth* were joined and screened by three Sea Kings of 826 Squadron, each of which carried a complete spare crew. Too large to land on the frigates' flight decks, the Sea Kings were to winch down their spare crews and refuel from the ships, using a technique which had been developed in the late 1960s, picking up a fuel line by means of the winch, connecting it to the aircraft fuel system and then easing out over the ship's quarter to take in the Avcat while keeping station on the big 'tanker'. In this way the Sea Kings remained airborne for over ten hours while the frigates quartered the area. Although the search was complicated by the very uneven nature of the seabed, Captain Coward's *Brilliant* and Commander A. Morton's *Yarmouth* both obtained promising contacts which were checked by the Magnetic Anomaly Detectors (MAD) carried by the Sea Kings and then attacked, using the *Yarmouth*'s 'Limbo' mortar, her Wasp's depth-charges, or homing torpedoes released by the *Brilliant* or her aircraft. The hunt went on until after dark, when it had to be discontinued to give the frigates time to rejoin the carriers before dawn.

The *Glamorgan* and the two type 21s quite narrowly missed an opportunity to intercept two Argentine blockade-runners as they escaped from Port Stanley. The *Formosa* had unloaded 20,000 tons of material at Port Stanley since 20 April and had only completed the task at the time that the Vulcan attacked. The rather smaller *Rio Carcaraña* had arrived on 25 April and most of her material was still on board. Both ships, owned by the

The Argentine Navy's German-designed Type 209 submarines were respected by the Royal Navy, but after 1 May, when the *San Luis* was fortunate to escape the attentions of the *Brilliant* and *Yarmouth*, there was only one encounter. The *Salta*, shown here at Puerto Belgrano, was reported to have experienced torpedo fire-control problems and undertook no operational patrols *(Argentine Navy)*

* *Flight Deck*, op. cit. p. 32.

state shipping line, were sailed as soon as possible, the *Rio Carcaraña* at 1300 and the *Formosa* at 1440, rounded Cape Pembroke and made off along the south coast of East Falkland, unobserved by the CAP or the reconnaissance helicopters.

The CAP was directed after several contacts during the morning but all turned back before the Sea Harriers came within radar range and it was not until shortly after midday (at 1545Z) that the next Argentine aircraft were seen. The CO of 801 Squadron, Lieutenant-Commander N. D. Ward AFC and Lieutenant M. W. Watson, were sent out to investigate a fleeting contact over the north coast of East Falkland and, searching at low level under the cloud, they sighted three aircraft which they identified as Pucaras. The Argentine aircraft, which were actually Turbo-Mentors from the naval field on Pebble Island, saw the Sea Harriers as they closed and 'immediately evaded wildly, dropping ordnance and entering cloud'. Ward and Watson followed them into the cloud and managed to get in a couple of bursts of 30mm Aden cannon fire at fleeting targets glimpsed in the murk, but the risk of collision or firing on one another was too great and the Sea Harriers pulled away, leaving 'twitched' *Armada* pilots, one with a rear cockpit canopy holed by a 30mm shell.

Climbing back to 20,000 feet, Ward and Watson were soon afterwards vectored towards a pair of aircraft forty-five miles to the west of them, approaching at about 35,000 feet. The Sea Harriers turned away, in the hope that the enemy would chase them to close range, and gradually descended to 15,000 feet, where they would have a considerable advantage in a subsonic turning fight. When the Mirages were twenty miles astern, the CAP reversed towards them but the Argentine fighters were warned by the *VYCA 2* controller and made no attempt to descend, instead firing three missiles – possibly a Matra 530 and a pair of Matra R.550 Magic infra-red missiles – far out of range. The two naval pilots watched the trails of the rockets as they fell a couple of miles ahead of the Sea Harriers, but the Mirages were never sighted.

By now the Argentine Air Force had an idea where the Carrier Battle Group was operating. Several low, slow aircraft contacts had been detected by the ships' radars but had not been found by the CAP, and the TPS-43 radar, watching the carrier fighters' movements, was able to provide a good general position report. From the mainland bases twenty-eight A-4s and six Canberras took off, as well as a dozen Daggers, not all of which were armed with bombs. Those which reached the Falklands – twenty-five of the forty-six, according to Argentine sources – began to appear on the ships' radar screens from mid-afternoon, as the *Glamorgan* group came within 4.5in gun range of Port Stanley airfield.

The big guided-missile destroyer was controlling an 801 Squadron CAP (Lieutenant S. R. Thomas and Flight-Lieutenant P. C. Barton RAF) which was sent out to intercept a pair of 'bogeys' assessed as Mirages, approaching over West Falkland. A few minutes later the *Hermes*, controlling her own CAP, vectored Flight-Lieutenant A. R. Penfold RAF and Lieutenant M. W. Hale towards another pair of high-level fast-movers. No ship detected a third formation, of three Daggers, low down over the Falkland Sound and heading towards Port Stanley.

Thomas and Barton approached their targets at 15,000 feet, knowing that the enemy were at the same level. To their surprise, when they saw the Mirages over San Carlos Water, the latter were in a most inappropriate formation, with the No 2 (*Primer Teniente* Carlos Perona) a mile on his Leader's quarter. From that position he was unable to fire a heat-seeking missile, lest it endanger his leader (*Capitan* Garcia Cuerva), and if a Sea Harrier got behind him he could expect no assistance from the man in front. The leading Mirage fired his Matra 530 missile head-on at a range of five miles and pressed straight on at Thomas, whose Sidewinders did not 'see' the Mirage's exhaust plume. As the range closed, Thomas pulled up and turned hard to starboard, passing about 100 feet above the Mirage, which was turning to port and beginning to dive. A Sidewinder acquired as the Sea Harrier straightened out, 1,000 yards behind the Mirage, which was in a steep dive for the cloud tops, 3,000 feet above the sea, and Thomas fired, watching as the missile passed close to the Argentine fighter's jet-pipe as it disappeared into the cloud.

Flight-Lieutenant Barton had turned outwards when Garcia Cuerva had fired and then turned back to make a stern attack on Perona, firing his cannon as the Mirage crossed ahead at a range of 1,000 yards. Barton's Sidewinder acquired as he came astern of the trailing No 2 and he fired at a range of 2,000 yards. The missile tracked Perona as he turned to port to follow his leader down and then hit the Mirage's rear fuselage. The victim caught fire and began to break up but Perona ejected safely, slightly injuring his legs in the landing on the shore of West Falkland. The first air-to-air victim of a Royal Navy fighter for nearly thirty years,* Perona was the first Argentine Air Force pilot ever to be shot down in a foreign war.

Garcia Cuerva was unluckier. His aircraft had been seriously damaged by fragments when Steve Thomas's Sidewinder's proximity fuze detonated at close range. The Argentine pilot decided to divert to Port Stanley and ran in towards the town from the west. It is possible that *VYCA 2*, having watched the combat, thought that the approaching aircraft was a Sea Harrier returning to the carriers and alerted the AA defences. As Garcia Cuerva reached the town, the guns opened up and, hit repeatedly, the Mirage crashed on the outskirts, the pilot losing his life.

A few minutes earlier, as the damaged Mirage was closing Port Stanley, three Daggers of VI Air Brigade had overflown Cape Pembroke. Flying at low level, they had been tracked intermittently by the ships' radars and the *Invincible* scrambled a pair of Sea Harriers to deal with the

* The previous 'kill' had been on 9 August, 1952, when Lieutenant P. Carmichael RN, flying a Hawker Sea Fury from HMS *Ocean*, shot down a Chinese MiG-15 fighter.

raid, which appeared to be heading for the Carrier Battle Group. The Daggers soon turned back and headed south-west, towards the *Glamorgan* and her consorts less than ten miles away.

The three ships, led by Captain M. E. Barrow RN, were just completing the first leg of a bombardment of Port Stanley airfield, firing airburst shells over defensive positions and on the buildings. As they turned away before beginning another run, spotters in *Glamorgan* saw the destruction of Garcia Cuerva's Mirage and then, too late, the three Daggers as they came in right down on the sea at seven miles a minute. None of the ships, each of which was singled out by one Dagger, was able to fire a Seacat and only Commander P. J. Bootherstone's *Arrow* opened fire with its one 20mm gun on the exposed beam, while Commander C. J. S. Craig's *Alacrity* got one of its bridge machine guns into action. The Daggers fired their 30mm cannon before releasing two 1,000lb parachute-retarded bombs each as they crossed their targets and made off. The *Glamorgan* and *Alacrity* were both near-missed, the latter sustaining minor shock damage which was quickly rectified. Not until she was docked on return to the United Kingdom was the extent of the *Glamorgan*'s underwater damage realized, but in the meantime the extensively 'dished' plates gave no trouble. The strafing caused superficial damage to the *Glamorgan* and *Arrow* and wounded the latter's Seacat aimer. The Daggers returned safely to base.

The strike had been covered by two Daggers of the same Brigade. These had lagged behind slightly, so that the bombers had arrived between them and the VIII Air Brigade Mirages, whose presence was co-incidental. As the 800 Squadron CAP approached, under *Hermes'* control, the Daggers, advised by *VYCA 2*, jinked several times, presumably to commit Penfold and Hale to a turn which the Argentine pilots could exploit to achieve a good missile-firing position. The Sea Harriers, at 20,000 feet, held on and it was the Daggers who finally committed themselves to a head-on attack, beginning their descent from 35,000 feet. At about five miles the Daggers fired two Israeli-made Shafrir heat-seeking missiles, one of which 'saw' Martin Hale's exhaust plume and began to home on his aircraft. Hale promptly broke downwards, heading for the cloud tops 15,000 feet below and anxiously watching the missile which continued to close until its fuel burned out and it fell away, well clear. The Daggers appear not to have seen Penfold, 2,000 yards on Hale's beam when the Shafrirs were launched, for they began a gentle turn across his Sea Harrier's nose. Penfold turned with them but so fast were they travelling, with afterburners on, that he was three miles astern when his Sidewinder acquired and he fired in hope rather than expectation. Climbing back into the fight, Hale watched the missile overhaul its hot, bright target in the thin air and destroy the unsuspecting Dagger over Pebble Island. The pilot, *Primer Teniente* Jose Ardiles, the cousin of the star of the 1978 World Cup, Osvaldo Ardiles, was lost with his aircraft.

Only thirteen minutes had elapsed between Paul Barton firing his Side-winder (at 1928) and Tony Penfold seeing his strike. In that brief period the air superiority campaign was, effectively, won and lost.

Half an hour after the Dagger had been splashed, HMS *Brilliant* reported that she was being circled by three Canberra light bombers at low level. She and the *Yarmouth* were still probing for the submarine,* about ninety miles to the north-west of the carriers. The only CAP airborne was the 801 pair which had been scrambled to counter the Dagger strike and these aircraft were held back until the Argentine bombers' intentions became clear. The *Invincible* next detected an inbound formation of aircraft on a different bearing and when these faded at a distance of 110 miles it was assumed that they had descended to low level. The *Hermes* scrambled an 800 Squadron CAP and the 801 Sea Harriers already airborne were sent out to look for the new raid, the pilots, Lieutenant-Commander Mike Broadwater and Lieutenant W. A. Curtis, using their intercept radars to search for the intruders. After flying about fifty miles, another formation of three Canberras was detected, flying not south-east towards the carriers but west towards the Falklands. At 2040 the two Sea Harriers began their attack unobserved and were not seen until Lieutenant Curtis fired a Sidewinder at the left-hand wingman from a range of about a mile. The Leader and the Canberra on his starboard wing jettisoned their bombs and wingtip tanks and accelerated as they broke away in opposite directions. The first Sidewinder appeared to miss the No 2, but as Curtis fired his second missile he watched it score a direct hit and the second Sidewinder flew into the fireball. Broadwater chased the Leader but he was by now short of fuel and could not afford a tail-chase at low level. He fired both Sidewinders at a range of two miles but both fell short.

When he was sure that the Sea Harriers had broken away, the Leader, *Capitan* A Baigorri, returned to search for his downed wingman, *Teniente* Gonzalez, and his navigator, *Teniente* de Ibanez, but was unable to find any trace of them. At 2054 HMS *Brilliant*'s Lynx, which was airborne for an attack on the *San Luis*, sighted the Canberra on the horizon, orbiting at low level, apparently with bits falling off. This gave rise to the belief that Lieutenant-Commander Broadwater's target had been hit and possibly lost.

An hour before, off Cape Pembroke, HMS *Alacrity*'s Lynx had also been in action. The helicopter had been spotting for the continuing bombardment of Port Stanley airfield and during a lull sighted the Coast Guard patrol boat *Islas Malvinas*. Lieutenant-Commander R. G. Burrows must be given credit for making the first attack on an Argentine surface vessel but he nearly became the first helicopter casualty, for, in the brisk exchange of fire, his door-mounted GPMG was out-matched by the patrol boat's 0.5in machine guns and the helicopter was forced to return

* Now known to have been the *San Luis*.

with a hole in its windscreen, damage to a rotor blade and the cockpit floor awash with fuel from a punctured tank.

The bombardment group, having survived the Dagger attack at the beginning of its operation, made firing runs which inflicted a few casualties and prevented any repair work on the runway. The defenders fired back with their 105mm howitzers but as yet lacked experience in firing at moving targets.

The *Glamorgan* continued to track Argentine aircraft and give warnings to the carriers. At about 2030, an hour after the Dagger attack and as the 801 CAP was closing in on the Canberras, the destroyer detected a formation of aircraft over West Falkland. These turned to the south-east, disappeared from the radar in the vicinity of Fitzroy and were not seen again by the ships. At 2040 (1740 Argentine time) the blockade-running freighter *Formosa* was off the south coast of East Falkland when she was attacked by what she reported to be a single Sea Harrier which made two separate bombing runs, dropping two bombs on each occasion, and then came back for strafing passes. The second attack scored hits with both bombs, one bouncing off the head of a crane into the sea while the other went through a hatch cover and into the hold, where it came to rest without exploding. *Capitan* J. C. Gregorio of the *Formosa* may be forgiven for believing that the aircraft which bombed his ship were British. They were, in fact, Argentine A-4B Skyhawks of V Air Brigade, three of which, flown by *Capitan* Pablo Carballo, *Primer Teniente* Cachon and *Teniente* Carlos Rinke, had made at least *five* passes, by their own admissions, but not until the following day were they made aware that the target had been an Argentine ship or that they had hit it! All three pilots were to inflict considerable damage on the Royal Navy and Royal Marines in the weeks which were to follow, but no lesson was learned from the non-exploding bomb, as will be seen.*

The other escaping freighter, the *Rio Carcaraña*, had reached the Falkland Sound and anchored off Port King, Lafonia, an hour before the *Formosa* was bombed. The cargo she was carrying had to be laboriously transferred, using her cranes and muscle-power, to the smaller *Isla de los Estados* lying alongside.†

The bombardment group kept up a drizzle of shells on the Argentine positions in the Port Stanley area until well after dark, the last gun being fired at about 0135. The activity covered the landing of reconnaissance teams by the Sea Kings of 846 Squadron, but some of the latter were detected by the shore radars before they crossed the coast. The Argentine garrison was understandably concerned about the offensive potential of the SAS (disguised as sheep or not) and an entire infantry regiment was tied down at Port Stanley airfield throughout the campaign to guard against 'commando'-style raids. Nevertheless, on this and all the succeeding

* i) M. Fernandez Sarrion, *Defensa*, Madrid 1982; ii) BARG, *Falklands, The Air War*, p. 117.
† M. Fernandez Sarrion, *Defensa*, Madrid (1982).

nights, the night-flying helicopters were never prevented by Argentine action from carrying out their missions throughout the Falklands in all weather conditions.

The first long day had ended well for Admiral Woodward's force. The submarine threat still existed, but it was believed that the submarine had been thoroughly shaken by *Brilliant*, *Yarmouth* and their helicopters. In the air, although there had been many alerts, none of the Argentine sorties had got near the carriers, while out of twenty-five Argentine aircraft which had reached the Falklands four had been lost. Particularly worrying for the Argentine Air Force was the loss of the last of the five pairs of Mirages to be sent out. If air superiority was to be gained over the Sea Harriers, then this was the only fighter really capable of winning it, with its air-to-air radar and 'head-on' radar-homing R.530 missile. But no more than a dozen were available at the beginning and the loss of just two of this small force, which was all there was for the night and all-weather defence of mainland Argentina, was insupportable. VIII Air Brigade was therefore kept in hand for the defence of the southern airfields (and, according to some British 'light-blue' commentators, the Buenos Aires area) and the only offensive missions after 1 May were high-level diversionary sorties, above the Sea Harriers' reach, to cover (but not protect) the low-level strikes.

The hole in the runway caused by the Vulcan's 1,000lb bomb proved to be a nuisance to the temporary airport management but it did not prevent the movement of Air Force and Navy transport and light attack aircraft, turboprop C-130s, Lockheed Electras and Pucaras and jet Fokker F.28s and Macchi MB339s landing and taking off when the opposition was absent. 'BAM Malvinas' had never been a serious proposition for the operation of the fast strike aircraft; although the Navy's Super Etendard and A-4 squadrons had conducted trials which showed that these aircraft *could* land and take off from a 1,200 yard strip, this was practical only on a dry runway with no cross-wind, conditions frequently absent at Port Stanley in the late autumn. Quite apart from the limitations of the small runway, there was also the risk, obvious from 1 May, from naval gunfire. The Argentine air forces had no night or bad-weather strike capability and British ships could make their approach and getaway under cover of darkness, to deliver a bombardment which could inflict damage which would be unrepairable at such a primitive base as Port Stanley.

Chapter Five

'Lombardo's Fork'

As 2 May began, Admiral Woodward was aware that the Argentine Fleet was out against him in full strength and, furthermore, he knew the nature of the threat, so that he could anticipate the timing of the first thrust.

Argentine naval operations were being directed by *Contralmirante* J. J. Lombardo, the Fleet Commander who was technically responsible for all Argentine operations in defence of the occupied islands. His plan, to be implemented when it was apparent that the Royal Navy was about to, or had already, begun the amphibious assault, was for a succession of blows from separate directions – rather than a simultaneous 'pincer' attack, it would resemble an oblique fork. The appearance of the *Glamorgan* and the two Type 21s off Port Stanley on the 1st and the detections and sightings of many helicopter movements persuaded the Argentine command in the islands that invasion was at hand and Lombardo set his countermeasures in motion, creating four task groups, each with a stand-off attack capability and an oiler in support to provide endurance and mobility.

Task Groups 79.1 and 79.2 remained in company for the time being. Led by the carrier *25 de Mayo*, with her screen of the two Type 42 AA destroyers, these ships had been loitering off Deseado, 400 miles to the north-west of Port Stanley, but were now approaching to open the battle

ARA 25 de Mayo and her A-4Q Skyhawks were initially seen as the Argentine Navy's main threat to the British carriers. An 'aunt' (rather than sister) of the *Hermes*, this Light Fleet carrier had seen action off Hong Kong in late August 1945 as HMS *Venerable* and had served with the Royal Netherlands Navy as the *Karel Doorman* for 20 years before beginning her new career *(via MoD)*

with a dawn Skyhawk strike, possibly in combination with a Super Eten-dard AM.39 Exocet strike from Rio Grande. The object of this first stage was to eliminate the two British carriers and it would be followed up by attacks by the two MM.38 Exocet-armed destroyers of TG79.2 (*Segui* and *Comodoro Py*). To the north of the Argentine carrier group was the newly-formed TG79.4, made up of the three 24-knot A.69 corvettes, *Drummond*, *Granville* and the recently-repaired *Guerrico*, each armed with a quartet of Exocets and one 100mm gun.

The big guns, those of the 6in cruiser *General Belgrano*, were closer to Admiral Woodward's TG317.8. The cruiser and two more Exocet-armed destroyers (*Piedra Buena* and *Hipolito Bouchard*) were operating from Ushuaia, the naval base on the disputed Beagle Channel, and had been in a holding position off Isla de los Estados (Staten Island) 300 miles to the south-east of Port Stanley, but had begun to make ground to the east,

The Argentine Navy's other major unit, the cruiser *General Belgrano*, was even older than the venerable *25 de Mayo*, having been the US Navy's *Phoenix* from 1938 until 1951, when she was sold to Argentina. Her five triple 6in (152mm) gun turrets and 4in (102mm) armour made her a potentially highly dangerous adversary for any British surface force *(via MoD)*

skirting the southern edge of the Total Exclusion Zone. By midnight on 1/2 May, *Capitan* Hector Bonzo's Task Group 79.3 was to the south of the Falklands, poised for a run to the north or for a descent on South Georgia, two days' steaming to the east. Unbeknown to the Argentinians, however, *Belgrano*, her destroyers and the oiler supporting them had had company for some hours, in the form of the submarine HMS *Conqueror*, which was quietly following, and reporting, the zig-zagging progress of the group.

Contralmirante Allara's carrier and destroyer groups had managed to elude detection by the British submarines to the west and north of the Falklands, but from the interpretation of wireless traffic patterns and ob-servation of the direction of approach of shadowing aircraft from the *25 de Mayo*, Admiral Woodward was able to assess the position and progress of TGs 79.1 and .2. With his rear covered by the *Conqueror*, he could make the necessary dispositions to welcome the first Argentine arrivals. The British fully expected that the Argentine Air Force would make a major effort in support of the Navy, but this took no account of the latter's ambition to save 'las Malvinas' almost unaided. Whether by intent or poor staff work, the Air Force was apparently not informed of the master plan, for the Southern Air Force Command (*CdoFAS*) planned only nineteen sorties for this crucial day, compared with fifty-six on 1 May.*

At 0325 on 2 May (half-an-hour before midnight, local time) a Sea Harrier was scrambled to investigate a radar contact detected to the north of the carriers and suspected to be one of the *25 de Mayo*'s Grumman S-2E Tracker search aircraft. No interception was achieved, but Admiral Woodward ordered a surface search mission to be launched by the *Invincible*.

The Sea Harriers flew out at low level, not using radar but relying upon their passive radar warning receivers for a silent search until they were about 150 miles out, when they were briefed to 'pop up' and carry out a radar search for the Argentine carrier. At 0425, Flight-Lieutenant I. Mortimer RAF, searching in the north-west sector, duly climbed and switched his Blue Fox radar from 'standby' to 'transmit', whereupon he immediately detected a group of four or five ships less than ten miles ahead. Almost as promptly his warning receiver told him that he was being illuminated by a Type 909 Sea Dart tracking radar. As the nearest friendly 909 was 120 miles astern, this could only be the *Hercules* or *Santissima Trinidad*. It was indeed the former; the approaching 'SHAR' had been detected by the Argentine task group, the returning Tracker had been vectored out of the fighter's path and the *Hercules* had been allocated the target. Mortimer gave no opportunity to engage, for he immediately broke away hard and dived to low level, to increase the missile system's firing problem.

Admiral Woodward, who had been about eighty miles to the northeast of Port Stanley when the Tracker had detected the Carrier Battle Group, made ground to the south-east, moving towards the edge of the TEZ to increase the distance which Argentine strike aircraft would have to cover. By 0700 he had been rejoined by the five ships which had been detached for bombardment and the anti-submarine hunt, so that the Battle Group was in good order four hours before the *25 de Mayo*'s strike could be expected, at dawn. The three Type 42s were stationed about thirty miles up-threat, to act as a picket line, and the *Glamorgan*, *Yarmouth*, *Alacrity* and *Arrow* formed an anti-aircraft and anti-submarine screen to protect the main body – the RFAs *Olmeda* and *Resource* and the two carriers. Tucked close in to the *Hermes* and *Invincible* were their two

* Sources for Argentine intentions on 2 May include: R. L. Scheina, *US Naval Institute 'Proceedings'*, May, 1983; Adm J. J. Lombardo, BBC TV 'Panorama' interview, 16 April, 1984; S. Mafe Huertas, *Air International*, May, 1983.

'goalkeepers', the two Type 22s with their Sea Wolf missile systems to provide close-range point defence. The *Invincible/Brilliant* combination was particularly potent, for the carrier was armed with Sea Dart, providing area defence behind the picket line. Only one essential asset was missing – airborne early warning to control the first line of defence, the Combat Air Patrols. The A-4Q Skyhawks, should they come, would do so at very low level. Beyond the radar horizon, which the picket line pushed out to about sixty miles from the carriers, the Sea Harriers would have to search visually and with their own intercept radars for the inbound enemy.

The first CAP sections were flown off well before first light and took up their stations, while other pilots awaited on deck, strapped into their fighters, at immediate readiness to scramble to reinforce the standing patrols. The weather was good, but the attack, for which both sides were keyed up, never came. The *25 de Mayo*, about 180 miles to the north-west, was ready to launch her eight Skyhawks but instead of the accustomed stiff breeze of these latitudes, the wind had fallen away almost to nothing. The carrier's own speed and the catapult together could give the attack aircraft about 100 knots, but with sufficient fuel for the round trip and a load of three 500lb bombs, the Skyhawk needed at least 25 knots of natural wind as well. The Argentine command's choices were to launch the strike with sufficient fuel for the mission but no bombs, to launch the aircraft loaded with bombs from a range of seventy miles, or to wait for the wind to return. The first would have been pointless and the second suicidal, so the frustrated strike pilots whistled for a wind all day, while the Royal Navy fighter pilots, whose answer to lack of wind was to increase the length of their take-off run, investigated Tracker and P-2H Neptune radar transmissions and wondered where the Skyhawks were. The only Skyhawk sorties on the 2nd were by lightly-loaded aircraft launched for *Patrullas Aereas de Combate* (Spanish CAPs), armed with old-model (AIM-9B) Sidewinders and their built-in 20mm cannon.

The Carrier Battle Group turned back to the west shortly after noon (1600 GMT) to prepare for another bombardment operation. The RFAs were left on the edge of the TEZ and the *Plymouth*, which had been detached late on the 1st to reinforce the South Georgia defences, was recalled to screen them. RFA *Fort Austin* was approaching the TEZ from the north-east and the *Yarmouth* was despatched to shepherd her in.

The Argentine Navy Neptune shadower noted the Battle Group's turn to the west and reported it to the naval air base at Rio Grande. Early in the afternoon *Capitan de Corbeta* J. J. Colombo led the Argentine Navy's first Super Etendard/Exocet attempt. As the Royal Navy correctly believed, the Super Etendard's normal radius of action was barely sufficient to reach the longitude of Port Stanley, but this did not take into account the aircraft's air-to-air refuelling capability, of which the 2nd Fighter-Attack Squadron intended to make full use. On this occasion, however,

Hermes' 'goalkeeper', HMS *Broadsword*, tucked in close. Although intended as specialised anti-submarine vessels, the Type 22s were particularly valued for their Sea Wolf close-range AA system – the forward 'six-pack' launcher can be seen between the four Exocet launchers and the bridge – and their lack of a medium-calibre gun did not prevent their use as general-purpose ships inshore *(MoD)*

although the two naval missile attack aircraft rendezvoused with the Air Force KC-130H Hercules tanker, the latter had technical problems which prevented refuelling and the mission had to be aborted.*

By mid-afternoon on 2 May, therefore, the opening moves of the Argentine Navy's plan had been thwarted by lack of wind and technical difficulties. Admiral Lombardo ordered the three separate groups to withdraw, possibly to await an improvement in conditions which would permit a further attempt on the following day. Admiral Woodward kept his screen intact until 2200, by which time it was clear that the *25 de Mayo* had not launched a dusk strike, and then detached the *Alacrity* and *Arrow* to bombard Port Stanley airfield. As it transpired, the Argentine carrier was never to launch a strike, for already the naval situation had been changed completely.

The *Belgrano* group, on the southern edge of the TEZ, had been causing the British naval commanders some concern. The cruiser and her two destroyers, trailed by the *Conqueror*, had been about 300 miles from the Battle Group since dawn and although she had been slowly making her way to the west during the 2nd, were she to turn to the north-east at nightfall, she would have fifteen hours of darkness to cover a run-in at twenty knots. As well as posing a threat to the Carrier Battle Group, the *Belgrano* was also well placed for a raid on South Georgia, 850 miles to the east – a move which could not be countered as long as the British carriers had to mark the *25 de Mayo* group. Her presence, together with the two Exocet-armed destroyers, would alter the balance of forces in the TEZ appreciably, for although she was an old ship, scarcely capable of twenty-five knots, her 6in guns fired 105lb shells to a greater range than the British 4.5in guns and, the only armoured ship on either side, the *Belgrano* was almost impervious to their 55lb shells and well-protected against the ship-launched Exocets. Admiral Woodward had only two ship-killing weapons to cope with the cruiser – the submarines' 21in torpedoes and the Sea Harriers' 1,000lb bombs. The aircraft were none too numerous for their all-important air defence task and any diversion of effort would possibly prove to be expensive; while one submarine was already in contact it would face an immediate tactical complication if the *Belgrano* group was to turn to the north-east for a high-speed run into the TEZ.

To the south of the Falklands there lies a submerged ridge known as the Burdwood Bank, believed by some modern geologists to mark the boundary between the African and South American tectonic plates. The bank extends some 240 miles from east to west and is about sixty miles wide at its closest point to East Falkland, 100 miles to the north. To the south of the shelf the water is more than 10,000 feet (3,000 metres) deep but this shoals very rapidly to a depth of about 360 feet (110 metres) and

* Scheina, op. cit.

the contours of the Bank are so uneven, with underwater cliffs and pinnacles, that this decreases to as little as 150 feet (45 metres) in places. For readily-apparent reasons, the Burdwood Bank is no place for a fast-moving submerged submarine, particularly when it relies upon its own ability to run at great depths to remain undetected while shadowing a high-speed enemy. There was thus a distinct possibility that the *Belgrano* could shake off the *Conqueror*, which would have as little as five hours in which to relocate and overhaul the Argentine ships once the latter were clear of the bank and making for the waters to the east of Port Stanley.

The indications of an Argentine 'pincer' movement, and the tactical difficulties which this would involve, obliged Admiral Woodward to request an extension of the Rules of Engagement which would permit the *Conqueror* to eliminate the threat from the south-west. The request was passed up the chain of command and the Chief of the Defence Staff, Admiral of the Fleet Sir Terence Lewin, himself explained the scenario to the War Cabinet: there was evidence that the Argentine Navy intended to attack the Carrier Battle Group from widely separated directions and the present courses and speeds of the Argentine groups were irrelevant. Tactical circumstances made an early revision of the Rules necessary. The War Cabinet approved the amendment to the rules to permit the submarine to attack the cruiser and the appropriate signal was transmitted to HMS *Conqueror* at 1330 GMT (mid-morning off the Falklands).

[Much was made after the war of an allegation by the then Minister of Foreign Affairs in the Argentine Government, Dr Nicanor Costa Mendez, that, by authorizing the attack on the *General Belgrano*, the British Government 'scuttled' a peace plan offered by President Belaunde Terry of Peru and which was on the point of acceptance by the Junta, if indeed it had not already been accepted. The argument ran on to claim that the sinking of the cruiser was the biggest single act of escalation and that thereafter the Junta could not accept any formula if it were to appear that Argentina was negotiating under duress. In fact, President Belaunde offered his plan direct to the Junta, only afterwards presenting it to the British Government through an intermediary (the US State Department). Furthermore, he publicly announced its existence before the Argentine leaders had replied or the British Cabinet even knew of its terms. Tactical situations tend to develop at a more urgent pace than diplomatic manoeuvres and although the Argentine Navy had attempted to make the first 'escalatory' moves on 2 May – the Air Force strike missions on the 1st might have been unsuccessful but they too were in deadly earnest – it was the Royal Navy which struck first on that day.]

Commander C. L. Wreford-Brown, commanding HMS *Conqueror*, received the 1330 signal amending the 'RoE' but, due to communications difficulties, it was not until 1730 that the amendment was clearly understood. The attack was set up with great deliberation, the submarine closing in to attack the zig-zagging cruiser while giving the widest possible berth to the two screening destroyers. By 1857 an ideal position had been reached, 1,400 yards on the *Belgrano*'s port bow, and Commander Wreford-Brown fired a salvo of three Mark 8** torpedoes. With the size of the salvo and the pattern used, it was expected that one hit would be obtained.

The *Belgrano*, thirty-five miles outside the TEZ and forty miles from one of the 150-foot patches on the Burdwood Bank, was dawdling at ten knots towards Isla de los Estados, off Tierra del Fuego, whither she had been ordered, presumably until the attack operation could be resumed. In spite of being so close to an area declared to be dangerous, the cruiser was not at a high state of damage control readiness and many of her sailors were gathered in the canteen space and on the mess-decks, enjoying an afternoon stand-easy. No look-out saw the track of the torpedoes and the two hits on the port side came as a total surprise. The destroyer *Bouchard* claimed that she too had been hit, by the third torpedo, which failed to explode.

Wreford-Brown had achieved far more than he had expected and he now took the *Conqueror* out of the area to avoid detection and counter-attack. His torpedoes were almost identical to those used in the Royal Navy's last attack on a cruiser – the Japanese *Ashigara*, in June, 1945 – and had been in service since 1932, longer, indeed, than their target. The cruisers of the US Navy's 'Brooklyn'-class had survived very severe damage from bombs, large-calibre shells, Kamikazes and Japanese torpedoes much more powerful than the old Mark 8. It was widely believed that the *Belgrano* could well survive these two hits, particularly as she had two intact destroyers with her, the sea was not particularly rough and she was within 100 miles of the lee of Isla de los Estados and only 240 miles from the naval base at Ushuaia.

To those on board the cruiser there was, from the first, no real prospect of saving the ship. The first torpedo had struck right forward, between the bows and the foremost 6in turret, and the second exploded under the after superstructure, in line with the engine rooms. Argentine sources had described a 'heat wave' or 'fireball' spreading through the ship. Whatever the cause of this phenomenon – the ignition of inflammable vapour or dust – it indicates that doors and hatches, which were designed and installed to contain flame or heat, as well as water, were open over a considerable part of the ship. Most of the 321 men lost with the ship were killed in the canteen or on their mess-decks by the initial explosion or the fire.*

The flooding of the machinery spaces deprived the ship of all power and quickly brought her to a standstill. The auxiliary generators, which should have provided emergency power for fire-fighting and counter-flooding pumps, could not be started, and all normal lighting and com-

* Scheina, op. cit. Later sources, particularly those continuing the political controversy, have quoted up to 368 men killed and missing.

munications failed. *Capitan* Hector Bonzo and 879 of his ship's company abandoned the ship but took thirty minutes to do so – a long time, even in darkness lit only by emergency lanterns – before they were all aboard thirty thirty-man inflatable liferafts. The flooding spread unchecked through the ship as the men left and she had a heavy list to port by the time that the last man was clear. Fifteen minutes later the *General Belgrano* rolled over on her port side and plunged by the bows, a remarkably fast end for a 10,800-ton cruiser with a high reserve of buoyancy.

The two destroyers, *Bouchard* and *Piedra Buena*, did not witness the end. They hunted for the *Conqueror*, initially to the west of the position of the attack (thus giving rise to the canard that they had promptly headed for home), but thereafter spreading the search wider, dropping small patterns of depth-charges or single charges from time to time. The peculiarities of the channelling of underwater explosions led to some of the depth-charges being felt quite strongly by the submarine, but the destroyers were never close enough to be any real danger and the *Conqueror* quietly moved away from the scene, so that she too neither saw nor heard the cruiser's last moments.

After hunting for two hours, the *Bouchard* and *Buena* returned to the scene of the torpedoing but were unable to find any trace of the cruiser (which had foundered more than an hour previously) or of the thirty brightly-covered liferafts. Darkness had now fallen and the weather began to deteriorate, the wind increasing to up to sixty knots in gusts and the waves building up. The liferafts were buffeted by wind and sea but, although they were uncomfortable, their occupants were protected from exposure by the inflatable bottoms and roofs and all who got off the *Belgrano* survived. However, their ordeal was to last for twenty-four hours after the sinking before the first raft was sighted by searching ships and another day was to elapse before all were picked up.

Admiral Woodward, when he received the *Conqueror*'s report of the successful torpedo attack, knew that the threat from the south-west had

HMS *Conqueror* returns from her South Atlantic patrol. For the expenditure of three torpedoes of even greater antiquity than their victim she ensured that the Argentine surface fleet would not again challenge the Royal Navy *(MoD)*

been 'taken out', although he, like the rest of the world, was not to know that the *Belgrano* had sunk. That still left the carrier force to the north-west and the three A.69 corvettes. At 2300 radar contact was made with what appeared to be a group of ships to the north-west and the Carrier Battle Group prepared for a surface action, the two Type 21s being recalled from their bombardment mission.

In retrospect, it seems likely that the contacts, which faded, were caused by climatic conditions* or even large flocks of birds, but they led to the next encounter with the Argentine Navy. At 0130 a Sea King of 826 Squadron engaged on a surface search to the north of the Falklands reported a radar contact and closed to identify visually. A darkened ship was seen and, as the helicopter approached, it opened fire. The Sea King opened the range, reported that the contact was definitely hostile and settled down to shadow.

The Lynxes from, first, HMS *Coventry* and then HMS *Glasgow* were flown off, armed with two Sea Skua missiles each, to investigate the ship and attack if necessary. Homed by the Sea King, *Coventry* Flight picked up the target and, when fired upon by a medium-calibre gun, fired both Sea Skuas. The pilot and Observer watched as the radar-guided missiles homed and hit and the ship sank in a large explosion. Half-an-hour later the *Glasgow*'s Lynx, which had been delayed by radio problems, gained contact with another vessel in the same area and was also fired upon. The Lynx, an hour's flying from the destroyer, was low on fuel, but the crew worked round to a good firing position and was rewarded with an observed hit by one of the two Sea Skuas fired.

Glasgow Flight's target had been the Argentine patrol vessel *Alferez Sobral*, a 700-ton ocean-going tug which had been transferred from the US Navy and was rated by her new owners as a 'corvette'. The Sea Skua had

* In certain circumstances the radar pulses become trapped under a temperature layer and follow the curve of the Earth; the reflections do not always return in an order which can be sorted out by the receiver circuits into an intelligible picture and very convincing contacts are displayed on the radar screen.

The Lynx/Sea Skua combination proved to be successful in its first engagements even though the full acceptance trials of the missile were not officially complete ('*Soldier*' Magazine)

hit her in the bridge structure, killing the commanding officer and seven ratings, but she managed to reach Puerto Deseado two days later. There is considerable mystery as to the identity of the *Coventry*'s Lynx's target: it was believed that this was the *Sobral*'s sister-ship *Comodoro Somerella*, both ships being employed on air-sea-rescue duties at the time of the attack (though this was not known at the time), but the latter has been seen since the war and was therefore not the victim. The aircrew believed that their target was larger than the patrol craft and it has been suggested that they had attacked an A.69, which would tally with the report of a larger gun than the 20mm cannon arming the *Sobral*, and that the heavy explosion was caused by a hit on an Exocet canister.

The British ships were unable to attempt any rescue operations, but in the hope of minimizing loss of life from the sunken ship the flagship broadcast a life-saving message on all International Distress radio and wireless frequencies, giving the time and position of the attacks.

To date, the Royal Navy had damaged a submarine with forty-year-old depth-charges, sunk a cruiser with fifty-year-old torpedoes and shot down three aircraft with an up dated version of twenty-five-year-old missiles. The *Sobral* and the unidentified ship had been hit with a weapon which was not yet officially in service, for the Sea Skua had not yet completed the full range of trials needed for Service clearance for use! Another such weapon was on its way south. The Stingray lightweight anti-submarine torpedo had been given an abbreviated and accelerated trials programme to clear its release from Lynx and Wasp helicopters and from RAF Nimrods and from mid-May several frigates would be equipped with this advanced weapon.

The weather which had given the *Belgrano*'s survivors such an uncomfortable night reached the Carrier Battle Group's operating area during the morning of 3 May, bringing low cloud and visibility of no more than a mile, as well as high winds and rough seas. The British ships attempted no offensive operations, replenishing while the Sea Kings maintained their surface and anti-submarine search patrols. The CAP was scrambled once to look, unavailingly, for a fleeting contact on a shadowing Neptune and then, at dusk, for a search for shipping which took them 240 miles to the south-west of the carriers.

The *25 de Mayo*, having had insufficient wind on 2 May, had too much on the 3rd and was unable to operate her fixed-wing aircraft. Following the news of the attack on the *Belgrano*, all Argentine warships were pulled back to the west, to operate in shallow water where the big Fleet submarines would not follow. In effect, the latter had won the first major victory by torpedoing the cruiser. As the news of the heavy loss of life reached the world, Argentina began to enjoy widespread public sympathy, but this does not win wars and the Junta could not afford the loss of prestige which would have attended the sinking of *25 de Mayo* or the Type 42 destroyers and they played no further effective part in the war.

Chapter Six

First Losses

Up to 4 May the Royal Navy's successes had been gained at no cost but the expenditure of ammunition and one man slightly wounded. Any optimism which may have been felt as to the prospects of a cheap victory was dashed on this day, when the honours went to Argentina.

The day's action began with another RAF Vulcan attack on Port Stanley airfield. As on 1 May, the big bomber achieved surprise but the stick of twenty-one bombs fell more than 600 yards to the west of the centre of the runway, considerably frightening the crews of three AA guns which were narrowly missed but inflicting no damage on the airfield or installations. The Vulcan and its eleven Victor tankers all returned safely to Ascension.

Admiral Woodward hoped to repeat the success of the first day, his main aim being to reduce the strength of the Argentine Air Force. The Carrier Battle Group ran in to the west during the night and by mid-morning the *Hermes* and *Invincible* were within 100 miles of Port Stanley, with the three Type 42s twenty miles up-threat, forming a picket line. The Sea Harriers flew CAP missions from before first light but the Argentine Air Force was not going to react to their presence alone. Apart from reconnaissance, the only Air Force activity on this day centred on the re-opening of the Port Stanley runway, a Hercules flying in to bring stores and evacuate wounded men.

The Argentine naval air arm was also flying reconnaissance sorties and a Neptune soon found the British ships, the position reported at 1215 corresponding to that of the Type 42s. A pair of Exocet-armed Super Etendards took off half-an-hour later from Rio Grande and rendezvoused with an Air Force tanker 130 miles to the east. After refuelling, the strike aircraft dropped to low level to close the ships, 250 miles distant. The Neptune, which was struggling to keep its old radar working, up-dated the position of the Type 42s, informing *Capitan de Corbeta* A. Bedacarratz and *Teniente de Navio* A. Mayora that three ships, one of which appeared to give a larger 'echo', were sixty miles to the south of Port Stanley, 115 miles to the east of the strike aircraft. The Super Etendards were experiencing bad weather, with interspersed fog and rain showers reducing visibility to under half a mile below a 500-foot cloudbase.

The picket line, and the carriers twenty miles to the east, were in better weather, with ten miles visibility, solid cloud at 1,000 feet, a quite light breeze and a gentle ten-foot swell. The Type 42s were spread out, fifteen miles apart, with the *Coventry* forty miles south of Port Stanley and the *Sheffield* on the other end of the line, beyond the *Glasgow*. Four Sea Harriers were on CAP at medium level but there were no 'Bogeys' on any of the radar screens, nor were there any 'Rackets' – the code-name for unidentified or enemy radar transmissions. On several occasions during the preceding days the ships of the Carrier Battle Group had gone to 'Action Stations' on the detection of what was believed to be the Super Etendard's 'Agave' radar, but these had all been false alarms. The Argentine pilots were aware that they would be betrayed by this means and their radars were accordingly warmed up but left on standby, ready for the brief transmission that would be needed to verify the presence of a target and to feed the range and bearing to the Exocet fire-control computer.

The first warning of the attack was given by HMS *Glasgow*, when the enemy aircraft were about twenty-five miles to the west of her, flying at sea level towards the *Sheffield*. The CAP was sent out to investigate above the cloud while the two Type 42s attempted to acquire the very difficult targets with their Sea Dart systems. The *Sheffield* had been using her satellite communications equipment until the *Glasgow*'s warning, when it was switched off to avoid possible interference with her passive radar warning gear, but she already had radar contact when the two Super Etendards 'popped up' inside twenty miles to use their radars for two or three 'sweeps' to set up the Exocets, returning to sea level after this brief look from 100 feet. When they reached a range of about twelve miles, each aircraft fired a missile and they then split in opposite directions to make their escapes. No attempt was made to select a high-value target, or even to check the identity of the ship at which they had launched 40% of the Argentine Navy's inventory of this irreplaceable weapon. They had simply fired at the first contact to appear and then made off.

Fired at such short range, the Exocets had little more than a minute's flying time to reach the *Sheffield* and the only brief warning of the nature of the attack was the sighting of the smoke trail and one missile about six feet above the sea, less than a mile from the ship. There was no time to fire chaff rockets to decoy the missile and only just enough to broadcast 'Missile Attack – Hit the Deck!' before the Exocet, fulfilling its designers' intentions exactly, hit the destroyer dead amidships. The other Exocet had not seen the *Sheffield*, nor was it seen by that ship, but it was watched a minute or so later by the *Yarmouth*, some twenty miles to the east, as it flew parallel to her and ditched at the end of its 'training run'.

The missile which scored the hit had approached from *Sheffield*'s starboard bow and on entering the ship's side tore a hole four feet deep and fifteen feet long, extending from the Auxiliary Machine Room to the

Minutes after the missile hit, the *Sheffield* lies dead in the water, thick black smoke pouring out of the hole made by the Exocet and lighter-coloured smoke coming from the upper-deck ventilation exhausts. Fenders have already been rigged over the starboard side in preparation for the *Arrow* coming alongside *(MoD)*

A close-up, from the *Arrow*, of the long gash in the *Sheffield*'s side and the discoloured areas where the heat of the initial fires has stripped off the paint on the hull and bridge structure *(MoD)*

Forward Engine Room. The 370lb warhead did not explode, but the kinetic energy released by the impact and deceleration* was more than enough to ignite the remainder of the Exocet's fuel, which exploded, causing blast damage which extended up as far as the bridge structure and spreading dense choking smoke throughout the centre section of the ship. Fires broke out in the two machinery spaces, fed by a fuel supply tank, and in the galley above, but the complete loss of firemain pressure due to the rupture of the ringmain system meant that until outside assistance arrived the fire-fighting parties would have to rely upon the ship's two emergency pumps. The Olympus engines continued to run, although they could no longer be controlled from the bridge, and an undamaged generator maintained electric supplies. Steering from the bridge was also lost, but a little group of men in the tiller flat steered the ship by means of emergency controls, their instructions being passed in a variety of unconventional ways as the situation deteriorated.

There were many devoted bands of men working to save their shipmates' lives that forenoon, fighting the fires, entering smoke-filled compartments to rescue men or to attempt to retrieve salvage and firefighting

* The equivalent of a 75-ton locomotive being brought to a standstill from 60mph in 10 yards.

gear. One such team was led by Petty Officer D. R. Briggs,* who made several trips to the smoke-laden Forward Damage Control Section Base to collect equipment before he was overcome. Unconscious, he was pulled clear by Petty Officer G. A. Meager, the ship's senior medical rating, who had already rescued another man from a smoke-filled compartment. Sadly, he could not revive PO Briggs, who was posthumously awarded a Distinguished Service Medal for his courage; PO Medical Assistant Meager's devotion was rewarded by a Queen's Gallantry Medal. Others gave their lives to keep the ship's defensive systems operational while the fires were fought. The computer room team stayed too long and were overcome by the smoke, which was remembered by most of the survivors as the worst effect of the aftermath of the Exocet hit.

The communications system was another immediate victim of the hit and the first outsiders to realize that something was badly amiss were the crew of a Sea King of 826 Squadron, on anti-submarine patrol seven miles away. Perhaps because of the nature of their mission, and not knowing of the air-raid warning, their initial impression was that she had been torpedoed. The sonar operator was lowered to the *Sheffield*'s forecastle and returned to inform the pilot of the cause and nature of the damage, which was relayed to the *Hermes* at 1412, ten minutes after the missile had struck.

Assistance arrived quickly thereafter, Sea King 4s flying in more gas-turbine pumps, foam and breathing apparatus, followed by HMS *Arrow* and then the *Yarmouth*. The two frigates came close alongside, the *Arrow* to port and the *Yarmouth* to starboard, and played water from their hoses on the sides and deck of the *Sheffield* to prevent the heat from spreading ahead of the fire. The *Arrow* was able to pass three hoses over to fight the fires from the forward end but all these efforts were insufficient – the fire continued to spread. To complicate matters, the *Yarmouth* was obliged to break away at 1526 when a torpedo track was reported. She carried out a mortar attack on a possible submarine contact and then returned to the *Sheffield*, leaving the 'submarine' to the Sea Kings and her own Wasp, which had up to then been ferrying injured men from the damaged destroyer's flight deck. The hunt for the submarine went on for two hours, during which the *Yarmouth* broke off once more to add her accurate weaponry to the attack.

The anti-submarine activity had no bearing on the *Sheffield*'s fate, however distracting it may have been. At about 1800 the surviving generator finally died, leaving the blazing ship with no power for her weapons system, steering or internal communications. It was mid-afternoon, in favourable weather for another Argentine air attack, and Captain Salt was concerned that he was occupying too great a proportion of the Battle Group's assets. More immediately, the fire was getting close to the Sea

---

* His full rank was Petty Officer Marine Engineering Mechanic (Machinery) – the modern title for what was known as a Petty Officer Stoker in less sophisticated days.

Dart missile magazine and the 4.5in gun ammunition. He therefore gave the order to abandon ship and Commander Bootherstone brought the *Arrow* alongside the *Sheffield*'s forecastle to take off 225 men; Sea Kings from the *Hermes* took off thirty-five more, including Captain Salt, and *Yarmouth* already had six on board. Twenty-four of the survivors were wounded; twenty men had died.

The *Hermes* had been preparing to launch a strike against Goose Green when the *Sheffield* was hit. The take-off was postponed until the air defence picture was clear, to ensure that the aircraft were available for CAP if necessary. Three 800 Squadron Sea Harriers finally took off at 1530, two armed with cluster bombs and the other with three retarded bombs. About half-an-hour later, noon at Goose Green, Lieutenant G. W. J. Batt and Lieutenant N. Taylor approached from the south-east at low level to drop their cluster-bomb containers on parked aircraft and vehicles, while Flight-Lieutenant E. H. Ball RAF attacked a few seconds later from the south-west, laying his parachute-retarded bombs on the grass runway.

The pair led by Lieutenant Batt was tracked for most of its inbound flight by the Port Stanley TPS-43 radar and the *VYCA 2* team warned the Goose Green AA batteries of approaching trouble. The Army-manned Skyguard radar detected the Sea Harriers at a range of ten miles and the 35mm Oerlikon cannon opened fire as the fighter-bombers crossed the coast, hitting Lieutenant Nick Taylor's aircraft, which burst into flames and crashed on the airfield, killing the pilot. The Air Force 20mm crews did not see Flight-Lieutenant Ball's approach in their sector and opened fire on Lieutenant Batt only as he was departing, claiming to have scored hits. Neither of the two Sea Harriers which got away was touched by the AA and both landed safely at 1640. Lieutenant Taylor's body was retrieved from the wreckage of his aircraft (XZ450) and was buried with military honours on the edge of the airfield.

The loss of the Sea Harrier was a serious matter for the Battle Group, which had only twenty to begin with and no prospect of replacements for nearly three weeks. The degree of the Argentine Air Force's unwillingness to take on the naval fighters in air combat was not yet appreciated and it was believed that it was necessary to husband the carriers' (and the Group's) principal weapon of attrition for the big battle for air supremacy.

The Argentinians were meanwhile monitoring the activity around the *Sheffield* with considerable interest, listening to the radio traffic, watching the helicopter movements on the TPS-43 radar and tracking the ships by means of a shadowing Neptune. However, they had no idea of the identity of the victim until it was volunteered by the Ministry of Defence spokesman who announced that the *Sheffield* had been hit and abandoned. The announcement, broadcast on radio and television, was made at 9.16pm (British Summer Time), as the sun was setting in the Falklands, and it coincided with a decision by Admiral Woodward that the derelict should not be sunk by gunfire, as he had originally intended, but would be left afloat to act as a 'tethered goat', to lure submarine or air attack.

As he withdrew to begin a major RAS, Admiral Woodward had much food for thought. The Exocet had been proved beyond doubt to be a potent weapon, which could be delivered with little or no warning thanks to the Royal Navy's complete lack of any airborne early warning radar system. The loss of one of his three modern anti-aircraft ships reduced not only the AA firepower but also the picket strength and coverage. The only weapon saved from the ship was her Lynx, which had taken off, still armed with its Sea Skuas, after the missile had hit and was now aboard the *Fort Austin*. The loss of the Sea Harrier meant that, in future, low-level attacks on defended targets would be delivered only when the gains were commensurate with the obvious risk.

In the United Kingdom countermeasures to deal with the air-launched Exocet were investigated and, where they showed promise, developed. Analysts used data from the Battle Group to devise chaff patterns and ship manoeuvres to distract the homing head; radar reflectors and jammers to seduce it were fitted in helicopters and successfully tested in firings by RN Exocet-fitted ships, and the Navy and Thorn-EMI got together to modify the Nimrod's Searchwater radar for installation in a Sea King helicopter, to produce an AEW aircraft which could operate from the carriers.

The first major reinforcement group was preparing to leave Home Waters but a replacement for the *Sheffield* was a little closer to hand. On 5 May the Type 42 *Exeter* was ordered to leave her patrol off Belize and proceed to join Task Group 317.8. Captain H. M. Balfour MVO RN had expected the summons and was already quietly working his ship's company up for the operation. Her efficiency and her superior Type 1022 warning radar were to make her particularly welcome but she would not arrive for another seventeen days.

Another Type 42, the *Cardiff* (Captain M. G. Harris RN) was on her way through the Mediterranean, returning from a tour of duty off the Straits of Hormuz, where a Royal Navy presence was being maintained to protect merchant shipping in the event of the Iran–Iraq war spreading to the entrance to the Persian Gulf. She was ordered to proceed to Gibraltar to undertake a maintenance period and to store for the South Atlantic. On leaving the straits, she would turn to port, instead of starboard, as originally intended. The *Cardiff* was alongside from 7 to 12 May and then sailed to join the group which had left Portsmouth and Devonport on the 10th. Only two of the original six Type 21s were not yet allocated to 'Corporate': the *Birmingham* was completing a refit but was earmarked to join the task force at the end of June and the *Newcastle*, whose Lynx Flight was embarked in RFA *Fort Austin*, was in the third month of a year-long refit which was actually completed in seven months.

Led by HMS *Bristol* (Captain A. Grose RN), this group comprised the Type 21s *Avenger* and *Active*, three 'Leander'-class frigates – the *Minerva* and *Penelope* armed with MM-38 Exocets and the recently-converted *Andromeda* with Sea Wolf as well as Exocets – and the fast fleet oiler RFA *Olna*. The oiler carried two Sea Kings of 824 Squadron and four of the frigates carried a Lynx each, only the *Active* being equipped with the older Wasp. The *Minerva*'s Lynx crew had joined the ship by a very narrow margin; they had already been down south, flying from the *Fort Austin* in the opening days, and had just returned via Ascension. The Type 82 guided missile destroyer *Bristol*, the first ship to be armed with Sea Dart, had no hangar or embarked flight, but her flight deck had been extended and strengthened to operate a Wessex. The big ship's particular attribute, besides her air defence system, was her comprehensive command capability, which would provide Admiral Woodward with an alternative flagship if required.

The eight ships worked up as they went south, benefiting not only from the Carrier Battle Group's current experiences, on which the ships were continually up-dated, but also from the presence of a team of 'Sea Riders' – operational sea training specialists from Portland, who remained until the group reached Ascension on 18 May.

Chapter Seven

Bad-weather Blockade

The Carrier Battle Group moved out to the east of Port Stanley during the night of 4/5 May and operated in good weather during the following morning, flying surface search missions with the Lynxes and Sea Kings, while other Sea Kings provided an anti-submarine screen for the carriers or discreetly patrolled around the derelict *Sheffield*. The Argentine bases nearest to the Falklands were 'weathered-in' and the only intruders were reconnaissance aircraft which turned back well before the few Sea Harrier sorties could get near. The weather in the TEZ deteriorated as the frontal system moved east and by afternoon the visibility had deteriorated to less than a mile under very low cloud.

During the forenoon the Argentine Navy had its own private battle. A Tracker from *25 de Mayo*, operating close inshore along the coast to the north of Comodoro Rivadavia, gained contact with a submarine and dropped depth-charges and a homing torpedo. A fresh contact was then picked up by a second Tracker, which was joined by Sea Kings from the carrier, and further attacks were delivered. No British submarine was near the position and it is possible that the Argentine aircrew, in spite of their local knowledge, were as deceived by 'marine life' – often whales – as their Royal Navy opposite numbers. The latter, and the ships' sonar teams, were learning to tell the subtle difference between a noisy whale and a 'quiet' submarine and the number of submarine alerts soon diminished.

During the afternoon of the 5th the *25 de Mayo* flew off her eight A-4Qs and began to make her way north to her base at Puerto Belgrano, remaining close inshore. Whether or not she had mechanical problems, as was alleged afterwards by the Argentine Navy, her departure was a victory for the nuclear-powered submarines, for she did not sail again during the conflict. Her Skyhawks went to BAN Rio Grande, where they were to be based for strikes on British ships in the Falklands area, providing the only fully-trained anti-shipping bomber force.

The *Sheffield* was visited during the day by a Sea King 4, which lowered the ship's Engineer Officer and the Flight Commander to retrieve fire-fighting equipment which had been left and some aviation gear from the hangar. The ship was still on fire forward but during the afternoon one of the anti-submarine Sea Kings reported that the smoke had died down. Any idea that the fire may have gone out was dispelled by a report from an aircraft returning after dark that the destroyer's hull was glowing red.

The low cloud and poor visibility continued through the night, while the surface search Sea Kings looked for possible blockade-runners. At about midnight an alert Observer picked up a small contact and vectored a Lynx from RFA *Fort Austin* to investigate. The probing helicopter had a new piece of kit – a low-light television, with which it was established that the contact was an uncharted small rock which was just awash.

The dawn CAP from the *Invincible* on 6 May was directed to investigate another contact reported about fifty miles to the south of the carriers. The two Sea Harriers were not in formation and entered the area, in which the fog was appreciably thicker, separately. Both disappeared, leaving no trace of the aircraft or their pilots, Lieutenant-Commander John Eyton-Jones (the Senior Pilot of 801 Squadron) and Lieutenant Bill Curtis. It was presumed that these two vastly experienced pilots, who would be greatly missed, had collided in the bad visibility. The loss of the two fighters was another serious blow which could not be afforded. The carriers had only a slender margin of offensive striking power left over the absolute minimum needed for the defence of the Battle Group.*

The weather remained bad throughout the rest of 6 May and the following day. Admiral Woodward was unable to close in to harass the occupiers: his ships could lay down accurate gunfire on whatever spot they chose, but Forward Observation Officers were needed to ensure that there was something worth shooting at on that spot. Only the helicopters were able to operate on their main tasks of surface and anti-submarine search, while the Sea King 4s of 846 Squadron, supporting the SAS and SBS teams on the islands, found the conditions to their liking, the difficulties caused by the weather hampering the Argentinians more than themselves. Two Sea Harriers were scrambled from the *Invincible* during the afternoon of the 7th to intercept a contact which, in the event, failed to close. The recovery of the CAP, through a fortuitous hole in the fog, was an epic of ingenuity, skill and luck, taking full advantage of the Sea Harrier's unique characteristics. It could not have been achieved by a conventional fighter and carrier.

---

* The reporting of this accident, in a London evening paper, on the night of the occurrence, was a sorry example of the irresponsible attitude which persisted in some quarters of the British Press. Correspondents were requested not to release any details, not only because it was undesirable that the Argentinians should learn of the losses, but also to ensure that the pilots' families should be properly informed before the news became public knowledge.

Advantage was taken of the continuing bad weather to detach RFA *Olmeda* to replenish from the *Appleleaf*, which, it may be recalled, had been sent off on 30 April to top up from the BP tanker *British Esk*. The latter was delayed and this resulted in a reorganized sequence of transfers which illustrate the complexity but flexibility of the fuel replenishment arrangements and allocation of escorts.

On 2 May the *Appleleaf*, escorted by HMS *Plymouth*, had met up with the *Antrim* and *Tidespring* to the north of South Georgia. The big Fleet oiler's cargo of aviation fuel was unsuitable for winter use and she had exchanged loads with the storm-damaged *Brambleleaf*, which was on her way back to repair in the United Kingdom. The ex-*Brambleleaf* 'winter' fuel was now transferred by the *Tidespring* to the *Appleleaf*. The group was joined by the southbound RFA oiler *Blue Rover* on 4 May and did not split up until the 6th, when the *Plymouth* took the *Appleleaf* and *Blue Rover* south, leaving the *Antrim* and *Tidespring* to proceed north with their prisoners, BAS scientists, TV crew and ducks towards Ascension, where the 'passengers' would be landed and the oiler would pick up a fresh load of fuel. The *Plymouth* rendezvoused on 8 May with RFA *Fort Austin*, the latter acting as an escorting helicopter carrier for RFA *Olmeda*, which began to pump-over the thrice-transferred fuel from the *Appleleaf*.

The *Plymouth* headed north once more to join the next southbound group. This had been led by the Type 21 *Antelope*, still shepherding the five LSLs and RFA *Pearleaf*, all of which had left Ascension on 30 April. The group had been overtaken on 7 May by RFA *Regent* and the hospital ship *Uganda* and had then met the *Antrim* and *Tidespring*. It had been decided that the LSLs required more protection than was offered by the Type 21, which now exchanged the Britons from South Georgia, the wildfowl, the 'special category' prisoner Astiz and the oiler with the *Antrim*, which got the convoy in exchange. The *Antelope* and *Tidespring* arrived off Ascension after dark on 12 May and transferred the prisoners to an awaiting chartered DC-10 airliner, which flew them to Montevideo. Astiz remained in solitary confinement at Ascension until it could be decided what was to be done with him, in the light of urgent French and Swedish requests for facilities for interrogating him.

The *Antelope* 'steamed' over 11,000 miles during her 37-day deployment; of this a sizeable proportion was covered during her trip back to Ascension with the *Tidespring*, taking the South Georgia Argentine marines and civilian workers to the island for repatriation *(MoD)*

The LSLs, now in HMS *Antrim*'s charge, loitered on about latitude 30° South, awaiting the main Amphibious Group, which sailed from Ascension on 7 May. During the early forenoon of the 8th the *Antrim* picked up an aircraft which homed on her group, behaving like no civil airliner, but which came no closer than 115 miles. Five hours later, at 1645, a second aircraft, also assessed as a Boeing 707, went through the same routine but pressed on in to twenty miles, just outside the range of the Seaslug system, before turning away, to the chagrin of the guided-missile destroyer's operations team. Between these visits by the shadower, an RAF Nimrod from Ascension had spent some while with the LSLs, ensuring that no surface threat was developing.

The Argentine Air Force was also playing cat-and-mouse with the Carrier Battle Group on the 8th, although the purpose of their operations on this day appears to have been the resupply of Port Stanley by air. The weather was still poor, with low cloud and fog, but Sea Harriers were launched at midday to stalk a 'bogey' which was orbiting in the Port Stanley area, possibly awaiting a break in the weather. The alert *VYCA 2* saw the CAP coming and warned the intended victim, who made off to the west before the fighters could get near. Three hours later, the CAP went after the escort of a C-130 which was mistakenly thought to be dropping supplies by parachute, but again the Sea Harriers were frustrated, although they were in to twelve miles before their quarry turned and made off.

It was now apparent that Port Stanley airfield was in use again, hole or no hole, and, as the fog began to show signs of lifting at last, Admiral Woodward went over to the offensive once more. At 1900 the *Brilliant* and *Alacrity* were detached, the former to patrol off the northern entrance to the Falkland Sound and the latter to shell Argentine bivouacs on Port Stanley Common. These harassing actions, as well as giving the Argentine soldiers a sleepless night, would cover another activity, the salvage of the *Sheffield* by HMS *Yarmouth*, which had left the carrier group at 1700.

C-130 'TC-68' of the Argentine Air Force, its engines running, unloads stores while ambulances wait with their load of sick and wounded to be flown out to the mainland. Low cloud and poor visibility cloaked many daylight blockade-breaking flights and are evident in this photograph *(FAA via J.C. D'Odorico)*

The destroyer, which had been visited every day since she had been abandoned, was floating on an even keel and her fires had apparently burned themselves out without reaching the gun or missile magazines. On 8 May towing gear was laid out on her fo'c'sle by a team winched down from a Sea King and before midnight the *Yarmouth* had the *Sheffield* in tow to the east and was soon making six knots.

The diversions went as planned, the *Alacrity* firing 90 4.5in shells, spotted by an observer in her Lynx. All went into the intended target area. The *Brilliant*, which had taken along the *Glasgow*'s helicopter, conducted a noisy demonstration off Port Howard, the two helicopters dropping flares and firing their GPMGs at positions believed to be occupied by Argentine troops, but provoking no response. The final diversion of the night, delivered a couple of hours after midnight, took the form of the illumination of Darwin and Fox Bay, on West Falkland, by Sea Harriers of 801 Squadron, which lofted high-intensity Lepus flares to enliven the garrisons' night.

Even as the frigates and the Sea Harriers were returning to the main body, the next 'wave' was on its way in. This comprised the *Broadsword* and *Coventry*, which were to act as a team to harass the Port Stanley area and prevent the use of the airfield by transport aircraft, the Type 42's gun and Sea Dart taking care of these two tasks while the Type 22's radar, which had a better overland coverage, and Sea Wolf system would protect the two ships from direct attack. They were to remain on station throughout the day, controlling their own CAP. The Sea Harriers were also to take a hand in stepping up the pressure on the Argentinians. Those briefed for patrols over East Falkland were armed with a 1,000lb on the fuselage pylon and would drop the bomb on arrival on station. To remain well clear of the AA guns and Roland missiles, the fighters would bomb from high level – the last British naval aircraft to use this method had been Fairey Swordfish, in 1940, but the Sea Harrier, with its navigational aids, radar and computer, could expect considerably greater accuracy, as well as delivering twice the load.

The system was not proven, however, and so when Lieutenant-Commander Batt and Flight-Lieutenant D. H. S. Morgan RAF arrived half-an-hour after dawn on the 9th to find the Port Stanley area completely blanketed by cloud, they did not drop their bombs, even the slight risk that they may have landed near the town being unacceptable. The bombs were retained and the CAP settled down to patrol at medium level.

Meanwhile, the *Yarmouth* was still towing the *Sheffield*, by now to the south-east of Port Stanley. In the same general area was the Argentine trawler *Narwal*, which had been dogging the movements of the British ships since 30 April. No action had, so far, been taken against her as she was wearing a merchant ensign, but the rules had changed with effect from 9 May, the Argentine Government having been warned that the zone in which its warships might be attacked had been extended up to a line twelve miles from the continental coast and that any ship supporting the illegal occupation of the Falklands might be attacked if found within 150 miles of the centre of the TEZ.*

The 800 Squadron CAP had been on station for about twenty minutes when a surface contact was detected fifty miles to the south of Port Stanley and reported by Batt and Morgan to their controlling ship, the *Coventry*. It was confirmed that no British ship was in that position and the Sea Harriers let down through the cloud into the gloom below to identify the vessel, which turned out to be the *Narwal*. Permission to attack was sought and obtained and at 1150 the two fighters dropped their bombs in a low-level attack. One missed, the other hit and lodged in the trawler's engine room. Neither exploded as the bomb fuses had not had time between release and impact to be armed. No damage was

9 May: the Argentine 'spy trawler' *Narwal* is seized by an SBS team flown in by an 846 Squadron Sea King 4 (right) and an 826 Squadron Sea King 5, covered by a second Mark 4 *(MoD)*

apparent to the two pilots, who returned and damaged the ship further by strafing with their 30mm cannon. The *Narwal* was brought to a standstill and her crew prepared to abandon ship, launching a liferaft. Two hours later another pair of Sea Harriers made strafing runs. Visibility was poor and the pilots did not see the liferaft until after they had opened fire on the trawler which, although stationary, was apparently intact and was still flying her national flag.

At noon the two carriers flew off three Sea Kings, a pair of 820 Squadron's Mark 5s and one of 846 Squadron's Mark 4s, with an assault party provided by the SBS from HMS *Hermes* and a prize crew from the *Invin-*

* The extended zone did not extend into the waters of the River Plate, which was regarded as an international waterway, in which all traffic was entitled to proceed without risk from hostile action.

cible. The Marines abseiled down to the trawler from the Sea King 4, covered by the Mark 5s' GPMG door gunners, but encountered no resistance from the crew. One man had been killed by the bomb hit and eleven others were wounded by the strafing. Among the twelve unwounded prisoners was the Argentine naval officer under whose orders she had been sailing. In spite of so much enforced leisure following the 1150 attack, he had neglected to destroy his orders, which not only confirmed the *Narwal*'s role as a 'spy ship' but also identified two other trawlers with the same task. The prisoners were winched up to the 820 Sea Kings, the Marines returned to their aircraft and the helicopters headed back towards the carriers, 150 miles away, leaving the 'prize crew' to attempt to make temporary repairs and get the *Narwal* under way.

The Sea Kings had been operating at the limit of their radius of action and as they returned it became apparent that the Mark 4 had insufficient

The *Narwal*'s genuine fishermen were accommodated in the *Invincible* until they could be repatriated via Montevideo. During their stay, they were kitted out in Royal Navy action dress, complete with life-jackets, survival suit and anti-flash gear, the last giving them a clerical air which accords with their surroundings, the carrier's chapel, which served as their mess *(MoD)*

fuel remaining to make it all the way back. The *Glasgow* was detached from her picket station and made towards the helicopters at her best speed while the Sea King pilots conferred as to how the Mark 4, which was not equipped for in-flight refuelling from small ships, was to pick up the *Glasgow*'s hose. No improvisation was possible, so the Sea King had to be landed on the Lynx-sized deck. That this was achieved, with less than three feet of clearance between the tips of the rotor blades and the destroyer's hangar door, was due to the skill of the pilot and the courage of the Flight Deck Officer who controlled the landing. Enough fuel was transferred for a safe return to the *Hermes* and the Sea King took off again, a manoeuvre which was almost as tricky as the landing.

While the *Narwal* incident had been under way, the *Coventry* had been in action and she too had scored a notable 'first'. With HMS *Broadsword* in close company, she carried out several firing runs against Port Stanley airfield. At about noon the two ships detected aircraft to the west, approaching over West Falkland. These were assessed to be a C-130 and its escort, possibly A-4C Skyhawks from their radar 'signatures', the latter flying appreciably higher. At 1420 the *Coventry* opened fire with her Sea Dart system, engaging first the low-flying Hercules with one 'bird' and then the escort with two more. The first missed its difficult target, which turned away; one of the two fired at the fast jets also missed, but the other appeared to go between the two contacts, which split up, one turning to the south over Falkland Sound and losing height until it disappeared off the radar, the second turning all the way to the west as it lost height and then faded. Captain D. Hart-Dyke MVO RN of the *Coventry* claimed two possible kills but these were not officially recognized or included in the final 'tote' of Argentine losses. It was not until July, 1983, that it was confirmed that two IV Air Brigade A-4Cs had been lost on 9 May, supposedly in bad weather. The body of one of the pilots, *Teniente* J. E. Casco, was recovered near the wreckage of his aircraft on the precipitous South Jason Island, off the north-west coast of West Falkland, but that of *Teniente* J. R. Farias must be presumed to have been lost to the south of the Falkland Sound.

The *Coventry* resumed her steady shelling of the Port Stanley area but broke off once again at about 1900, when a low-flying helicopter was detected heading away from Port Stanley towards the Goose Green area. The Type 42 turned and headed after it and when it crossed the coast and became a better target she fired a single Sea Dart, scoring a direct hit at a range of well over ten miles. The victim was an unfortunate Argentine Army Puma on a search-and-rescue sortie, possibly to look for Farias, whose Skyhawk had last been seen in the area towards which the helicopter had been heading. All four of the Army aircrew were killed.

Late in the evening of the 9th the *Brilliant* and *Glasgow* arrived off Port Stanley to relieve the successful *Broadsword*/*Coventry* combination on the 'gun-line'. At about the same time the *Alacrity* and *Arrow* took up stations to patrol off the ends of the Falkland Sound to ensure that no supplies arrived or left by that route. During the night the Lynxes of all four ships reconnoitred the harbours and bays on the north and south coasts of both main islands but drew no fire and saw no activity. The Sea King 4s were, as usual, quietly ferrying men and equipment for the Special Forces reconnaissance teams which were established in observation hides overlooking most of the Argentine positions.

The weather deteriorated towards midnight, the wind freshening and the sea becoming rougher. At 0230 Commander Morton of the *Yarmouth* decided that it was prudent to remove the towing party from the *Sheffield* and an anti-submarine Sea King transferred the men to his frigate. He continued to tow the destroyer, albeit with some difficulty in the 35-knot wind and 10–15 feet waves in which the high-sided dead ship tended to 'sail' downwind and roll excessively. Inevitably quantities of water entered the hole on her starboard side and by 0545 she had a 5° list which increased to 25° during the next hour. The hole was now submerged and the end was just a matter of time, but the *Yarmouth* persisted for another quarter of an hour, until it was obvious that the ship was about to sink, and the tow was then slipped. Two minutes later, at 0702, the *Sheffield* suddenly rolled to starboard, capsized and sank. The *Yarmouth* had towed her for twenty-seven hours and had almost reached the eastern edge of the TEZ. Had the weather held for even another day emergency measures could have been taken to patch the hole and then to prepare the *Sheffield* for the longer tow to South Georgia; as it was, much was learned of the effects of fire and explosion on modern structures and fittings and immediate steps were taken to replace material which gave off toxic smoke in excessive quantities and to provide a new pattern of emergency breathing apparatus for every one of the 20,000-plus men of the 'Corporate' ships' companies.

The Argentine Air Force was unable to get through to Port Stanley due to the weather and no contacts were detected to the east of the Falkland Sound all this day, or the next. The bad weather became a full storm which prevented the carriers from operating their fighters except in the event of a raid (which did not come), but the helicopters continued to fly their anti-submarine, surface search and 'island airways' missions. The last daylight activity on 10 May was the retrieval of the prize crew from the *Narwal* by 820 Squadron's Sea Kings. The damaged trawler was in imminent danger of foundering in the heavy seas and her end was hastened by scuttling, the vessel sinking at sunset.

The weather did not prevent the *Glasgow* from conducting three bombardments on the 10th. With spotting provided by a Royal Artillery officer in the *Brilliant*'s Lynx, she fired 222 rounds of 4.5in at Army bivouacs, AA gun sites and the former Royal Marine 'barracks' at Moody Brook, where the new occupants had established their headquarters. Argentine return fire, which included AA fire at the Lynx, was ineffective.

During the late afternoon of 10 May Admiral Woodward detached the *Alacrity* and *Arrow* for nocturnal inshore operations. Commander Paul Bootherstone took the latter along the north coast of East Falkland and as far west as Pebble Island, his Lynx reconnoitring ahead out to the Jason Islands, without either the frigate or the helicopter noting any enemy activity.

The *Alacrity*'s mission was more eventful, for hers was the most hazardous yet ordered as it took her through the Falkland Sound from south to north. Navigation in these reef- and rock-strewn narrow waters was in itself sufficiently challenging on a dark night in low visibility without the possibility of mines, but the Argentine Navy had not mined the approaches to the Sound and, although Commander Chris Craig kept as many as possible of his ship's company well above the waterline, this was never an actual risk.

At about 0100 on the 11th (9.00pm on the 10th, local), the *Alacrity* was rewarded by the detection of a ship underway off the Swan Islands, apprently making for the dubious protection of the West Falkland coast. An attempt to illuminate the vessel by starshell was only partly successful, due to the very low cloud base, but it was obvious that this was an Argentine ship and the *Alacrity* opened fire with high-explosive shell a few minutes later. The 4.5in Mark 8 gun fired fast and very accurately, scoring hits on the target's deck cargo, which included several thousand litres of cased aviation fuel. The ship, which had by now been identified as the 834-ton transport *Isla de los Estados*, caught fire and then suddenly blew up at about 0115, the fireball extending into the cloud. The sinking occurred within a mile of the coast and about five miles from Port Howard, whose garrison, it was thought, could scarcely have failed to notice the explosion, and the *Alacrity* continued her passage of the Sound, leaving the Argentinians to rescue any survivors.

The *Isla de los Estados* had only completed unloading the *Rio Carcaraña* at Port King, Lafonia, on the 10th and was ferrying her dangerous cargo to Fox Bay and Darwin when she was found and sunk. The Argentine authorities were not aware that anything was amiss until she failed to respond to radio calls on the 11th and, although the captured tender *Forrest* was sent out immediately to search for her, it was not until the 13th that the only two survivors were found and the story of their ship's loss pieced together.

It took rather longer for the Royal Navy to realize, gradually, that the Argentine Navy came quite close to squaring the account three hours after the loss of the transport. The *Alacrity* passed out of the Sound without being detected by the observation post on Fanning Head and met up with the *Arrow* off Cape Dolphin, both ships then turning to the east for the run back to the Battle Group. Ahead of them was the submarine *San Luis*, which had tracked both frigates as they approached the rendezvous and was now in an ideal position for an attack. Fortunately for the latter, the *San Luis'* fire-control computer was unserviceable and although a manually-calculated attack was possible, not more than one wire-guided SST-4 torpedo could be fired and controlled at a time. *Capitan de Fregata* F. M. Azcueta fired at a range of 5,000 yards at about 0430, selecting the southerly of what he believed to be two destroyers. At no time did he use the periscope, all tracking and firing data being provided by his sonar. According to Azcueta's account,* the guidance wire broke after two and a half minutes, which corresponds with a torpedo: target closing speed of about 60 knots over two and a half miles. A few minutes later, when the frigates were close to the submarine, a 'small

---

* Interview, *US Naval Institute 'Proceedings'*, March 1984 edition, p. 119.

metallic explosion' was heard. Neither of the British ships reported any incident during this period but Paul Bootherstone recalls that when the *Arrow*'s towed torpedo decoy was retrieved later it was found to be badly damaged. At the time it was believed that it had touched the sea bed, but it now seems possible that the damage was caused by the *San Luis*'s torpedo. The submarine was unable to reach a firing solution in time for another manual attack before the frigates were drawing away from her, still ignorant that they had been so close to the enemy.

The *San Luis* had by now been in the patrol area to the north of East Falkland for a month, during which time she had surfaced only once, to effect repairs. After the first attacks, on 1 May, she had neither found, nor had she been detected by, British forces, whose activities had been mainly to the south and east of East Falkland. She had delivered one anti-submarine attack against a very doubtful target which had been tracked on sonar. As no Royal Navy submarine was in the vicinity of the Falkland Sound at the time of the attack, on the evening of 8 May, it must be presumed that the unfortunate victim was a whale. The submarine left for base on 11 May and was not relieved on patrol as the *Salta* was suffering from noise problems which were not to be cured until after the end of hostilities. There was thus a break in the watch on the approaches to the Falkland Sound at the critical period before and during the assault and build-up phase of the British operations. The *San Luis* did not turn round particularly quickly and she was not able to sail for a second patrol before the end of the fighting.

Capitan de Fregata Azcueta's modest claims of thwarted success were inflated by the Argentine propaganda machine and there arose a legend that the *Invincible* had been hit by a torpedo which failed to explode. This was seized upon by the British media and by the British Atlantic Committee, some of whose members persisted in restating the fiction long after the *Invincible* had been dry-docked and a minute examination of her hull had revealed no impact damage.*

The *Alacrity* had become the first ship of Task Group 317.8 to circumnavigate East Falkland, but before she rejoined the main body two more ships had proceeded further to the west. Argentine aircraft had flown over West Falkland during 10 May but had remained out of reach of the *Glasgow*'s Sea Dart. To remedy this lack of reach the *Broadsword* and *Coventry* were despatched to operate to the west of West Falkland between dawn and dusk on the 11th. Unfortunately for Admiral Woodward's plan to increase the rate of Argentine air attrition, the weather on this day was too foul at the mainland bases and there were no incursions at all, so the trap remained unsprung. The two ships returned to the carrier group early on 12 May.

The Carrier Battle Group was joined on the 11th by two supply ships,

British Atlantic Committee, *Diminishing the Nuclear Threat*, February, 1983.

A No 55 Squadron Victor tanker refuels a Nimrod over solid cloud (*MoD*)

Above right The *Uganda* in rough weather in the 'Red Cross Box', to the north of the Falkland Sound (*via Lt Cdr L.E. May RN*)

the stores RFA *Regent* and the BP STUFT tanker *British Esk*, which was to pump her cargo over to the *Olmeda* and *Appleleaf* when the weather moderated. Another arrival was the *Uganda*, but her non-combatant status forbade her joining the task group and she remained on the edge of the TEZ, awaiting an opportunity to embark the twenty-four wounded from the *Sheffield*. The unwounded survivors would be transferred to the *British Esk* and given passage to Ascension, whence they would be flown to the United Kingdom.

Further to the north, the second flight-refuelled Nimrod sortie, supported by four Victor tankers, gave support to the *Fearless* and *Antrim* groups by conducting a radar surface search out to a distance of nearly 3,000 miles towards South Georgia. Of more immediate benefit was the first long-range Hercules supply drop to the *Fearless*, then 1,300 miles south-west of Ascension. Thanks to the activities of the Fleet submarines, the Royal Navy had a good picture of the whereabouts of the main Argentine naval units, all of which were either in harbour or careful to remain inside their twelve-mile sanctuary zone. Commodore Clapp's other aerial visitors were a pair of Soviet Bears, taking a final look so far south.

Another high-level reconnaissance sortie was flown by an Ascension-based Nimrod on 12 May, this trip reaching a position 350 miles to the north-east of the Falklands. At 1247, when returning, 250 miles to the north-west of the *Antrim* group, the RAF crew sighted the enemy for the first and only time. This was no less than their opposite number, an Argentine Air Force Boeing 707 engaged on a surface search and shadowing mission. It is not known whether the 707 crew saw the Nimrod, but a direct result of this unique encounter was the fitting of Sidewinder missiles to qualify the Nimrod as the largest fighter of all time.

The weather in the TEZ during the morning of 12 May was still poor. The *Brilliant* and *Glasgow* appeared off Port Stanley for their day on the line, the Type 42 opening fire before daybreak. By noon the weather had

An 800 Squadron SHAR begins its take-off run from the *Hermes'* rolling deck for a CAP and harassing strike sortie, armed with a pair of Sidewinders on the outboard pylons and a 30mm Aden cannon in each of the two under-fuselage fairings. The two 100-gallon (454-litre) jettisonable tanks were a standard load for all missions and this aircraft is also carrying a 1,000lb (454 kg) bomb on the fuselage centre-line *(MoD)*

improved sufficiently for the *Hermes* to launch the first routine CAP since the 9th and these aircraft carried out the first high-level raid on the airfield area, four 1,000lb bombs being dropped by radar aiming.

Three-quarters of an hour later the *Brilliant* detected a raid heading towards her, approaching overland from the north-west. She and the *Glasgow* were fifteen miles south of Port Stanley, 'resting' between bombardments, and thus had plenty of sea-room for their missile systems to acquire, track and fire before the attackers could reach bomb-release point. The CAP would not have time to engage before the raid entered the 'missile engagement zone'.

The *Glasgow*'s Type 909 directors picked up the target – four A-4Bs of V Air Brigade – but the Sea Dart loading system then failed safe, the launcher computer refusing to accept the two missiles. As soon as the Skyhawks came within range, fire was opened with the 4.5in gun. This had fired sixty-seven rounds without trouble during the morning, but it now jammed after eight rounds. Two automatic systems had now failed, leaving the *Brilliant*'s Sea Wolf as the next-to-last-ditch defence. With the strike aircraft little more than a mile away, the *Brilliant*'s system fired three missiles in rapid succession. Two of these scored direct hits, blowing their victims apart. The target of the third, flying at wave-top height, took violent evasive action and flew into the rough sea. The system could not re-engage the surviving Skyhawk in time to prevent it from releasing a 1,000lb bomb at the *Glasgow* – too early, for the bomb ricochetted off the water over the roof of the destroyer's hangar. The aircraft escaped undamaged and the pilot, *Alferez* A. J. A. Vazquez, made his lonely way back to base (where he ran off the runway on landing) to report the loss of his leader, *Primer Teniente* M. O. Bustos, and his fellow-wingmen, *Tenientes* J. R. Ibarlucea and M. V. Nivoli.

This attack was delivered at 1644. Twenty minutes later another raid was detected heading for the two ships. The *Glasgow*'s weapons engineers were still working to clear the launcher snag and the jammed gun, but the *Brilliant*'s success had given everyone confidence in the Sea Wolf system. The next four A-4Bs to attack, led by *Capitan* Zelaya, adopted a different approach, weaving to upset the close-range gunners' aim. The Sea Wolf system was also confused. It had been designed to deal with multiple missile attacks, but missiles do not indulge in mutual weaving and the computer was perplexed. As a computer understands only 'yes' or 'no', whereas a human operator would think 'Let's give it a try', the *Brilliant*'s GWS25 system decided to do nothing and, figuratively, folded its arms. In practice, at the moment when it was expected to fire, the system trained the launchers, which had been pointing at the approaching Skyhawks, to their fore-and-aft positions. The emotions of those who were aware of what had happened are better imagined than described, particularly as they were also aware that there was no time left to re-engage with television guidance.

The last-ditch defences were already in action. These consisted of a single 40mm Bofors on the *Brilliant*'s upper deck, one 20mm Oerlikon on the *Glasgow*'s bridge-wing and an assortment of GPMGs, LMGs and rifles. These scored hits on at least one aircraft, but they could not stop the attack and bombs were released at both ships. At least one bomb skipped over the *Brilliant* but the *Glasgow* was hit amidships by a 1,000lb bomb which entered the side three feet above the waterline and left through the other side at about the same height, without exploding.

The four Skyhawks did not attempt a re-attack but flew off to the northwest, still at low level to avoid the Sea Harrier CAP, and crossed the coast near Goose Green. Their approach had been detected by the Army AA battery's Skyguard radar and handed off as a target to the Super Fledermaus fire-control system. The Skyhawks had approached from a direction used by Sea Harriers in their two attacks on Goose Green, *VYCA 2* had not given warning of 'friendlies' in the area and the incoming aircraft were not recognized before the twin 35mm guns opened fire. The aircraft flown by *Primer Teniente* F. Gavazzi, who had led the section which scored the hit on HMS *Glasgow*, was hit and crashed on the airfield. The unfortunate pilot was buried next to Lieutenant Nick Taylor.

The *Glasgow* had had what appeared to be a near-miraculous escape but her problems were by no means at an end. The bomb had passed through the upper part of the Auxiliary Machinery Room, demolishing high-pressure airlines, the intakes for the Tyne gas-turbine engines and a diesel fuel tank, whose contents drenched the watchkeeper in the compartment, Mechanician Waddington, who otherwise escaped injury. Fortunately, there was no fire. The destroyer still had propulsive power, she would be able to fight when the Sea Dart and gun problems had been sorted out and her immediate pre-occupation was preventing the ingress of water through the three-foot holes on each side. The well-drilled damage control parties quickly improvised plugs as the ships withdrew on a course intended to minimize rolling, but long-term waterproofing would not be possible until the immediate threat of further attack was past and outside help was available.

At 1800, three-quarters of an hour after the second attack, a third Argentine formation was detected. Captain Coward declined the *Hermes'* offer of a reinforced CAP; he had full confidence in his Sea Wolf's back-up TV guidance system and the *Glasgow*'s main weapons were once again operational. The Argentine strike circled over West Falkland and then withdrew without attempting to approach. The *Brilliant* and *Glasgow* rejoined the Battle Group after dark and technical teams and equipment were flown to the latter to assist with repairs.

The V Air Brigade's strikes had been successful in their object, which had been to drive away the bombardment group, which was inflicting a steadily increasing number of casualties and appreciable damage. Admiral Woodward had now only one intact Type 42 destroyer (the *Coventry*) and this ship could not be risked for offensive operations until reinforcements were nearer at hand. The nearest, the *Exeter*, was still two days to the north-west of Ascension and the *Cardiff* had only that day left Gibraltar. Doubts had also been raised about the Sea Wolf system, but the *Brilliant*'s own operators and engineers very quickly identified the cause of the failure and devised an effective remedy which considerably broadened the computer's outlook and enabled the *Brilliant*'s missiles to be used against weaving attacks.

The *Glasgow*'s story over the few days which followed was an epic of hard work and ingenuity to overcome multiplying difficulties. The slight improvement in the weather gave way to another gale and the shipwrights labouring to weld patches over the holes spent long hours soaked by the incoming water. Not until early on 15 May was the work completed and the destroyer regarded as fully seaworthy. She still had serious problems even then. At the time of being hit, one Olympus main engine was inoperative with a suspect main bearing and the other was giving cause for concern. With both Tynes unusable after their air intakes had been ruptured, the ship was now entirely dependent upon the remaining Olympus and a failure in the propeller shaft automatic speed control meant that this had to be controlled manually. The replenishment fuel line had also been destroyed by the bomb and a lash-up rig had to be improvised before Captain Hoddinot could attempt a much-needed RAS, in a full gale, on one engine and one hand-controlled propeller.

The gale added another ship to the 'sick list', further reducing Admiral Woodward's offensive capability. The frigate *Arrow* had developed some structural cracking during the bad weather experienced on the way south and during the earlier operations in the TEZ, and this had been exacerbated by her grinding against the *Sheffield* during the firefighting and rescue operations, which had added ten dents and three small holes forward, as well as buckling some frames. The frames had been shored, the holes patched, and the cracks drilled to prevent them from running further. The gale on 13 and 14 May extended the cracks in the decks so that they went beyond the aluminium superstructure and threatened the integral strength of the steel hull. Proper repairs were beyond the Battle Group's resources and would have to await the arrival of the repair ship *Stena Seaspread* and her 162-strong team of naval technicians, who were by now at South Georgia, picking over the scrap metal with the *Endurance*'s engineers, looking for suitable plates and girders to supplement their stock of raw material. Until assistance could arrive, the *Arrow* had to be handled with care, although she remained fit for combat. Her sister-ship, the *Alacrity*, was also suffering from cracking and although her defects were as yet less serious, they were treated with considerable respect.

During the excitement in the immediate aftermath of the second attack on the *Glasgow*, the *Hermes* lost a Sea King of 826 Squadron. The aircraft ditched while on the anti-submarine screen but was seen by the crew of another helicopter: the four members of the lost aircraft's crew were re-covered without fuss and returned to the carrier by 1800.

The *Uganda* received her first casualties on the 12th, these being the injured (mainly burned) from the *Sheffield*, transferred from the care of the Surgical Support Team in the *Hermes* to an atmosphere more closely resembling a hospital, complete with Queen Alexandra's Royal Naval Nursing Sisters (QARNNS). On the next day the *Uganda* was joined by the ocean survey ship HMS *Hecla* which, as an 'Ambulance Ship', was to ferry convalescent casualties to Ascension, whence they would be flown to the United Kingdom.

Elsewhere, the third-oldest ship in Admiral Woodward's force, the *Plymouth*, celebrated her 21st birthday in company with the LSLs, which were being brought further south to a position where they would meet up with the faster ships of the Amphibious Group, now five days outbound from Ascension. RMS *Queen Elizabeth 2* sailed from Southampton with the three battalions of 5 Infantry Brigade on board. The *Canberra* had already received the nickname of 'The Great White Whale'; uncharitably, 3 Commando Brigade bestowed that of 'The Black Pig' on the pride of the Cunard fleet. One of the ships supporting this second landing force, the RFA helicopter support ship *Engadine*, had sailed from Devonport on 9 May with four Wessex 5s and the personnel of 847 and 825 Squadrons on board. She broke down to the north of Cape Finisterre on 12 May, but her small engine-room staff managed to carry out a major component change within twenty-four hours, a task which would normally have required her to seek dockyard assistance.

The tugs *Salvageman* and RMAS *Typhoon*, which had been loitering to the west of Tristan da Cunha for several days, were ordered to close South Georgia, the *Salvageman* to be prepared to come to the edge of the TEZ to assist HMS *Glasgow* if need be. The big merchant tug put into Grytviken on 15 May, a day ahead of the slower *Typhoon*, and sailed on the 16th, after refuelling from the newly-arrived RFA *Blue Rover*. The *Endurance* was no longer alone at South Georgia, as she had been since 2 May (apart from Mike Company of 42 Commando), and Captain Nick Barker was beginning a busy period which was to last until the end of the campaign, in which he served as Senior Naval Officer and ex-officio Queen's Harbour Master, co-ordinating local movements and stores and personnel transfers in anchorages which were among the roughest and most exposed and inhospitable in the world. He had left his largest survey boat, the *James Caird*, at Port Stanley, but her place was taken by a day-glo orange LCVP (Landing Craft, Vehicles and Personnel) left behind by the evicted Argentinian scrap dealers and rechristened '*James Turd*' by her new owners. Among the most useful of his 'auxiliary craft', however, were the five 'Ellas', the STUFT and commissioned minesweeping trawlers, which left Ascension on the 13th and proceeded direct to South Georgia.

Other southbound departures on this day were the *Antelope* (for the second time) and her sister-ship *Ambuscade*, which had served as guardship at Gibraltar and then at Ascension until the arrival of the new HMS *Dumbarton Castle*. *Sir Bedivere*, after her 'dashes' across and down the Atlantic, sailed unescorted and another solo departure was that of HMS *Onyx*, the only 'conventional' diesel-electric submarine to be deployed for 'Corporate'. She was, in fact, the fifth Royal Navy submarine to cross the Equator, having been preceded by the fourth nuclear-powered vessel, HMS *Valiant*.

The weather on 13 May was bad in the TEZ and at the continental airfields, so that neither CAP nor strike sorties were flown, and the main preoccupation of the Battle Group was with the *Glasgow*. During the forenoon of the 14th 801 Squadron CAP missions tossed eight 1,000lb bombs at Port Stanley airfield and another two were added by 800 Squadron during the early afternoon. Photographs of the airfield taken from medium altitude on 12 May by 800 Squadron had revealed that the original crater caused by the Vulcan attack on 1 May had not been filled in but it was assessed that the full length of the reduced-width runway was available for C-130 landings and take-offs. Lobbing air-burst and long-delay-fuzed bombs could not be expected to close the runway, but they certainly discomfited the enemy and were the only form of harassment possible until the arrival of more gun-armed vessels to resume the bombardments.

At 1830 on the 14th the *Hermes*, with the *Broadsword* as her close-range 'goalkeeper' and the *Glamorgan* in support, detached from the Battle Group and steamed to a position to the north of East Falkland. The carrier flew off two of her four Sea King 4s on 'routine' Special Forces support missions and, half an hour before midnight, the other two, with forty-five men of D Squadron SAS and a naval gunfire support team on board

These parties were landed on the north coast of Pebble Island, three miles from the Argentine base on the airstrip, and set off overland. They arrived undetected and were able to place demolition charges on eleven aircraft – six Pucaras, a Coast Guard Short Skyvan light transport and four aircraft which they could not identify but reported as 'Macchis' (they were actually the T-34C Turbo-Mentors of the Navy's 4th Naval Attack Squadron) – among a dump of about a ton of assorted ordnance and, in groups of three, at the thresholds and intersection of the two landing strips. Not until the charges were detonated (with complete success) did the Argentine garrison react, opening fire with small arms and setting off their own prepositioned defensive charges. The NGS team called down fire from the *Glamorgan*, which fired ninety rounds of 4.5in to cover the retreat and extraction of the raiders. The helicopters, which had returned to the *Hermes* after the initial insertion, arrived to pick up the troopers and gunnery spotters and all were back on board an hour before dawn, seven hours after leaving the ship. One man had a gunshot wound, another was suffering from slight concussion from the explosion of the Argentine defensive mines.

This successful raid heartened everyone involved in the operation, in the South Atlantic, on their way out and in the UK headquarters organization. Never before had such a distant operation been followed in 'real time', all the delay and suspense being overcome by satellite voice communications and morse transmission and signals distribution. Admiral Fieldhouse and his Fleet staff at Northwood were in firm control of the overall campaign, with its many interwoven and interdependent components, under the general direction of the Chiefs of Staff, who were, in turn, responsible through the Chief of the Defence Staff, Admiral of the Fleet Sir Terence Lewin, to the 'War Cabinet'. The Navy Department had a well-practiced crisis management system which provided material, men, fuel and stores. Naval officers and civil servants surveyed, requisitioned and converted merchant ships, co-ordinated *ad hoc* trials to prove tactical and technical improvements and advised on their front-line use, and obtained diplomatic clearance for necessary visits to neutral countries. This comprehensive service was provided twenty-four hours a day, while the normal peacetime business continued to be conducted, leaving the Commander-in-Chief free to direct the conduct of the war and to decide how best to use all the men, material and advice.

One of the decisions secured was for the declaration of 'Active Service' at midnight on 14/15 May. Everyone at sea, Merchant Navy crews, NAAFI staffs, Chinese laundrymen and even the media correspondents, was now subject to Service discipline (although this would be exercised only *in extremis*), was covered by the provisions of the Geneva Convention and was, if the worst came to the worst, assured that his estate was free from death duties.

The weather on 15 May continued poor, with cloud preventing

planned photographic reconnaissance sorties to cover Port Stanley, Pebble Island and Fox Bay, where a merchant ship had been reported. The high-level bombers were in action, 801 Squadron dropping seven 1,000 bombs on Port Stanley airfield, Sapper Hill and a helicopter support base discovered near Mount Kent. 800 Squadron CAPs tossed six air-burst bombs at the airfield during the afternoon, upsetting the residents. As on the previous day, one of the bombs appeared to detonate prematurely when passing through 10,000 feet. At the time this was surmised to be a fuze failure, but subsequent claims made by the French Aerospatiale company suggest that one of the bombs was destroyed by one of their Roland missiles and it may be that this was the cause of the other 'premature' as well.

The Carrier Battle Group operated to the east of the Falklands in rough seas, untroubled by any Argentine activity. The *Glasgow*'s patches were standing up well to the stress and, now running on both of her Olympus main engines, she was able to resume her place on the picket line with the *Coventry*. Distant support was again provided by a flight-refuelled Nimrod, which took off before dawn and flew to a position just outside the TEZ before sweeping north within radar range of the Argentine coast to confirm that no hostile warships were out. Three contacts detected 600 miles north of the Falklands were assessed by the naval staffs as being merchant ships. The fourth nuclear-powered submarine, HMS *Valiant*, joined the close blockade during the third week in May, giving further insurance against a surprise sortie by the disheartened Argentine surface fleet.

A further blow to the Argentine Navy was the loss of its long-range air reconnaissance and shadowing capability. On 15 May the last serviceable Neptune finally gave up the ghost, never to fly operationally again. Two Embraer EMB.111 offshore patrol variants of the Bandeirante light transport aircraft had been leased from the Brazilian Government for the duration of hostilities, but these lacked the endurance needed for long hours of shadowing at up to 500 miles radius from base and, although they flew many sorties during and after the war, they were returned to Brazil and no new aircraft were ordered. The Super Etendards were thus without a targeting link and an alternative source of up-to-date information had to be sought.

For obvious reasons the Boeing 707s could not provide a tactical reconnaissance service, and two of their later strategic missions could have proved to be disastrous. The first of these occurred on 15 May when a 707 overflew the main body of the Amphibious Group. One Sea Harrier of 809 Squadron had not been swaddled in a DriClad protective cocoon for the passage south but was available for defensive sorties aboard the *Atlantic Conveyor*. Unfortunately, when the Argentine aircraft overflew at 1630 on the 15th, the weather was too bad to attempt a vertical take-off and recovery on the ship's relatively small platform, much to the chagrin of her Senior Naval Officer, Captain Mike Layard RN, and her Master, Captain Ian North, whose enthusiasm for his unaccustomed role knew few bounds.

The weather began to clear in the Falklands area during the late afternoon of the 15th. Two ships detached from the Battle Group for inshore operations, first the *Alacrity*, to repeat her transit of the Falkland Sound and then, an hour after sunset, the *Brilliant*, to investigate the ship reported at Fox Bay. Commander Craig had an uneventful northbound passage through the Sound and dropped off two Gemini-loads of Marines of the SBS in Grantham Sound without attracting the attention of the Argentinians. After recovering the inflatables, he launched his Lynx to stir up the defenders of Port Howard while the *Alacrity* ran through the 3-mile-wide northern exit in bright moonlight, under the Argentine observation post on Fanning Head.

The *Brilliant* was approaching the southern entrance to the Sound as the *Alacrity* was leaving, at about an hour after midnight. She launched one of her Lynxes to look into Fox Bay but the defenders here were alert and the helicopter was unable to get close enough to drop flares to identify the ship, due to heavy and accurate AA fire. Thwarted, Captain Coward returned to the Battle Group by dawn, as did the *Alacrity*.

The 801 Squadron CAP dropped three more 1,000lb bombs on Port Stanley airfield during the forenoon of 16 May. As soon as it became apparent that the Argentine Air Force was not going to take advantage of the better weather, *Hermes* flew off two armed reconnaissance missions, each comprising a pair of bomb-armed Sea Harriers. At 1650 the first pair saw a large merchant ship off Port King, on the East Falkland shore of the Falkland Sound and attacked it first with bombs and then with cannon. The target was the freighter *Rio Carcaraña*, now empty but unwilling to run the blockade back to Argentina: although the 800 Squadron pilots believed that they had scored only near misses with their bombs, they had actually hit her with two bombs, destroying a substantial part of the accommodation and causing flooding. The crew abandoned their vessel and made their way to Port Howard. An hour later the second Sea Harrier pair finally managed to identify the Fox Bay target, which was not the *Bahia Paraiso* (declared as a hospital ship since 8 May) as had been reported but the older, Canadian-built *Bahia Buen Suceso*. The 3,000-ton naval auxiliary was secured too close to the civilian settlement at Fox Bay West for the Sea Harrier pilots to use their bombs without risk of hitting the houses and they therefore attacked only with their 30mm guns. The heavy explosive shells were sufficient to cause considerable damage in the engine room, which caught fire, and extensive superficial damage to the upper deck fittings. The AA fire was heavy and accurate, one fighter returning with a bullet hole in its fin.

Later in the afternoon another 800 Squadron sortie was flown to photograph the two damaged ships, Port Darwin, Moody Brook and Port

Stanley airfield. The shots brought back appeared to show another bomb crater on the runway. The Argentine Air Force unit running the airfield had become cunning and was artistically simulating bomb craters, using bulldozers to build piles of mud which were then shaped to deceive cameras and the human eye and which could be scraped off at night to permit the landing of Air Force C-130s and Navy Lockheed Electras.

The almost-nightly air transport runs from the mainland to Port Stanley had by mid-May been developed into a well-drilled routine. A minimum of radio communications was used and the navigational radio beacon was turned on only briefly at the inbound aircraft's request. *VYCA 2* monitored the approach and departure, warning of the presence of Sea Harriers and advising the AA defences, so that they would not engage the friendly transport. The field hospital was also alerted and sick and wounded were brought up to the airfield in ambulance vehicles to be ready for embarkation. Airfield lighting was minimal, with just five dim lights across the ends of the runway and pairs of low-intensity lead-in and overshoot lights to assist the pilots to line up with the runway. High-intensity approach lights were available but could rarely be used as they could be seen from a great distance by the blockading forces as well as the inbound aircraft. Once on the ground, the aircraft kept their engines running and did not leave the runway while they were being unloaded and then embarked personnel. The turn-round rarely exceeded 10–15 minutes. From 1 May the C-130s provided the only source of aviation fuel brought into the islands, their surplus over what was needed to get them back to the mainland safely being drained off and stored in drums and flexible 'pillow tanks' hidden underground and in natural gullies around the airfield. Even after the loss of the *Isla de los Estados*, with nearly 90,000 Imperial gallons of aviation fuel, *BAM Malvinas* never ran critically short.

As well as the reception of aircraft and the construction of dummy craters, the Air Force detachment appears to have been responsible for most of the repair work on the peninsula. The damage inflicted on the parking and taxiing areas, the AA crews' bunkers and airfield buildings had to be repaired during daylight hours, the nights being taken up with cargo reception or the ships' bombardments which caused most of the damage and inflicted most of the Air Force casualties, which amounted to five men killed and eighteen wounded during the campaign.

During the night of the 16/17th, Admiral Woodward resumed bombardments, sending the *Glamorgan* inshore to harass and interdict the southern coast of East Falkland. This night's activity, during which 130 rounds of 4.5in were fired at targets in the Darwin, Fitzroy and Port Stanley areas, was the beginning of a series in which the *Glamorgan*, commanded by Captain M. E. Barrow, was to make this sector peculiarly her own. The Argentine artillery usually replied to her fire and she was the first ship to be engaged by 155mm guns, flown in from 15 May, but she was not touched until her ninth bombardment mission, when a more accurate weapon was used. Her Wessex 3 helicopter was employed for spotting the fall of her shot and frequently came under AA fire, but it too escaped damage by the guns.

16 May had been particularly successful for the Carrier Battle Group and it also marked the concentration of all the units of the Amphibious Group for the final approach to the TEZ. The *Antrim* Group had been joined on 14 May by the water tanker *Fort Toronto* (whose bright green funnel had not been altogether welcome) so that when Task Group 317.0 was finally 'integrated', an hour after sunset, there were fifteen RFAs and STUFT, led by the landing ships (LPDs) *Fearless* and *Intrepid* and screened by the *Antrim*, *Plymouth*, *Argonaut* and *Ardent*. Although only 700 miles south-east of Mar del Plata, the assembled Group was not found by the Argentine Air Force on this or the following days. Commodore Clapp briefed his commanding officers and RFA and merchant Masters during the next day, so that the transports, escorts and troops to be landed would have a clear understanding of their personal roles and objectives on 'D'-Day, now only four days away.

17 May is Argentina's 'Navy Day', usually the occasion for a public holiday. It was reasonably expected by the British that this particular Navy Day would be marked by some determined offensive action and, as it was known that the surface fleet was bottled up and suspected that the submarine force was in harbour,* it was anticipated that this would take the form of a Super Etendard Exocet attack. The carriers' offensive air activity was limited to a pre-dawn mission by a pair of *Invincible*'s Sea Harriers which tossed Lepus flares to cover Special Forces movements and then a couple of 1,000lb bombs lofted at Port Stanley airfield by the same ship's first CAP of the day. Thereafter, the only mission to cross the coast was an 800 Squadron photographic trip, which brought back pictures of Fox Bay, Goose Green, Port King and settlements in Lafonia, returning just after noon. The Sea Harriers were otherwise retained for defensive CAP over the Battle Group, to guard against Exocet attack, two fighters being airborne on station at all times up to dusk.

The Argentine Navy did attempt a Super Etendard attack. Since 1 May a naval operations cell with *VYCA 2* had been providing a rough plot of the carriers' movements by observing the tracks of the CAPs and strikes. The information had been passed to BAN Rio Grande and used to plan the Neptunes' shadowing missions but, with the demise of these aircraft, no 'fine tuning' was now possible. The senior aviators in the British carriers – Captain Linley Middleton RN of the *Hermes* (the only naval pilot in TG 317.8 with previous fixed-wing combat experience), the Commanders (Air) of *Hermes* and *Invincible*, Robin Shercliff and Francis Milner, and

---

* There was some slight doubt concerning the old submarine *Santiago del Estero*, which was thought to be unfit for any form of service. To be completely safe, however, HMS *Endurance* was warned to take precautions against an attack on South Georgia, the only possible 'safe' target for the submarine.

the Admiral's Staff Aviation Officer, Commander Christopher Hunney-ball, were well aware of the dangers of a regular traffic pattern and simple but effective deception measures had been taken to mislead the radar watchers at Port Stanley. Thus, when the pair of Super Etendards popped up to target their Exocets, their Agave radars swept a completely empty sea, instead of showing the ships which had been expected. HMS *Brilliant* detected and correctly identified the Agave transmissions, but no radar contacts were picked up by any ship or by the CAP which had been sent out down the bearing of the 'racket'. The Super Etendards, having failed to find the task group, did not invite interception by persisting with a search and returned to base with their missiles.

During the afternoon, some of TG 317.8's helicopters were re-shuffled, in anticipation of the arrival of the *Atlantic Conveyor*'s cargo. The *Hermes*, whose hangar and flight deck parking space would be strained by the additional Sea Harriers and RAF Harriers, detached four Sea King 5s of 826 Squadron to RFA *Fort Austin*, in exchange for three smaller helicopters, two Lynxes and the Wessex 5 'gunship' of 848 Squadron. Two 846 Squadron Sea King 4s were loaned to *Invincible* for the night. The *Invincible* also embarked the *Fort Austin*'s third Lynx, which, like one of the two transferred to *Hermes*, was fitted with a jammer tailored to counter the Exocet homing head. Another anti-missile device was a radar reflector being fitted to anti-submarine Sea Kings. The Exocet radar and computer had no way of telling that a contact in its field of view was not actually touching the sea and, if distracted, would fly harmlessly under the helicopter, away from its intended target.

The *Hermes* and *Invincible* parted company in late afternoon, the former to rendezvous outside the TEZ with the *Atlantic Conveyor* and the latter on a special operation. Another of *Hermes*' Sea King 5s was lost during the evening, the crew being picked up after their helicopter ditched due to an instrument malfunction. The aircraft floated but could not be salvaged and had to be sunk by gunfire.

The *Invincible*, with her 'goalkeeper' HMS *Brilliant* in company, was meanwhile heading west at high speed, darkened and with all radars silent but ready for immediate operation should any Argentine radar transmissions be intercepted. During the night, when well to the west of the islands, the carrier increased speed, surpassing the best she had exceeded on trials, to fly off a heavily-laden Sea King 4. The carrier and frigate then turned back to be well clear of the early morning reconnaissance missions before dawn.

The purpose of the Sea King's one-way sortie has been the subject of much speculation since the damaged aircraft was found on a sand-spit 10 miles to the east of Punta Arenas on 20 May. The two pilots and the air crewman gave themselves up to the Chilean authorities, who, after interrogation and allowing the Press to interview them, released the three men. According to their statements, they had become lost in bad weather while reconnoitring the coast of Tierra del Fuego and, short of fuel, had flown up the Straits of Magellan until they found a suitable landing area in neutral Chile. The Britons were deported to the United Kingdom, where they enjoyed a brief leave before returning to the South Atlantic to rejoin 846 Squadron. After the campaign, all three were decorated: Lieutenant R. Hutchings RM and Lieutenant A. R. C. Bennett RN, the pilots, received Distinguished Service Crosses, while Leading Aircrewman P. B. Imrie was awarded a Distinguished Service Medal.

The *Invincible* was still well within the TEZ at daybreak on 18 May. She had begun flying some three hours earlier, flying off two Sea Harriers to divert Argentine attention with a Lepus flare display. The first three CAP missions dropped another six 1,000lb bombs on Port Stanley airfield, but thereafter 801 Squadron flew only two more sorties on that day.

During the morning the first of four Sea Harriers of 809 Squadron landed on board the *Hermes*, having taken off from the *Atlantic Conveyor*. The aircraft transport had proceeded ahead of the Amphibious Group, with the MARTSU team and a score of RAF Harrier maintenance personnel preparing the fourteen fighters for transfer, removing the protective covers and carrying out routine checks. Many of the RN Wessex and RAF Chinook ground crews were aboard the STUFT *Europic Ferry*, astern with the Amphibious Group, and the preparation of the helicopters would have to wait until they caught up and could be transferred to the *Atlantic Conveyor*, by which time the jets would be out of the way. Three more Sea Harriers and four RAF Harriers took off from the transport and landed aboard the *Hermes* during the next two hours. The Commanding Officer of 809, Lieutenant-Commander T. H. Gedge, flew the first of the reinforcements for *Invincible*. His squadron, which had been in existence for only thirty-seven days, twenty-one of them spent on passage, was to be integrated into 801 and 800, which between them had already absorbed 899 Squadron's aircraft and personnel.

Three hours after their arrival, the *Hermes'* new pilots, who had had no practice since leaving the United Kingdom, were flown off for refamiliarization – an interception exercise, air combat manoeuvring and deck-landing practice being packed into a 75-minute flight. At 1900, while they were airborne, the Carrier Battle Group (TG 317.8) and the Amphibious Group (TG 317.0) rendezvoused. The thirty-two ships in company provided an unforgettable sight for those privileged to be present.*

---

* The Argentine Air Force missed the occasion, but any gap there may have been in the opposition's knowledge was promptly filled by the Overseas Service of the BBC, which told the world that 'the troopships have now joined the main force of warships'. Very few of those aboard the ships admired such determination to tell the truth whatever the consequences.

During the night of 18/19 May the *Glamorgan* again closed the southern coast of East Falkland and fired 100 4.5in shells at targets between Port Stanley and Lively Island. 846 Squadron flew the last of its pre-invasion covert support sorties from the *Hermes*. Twenty-six such flights had been made on twelve nights since 1 May. The *Brilliant* and *Alacrity* patrolled to the north of the Falkland Sound but they saw no sign of Argentine activity and withdrew quietly, without trying to provoke any.

One of the four Nimrod 2P (the suffix denoted that the aircraft was fitted with a flight-refuelling probe) aircraft at Ascension flew an eighteen-hour surface search which brought it within fifty miles of the TEZ and then returned 250 miles off the Argentine coast. Although the Amphibious Group was now safely arrived, there was a stream of warships, RFAs and STUFT south of Ascension which needed some form of surveillance support, however slight the risk from surface or submarine attack. The 'ambulance' HMS *Hydra* was closest to the TEZ, her sister-ship *Herald* having detached to land an injured crew member at Rio de Janeiro on 18 May, but behind her and south of the latitude of the River Plate (35° South) were the STUFT support tanker *Anco Charger*, the 'despatch vessel' HMS *Leeds Castle*, the Type 21s *Ambuscade* and *Antelope*, the 'Ellas', RFA *Sir Bedivere* and HMS *Exeter*. Further north, but due to pass 35°S by D-Day, were the tankers *British Dart* and *British Test*, the Post Office despatch vessel *Iris*, the stores ship *Saxonia* and, bound for South Georgia, the ammunition ship *Lycaon*.

There was one ship northbound, the *British Esk*, carrying the *Sheffield*'s survivors and a solitary correspondent. The latter had complained, jointly with the BBC TV and ITV reporters, of the lack of facilities and had been offered a passage home. Unlike the television representatives, this news agency man had accepted and left the scene of action less than a week before the invasion. His cameraman decided to remain and was thus on hand to take what was without doubt the most dramatic photograph of the war. The *Esk* refuelled the *Exeter* on 19 May and Captain Balfour of the latter took the opportunity to discuss the *Sheffield*'s experiences with Captain Salt and, consequently, to modify his ship's company's training and damage control preparations.

The Battle and Amphibious Groups spent 19 May about 300 miles to the east-north-east of Port Stanley, reshuffling aircraft, assault units and any weapons and equipment that could be re-positioned in the time available. Inevitably the helicopters were heavily involved in the moves, but the major troop movements, from the *Canberra* to the *Fearless* and *Intrepid*, were carried out by the landing ships' LCVPs and LCUs (Landing Craft, Utility). This was not entirely popular with the soldiers and Marines. 3 Para, transferred to the *Intrepid*, regarded the LCUs with distaste, referring to them as 'rubbish skips', while 40 Commando RM, although more accustomed to this form of transport, spent two hours in *Fearless*' LCUs, an uncomfortable experience in the open ocean.

19 May 1982: RFA *Tidepool*, recalled while on passage to join the Chilean Navy, refuels HMS *Fearless* while HMS *Ardent* approaches to begin refuelling from one of the oiler's port rigs; RFA *Stromness* is in the background *(MoD)*

Sea King 4 'VT' of 846 Squadron floats inverted after crashing while approaching the *Intrepid* at dusk on 19 May *(MoD)*

Tragedy attended the only major troop movement by helicopter. Two hours after sunset an 846 Squadron Sea King transferring troopers of D Squadron 22 SAS from the *Hermes* to the *Intrepid* struck a large bird and crashed into the sea. The pilots, the aircrewman and five passengers were rescued by HMS *Brilliant*'s seaboat and the *Intrepid*'s LCVPs, but twenty-two others were lost, a toll which exceeded the loss of life in the *Sheffield*. Many of those on board the Sea King had already survived the two crashes on Fortuna Glacier and had taken part in the assault on Grytviken and the Pebble Island raid.

HMS *Hermes* was now up to her full strength of fifteen Sea Harriers and embarked another Harrier GR3 of No 1 Squadron during the 19th. Her two remaining Sea King 4s were flown off to the *Canberra* and the *Norland* embarked a spare Mark 4 which had been brought south in the *Elk*'s 'hangar'. COMAW's other immediate helicopter assets were four Wessex 5s of 845 Squadron, at present on board the *Resource* and *Tidepool*, and the eight other Sea King 4s of 846, already aboard the two LPDs. The six Wessex 5s of 848 Squadron and the four Chinooks of No 18 Squadron RAF would have to remain on board the *Atlantic Conveyor* until dispersals and refuelling facilities could be provided ashore, there being no flight deck space left on the amphibious shipping.

The *Invincible* remained inside the TEZ, covering the activity. An hour after dawn she launched four Sea Harriers, each armed with two 1,000lb air-burst bombs, for a strike on the Argentine helicopter forward operating base in the Mount Kent area, fifteen miles west of Port Stanley airfield. The islands were completely covered by low cloud and the bombs were lofted blind, using radar offsets to 'feed' the bomb-release and aiming computer. The remaining Sea Harriers of 809 Squadron were embarked in the *Invincible* from the *Atlantic Conveyor* later in the day (giving her ten fighters) and their pilots were flown on combined CAP and refamiliarization sorties.

The *Hermes*, now with twenty jets on board, used the day to acquaint the Air Force pilots of No 1 Squadron RAF with her procedures, and the sixteen Harrier GR3 familiarization sorties provided targets for the twenty-five Sea Harrier CAP sorties flown by her 'old' and 'new' pilots. The forty-one fighter sorties constituted a record for the *Hermes* at the time, but it was to be exceeded two days later in the campaign and never again were the RAF Harriers to fly so many sorties in one day. The GR3s (the Sea Harrier had already been abbreviated in signal and speech to 'SHAR') had been modified to carry and fire the AIM-9L Sidewinder, but their main role was 'offensive air support' for the assault force and it was not intended that they should be used in the interceptor of air superiority roles unless dire necessity (which meant catastrophic Sea Harrier losses) forced it upon the command. The GR3, besides being slightly slower than the SHAR, lacked the search and fire-control radar (which actually

The engine of an RAF Harrier GR3 is changed in the *Hermes*' hangar (the aircraft's wing is lashed to a trestle at the right of the picture). Behind, a Sea Harrier of 800 Squadron undergoes maintenance, while one of the Lynxes embarked on 19 May for electronic warning is parked on the far side of the hangar, under stowage racks for Sea King rotor blades *(MoD)*

pointed the Sidewinder's heat-seeking homing head at a target) and had a poorer all-round view from the cockpit. The pilots of No 1 Squadron had had only the briefest offensive air combat training in the Harrier, their normal air-to-air training being defensive, to stay out of trouble. Nevertheless, during the afternoon of 19 May, the Commanding Officer, Wing Commander P. T. Squire AFC, and Flight-Lieutenant J. Glover were launched, on their second familiarization trip, to intercept the Boeing 707, which had been detected at very long range and which turned back long before the fighters were able to get close. The GR3 was not employed in this fashion again.

During the night of 19/20 May Captain Barrow took the *Glamorgan* inshore again to disturb and damage the Argentine defenders between the entrance to Choiseul Sound and Cape Pembroke. One hundred and one 4.5in shells were fired before the destroyer broke off to return to join the Battle Group and re-ammunition.

'D Minus One' dawned with an overcast sky and visibility of two to three miles at sea level. Two hours later, at 1300, Admiral Woodward and Commodore Clapp were informed that the Prime Minister and her Cabinet had approved the invasion plan and that Operation 'Sutton', the assault on East Falkland, was to be mounted at 0630 the next day. The two Groups were still together, having entered the TEZ shortly after dawn, and at 1415 the Amphibious Group turned to the west, leaving the Carrier Battle Group to continue to the south-west, escorted only by the *Coventry* and *Glasgow* as radar pickets, the *Arrow* and *Alacrity* as 'goal-keepers' and the *Glamorgan* in support.

The last of the six GR3s of No 1 Squadron embarked in the *Hermes* at 1400 and an hour later the first offensive mission flown by the Royal Air Force from an aircraft carrier since October, 1918, was launched. Three GR3s armed with cluster-bomb units delivered a completely successful attack on a large, dispersed fuel dump at Fox Bay and returned without damage. One Sea Harrier flew a round-robin low-level photographic mission over the Falklands, but this was the only SHAR operation away from the Carrier Battle Group. Two aircraft were maintained on CAP until the late afternoon, with further sections held at immediate readiness on deck in case they were needed to defend the Amphibious Group. The only Argentine aircraft to be detected within the TEZ was a C-130 engaged on surface search, seventy-five miles south of Port Stanley, and over 150 miles from the carriers and even further from the invasion force on the other side of East Falkland.

At dusk the *Glamorgan* again detached for her south coast beat. From midnight she drew undivided attention, simulating landings by her helicopter and firing twenty-one 4.5in starshells and seventy-six high-explosive shells to divert the Argentine command from events developing in the north end of the Falkland Sound.

The three-week 'precursor' phase of operations had succeeded in two of its major objectives: the Argentine occupying forces were cut off from supply from the mainland, other than what could be flown in by the few transport aircraft, and the Argentine Navy was effectively eliminated as a serious opponent, although as long as it remained 'in being' forces had to remain allocated to deal with a possible sortie. Damage and casualties had been inflicted by ship bombardments, during which over 1,500 4.5in shells had been fired, and by Sea Harrier attacks, which had contributed over thirty tons of ordnance against land targets. The two RAF Vulcan attacks had delivered a further twenty-one tons, but only the first raid had been effective, at very high cost in fuel. So far the Argentine defences had been successful only in shooting down one Sea Harrier and possibly two 1,000lb bombs. The garrison was aware that Special Forces patrols were active on the main islands but had as yet found few traces of the reconnaissance teams and had not managed to track one down. The general level of alertness was low – the explosion which destroyed the *Isla de los Estados* had gone unnoticed, the Fanning Head look-outs failed to see the *Alacrity* less than three miles away in bright moonlight and the defenders of Pebble Island were taken completely by surprise.

Less satisfactory were the unwillingness of the Argentine Air Force to come out and suffer attrition and the manifest ability of the Navy Super Etendards to come out and inflict attrition. The Air Force had lost ten mainland-based jets out of the fifty-one which had reached the islands – a wastage rate which could not be sustained when there were no apparent compensating successes (news of the damage to the *Glasgow* was successfully withheld). The Super Etendards, on the other hand, had scored a spectacular and well-publicized success in hitting the *Sheffield*, but only one of their three missions had found a target and then only one of the two missiles fired had scored a hit. This attack was to influence the Carrier Battle Group's employment throughout the remainder of the campaign. Had some form of airborne early warning been available, the Super Etendards would have lost the invulnerability to interception which they enjoyed and the carriers could have operated farther to the west, with their Sea Harriers providing a continuous 'Blue Blanket' during daylight hours. As it was, they had to remain well to the east of Port Stanley, to force the Super Etendards to operate at least 450 miles from Rio Grande, beyond the strike aircraft's maximum unrefuelled radius of action. Even at this distance, the two carriers, with twenty-five SHARs between them, could maintain a standing CAP over the islands from dawn to dusk, but they would be unable to reinforce the defences quickly to meet specific raids on the amphibious operations.

The *Comando de la Fuerza Aerea Sur*, on the eve of the San Carlos invasion still had thirty-eight A-4 Skyhawks, two dozen Daggers and six Canberras available for strikes from the mainland, as well as the seven naval Skyhawks disembarked from the *25 de Mayo*, still operating under naval control. This force, if properly briefed and co-ordinated, and ready to learn swiftly from its experiences, was more than sufficient to inflict debilitating losses on the Royal Navy and its auxiliaries.

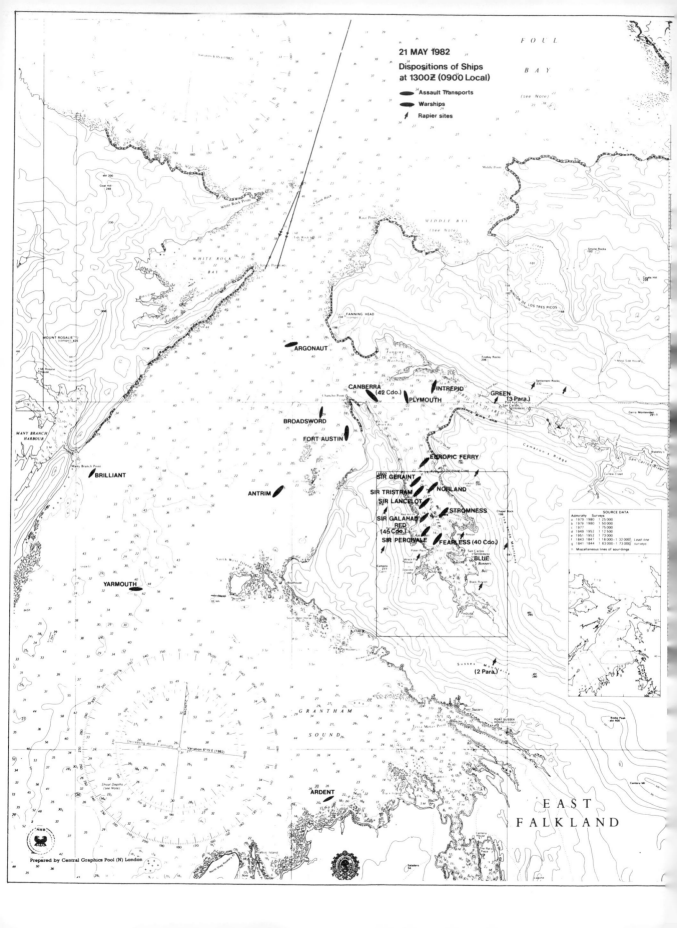

21 MAY 1982

Dispositions of Ships
at 1300Z (0900 Local)

Assault Transports

Warships

Rapier sites

FOUL BAY

ARGONAUT

CANBERRA
(42 Cdo.)

INTREPID

PLYMOUTH

GREEN
(3 Para.)

BROADSWORD

FORT AUSTIN

EUROPIC FERRY

BRILLIANT

SIR GERAINT

SIR TRISTRAM

SIR LANCELOT

NORLAND

ANTRIM

STROMNESS

SIR GALAHAD
RED
(45 Cdo.)

SIR PERCIVALE

FEARLESS (40 Cdo.)

BLUE

YARMOUTH

SOURCE DATA

	Admiralty	Surveys	
a	1979	1980	1 25 000
b	1979	1980	1 50 000
c	1977		1 75 000
d	1949	1952	1 12 500
e	1951	1952	1 73 000
f	1843	1847	1 18 000–1 32 000	*Lead line*
g	1841	1844	1 83 000–1 73 000	*surveys*
h	Miscellaneous lines of soundings		

GRANTHAM

SOUND

Sussex Mts.
(2 Para.)

ARDENT

EAST
FALKLAND

Prepared by Central Graphics Pool (N) London

PART IV

Chapter One

'D'-Day

Commodore Clapp began the run-in to the northern end of the Falkland Sound at 1415 (10.15am local time) on 20 May, when he detached from Admiral Woodward's Battle Group and turned to the west. Brigadier J. H. A. Thompson, the landing force commander, was in the *Fearless* with his Brigade headquarters and 40 Commando RM. This Commando and 2 Para, in the *Norland*, would constitute the first assault wave and would be followed by 45 Commando, split between RFA *Stromness* and HMS *Intrepid*, and 3 Para, in HMS *Intrepid*. 42 Commando, a company short since the detachment of M Company for the South Georgia operation nearly a month before, would remain aboard the *Canberra* in reserve until called forward. Supporting units – including the unique Commando Logistics Regiment, the eighteen 105mm guns of 29th Commando Regiment RA, the Royal Engineers of 59 Independent Commando Squadron, the light helicopters of the Commando Brigade Air Squadron and 656 Squadron Army Air Corps, 16 Field Ambulance RAMC and the Rapier missile troops of 'T' Battery, 12 Air Defence Regiment RA – were embarked in the *Europic Ferry* and the LSLs *Sir Galahad, Sir Geraint, Sir Lancelot, Sir Tristram* and *Sir Percivale*. These smaller vessels, the North Sea ferry and the purpose-built landing ships, were also carrying the vast stocks of provisions, stores and munitions needed to keep the five 'infantry' units and their supporting arms in the field for a lengthy campaign.

Close escort during the 12½-knot passage to the west was provided by the *Antrim, Broadsword, Brilliant, Plymouth, Yarmouth, Argonaut, Ardent* and RFA *Fort Austin*, the last-named providing continuous anti-submarine and surface clearance patrols, assisted by the *Antrim*'s Wessex 3, which was having to share the destroyer's none-too-generous deck and hangar space with a troop-carrying Wessex 5 of 845 Squadron. Close-range weapons crews closed up in all ships at noon but no Argentine aircraft or surface vessels were detected and the convoy passed unnoticed sixty miles north of Port Stanley. 'Darken Ship' was ordered early in the gloomy afternoon and, as sunset approached, the ships began to take up fresh dispositions as a preliminary to altering course for the run-in to the assault area.

At 4.00pm HMS *Antrim* and *Ardent* detached from the convoy and proceeded independently for the Falkland Sound, to reach their ordered positions. Four hours later the main body turned to the south-west, dividing into three separate columns, to arrive in successive waves. The first was made up of the two LPDs, escorted for the first part of their approach by the *Yarmouth*. These ships had the only landing craft – eight LCUs and eight LCVPs – and they required time to float out the LCUs and lower the LCVPs before the other troop-carrying ships came up. The second wave, consisting of the *Canberra*, *Norland* and *Stromness*, preceded by HMS *Plymouth* and with the RFA *Fort Austin* and the *Brilliant* bringing up the rear, was to arrive in the lowering area forty-five minutes later. Finally, the LSLs and *Europic Ferry*, escorted by the *Broadsword* and *Argonaut*, would begin to pass through the narrow entrance to the Falkland Sound four hours after the second wave.

A silent, unobserved approach was planned for the LPDs and 'troop-ships'. To ensure that any activity on the part of the Argentine contingent on Fanning Head was brief, Marines of 3 SBS and a bombardment observation team were landed as a special assault force. At 7.00pm the *Antrim* flew off her guest Wessex 5 with the first 'stick' of Marines, followed soon afterwards by her own Wessex 3. By 10.45pm the Wessex 3 had landed two sticks and had been stowed out of the way in the ship's hangar, while the Wessex 5 had landed the last of its five sticks and was on its way back to the ship, landing at 11.10pm. The flights had not been noticed by the Argentinians and the thirty-two men ashore advanced to lying-up positions to await the next stage of their operation.

Meanwhile, Commander A. W. J. West had taken the *Ardent* through the 2¼-mile-wide entrance to the Falkland Sound, under the 770-foot, steeply-sloping headland which dominated not only the Sound but also the entrance to the San Carlos inlets. His passage, at 8.00pm, went unnoticed, although at 30 knots the *Ardent* was leaving a broad wake and her progress was by no means silent. By 9.00pm she too was in position for her next phase, gunfire support for an SAS diversionary raid on Darwin. These troops were flown off from the LPDs by 846 Squadron and inserted undetected, but the ships were delayed by the need to find 'the right wind' for launching and recovering the Sea Kings and they were hard-pressed to make their scheduled entry time at the narrows. The *Antrim* entered the Sound at about 10.15pm, closely followed by the *Yarmouth*, which carried out an anti-submarine sweep, supported by two 826 Squadron Sea Kings from the *Fort Austin*, and established a patrol line between the North West Islands and Poke Point on the West Falkland shore. The destroyer closed the East Falkland coast and, from a position near Cat Island, covered the entrance of the first two waves of assault ships.

Captain E. S. J. Larken brought the *Fearless*, followed a mile astern by the *Intrepid*, through the narrows at 10.45pm, passing within 500 yards of

Jersey Point, opposite Fanning Head. Only when they were well inside the Sound did the two LPDs turn to close the East Falkland shore and run north again, past the *Antrim*, to anchor to the west of Chancho Point at 11.20pm and begin 'docking down' to float out their LCUs.

The next wave was already entering the narrows and the last ship, HMS *Brilliant*, was into the Sound ten minutes after midnight. She remained under the cliffs on the West Falkland side while the other five ships circled to the east, the *Fort Austin* anchoring inshore between Chancho Point and Cat Island and the *Norland*, *Canberra* and *Stromness* in a line off the entrance to the San Carlos inlet. The *Plymouth* entered the enclosed waters and took up a position from which her 4.5in guns commanded both arms – Port San Carlos to the east and the longer, broader San Carlos Water running to the south-south-east. The two ships which had provided covering fire for the Grytviken assault were therefore once again entrusted with this task.

The sky had cleared during the approach to the Sound and, although the new moon did not rise until two hours before dawn, visibility in the starlight was very good. Nevertheless, the Argentine look-outs on Fanning Head and the 1,400-foot Mount Rosalie on the West Falkland had failed to see or hear the passage of eleven ships, among which was one of the largest and most conspicuous passenger liners in the world, had not heard the helicopters clattering around (and below) their positions and had missed the unmistakeable din of ships anchoring less than two miles away. At 00.52am their slumbers were rudely disturbed as the *Antrim* fired two ranging salvoes at Fanning Head and then began to fire for effect on the directions of the observation team ashore. Steaming slowly in the Sound, about six miles from her target, the destroyer poured in 268 4.5in shells during the next half-hour. As soon as the bombardment was lifted, the SBS team stormed the position, where they found nine wounded and dazed defenders and twelve dead. A handful of others, some wounded, had made off during the shelling and were picked up during the days which followed, many of them suffering from exposure and frostbite. The observation post was found to be armed with a 106mm recoilless gun and 81mm mortars and to have modern night-viewing equipment. But for the incredible laxity of its occupants, it could have made life difficult for any of the ships passing through the narrows or for the assault ships as they came to anchor to the south of Fanning Head.

The Head was securely in the Marines' hands by 1.30am, an hour before the first troops were scheduled to 'hit the beach'. As the *Antrim*'s shells passed far overhead, the *Intrepid*'s landing craft moved over to the *Norland* to embark 2 Para. Delays were inevitable, for the soldiers' exercises with the ship had been curtailed and, although carefully briefed, they were not familiar with the drills. Nevertheless, the Royal Marine senior NCOs commanding the LCUs and LCVPs made up well for lost time. 40 Commando was able to embark while their LCUs were in the *Fearless'* dock.

Responsible for piloting the landing craft was Captain S. E. Southby-Tailyour RM. By one of those fortunate coincidences that sometimes attends enterprises such as 'Corporate', Ewen Southby-Tailyour was a skilled amateur yachtsman who, during a tour with the Falklands garrison, had compiled a cruising guide to the coasts and inlets of the islands. Not entirely surprisingly, no publisher had taken up a book which, up to April, 1982, had such a limited commercial appeal. The manuscript now became a major planning tool in the hands of Commodore Clapp's and Brigadier Thompson's staffs. Captain Southby-Tailyour acted as a principal adviser up to the landings and was thereafter given charge of the landing craft operations.*

Covered by the *Plymouth's* guns and with the Scorpions and Scimitars of the Blues and Royals in the bows of the LCUs to provide close support fire with their 76mm and 30mm guns, the craft made their way down the eight-mile arm of San Carlos Water. The Marines of 40 Commando went ashore at San Carlos Settlement, on the east side of the Water, at 3.30am, a few minutes after 2 Para, who had less distance to go to their beach as the *Norland* was anchored closer inshore than the *Fearless*, had reached the southern end and waded through the last few yards of shallow water. No opposition was encountered on either beach and while the Marines made their presence known to the residents, ran up the Union Flag and prepared defensive positions, the Paras climbed the Sussex Mountains, the 600-foot ridge from which they could look down on the most likely approach for a counter-attack by the nearest Argentine infantry units, from Darwin and Goose Green. These enemy troops by now had been aroused by what they thought was a battalion attack but which was a 'son et lumiere' production by D Squadron, 22 SAS, led by Major C. N. G. Delves. Much further away, the main force at Port Stanley was alert and anticipating landings in what the Argentine Governor and military commander, Brigadier Menendez, believed to be the most likely sector; the *Glamorgan's* starshell and high-explosive display was currently confirming that view.

The landing craft, whose real movements were still unknown to the defenders, made their way back to the landing ships. The *Fearless'* LCUs embarked two companies of 45 Commando from the *Stromness*, picking up the third company and independent Troops from the *Intrepid* on the way. The *Intrepid's* assault battalion, 3 Para, embarked in that ship's craft and the second 'flight' set off, the Marines for Ajax Bay, on the west shore of San Carlos Water, and the Paras for Port San Carlos. The LSLs entered the Falkland Sound under Fanning Head at 5.30am, as these troops were embarking, and after loitering under the West Falkland cliffs, they too

---

* Southby-Tailyour, *Falkland Islands Shores*, Conway Maritime Press, 1985.

A heavily-laden LCU, identifiable by its 'tiger stripes' as one of the *Fearless'*, runs in towards San Carlos Settlement *(MoD)*

approached the San Carlos inlet.

The *Canberra* moved into the inlet as the LSLs entered the Sound, thus becoming the first of the big ships to see San Carlos Water. She was, indeed, too big to risk right inside and she anchored again at 6.00am, three miles south-east of Fanning Head, a mile inside Chancho Point. As she did so, the *Norland* weighed anchor, followed by the *Stromness*, and these two ships passed into the Water astern of *Fearless'* second flight of landing craft, anchoring at about 6.30am. Some of the LSLs were already rounding Chancho Point, sticking to their timetable although the operation was running a little late. Thus the *Sir Percivale* (Captain A. F. Pitt RFA) overtook 45 Commando's LCUs and arrived off Ajax Bay at 7.00am, several minutes before they touched down. Turning his ship to bring his 40mm Bofors gun on the port side of the forecastle to bear on the beach, Captain Pitt made ready to lay down supporting fire if required. This landing, like the earlier ones in San Carlos Water, was unopposed and the gallant *Sir Percivale* was not called upon to succour the Marines in distress.

The only Argentines were at Port San Carlos, a half-company of infantry supporting the Fanning Head position. They did not react to the bombardment and seizure of the observation post, but appear to have realized that 'something was up' as 3 Para approached in the *Intrepid*'s landing craft, at about 6.45am, and hurriedly began to withdraw up the San Carlos River, exchanging shots with the leading paratroops.

The landing craft returned to their parent LPDs in preparation for what was to be a very long day's work, ferrying men and materials ashore. The LPDs themselves were preparing to move into San Carlos Water and the *Fearless* weighed anchor at 7.15am. Followed in by the *Europic Ferry*, which had remained out in the Sound after the LSLs had gone in to anchor, Commodore Clapp's flagship, with 3 Commando Brigade's HQ still on board, proceeded to the head of the Water and took up a position between San Carlos Settlement and Ajax Bay. The *Intrepid* was at the other end of the line of LSLs and store ships (as the *Stromness* and *Norland* had become after the landing of their troops).

It was now growing lighter and the men ashore and on the ships could see more of their surroundings. San Carlos Water extends five miles from Doctor's Head to the head of the inlet, shoaling to less than 33 feet (10 metres) depth in its last mile and a half. The width of the inlet is about a mile, with deep water close inshore as far up as the northern side of Ajax Bay. The only flattish areas of land with deep water approaches and beaches free of kelp are around the Settlement and the Refrigeration Plant at Ajax Bay, both at the foot of steep slopes which close in to the water's edge at the northern end of the water. The ridges which enclose the arm of the sea, Campito to the west and the Verde Mountains to the east, rise to over 650 feet and the 500-foot contour lines on either side are never more than three miles apart. Apart from the mile and a half-wide opening between Fanning Head and Chancho Point, which would give attacking pilots only two miles – fifteen seconds at 480 knots (550mph) – to complete their turns, select targets and line up for the attack, the only line of approach for low-level strikes was from the south-east, down the valley which ran along the northern side of the Sussex Mountains. Here pilots approaching at very low level would be able to see ships off Ajax Bay at least six miles away and would have to descend a relatively gentle slope to get down to near sea level.

So far the only ship to have engaged the Argentinians had been the *Antrim*, the lack of opposition leaving the watchful *Plymouth* without targets. As first light approached, however, the defenders of Darwin and Goose Green prepared to take on their assailants and the forward observer with the SAS called for fire from the *Ardent*, to interdict Goose

The LSLs off Ajax Bay, with Fanning Head in the background, seen from the *Fearless'* bridge-wing *(MoD)*

Green airfield, where Pucaras were preparing for take-off. The frigate was already in position, close to the kelp beds on the southern shore of Grantham Sound, 22,000 yards from the target. At this range, over a distance once attainable only by heavy cruisers and battleships,* Commander West's ship not only hit the runway area but destroyed an aircraft lining up for take-off. The bombardment, which began at 7.23am, was checked after twenty rounds but the flurry of activity which it provoked at Goose Green lasted for some while as the Air Force AA fire control radar was repositioned, its crew believing that this, rather than the Pucaras, was the main and most valuable target. The retiring SAS troopers requested further support from the *Ardent*, which fired over 150 rounds of 4.5in during the forenoon and early afternoon, despite the distraction of air attacks. She did not, however, manage to prevent the Pucaras from operating and at least four pairs managed to get airborne. The first of these came too close to the SAS and one was shot down by a Stinger shoulder-fired heat-seeking missile at about 7.55am. *Capitan* J. Benitez was the first Argentine pilot to be shot down on D-Day and was fortunate to survive and reach his base on foot.

The Argentine Army's potential for swift reaction to the landings, when the scale of the latter was at last realized, was reduced by a successful attack on the helicopter base near Mount Kent. Two GR3s of No 1 Squadron RAF struck at 7.45am, making several strafing passes to destroy a Chinook and a Puma and damage a second Puma, which was later finished off by 801's SHARs.

The British forces had meanwhile suffered their first helicopter losses and fatalities. As soon as there was enough light the Sea Kings of 846 Squadron had begun to lift urgently-required weapons and material. One such lift, with part of a Rapier missile battery, was escorted to the Port San Carlos area by two Gazelle gunships of 3 Commando Brigade Air Squadron, operating from RFA *Sir Galahad*. The Royal Marine pilots, noticing movement up the San Carlos River, went to investigate and could not be contacted by 3 Para, who tried to warn them that enemy troops were ahead. The Gazelles passed over a party in a gully and were both shot down, one ditching in the river. Only one of the four NCOs survived, although wounded.

The Argentine soldiers managed to get away and had already alerted the command at Port Stanley that British forces had landed. Menendez still did not know the scale of the landings but he, or his Air Force subordinate, had already informed the *Fuerza Aerea Sur* that assistance was needed and half-a-dozen Daggers were on their way by 8.30am.

The *Hermes* flew off a second pair of GR3s to support the landings at about 8.15am. The leader had to return to the ship with technical prob-

---

* The *Bismarck* opened fire on HMS *Hood* at 23,000 yards but did not score a hit until the range was under 15,000 yards. Longer ranges were obtained against shore targets but involved high expenditure of ammunition to achieve direct hits on small target areas.

A Sea King 4 delivers a load to a 40 Commando forward position on the Verde Mountains *(MoD)*

lems but his No 2, Flight-Lieutenant J. Glover RAF, continued to the Amphibious Operating Area, where he was informed that there was no trade for his ordnance. He therefore proceeded to look for targets in the Port Howard area and, at about 8.40am, while making a second pass near the settlement to take photographs, he was shot down by a British-made Blowpipe missile fired by an Argentine Marine Corps special forces team.* Flight-Lieutenant Glover was extremely lucky to survive his low-level high-speed ejection but was badly injured and taken prisoner. Flown by helicopter to Port Stanley and then evacuated to Argentina in a C-130, he was the only British Serviceman to be taken during the recapture operations.

* Romero Briasco & Mafe Huertas, op. cit., p. 211. Glover believed at the time that he had been hit by automatic AA gunfire and this was still the UK Ministry of Defence official version in mid-1986.

Chapter Two

'The Battle of Clapp's Trap'

DAY ONE – THE LANDINGS

The first Argentine aircraft to be seen by the amphibious forces was a naval Macchi MB339 armed trainer from Port Stanley. *Teniente de Navio* G. Crippa ARA approached undetected by flying at low level around the north coast of East Falkland and quite suddenly appeared in the narrows, where the *Argonaut* was patrolling, at 8.45am. He fired eight 5in unguided rockets and his 30mm cannon at the frigate, causing slight damage to her forward Seacat deck area and wounding two men, before turning east under Fanning Head and flying up the Port San Carlos valley. As he passed, engaged by GPMGs and a Blowpipe missile from the *Canberra*, Seacat from the *Intrepid* and the *Plymouth*'s 4.5in guns, Crippa obtained a glimpse of the activity in San Carlos Water. He returned undamaged to Port Stanley to make his report. This had been preceded by a report radioed by a Goose Green Pucara, which had flown into the valley running south-east from San Carlos Water and had subsequently met the SAS and their Stinger.

The carriers had launched the first SHAR CAP at 6.35am, to provide cover against an attack at first light. For the remainder of the day there was always at least one pair of fighters either on or within five minutes flying time of one or both CAP stations. Controlled by HMS *Antrim*, the SHARs flew 'race-track' holding patterns to the west of Grantham Sound and to the north of Pebble Island, to be able to counter attacks approaching the Amphibious Operating Area from either the south-west or north-west. Unfortunately, the topography which gave a measure of protection to the ships limited the effectiveness of their warning radar, particularly in the sector between west and north-west, and prevented long-range visual detection of strikes approaching at low level. Some raids were detected far to the west of West Falkland as they descended to get below the radar horizon, but this gave only general warning of impending attack and seldom any idea of the direction of the final approach. The Sea Harrier pilots were very much dependent upon their own eyes for initial detection and were too often able only to react after an Argentine formation had delivered its attack. Once again the lack of airborne early warning placed the Royal Navy (and the land forces which it was supporting) at a disadvantage. With AEW a radar barrier could have been established to the west of West Falkland and even the small number of SHARs which could be held on CAP could have broken up the inbound strikes. Alternatively, the size of the CAPs and their time on station could have been increased if the carriers had been able to operate closer to the Amphibious Operating Area with AEW to give them warning of Super Etendard/Exocet attacks.

About a quarter of an hour after Crippa's Macchi had made its quick dash across Port San Carlos, the *Ardent* was approached by a pair of Pucaras from Goose Green, shaping for an attack. Any such intention was quickly frustrated by the frigate's Seacat and 4.5in gun, which drove off the two aircraft long before they could get close enough to fire their weapons.

A fleeting radar contact far to the west prompted the *Antrim* to call an 'Air Raid Warning RED' at 9.07am, but nothing more was detected or seen until 9.35am, when three VI Brigade Daggers, hugging the ground, swept around Mount Rosalie and flew across the five-mile width of the Sound, heading for the passage between Fanning Head and Chancho Point. The Daggers, led by Major Martinez, were the first section of a six-plane mission which had taken off from Rio Grande even before the first reports, from the Macchi and the Pucara, had been received at Port Stanley. These fighter-bombers, and the three following a few minutes behind, had been led by a pathfinder Learjet which had delivered them to a landfall off West Falkland and then broken off to return to base.

The Daggers were engaged by the ships in the Sound, but none of them was hit until the most northerly, flown by *Teniente* P. I. Bean, ran into a Seacat in the entrance to the anchorage. The *Argonaut* and *Intrepid* claimed shares in this first kill, but it is probable that the *Plymouth*, giving the *Canberra* close support, was responsible. The liner was herself blazing away with her own GPMGs and 42 Commando's machine-guns and Blowpipes. Bean did not survive.

The next Dagger (*Major* Martinez) attacked the *Broadsword*, strafing as it approached. Both 1,000lb bombs missed but the twenty-nine 30mm cannon shells which hit around the flight-deck and hangar wounded fourteen men and damaged the frigate's Lynx and one of the *Brilliant*'s which was 'visiting'. The third aircraft in the section veered to the south and went for the *Antrim*, on her own, three and a half miles south-west of Chancho Point, off Cat Island. This Dagger pilot scored the first direct hit of the battle for the amphibious landings, a 1,000lb bomb striking the destroyer's flight-deck, skidding through the flash-doors at the after end of the Seaslug missile magazine, where it gashed two missiles, and finally lodged itself in the seamen's after heads, without exploding. Only one minor casualty was caused but flying splinters created some damage and several fires were started. The two surviving Daggers escaped without hindrance, although the *Ardent* saw one of them as it ran southwards past

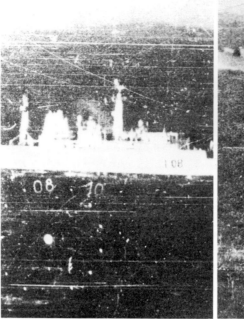

21 May: 9.36am – a Type 22 frigate seen through *Major Martinez'* gunsight as the Dagger pilot pulls up from his strafing run. The pendant number 'F 08', obviously 'touched in', was last used during the 1950s and '60s for the frigate *Urania*, but this ship is identifiable (by the protrusions on her funnel) as the *Broadsword* – 'F 88' *(FAA via J.C. D'Odorico)*

21 May: 1.46pm – HMS *Brilliant* under attack by the Daggers of 'Cueca' Division, who misidentified their target as being the ill-fated *Ardent (FAA via J.C. D'Odorico)*

the North-West Islands and hastened it on its way with a hopeful Seacat.

The *Antrim* quickly brought her fires under control and headed towards Chancho Point, to gain the protection of the *Broadsword*'s Seawolf. At 9.43am the next wave of Daggers was seen as they came over the West Falkland cliffs. The damaged destroyer fired one Seaslug at the oncoming aircraft as a deterrent, for the missile was not guided and was being jettisoned to reduce the fire hazard which it posed to the ship. Her port Seacat was out of action as the result of the previous attack and her 4.5in guns, the port 20mm and a number of GPMGs failed to prevent one of the Daggers from pressing its attack on her. The bombs missed, but the *Antrim* was sprayed with 30mm shells which started fires in a living space and the seamen's amidships heads and riddled the Wessex 3 with splinters. (The Wessex 5 had been flown off before first light to join the amphibious lift force.) Two men were seriously wounded and five others received minor injuries.

One Dagger made a dead set at the RFA *Fort Austin*, half a mile to the south of Chancho Point. Commodore Sam Dunlop prepared to beat off the attack with his two GPMGs and a battery of twenty-four rifles but was much relieved to see the Argentine aircraft break apart only 1,000 yards away, taken out by one of the *Broadsword*'s Seawolfs.* The frigate could

* This kill was not only witnessed by the *Fort Austin*, it was also seen by millions of British television viewers who watched the frigate's TV recording of the entire sequence of launch, guidance and missile strike. The Argentine accounts of the opening strike, as given in Ethell and Price's *Air War South Atlantic* and Romero Briasco and Mafe Huertas' *Falklands Witness of Battles*, describe it as a single wave, whereas the ships noted a lull between the two sections' attacks. All agree on the destruction of *Teniente* Bean's Dagger and the likely agent, but the Argentine Air Force has not (as of mid-1986) admitted the loss of the second aircraft.

not, however, save herself from attack and was hit by a few more shells and near-missed by bombs.

The two surviving Daggers were seen by the *Ardent* and engaged with the 4.5in, some of whose radar-proximity shells passed close enough to the aircraft to be triggered and burst. Even when they were past the *Ardent*, the Daggers were not completely safe, for the southerly CAP was sent after them by the *Brilliant*, which had assumed the air defence task when the *Antrim* had been damaged. The SHAR pilots saw the Argentine aircraft as they flew down the coast of Lafonia and dived after them. Lieutenant M. W. Hale (800 Squadron), the No 2, acquired with one of his Sidewinders and fired at long range, knowing that he would get no closer to the considerably faster Daggers. The range proved to be excessive for a low-level stern chase and the missile exploded harmlessly at the end of its run. The RN pilots kept up the pursuit until it became evident that their targets were not going to slow down.

There was now a long pause for breath, a lull which lasted for more than two hours, while the first Argentine strike returned to base. The pilots reported what they had seen, for the benefit of the next wave, to which the main striking force would be committed. Only the *Ardent*, still banging away at Goose Green, where she had destroyed another Pucara, would be attacked during this intermission.

Full advantage was taken of the pause by the Royal Navy. The *Antrim* went round Chancho Point into the entrance of Port San Carlos to effect what repairs she could, assisted by the *Fearless*, which sent across engineers and a bomb-disposal party from No 1 Fleet Clearance Diving Team, the latter arriving at 10.45am. Commodore Dunlop decided that the *Fort Austin*'s designated position in the Sound was too exposed and brought her into the inlet, anchoring half-a-mile offshore, between Hospital Point and Doctor's Head.

Within San Carlos Water work proceeded apace to unload the assault ships. The LCUs and LCVPs were joined in their task of shifting material to San Carlos and Ajax Bay by large motorized rafts – Mexeflotes – which had been brought out slung on the sides of the LSLs. The Mexeflotes' Army crews lived an uncomfortable existence, exposed without any form of shelter from the elements or attack, but shifted thousands of tons of ammunition, rations, weapons, fuel and vehicles direct from the ships to the beaches. Seven Sea King 4s were available for load-lifting, tasked by a support cell aboard the *Fearless*. In the nine hours of daylight on D-Day they picked up 288 loads, totalling over 220 tons, and 520 men from eleven ships and delivered these to twenty-one different sites. Among the most important of these cargoes were the 105mm Light Guns, which would be needed if the Argentine Army attempted to attack the beachhead, and all the elements of the Rapier battery, which was already required to assist in repelling air attacks but which would not be available, due to the need for 'settling-in' checks and adjustments, for several hours. Lighter loads were carried by the Wessex 5s of 845 Squadron, which could operate from the LSLs' midships deck as well as the large stern platform. One helicopter of each of these types was allocated for casualty evacuation, the Wessex for overland work, with a medical team on board, and a Sea King to bring wounded from the ships to the *Canberra*, where naval and military medical and surgical teams dealt with eighteen British and three Argentine patients during the day.

The main supply dump – the 'Brigade Maintenance Area' – was being built up at Ajax Bay, with its 'offices' in the disused refrigeration plant. This was also identified as a suitable location for the hospital facilities should they need to be moved from the *Canberra*.

At about 10.45am the *Ardent* was approached by another pair of Pucaras. These braved the 4.5in shells but broke away when a Seacat was fired and were chased away over a ridge by the missile. The Pucaras went off to rocket a derelict house near Darwin, believed to be occupied by the SAS, and then came back for another look at the *Ardent* at about 11.05am. The frigate was preparing to engage once again when three 801 Squadron SHARs appeared, vectored to the scene by the *Brilliant*. All three fighters concentrated on the leading Pucara, attempting to hit it with 30mm Aden cannon fire. The pilot, *Major* J. Tomba, managed to jink away from damage on the first three passes but Lieutenant-Commander 'Sharkey' Ward, the CO, set fire to the quarry's starboard engine on his second attack and got the port engine with his remaining ammunition on the third. Tomba ejected at very low level, over land, and walked home, the second fortunate III Brigade pilot to return on foot.

The long-suffering *Rio Carcaraña*, lying derelict in Port King, came under attack at about noon. *Capitan* Carballo had taken off from Rio Gallegos an hour previously, leading a V Brigade A-4B armed reconnaissance

A V Air Brigade A-4B, loaded with three 500lb (227 kg) bombs, 'hooked up' to a KC-130 tanker. The olive green and dark brown camouflage of this unit's Skyhawks was particularly effective at low level *(FAA via J.C. D'Odorico)*

mission. *Primer Teniente* Cachon's in-flight refuelling probe had iced up, so that he could not top up from the KC-130 tanker, and *Teniente* Rinke also had to turn back with fuel problems after the refuelling, leaving only *Alferez* Carmona to accompany the leader. Crossing the coast of Lafonia, Carballo at first believed that the *Rio Carcaraña* was a British transport unloading and made an attack. He had second thoughts at the last moment and did not release his bombs, but was unable to prevent Carmona from doing so. Carballo went on alone into the Sound, where he saw the *Ardent*, close to the shore, and descended to approach over land, taking advantage of what cover was provided. As a result the Skyhawk was not seen until it was less than two miles away, running in from almost dead ahead at very low level. Commander West ordered the helm to be put hard over to bring his port 20mm and the Seacat to bear, but the 4.5in gun, trained on the port beam, could not be slewed fast enough and only a few rounds of 20mm and machine-gun had been fired when Carballo dropped his bombs and pulled up to avoid the ship. The bombs missed, straddling the frigate, but the Skyhawk only narrowly avoided collision with its target, either the jet blast or an underwing tank knocking the Type 992 radar antenna, on top of the foremast, 30 degrees out of true. The antenna continued to rotate and provide a radar picture, despite its unusual alignment.*

The 800 Squadron CAP was arriving on station as the *Ardent* came under attack and the two SHARs were immediately sent out in pursuit by the *Brilliant*, descending as they crossed the coast of West Falkland near Fox Bay. When three miles south-east of Chartres Settlement, forty-five miles west-south-west of San Carlos, the No 2, Lieutenant-Commander M. S. Blissett, saw four Skyhawks crossing below him, from left to right. He called a break to starboard as the Argentine aircraft passed underneath and finished up ahead of his leader, Lieutenant-Commander N. W. Thomas,[†] and about 800 yards behind the Skyhawks, which had jettisoned their bombs and drop tanks and dispersed as soon as they had seen the two SHARs. Both naval pilots fired a Sidewinder and both scored hits, Blissett's target exploding while Thomas's caught fire and went out of control. *Teniente* N. E. Lopez had time to eject from his A-4C but his parachute did not deploy properly and he was killed on impact with the ground. *Primer Teniente* D. F. Manzotti's body was never found. Blissett was unable to acquire with his other Sidewinder and fired all his cannon ammunition without obvious effect at his second Skyhawk. Neil Thomas, who lost his other target, subsequently impressed upon the *Hermes* pilots the need to fire both missiles when multiple targets appeared. The Side-

---

* For the details of the individuals making up this, and subsequent, Argentine strike formations, information provided in Romero Briasco and Mafe Huertas' *Falklands Witness of Battles* is gratefully acknowledged.

† The CO of the absorbed 899 Squadron, Lieutenant Commander Thomas, served as the *Hermes'* Sea Harrier Chief Tactical Instructor.

winder was so accurate and reliable that there was no need to watch it all the way to the target; once the first was away from the launcher, they should look for another target.

This interception bought the Amphibious Operating Area another hour and a half's respite, during which the move ashore of 42 Commando Brigade from the *Canberra* to Port San Carlos was completed. At 1.15pm the *Brilliant* detected a formation 110 miles to the westward and sent out another 800 Squadron CAP towards Chartres to break up the raid at long range. This distracted the air warning organization and not until the last minute did anyone see six A-4Bs of V Air Brigade, which had approached at low level along the north coast of West Falkland, undetected at any stage of their flight from Rio Gallegos. Led by *Primer Teniente* Velasco, the six Skyhawks swept in from the open sea at 1.30pm and concentrated their attack on the first ship to be seen, the frigate *Argonaut*, on the easterly leg of her patrol line, close under Fanning Head. The ship completely disappeared behind the splashes of exploding bombs but reemerged with smoke pouring from her forecastle. The bombs which missed exploded, but the two which hit did not, although they inflicted very serious damage.

One 1,000lb bomb hit forward and lodged deep in the ship, in the forward magazine, where two Seacat missiles detonated, starting a major fire and causing heavy flooding. Of more immediate concern, however, were the effects of the second bomb, which struck the bulkhead between the engine- and boiler-rooms, for this deprived her of all power for steering or going astern as she headed for the Fanning Head cliffs with considerable way on the ship. With great presence of mind, the Officer of the Watch, Sub-Lieutenant P. T. Morgan, himself ran forward from the bridge, collecting two sailors as he went, and released an anchor. The *Argonaut* was brought up to a halt close under the cliffs – so close, indeed, that several other ships believed that she had run aground. There were fires and more flooding in the machinery spaces, with the added complication of severe steam leaks, but she was safely at rest and Captain C. H. T. Layman and his ship's company could concentrate on damage control. Two men had been killed and several others wounded.

As the Skyhawks were making their safe getaway, the 800 Squadron CAP was arriving in the Chartres area, whither they had been directed by the *Brilliant*. Lieutenant-Commander R. V. Frederiksen saw four aircraft at 1.35pm and led around behind the formation, rapidly overhauling what he thought to be Skyhawks, flying at low level under a layer of cloud which had descended during the early afternoon. The SHAR No 2, Lieutenant A. H. George, had fallen behind in the turn and although Frederiksen was able to despatch one of the Argentine aircraft with a Sidewinder and engage the leader of the formation with his guns, Andy George could not reach a firing position. The Argentine aircraft were, in fact, Daggers from Rio Grande and were quite unaware that they had

THE BATTLE OF CLAPP'S TRAP' · 193

been 'bounced', the disappearance of *Primer Teniente* H. Luna being attributed to his flying into the high ground. Luna, on the other hand, did know what had hit him and was lucky to have just sufficient time to eject at very low level.

In the AOA the events of the next few minutes, between 1.40 and 1.45pm, were hectic and confused, for the three Daggers which had escaped Frederiksen and George arrived over the Falkland Sound at much the same time as one or two formations of Skyhawks. For the first time Argentine aircraft got into the entrance to the amphibious anchorage in some numbers, giving very little warning of their arrival. All swept past the *Canberra*, possibly unwilling to believe that the British would have left a large white ship in such an exposed position unless she enjoyed the protection of the Geneva Convention as a hospital ship. Once inside Chancho Point, the raiders were faced with a concentration of warships in the two-mile-square at the mouths of Port San Carlos and San Carlos Water.

The *Antrim*, *Intrepid* and *Plymouth* all near-missed aircraft with Seacat missiles and the *Fort Austin* claimed to have hit a Dagger with her GPMG fire. The *Brilliant* had stationed herself off Doctor's Head. Her Sea Wolf system failed to 'see' the raids as they came through the gap opposite and a Sea Wolf fired by the *Broadsword* missed a Dagger which, in turn, missed the *Brilliant* with its bombs. The latter was, nevertheless, hit by sixteen 30mm shells which punched through the thin side plating to damage her Operations Room and most of her weapons systems, the Sea Wolf, Exocet and sonar all being put out of action. Providentially, the Type 967 radar was still operating and although the First Lieutenant, Lieutenant-Commander L. S. G. Hulme (who was acting as a fighter direction officer), was slightly wounded, he remained at his position, setting up his fourth successful interception of the afternoon even as the ship came under attack.

The amphibious ships had still not been attacked, although Argentine aircraft had passed down San Carlos Water after releasing their bombs and had been speeded on their way by the *Fearless*'s Seacats, and only the *Brilliant* had been damaged inside the anchorage. But out in the Sound the *Ardent* had been caught alone and exposed by the Argentine Navy's 3rd Fighter-Attack Squadron. At least one Dagger and one Air Force Skyhawk mission claimed to have damaged the frigate at about this time, but these do not tally with the ship's account, whereas the Navy A.4Qs' narrative matches it almost exactly.*

The naval Skyhawks approached the Falklands from west-south-west,

---

* There is, however, a minor discrepancy between the *Ardent*'s account and the most authoritative Argentine version (E. Villareno's 'Exocet', published as a special supplement to the weekly news review *Siete Dias*, in 1983). From circumstantial details, it is clear that the order of attack by the two Skyhawk sections was inadvertently reversed by the naval authorities, possibly due to the loss of all aircraft in the second to attack.

descending to sea level when within 100 miles of West Falkland. Unlike their Air Force counterparts, based further to the north and with a greater distance to the target, they had not refuelled during the approach. Undetected, they crossed the southern part of West Falkland and from Port Howard saw a Type 21 frigate in the Sound, 'to the south of "Bahia Ruiz Puente" (San Carlos Water)'. The *Ardent*, having completed her bombardment programme at 1.00pm, was heading for the North West Islands to join the *Yarmouth* in plugging the southern approaches to the San Carlos inlet.

At about 1.44pm, as the ships in the amphibious anchorage were beating off Air Force Skyhawks, the *Ardent* was attacked by *Teniente de Navio* B. Rotolo's three A-4Qs, manoeuvring to come in from astern. Commander West turned to put the aircraft on his port quarter but was unable to open the arc of the 4.5in gun. The Seacat launcher, which commanded the after arc and which had shot off three missiles already, now refused to fire, probably because the sight was depressed below the launcher's minimum safety angle (a problem which was subsequently overcome by a revision in firing drill). The A-4Qs, attacking in rapid succession, were opposed only by the port 20mm Oerlikon and two LMGs. Of nine 500lb 'Snake-eye' retarded bombs dropped, three hit the *Ardent*, two exploding in the hangar and the third, which did not explode, in the After Auxiliary Machinery Room.

The hit in the hangar killed instantly the Flight Commander, the Observer and two members of the Lynx maintenance crew, as well as the ship's Supply Officer, who doubled as the Flight Deck Officer, and about five other men. The Lynx was completely destroyed and the Seacat launcher was blown high off its mounting on the hangar roof and crashed back on to the flight deck. The fires which followed were confined mainly to the hangar area and some flooding was caused in the dining halls below the flight deck and in the main machinery control room from pipes fractured by the passage of the unexploded bomb, which also severely damaged the After Switchboard. The *Ardent*, running only on her Tynes at the time of attack, was still able to make the full 17½ knots on these engines and her steering was undamaged, but the electrical damage had put her 4.5in gun out of action and without her Seacat she had only the Oerlikons and three machine guns left for self-defence. She began to retire up the Sound to reach the protection of the ships at San Carlos, her damage control parties slowly getting the better of the fires.

The attack on the *Ardent* had not been detected by the *Brilliant*, but she picked up the next raid to the west of the islands and tracked it until it crossed the coast. The Pebble Island CAP was vectored to a holding position to the north of Port Howard and at about 2.00pm Lieutenant-Commander Ward and Lieutenant Steve Thomas saw first two and then a third Dagger approaching. The two 801 Squadron pilots carried out copybook attacks, using the Sea Harriers' low-level 'high-energy' manoeuvrability to get behind the Argentine fighter-bombers, which didn't have time to recover from their initial shock. All three were destroyed, two by Lieutenant Thomas, who claimed only a possible with his second missile as he did not see the Dagger crash. The pilots all ejected safely. Thomas, who now had three kills to his credit, including the Mirage III shared with the Port Stanley AA guns on 1 May, was himself hit by ground fire as he passed over the Port Howard area. His CO (with two kills on separate sorties on the 21st) had lost sight of him in the later stages of the combat and feared the worst when Thomas failed to reply to radio calls. In fact, the latter had been hit by three 0.5in machine-gun bullets, one of which had damaged his radio set, and he had set off to return to the *Invincible* nearly 200 miles away. Lieutenant-Commander Ward spent a short while looking for his No 2 and then himself turned east. As he did so, he caught sight of three white Skyhawks ahead of him but well out of range, heading down the Falkland Sound towards a burning frigate. He could do nothing to prevent the attack, apart from warning the *Brilliant* and the 800 CAP which was just arriving over Grantham Sound.

The Dagger section wiped out by Ward and Thomas had been half of the first raid by the San Julian-based No 2 Squadron of VI Air Brigade. The other three aircraft attacked the anchorage at 2.04pm but although they achieved surprise they scored no hits on the ships.

At 2.06pm the *Ardent* was a mile to the south-west of the North West Islands, bringing her fires under control, when a formation of Skyhawks was seen to cross the West Falkland coast at Many Branch Point. She immediately altered course to bring the aircraft dead ahead, to engage with the 4.5in and present the narrowest target. To *Capitan de Corbeta* A. J. Philippi it looked as though the frigate was actually among the rocky islets and was emerging to meet him.* He jinked away and circled anticlockwise at a distance of two miles (to stay out of Seacat range) and then ran in from astern, opposed only by one Oerlikon and two machine guns, whose view was partly obscured by smoke. The chaff rockets were fired in the hope of distracting the pilots and Philippi indeed believed them to be 'Seacat booster rockets', but nevertheless bored in, climbing to 300 feet inside the last mile to give his bombs time to arm and remain clear of their blast. At least one of his retarded 500-pounders hit and exploded, as did one of the next aircraft's (*Teniente de Navio* J. C. Arca), while *Teniente de Fregata* M. G. Marquez, bringing up the rear, may have scored more. As he flew over the frigate, Arca was hit in one wing by a burst of machine-gun fire delivered by the NAAFI Manager, Mr J. S. Leake, a former Regular soldier enrolled as a Petty Officer on the declaration of 'Active Service' six days earlier.

Even as the Skyhawks had set up the attack, the 800 CAP, Lieutenant C. R. W. Morrell and Flight Lieutenant J. Leeming RAF, alerted by

---

* Villareno, 'Exocet'; *US Naval Institute 'Proceedings'*, Naval review edition, May 1982.

Lieutenant-Commander Ward's call, had been diving hard to get down to intercept. This they were unable to do before the last Argentine pilot pulled away from the *Ardent*. Marquez tried to warn the two leading aircraft as he saw Morrell's SHAR drop in behind them but was himself cut down by three bursts of 30mm fired by the unseen Leeming. Philippi's aircraft was hit by a Sidewinder and he ejected safely near Port Howard, but Morrell's other missile malfunctioned and he had to close in and use his cannon against Arca's Skyhawk. No hits were claimed by the Royal Navy pilot but he had inflicted severe damage, hitting both of the little delta's wings. Arca, his fuel draining away, flying control hydraulics inoperative and, unknown to him, his port undercarriage shot away, tried to divert to Port Stanley airfield but had to eject over Port William, from which he was rescued with great difficulty by an Army UH-1 helicopter.

The last attack of the day was delivered by five A-4Bs of V Air Brigade at 2.15pm. These were engaged by the *Antrim*, *Plymouth*, *Intrepid* and *Fearless*, but neither side inflicted any damage, although the Argentine pilots made a bid for a share in the *Ardent*, eight miles away. During the hour and a half of daylight which was left the ships remained alert and the SHARs patrolled overhead but the Argentine air forces did not return.

This was a fortunate respite, for there were now two ships exposed in precarious positions, the *Argonaut* and the *Ardent*. The last 500lb bombs had started fresh fires in the after end of the latter – none struck forward of the hangar – and had killed or injured the entire after damage control party fighting the fires in the dining hall area.* The ship's steering gear was out of action, although both her Tyne engines were still under control; she was holed above the waterline aft and she had taken a five-degree list to starboard. Advised by his senior Heads of Department, Commander West decided to transfer the ship's company to the *Yarmouth*, on her way across the Sound to render assistance, when the latter arrived. In the meantime the fires were fought to prevent their spreading to the magazines and the engines were stopped. At 2.30pm the *Yarmouth* arrived alongside and the *Ardent* dropped anchor off the north-west corner of the small group of islands. During the next twenty-five minutes, thirty-seven wounded and 142 unwounded survivors crossed from the *Ardent*'s bows to the *Yarmouth*'s flight deck: twenty-two officers and men had died. Commander West was the last to step from ship to ship, at 2.55pm. The *Broadsword* had by now arrived on the scene to cover the *Yarmouth* and the two ships left the blazing frigate at 3.05pm.

Further up the Sound, off Fanning Head, the *Plymouth* had secured alongside the *Argonaut*. Power was supplied to raise the anchor and for other essential services and the damaged 'Leander' was moved into San

---

* Marine Engineering Artificer 1st Class K. Enticknapp, in charge of the party, was awarded the Queen's Gallantry Medal for his dedication to duty, despite wounds suffered in both attacks, and Able Seaman J. E. Dillon received the George Medal for the difficult rescue of a man who was even more seriously wounded than himself.

Carlos Water and re-anchored. During the tow the *Plymouth*'s galley provided hot meals to the damaged ship's men, who, like all the ships' companies, had had little to eat since before entering the Falkland Sound so long before.

By nightfall the only ship outside San Carlos Water was the *Broadsword*, standing sentry duty off Chancho Point. Inside, it had been decided even before the last series of attacks that the *Canberra* could not be allowed to remain, as had been intended, as a floating 'rest ship' and that she must sail that night with the other merchant ships. The *Ardent*'s survivors went on board at 4.30pm against the flow of traffic as the rear echelons of 3 Commando Brigade's units left with their tons of equipment and baggage, assisted by the personnel of Naval Party 1710 and the off-duty P&O crew and staff. The civilian crews had behaved magnificently through the day, the *Canberra*'s encouraged by the Senior Naval Officer's running commentary on the progress of the raids. Captain C. P. O. Burne RN had a style peculiarly his own and, whatever may have been the impression which he made on the military passengers, he was much admired by his Party and the P&O crew, who managed to match his apparent nonchalance.

The *Canberra*, *Norland* and *Europic Ferry* sailed from San Carlos Water at 10.30pm, escorted by the *Antrim*. The destroyer's unexploded bomb had been removed intact by Fleet Chief Petty Officer M. G. Fellows and his party from Fleet Clearance Diving Team 1 (FCDT 1) in a ten-hour operation, during which they had had to fight fires near the bomb, shield the wretched thing from being jarred during air raids and cut a path for its removal, all the while wearing breathing apparatus. The bomb was finally lowered into the water from the flight deck at 7.30pm. For his example and leadership, Mr Fellows, who already had a British Empire Medal for previous bomb-disposal exploits, was awarded the Distinguished Service Cross, the first to be awarded since the revival of the rank of Warrant Officer in the Royal Navy.

The *Antrim*'s inshore war was over. Without her Seaslug system, which was damaged beyond any early repair, she was of greater use as an anti-submarine and surface escort in the Replenishment Area outside the TEZ. Her own personnel and those from the repair ship *Stena Seaspread* patched the holes and tidied up the fire and flooding damage, while a MARTSU team from the *Atlantic Conveyor* helped the ship's Flight to repair the Wessex 3, which was flying again by 28 May.*

In San Carlos Water the *Fearless* was acting as the local repair ship, in addition to her duties as amphibious flagship, floating military headquarters, helicopter carrier and air transport controlling authority. The *Argonaut*'s own engineering staff had undertaken first-aid repairs, Chief

---

* The aircraft, still showing the scars, is to be seen at the Fleet Air Arm Museum, RN Air Station, Yeovilton, Somerset. The *Antrim* is further afield, serving in the Chilean Navy, to whom she was sold in 1983.

Marine Engineering Mechanic M. D. Townsend particularly distinguishing himself by patching the four-foot hole near the water line in the boiler room, working within five feet of the unexploded bomb. Once this was completed, as the ship came to anchor in San Carlos Water, he turned to the flooding caused by the bomb in the Seacat magazine, to reduce the volume of water in the ship and also to clear the way for FCDT 1's bomb-disposal party. Led by Lieutenant-Commander B. F. Dutton QGM, this party arrived by helicopter as the *Argonaut* was being towed in and remained for over a week. The bomb in the boiler room was soon removed and dumped over the side, but the other, surrounded by damaged ordnance in the diesel-fuel-soaked magazine, could not be defused *in situ*, nor could it be extracted using the normal access hatches, so that a special withdrawal route had to be cut to move the bomb first aft and then upwards. The clearance of the ordnance around the bomb, the cutting and the slow shifting took a week to complete and was at all times a hazardous operation. Brian Dutton's skill and courage were rewarded by the award of the Distinguished Service Order; he was the most junior officer to be so decorated in the main (October, 1982) Falklands honours and awards list.

The STUFT convoy, escorted by HMS *Antrim*, had been preceded out of the Falkland Sound some hours before by the *Brilliant*, which had sailed at 5.30pm, not to withdraw for repairs but to make a fast passage round to King George Bay, West Falkland, to insert Special Forces reconnaissance parties. She arrived half an hour before midnight and left three hours later, unobserved by the enemy. By dawn on the 22nd she was safely at anchor off Doctor's Head. Her Weapons Electrical Department had worked throughout the night on her various systems defects, rewiring whole sections and re-routing others, but several days would elapse before more than one Seawolf launcher would be available.

21 May had been, without doubt, a traumatic day for the Royal Navy. Not since May, 1945, had its ships been subjected to waves of determined air attacks breaking through the outer air defences and few could conceive the practical effects of bomb and cannon hits, however well known the theoretical penetration distances and damage radii may have been. Only two of the seven escorts engaged had escaped damage – the *Plymouth* and the *Yarmouth*, which had not been attacked directly but had engaged the Skyhawks which attacked the *Ardent* with long-range 4.5in gunfire – and, of those which had been hit, one had been abandoned and was to sink and only the *Broadsword* was still fully capable of steaming and fighting. The Argentine Air Force pilots' determination and courage had, paradoxically, saved the *Argonaut*, which could scarcely have escaped becoming a total loss if either of her bombs had exploded, and possibly the *Antrim*, for, as in the case of the *Glasgow* (and the MV *Formosa*) the bombs had been released so close that they had not had time to arm their fuzes.

The ships had been badly handicapped by the local terrain, which deprived them of radar warning during the last fifty miles of the aircraft's approach. Even when the Air Force Daggers and Skyhawks appeared in visual range, their excellent camouflage often delayed detection until the last moment, so that the missile aimers and gunners had insufficient time to open fire before relatively easy approaching targets turned into very difficult ones with a high 'crossing rate' as the aircraft flashed past at close range. Of the automatic AA weapons, only the old 40mm Bofors and 20mm Oerlikons had sights capable of allowing the gunners to work out deflection angles and there were all too few of these venerable but invaluable weapons. The rifle-calibre machine guns were fired with considerable elan and hope and actually worried the strike pilots, thanks to the amount of tracer used. Thousands of rounds were fired and many struck home, but such light projectiles could seldom inflict substantial damage on the aircraft. The ships had been presented with between thirty-two and thirty-eight aircraft and had destroyed two for certain, although more were claimed.

Another eight aircraft would have got through had it not been for the *Brilliant* CAP control, and even then fortune played a part. The First Lieutenant would have continued to understudy the Captain and co-ordinate the life of the ship if the *Antrim* had not been damaged. As it happened, this experienced Fighter Direction Officer was able to use a radar system which had not been intended for fighter control to set up four successful interceptions, three of which resulted in inbound raids sustaining losses while the fourth brought retribution on the strike which dealt the last blows to the *Ardent*. Lieutenant-Commander Hulme's success matched that of some of the best Second World War FDOs and, for all the sophistication of his radar compared with theirs, his basic methods were much the same.

The Sea Harrier pilots' problems would also have been recognized by their 1942 counterparts, who had also relied upon the skill of the controller to set them up for visual detection of an enemy who was often faster and always in superior numbers. The 1982 pilots were, however, operating at unprecedented (for the Royal Navy) distances from the carriers – over 200 miles at times – and they were invariably short of fuel after a few minutes' full-throttle low-level combat and they therefore needed to achieve quick kills, not only to protect ships in the Sound but also to return safely. The Sidewinder gave this capability, but the 30mm Aden cannon's heavy shells accounted for two of the fast jets and the only Pucara to be shot down by the naval fighters.

For all their undoubted courage and motivation, the Argentine pilots had failed. They had concentrated on the exposed escorts out in the Falkland Sound and then in the open roads at the entrance to the San Carlos Water anchorage, but apart from disrupting the steady flow ashore of men and material, halted during the brief passage of the attack waves, they had had no direct effect on the all-important amphibious build-up. The vital Assault Ships and Landing Ships had not been seriously threatened. Only one major effort had been attempted by the Air Force, eighteen aircraft reaching the Falklands and seventeen attacking the AOA between 1.30 and 1.45pm. Before and after that main 'show', at least twenty-five Daggers and Skyhawks took off from the mainland but only fourteen dropped their bombs, seven being shot down by the Sea Harriers and ships before the release point, while the other four either turned back early or fled. The Argentine Navy's effort was modest, but all six sorties got through to deliver successful attacks, at the cost of half the force.

The Argentine Air Force claimed to have mounted sixty-three fighter-bomber sorties on 21 May, but only seventeen Dagger and twenty-seven Skyhawk flights can be identified from existing sources.* It is likely that some of the 'missing' nineteen sorties returned early to base with technical difficulties, but this would not account for all of them. With the three aircraft known to have turned back bringing the total of non-effective sorties to a third of those taking off, the *Comando de la Fuerza Aera Sur* had serious cause for concern.

Aircraft losses were also serious – one out of five of those which reached the Falklands. The thousands of 7.62mm machine-gun rounds fired during the day had also damaged many aircraft which could not be repaired in time to fly against the ships on '"D" plus One'.† Of the Air Force units engaged on 21 May, only V Air Brigade had not lost an aircraft. The inventory was shrinking and, with the losses since the beginning of May, the Air Force was down to fourteen out of eighteen A-4Cs, thirty-two out of thirty-six A–4Bs and twenty-six out of thirty-three single-seat Daggers. The Navy still had all four of its flyable Super Etendards, but these were held back for Exocet operations only and its 'bread-and-butter' strike force had been reduced from seven to four A–4Qs. With no hope of early replacement of the lost aircraft and already short of essential spare parts to repair some of the badly damaged ones, neither the modest striking rate nor the heavy loss rate of 21 May could be sustained.

While the events in the Amphibious Operating Area attracted all the attention of the media and most of that of everyone else involved in 'Corporate', other activities continued. The carriers' usual goalkeepers, the two Type 22s, were inshore and their places were taken by the *Arrow* and *Alacrity*. During the day the *Antelope* and *Ambuscade* joined, giving a

* Romero Briasco and Mafe Huertas (op. cit.) correspond in their account with British Naval reports.

† *Aeroespacio*, Jan/Feb, 1984, p. 39.

remarkably homogeneous close screen of four Type 21s. Another arrival was HMS *Leeds Castle*, which had taken ten days on passage from Ascension due to an engine break-down. A replacement cam-shaft was air-dropped by an RAF Hercules on 18 May and the 'despatch vessel''s engineers completed the high-seas repair thirty-two hours later.

Off Ascension her sister-ship, the *Dumbarton Castle*, was at sea to rendezvous with the *Queen Elizabeth II* and pass stores and passengers, using a Sea King of No 202 Squadron RAF which she had embarked to assist the two Sea Kings of 825 Squadron aboard the liner. The *Dumbarton Castle* returned to Ascension and made a second rendezvous on the next day, it having been decided that the big ship should not come in sight of the island or the ever-present Soviet 'spy ship'. The two STUFT ferries, *Baltic Ferry* and *Nordic Ferry*, carrying 5 Infantry Brigade's heavy weapons and military stores, had called at Ascension and left on the 21st for South Georgia, taking a track well to the east of the straight line, to minimize the chance of their detection by the Boeing 707s.

DAY TWO – TAKING BREATH

At least two of the 707s were out on 22 May and both very narrowly missed disaster. In the early hours one approached the northern entrance to the Falkland Sound, presumably to see if there were any shipping movements. At the time, the only ship offshore was the destroyer *Coventry*, about ten miles north-east of Pebble Island and waiting to be joined by the *Broadsword*, with whom she would team up to act as a 'missile trap' to break up raids approaching from the west. The *Coventry* waited for the 707 to close in to twenty-five miles and then began the Sea Dart acquisition process, illuminating the target with both Type 909 tracking radars. All went well with the sequence until a flash-door failed safe, preventing missile loading on to the launcher. As the target did not wake up to the fact that it was in imminent danger until it was five miles closer and the fault could not be rectified before it was well out of range, there was bitter disappointment in the ship that the *Coventry* had been robbed of success against such a high-value target.

This near-engagement, which occurred at 3.00am, was followed, five hours later and 1,800 miles to the north-east, by an actual firing. The *Bristol* Group, which had been joined on the 21st by the *Tidespring*, hastening forward after getting rid of the South Georgia prisoners, detected what was undoubtedly not a civil airliner, for the track plot took the form of a series of loops and curlicues which brought the aircraft in from over 200 miles to thirty-five miles, its closest point of approach. Captain A. Grose RN, leading the Group, ordered the *Cardiff* to drop back and altered the disposition of his ships to disguise her 'disappearance'. The 707 duly obliged by coming within extreme range of the Type 42, which fired a Sea Dart salvo at about 1230Z. One of the missiles was seen on radar to have burst close to the target, which promptly broke away and dived to low level. Whether or not the warhead exploded close enough to damage the Boeing and cause the loss of cabin pressurization, as was suggested at the time,* the crew was certainly aware of the very narrow escape and the few 707s that were subsequently detected remained well beyond the range of all weapons.

22 May: *Vice-Comodoro* Otto A. Ritondale (extreme left) and his crew pose in front of the Boeing 707 before take-off on the reconnaissance mission which so nearly ended in disaster when they found the *'Bristol Group'* 1,400 miles (2,600 km) east-north-east of Buenos Aires. Only violent evasive action when the *Cardiff's* Sea Dart missile was sighted at the last moment saved the aircraft and crew *(FAA via J.C. D'Odorico)*

The *Broadsword*, which had stood by the *Ardent* during the night, watching the fires spread unchecked through the frigate, causing occasional explosions, left the Falkland Sound at about 2.00am to join the *Coventry* on the missile trap station off Pebble Island. The *Ardent* sank about half an hour later, leaving just the top of her mainmast exposed.

By dawn the *Brilliant* was back in San Carlos Water from her insertion mission to West Falkland. The entrance to the Water was guarded by the *Yarmouth* and the immobile but fully-armed *Argonaut*. Inside, under the hills on the western shore, was the *Plymouth* and the *Brilliant* positioned herself opposite, off Doctor's Head. A strong CAP was maintained all day, the carriers flying sixty such sorties (six more than on 'D'-Day and the greatest number on any one day of 'Corporate'). The defenders of the beachhead, unaware that bad weather on the mainland was preventing the Argentine air forces from launching any strikes, passed the day in

* *Aeroespacio*, Mar/Apr 84, pp. 34–36.

800 Squadron scored another anti-shipping success on 22 May, when a CAP caught the coastguard patrol craft *Rio Iguazu* in Choiseul Sound and drove it aground. The vessel was ferrying artillery to Goose Green and the coastguard crew managed to salvage the guns and remove their own AA gun, to add to the defences *(MoD)*

fine weather, wondering why the enemy aircraft did not come.

The good weather and freedom from attack permitted the unloading to continue uninterrupted. The Rapier battery move was completed and by noon the three sections, each with four 'fire units', were operational around the main troop concentrations, at Port San Carlos, San Carlos Settlement and Ajax Bay. The guns of 29 Commando Regiment fired their first task, against a group of 'LVT–7s' reported by a 45 Commando observation post overlooking Grantham Sound.* The transport helicopter activity was even more intense than it had been on the 21st, with the *Fort Austin*'s Sea Kings and the frigates' Lynxes contributing whenever they could be spared from anti-submarine patrols and surface searches, while the Marine and Army crews of the landing craft, Mexeflotes and the Rigid Raiding Craft which were being used as water taxis, were on the move from before dawn until after dusk.

There was still no attempt by the Argentine Army to harass or interfere in any way with the beachhead. Instead, most of their resources were devoted to strengthening the defences in the Darwin–Goose Green area. The Coast Guard patrol boat *Rio Iguazu* was sent from Stanley during the night of the 21st/22nd with a cargo of two 105mm pack howitzers and their ammunition. The boat failed to reach Darwin before first light and was sighted by the *Hermes*'s dawn CAP in Choiseul Sound. As there was no sign of activity on the part of the enemy air force and an 801 Squadron CAP was also available, Lieutenant-Commander Frederiksen and Lieutenant Hale strafed and damaged the *Rio Iguazu*, which was driven ashore among the kelp. The guns were subsequently recovered by the Argentine Air Force personnel at Goose Green, only to be captured three days later.

Goose Green itself was the target for the first four-aircraft GR3 strike. Led by Squadron Leader J. Pook RAF, one of the No 1 Squadron flight commanders, the Harriers were met by fierce AA fire but caused extensive damage to the fuel dump with their cluster bombs and escaped undamaged, despite an Argentine claim to have damaged one. The only

* These vehicles were probably Land Rovers, as the only LVTs used in the Falklands had been withdrawn after the initial amphibious assault

other GR3 mission was a low-level photographic trip by two aircraft over West Falkland between about 3.45 and 4.15pm.

Twenty miles to the north-west of Pebble Island the *Coventry* and *Broadsword* passed a fairly quiet day, much to the dissatisfaction of Captain Hart-Dyke of the former. Not until 1.40pm was there any sign of enemy air activity and even this 'raid' did not close within sixty miles. An hour and a half later, at 3.05pm, another 'raid' was detected, heading towards the trap. This was marked by a SHAR CAP but the fighters were hauled off by the *Coventry*, who wished to prove her Sea Dart system. In the end the Argentine aircraft turned back before coming within missile range.

At 4.10pm, without any warning, two Skyhawks appeared over the ridge to the east of Fanning Head, narrowly missed the surprised *Brilliant* and escaped in the twilight with hardly a shot fired at them. The photo GR3s were returning from West Falkland at about the same time and it is possible that, coming at the end of a quiet day, these 'confused the plot'.

The *Coventry* and *Broadsword* parted company shortly after this one attack, the frigate returning to San Carlos Water while the destroyer headed east to rejoin the Carrier Battle Group. The *Exeter* had arrived during the day, taking her place on the picket line with the *Glasgow*. The latter, with the assistance of the *Stena Seaspread*'s engineering specialists, was rebuilding the damaged Tyne engines' intake ducting, using plywood.

For most of the night the *Broadsword* had only the *Argonaut* with her to defend the AOA, the *Plymouth*, *Brilliant* and *Yarmouth* having put out for other tasks. Captain Pentreath took the first to King George Bay to extract an SBS team, accomplishing the task in spite of considerable complications. The *Plymouth* was back by dawn, having covered the 250-mile round trip in ten hours, but spent much of the next day clearing kelp and krill (small shrimp-like creatures) out of her condenser inlets.

The *Brilliant* and *Yarmouth* transited south through the Falkland Sound and sailed around Lafonia to intercept the next Argentine attempt to reinforce Goose Green. Radar contact was made in Lively Sound shortly before midnight and a Lynx was flown off to investigate. The aircraft came under machine-gun fire but did not shoot back, remaining to shadow out of range. By about 2.00am on the 23rd the frigates were within range and the ship was illuminated by the *Yarmouth*'s starshell and identified as the coaster *Monsunnen*, 'STUFT' from the Falklands Islands Company by the Argentine Army. The crew promptly ran the ship hard aground among the kelp and escaped over the rocks. The *Monsunnen*'s hull was cushioned by the weed and did not suffer serious damage, but the two frigates would not be able to tow her off before dawn and at 3.00am they left her and went their separate ways, the *Yarmouth* to return to her station off Chancho Point and the *Brilliant* to rejoin the Carrier Group.

DAY THREE – ARGENTINE AIRCRAFT RETURN

The number of escorts at San Carlos was not affected by the *Brilliant*'s departure, for the *Antelope* arrived shortly before first light with the first resupply convoy – the *Stromness*, *Norland* and *Europic Ferry*, which had spent all the 22nd with the *Elk* and RFA *Resource* on the edge of the TEZ, using every available helicopter, including the anti-submarine Sea Kings, to transfer hundreds of loads. The convoy, like all those which were to follow, was not discovered or approached by the Argentine forces.

Analysis of the previous afternoon's Argentine air traffic reported by the *Coventry* led Admiral Woodward's staff to the opinion that there had been a resupply air-drop in the Dunnose Head area. At 8.00am on the 23rd four GR3s took off from the *Hermes* and bombed the West Falkland airstrip but saw no signs of enemy activity or occupation. It was also thought possible that Pucaras had flown in to Pebble Island and that airstrip was treated to a GR3 strike later in the day.

The frigates at San Carlos launched strikes as well. The damaged *Argonaut*'s Lynx attempted the first Sea Skua missile attack on the *Rio Carcaraña* at Port King at 8.50am but was foiled by technical problems. *Antelope* Flight, attacking the same target an hour later, fired two Sea Skuas, both of which hit the ship. *Capitan de Corbeta* Philippi, who had paddled ashore after ejecting over the Sound on the 21st and was living rough on West Falkland, unable to find any of the 1,600 Argentine soldiers, saw the *Rio Carcaraña* burning and was under the impression that she was being bombarded by warships. He was mistaken; no bombardment of Lafonia was undertaken and the last attack of any kind on the abandoned ship had been by *Alferez* Carmona of V Air Brigade at noon on the 21st.

The day had dawned overcast but clear, but again the Argentine Air Force failed to make an early appearance and the newly-arrived stores ships were unloaded with little interruption. Among the most important items to be brought in by the *Stromness* were an aircraft fuel-handling installation and some tracking intended for assembly as GR3 landing pads. This material was taken ashore at Port San Carlos, where the Royal Engineers had identified an area for development as a helicopter forward operating base and now lost no time in putting the bits together. The dump at the Brigade Maintenance Area at Ajax Bay was still growing; with over 5,000 tons of stores already ashore or on their way and only the Mexeflotes and eight LCUs and eight LCVPs available for water transport, an increase in the number of helicopters was much needed but could not be provided until a base ashore could be established. Once this was available, the six Wessex and four Chinooks could be flown off the *Atlantic Conveyor*.

The Grantham Sound CAP found some 'trade' for itself at 9.30am, Flight-Lieutenants Leeming and D. H. S. Morgan RAF of 800 Squadron catching a glimpse of a helicopter over Shag Cove, 8,000 feet beneath them. On closing, the SHAR pilots saw not one but three helicopters, two Pumas and what they took to be a Bell 'Huey' (UH-1 Iroquois) but which was actually an Italian-built Agusta 109 gunship, escorting the other two Army helicopters as they made for Port Howard to deliver ammunition and bring back the Marine Corps special forces troop. The leading Puma caught sight of Morgan as he pulled up for a cannon run and in attempting to evade it crashed into the hillside which it had been skirting. The other Puma and the Agusta 109 landed and their crews scrambled clear before the SHARs returned to destroy the gunship and damage the Puma, which was finished off later in the day by 801 Squadron.

Some time after midday the *Antelope* flew off her Lynx to assess what damage had been inflicted on the *Rio Carcaraña*. The ship was found to be sinking and the Lynx returned up the Sound. At 12.40pm it was over-flown by four Skyhawks going in the same direction and the pilot broadcast an urgent warning of the raid. He was fortunate, for *Capitan* Carballo, leading his second strike against the landings, had attempted to

Capitan Pablo M. R. Carballo, the most successful division leader, mans an A-4B of V Air Brigade
(FAA via J.C. D'Odorico)

shoot down the Lynx, only to have his 20mm cannon jam after the first few rounds. Carballo's 'Nene' division shot past the entrance to San Carlos, going north through the narrows under Fanning Head, and then turned to starboard, to split up and make co-ordinated passes from the north and east.

The ships in the northern part of the water – the *Broadsword* off Hospital Point, the *Antelope* south of Fanning Island and the *Yarmouth* off Doctor's Head – were ready, despite the shortness of warning, and Carballo and *Teniente* Rinke, attacking down the Port San Carlos valley, were turned back by the barrage of 4.5in shells, Bofors, Oerlikon, GPMG tracer, Seacats and Rapiers. The *Antelope* claimed to have brought down one aircraft with her Seacat, but this was not the case. The second pair of A-4Bs, *Primer Teniente* L. Guadagnini and *Alferez* Gomez, now descended the ridge to the north and selected, respectively, the *Antelope* and the *Broadsword*. Gomez missed, but Guadagnini, though hit by 20mm fire, pressed home his attack and scored a direct hit about six feet above the frigate's waterline, on the starboard side, below the hangar. The Skyhawk failed to pull up sufficiently to avoid the tall pole of the main mast just ahead of the funnel and it was seen to blow up and fall into the water off the *Antelope*'s port side, together with the wreckage of the HF/DF aerial. Whether or not Gaudagnini would have survived the collision is debatable. What is practically beyond doubt is that his aircraft was also hit almost simultaneously by a Seawolf fired at Gomez and a Rapier. The 1,000lb bomb which had hit failed to explode.

The spray had scarcely subsided before a single Skyhawk, flown either by Carballo or Rinke, attacked almost unnoticed from the *Antelope*'s port quarter and, as the ship swung towards the attack, put another bomb into her, on the port side beneath the bridge; like Guadagnini's, this also failed to explode. The Skyhawk escaped, narrowly missed by a Seacat which also passed too close to the *Intrepid* for the latter's comfort. Both Carballo and Gomez had sustained machine-gun damage to their aircraft but were able to return to base.*

The *Antelope*, with one bomb in her Air Conditioning Unit and another somewhere in her devastated Petty Officers' Mess, remained in her sector for the next two hours. She had lost one man killed and one seriously injured, her gyros had failed and part of the ship was illuminated by emergency lighting but she was still able to fight and move.

The next inbound strike had started out as a four-aircraft division of naval A-4Qs from Rio Grande. After the experience on the 21st the squadron commander, *Capitan de Fregata* R. Castro Fox, decided that flight refuelling was necessary if the aircraft were not to be uncomfortably short of fuel on return. The Air Force laid on a KC-130 which the Skyhawks

---

* The Argentine account of this strike is derived from Romero Briasco and Mafe Huertas' work, which differs from that of Ethell and Price but corresponds more closely with British reports.

duly met 150 miles to the north-east of Rio Grande, but the No 4 was unable to take on fuel due to a transfer problem* and was ordered to return to base. The remaining aircraft coasted in over West Falkland as the V Air Brigade strike climbed out and heard 'Nene Leader' report that his No 3 had been shot down and that he himself had been damaged.†

The ships had about three minutes' warning of the attack, which came over the shoulder of Mount Rosalie, low across the Falkland Sound and climbed sharply to 300 feet as the aircraft came through the entrance, splitting up to attack the Broadsword, Antelope and Yarmouth. The extra height gave the bombs the time needed to arm the fuzes but at the expense of accuracy, for both the leader and No 2 missed short, while Capitan de Corbeta C. Zubizarreta did not press his attack on the Yarmouth and his bombs, for whatever reason, were not released. Castro Fox and his No 2 made their getaway, pursued by Rapiers from the Port San Carlos area, but the only damage seems to have been to the leader's drop tanks, the loss of fuel causing him some embarrassment during the return flight. He and his undamaged No 2 (Teniente Benitez) landed without incident, but Zubizarreta, attempting to bring his bombs back, burst a tyre landing on the wet runway in a strong cross-wind. As his Skyhawk swerved off the runway, he ejected and although the aircraft came to a halt only moderately damaged, the luckless Zubizarreta sustained fatal injuries. The Skyhawk's ejection seat, whose success record during the campaign was not such as to inspire confidence, gave insufficient 'time of flight' for the parachute to deploy at ground level.

The ships had only a ten-minute respite before, at 1.20pm, the southerly CAP gave warning of an inbound raid of four Daggers. The SHARs were unable to get down in time to catch the fighter-bombers before they entered the AOA gun and missile defence zone, but because only two Daggers actually came round the corner under Chancho Point it was at the time believed that the CAP had splashed two. Both went for Broadsword and, although her Sea Wolf missed, and she was near-missed, it was believed that the leader had been hit and brought down by 20mm fire from the Antelope and Yarmouth and the other by a Rapier, but both escaped. At the time it was claimed that 'all four aircraft' of the strike had been shot down, but the true score was none out of four.

There was a further raid at 2.05pm by three more Daggers, but these shied off without entering San Carlos or coming within range of the ships or the Rapiers. The 800 Squadron CAP over Pebble Island was alerted and the No 2, Lieutenant Martin Hale, caught sight of the leading Dagger as it crossed the island at high speed and started in pursuit. One of the Argentine wingmen, Teniente H. R. Volponi, was trailing far behind and Hale,

* This was a recurrent problem with the Skyhawks during the conflict and between 20 and 25% of the sorties launched against the Falklands were forced to turn back because of flight-refuelling difficulties.

† E. Villareno, Exocet.

who was being out-distanced by the leader, managed to get within Side-winder range and picked him off. Hit at low level and high speed, Volponi had no chance to eject. He was the seventh VI Air Brigade pilot to be shot down in the course of the twenty-one Dagger sorties which had reached the Falklands on 21 and 23 May. Such a loss rate could not be accepted for long and it would get even worse on the morrow!

The Navy's Super Etendards, blind since the grounding of the last Neptune on the 15th, finally received some targeting information after noon on 23 May. Two aircraft took off in mid-afternoon, armed with Exocets, and flew to a position to the north-east of Port Stanley, presumably directed by *VYCA 2* on the basis of analysis of the deliberately deceptive Sea Harrier traffic patterns. Not surprisingly, when the Super Etendards popped up, as dusk fell, to acquire targets, they saw only empty sea. The pilots continued a little to the east, then turned to make a wide sweep to the south of East Falkland. By the time that they reached Beauchene Island, it was almost completely dark and both pilots were startled when their radar warning receivers alerted them that they were being illuminated by 'fire-control radar'. It is possible that the radar intercepted was that of an 801 Squadron CAP, sent out at dusk to intercept a C-130 believed to be lurking to the south of Port Stanley. The Sea Harriers detected neither the C-130 nor the Super Etendards which reached Rio Grande without further incident.*

The Argentine Air Force did not return to San Carlos that day. The *Antelope* moved up San Carlos Water soon after the last appearance and anchored off Ajax Bay, near the *Fearless*. The serious casualty was moved to the 'Red and Green Life Machine' (the name given to the hospital in the refrigeration factory by the RAMC and naval medical teams, in allusion to the colours of the Paras' and Marines' berets) and two Royal Engineers bomb disposal experts came on board. Warrant Officer Phillips and Staff Sergeant J. Prescott had already rendered safe the *Argonaut*'s boiler-room bomb and now decided to tackle the thousand-pounder in the *Antelope*'s air conditioning unit. The ship's own engineers had braced the bomb so that it would not be moved by shock or vibration, a difficult and dangerous task in the damaged compartment filled with toxic refrigerant gas.

While the two Army specialists, assisted by two of the ship's senior engineers, Lieutenant-Commander R. F. Goodfellow RN and Mechan-ician H. B. Porter, attempted to defuse the bomb, the ship's company gathered on the fo'c'sle and the flight deck, only a skeleton team being left to man the armament and communications. The bomb proved to be recalcitrant and it was decided that a different technique was required. At about 5.15pm the four men attending to the bomb withdrew to fire a small defuzing charge. As they walked back to examine the results, the

* Villareno, *Exocet*.

bomb exploded. Staff Sergeant Prescott was killed instantly, Warrant Officer Phillips' left arm was badly injured (and was subsequently amputated at Ajax Bay), but the two 'Antelopes' sustained only minor injuries, although they were little more than thirty feet from the seat of the blast.

The ship's company had been moved to the flight deck for shelter from the biting wind and, although shaken by the explosion and the 'whip' which had lifted many of them off their feet, they broke out fire-fighting gear and began to tackle the inferno which had spread through three decks and across the width of the ship. The firemain had been cut by the blast and little pressure was available at the hoses, even when supplemented by an auxiliary pump and hoses plied by the crews of two of *Fearless'* LCUs, F1 and F4, commanded by Colour Sergeants M. J. Francis and B. Johnston RM respectively. The latter ignored instructions to lie off due to the intensity of the fire and the risk that the second bomb would explode; he was thus immediately available to evacuate survivors when, at about 6.20pm, the First Lieutenant ordered those on the flight deck to abandon ship. An LCVP took Commander Tobin and his small party off the fo'c'sle to report to Captain Pentreath aboard the *Plymouth* while the remainder of the survivors went to the *Fearless*.

Within ten minutes of the last man leaving the ready-use Seacat magazine appears to have exploded, and soon after that the main Seacat and torpedo magazine blew up.* The fires burnt on throughout the night, with minor explosions, but when dawn came the frigate was still afloat, severely scarred and smoking. Not long afterwards, however, another major explosion (possibly the 1,000lb bomb forward) occurred and, in a renewed conflagration, the ship's back broke and she sank with her bows and stern sticking out of the water, smoke pouring from the area of her 4.5in turret.

During the night of 23/24 May the *Broadsword* teamed up with Sea Kings of 826 Squadron from the *Fort Austin* to hunt for a submarine reported as being sighted from the heights overlooking the Falkland Sound. The *Plymouth* escorted the *Sir Percivale* out of the AOA and brought back the tanker *Tidepool* to replenish the warships which needed fuel. These two ships were followed by the RFA *Resource* and the *Sir Bedivere*, joining up at last with her sister-LSLs, the escort being provided by the *Arrow*, which had been sent into sheltered, if not quiet, waters to assist the defence and to await repairs.

The *Argonaut's* repairs had progressed to the point where she could move under her own steam on one set of machinery, although with severe limitations. The *Yarmouth* remained in San Carlos Water but moved up to the head, beyond the *Fearless*, to cover the approach from the valley to the south-east. At dawn on 24 May four frigates were avail-

* Associated Press Cameraman Martin Cleaver's dramatic photograph of this explosion is probably the best known of all the action shots taken during the campaign.

able for air defence in San Carlos Water, as well as the two LPDs and the Rapier batteries, which had claimed three kills during the previous day.

Port Stanley airfield had enjoyed a respite from attack since *Glamorgan*'s diversionary bombardment on the night of 20/21 May and it was suspected that Argentine strike aircraft might be using it as an emergency diversion. Four SHARs were flown off by *Hermes* at 7.00pm on the 23rd for a night attack on the airfield. The third aircraft, flown by Lieutenant-Commander Gordon Batt on what was to have been his thirtieth operational sortie and seventh low-level strike, crashed into the sea and blew up about a mile ahead of the carrier. The Sea Harrier crashed very close to the *Brilliant* and most of the ships with the Battle Group at first believed that she had been torpedoed and blown up, so intense was the flash. The *Brilliant* searched for the pilot for much of the night, unsuccessfully. The remaining three aircraft delivered their nine 1,000lb bombs accurately and returned safely and undamaged in spite of the usual heavy and accurate AA fire.

The airfield was attacked again at dawn on the 24th, in a co-ordinated strike by 800 Squadron and No 1 Squadron. The two Sea Harriers opened with a loft run from the north-east which attracted the attention of the AA defences and then kept their heads down with a shower of half-a-dozen air-burst bombs to allow two GR3s to make a low-level attack with retarded bombs from the north-west, followed by another pair of GR3s from due west twenty seconds later. Only the last section attracted AA fire and both aircraft sustained minor damage. The 1,000lb bombs scarred the runway surface and nibbled the edges but caused no significant damage.

The carriers' main contribution was, however, providing CAP for the Amphibious Operation Area, and after this strike, the only fixed-wing sorties were by thirty pairs of SHARs. Sea King anti-submarine patrols around the Battle Group continued around the clock and the same aircraft had to be employed for much of the load-lifting between stores ships, topping up those being convoyed in to the AOA and 'consolidating' the stocks of those providing the material. The six Wessex of 848 Squadron remaining in the *Atlantic Conveyor* were invaluable for this work and they were joined by the first Chinook of No 18 Squadron RAF to be restored to flying condition.

DAY FOUR – THE CRITICAL HALF-HOUR

24 May dawned clear in San Carlos Water and the unloading went uninterrupted for over two hours. Although some fifty Argentine fighter-bombers had reached the AOA up to this time, none had attacked ships in the anchorages between Doctor's Head and Ajax Bay, where all the LSLs and stores ships lay. The most dangerous attacks had come from the

24 May: the *Antelope*, with the damaged *Argonaut* behind, burns off Ajax Bay, her hull broken by the explosion of the first 1,000lb bomb and her Seacat ready-use magazine. Shortly after the first photograph was taken, the second bomb 'cooked off' and the frigate sank by the stern, her back broken. Work continued against this grim backdrop, Wessex and Sea King helicopters and the landing craft unloading the newly-arrived *Norland* and *Tidepool* (MoD)

north, through the northern entrance to Falkland Sound, or the west, over Mount Rosalie, but had been dissipated against the escorts in the broad mouth of San Carlos Water. To break up such raids before they could get close, the *Coventry* and *Broadsword* had again teamed up before dawn and taken up a 'missile trap' station off Pebble Island.

The Argentine Air Force commanders were aware of their lack of success and they therefore changed the pattern of their approach to benefit from the terrain instead of being restricted by it. By so doing they also took unwitting advantage of the Royal Navy dispositions: only three ships were fitted with long-range air-warning radar and of these the *Coventry* and *Broadsword* were to the north of West Falkland and the *Argonaut* was inside San Carlos Water, close to the protecting ridges which blanked off low-level cover in certain sectors. By approaching south of West Falkland and then up the length of Lafonia from George Island, the aircraft could reach the gap between ridges which led from Mount Usborne to the head of San Carlos Water with little risk of radar detection. One major strike was planned, with six Skyhawks from V and three from IV Air Brigades and four Daggers of VI Air Brigade getting into San Carlos Water from the south-east, while four more Daggers would approach and attack from the north-west. In the event one A-4B had re-fuelling problems and turned back and what little co-ordination there was between the Daggers and the Skyhawks seems to have been almost coincidental.

The first wave, of the five A-4Bs, was seen by the troops of 2 Para on the Sussex Mountains at 9.45am. Only a few seconds warning could be passed to the ships and the Rapier batteries as the Argentine aircraft swept down to the long inlet and over the line of LSLs off Ajax Bay. *Sir Galahad*, *Sir Lancelot* and *Sir Bedivere* were all hit, the first two by 1,000lb bombs which failed to explode but started fires and the last by a bomb which glanced off the head of the 20-ton crane forward of the bridge, cut

Above left 24 May: the Argentine Air Force finds its way into the transport anchorage and some bombs explode – in this instance between RFAs *Tidepool* and *Stromness* – but none aboard the ships *(MoD)*

Above 24 May: 11.05am – RFA *Sir Lancelot* is damaged for the second time in 20 minutes, this time by the Daggers of 'Azul' Division, led by *Capitan* Mir Gonzalez. Behind the LSL can be seen the distinctive shape of the RFA Stores Ship *Resource* and, stern-on, RFA *Fort Austin (FAA via J. C. D'Odorico)*

Left A Dagger overflies the newly-arrived *Sir Bedivere*, which survived a bomb which skipped off the head of her big crane and passed through a bulwark forward without exploding *(MoD)*

several aerial wires and then went through a bulwark and into the sea, where it did explode. Several of the Skyhawks were damaged but all returned to base.

The two LSLs were still fighting their fires, *Sir Lancelot* aft in her troop accommodation area and *Sir Galahad* forward under her vehicle deck, when the paratroops again gave warning of an attack, this time by the four Daggers, at 10.05am. The defences were now alert to the danger from the south-east and the aircraft were engaged as soon as they came within range, by Seacat, Rapier and automatic weapons of every calibre. As in previous attacks the Daggers strafed as well as bombed, hitting the *Fearless* and the *Sir Galahad*, but the only bomb hit was scored on the *Sir Lancelot* again, and again without the weapon exploding. Bombs fell near RFA *Fort Austin* and between the *Norland* and RFA *Stromness*, throwing up great columns of water as they *did* explode. Two Daggers were claimed shot down by the Rapiers and the Royal Marine Blowpipe Air Defence section aboard the *Sir Bedivere* claimed a 'probable'. The Argentine Air Force admitted that three of the aircraft were badly damaged by gunfire and missiles, but all got back to base.

As this battered division of Daggers left San Carlos Water via Chancho Point, pursued as they believed by a Sea Harrier (but more likely by the Seacats and gunfire of HMS *Plymouth* and *Arrow*), the other Dagger division was running into the arms of an 800 Squadron CAP off Pebble Island. The *Coventry* and *Broadsword* had tracked this raid inbound and the destroyer's Fighter Controller vectored the two SHARs to intercept. The Squadron Commanding Officer, Lieutenant-Commander A. D. Auld, saw the Daggers at their usual very low level approaching between Pebble Island and West Falkland and was able to pull around behind the leading pair and fire both Sidewinders in rapid succession. Even before the two victims crashed, Auld switched to the leader of the other Dagger section and, as the Argentine pair broke hard to starboard, fired at him with his guns. His own No 2, Lieutenant D. A. B. Smith, was well-placed to follow the Daggers' evasive manoeuvre and hit the leader with a Sidewinder. The fourth Dagger was just out of missile range when it rolled out on a westerly heading and it escaped by out-running the two Sea Harriers. Of the downed Argentine pilots, *Major* Puga and *Capitan* Diaz, the two section leaders, ejected safely, but *Teniente* C. J. Castillo lost his life.

This combat, at 10.15am, coincided with the attack by the three A-4Cs on San Carlos Water. Like the Daggers before them, they ran into intense gun and missile fire and this time no hits were scored on the ships. A confident claim was made by the *Fearless* that she had brought down one aircraft; the *Norland* reported that she had been hit by wreckage which had disintegrated overhead when hit by a Rapier (her own AA battery of riflemen had fired 1,200 rounds and claimed to have damaged a 'Mirage') and the Rapier sections claimed another aircraft destroyed. The Argentine version is that all three Skyhawks got away from the target area but that

Teniente J. A. Bono's aircraft went into a spiral dive and crashed into King George Bay with its pilot, apparently as the result of a Blowpipe hit. The leader, *Primer Teniente* J. D. Vazquez, was badly damaged by AA fire and, losing fuel from his holed tanks, had to be 'towed' back to San Julian by the waiting KC-130 Hercules tanker. The third Skyhawk, flown by *Alferez* Martinez, was also damaged.*

There were no further attacks on the 24th. The Argentine Air Force had had an excellent opportunity to inflict very severe damage on the amphibious ships and, indeed, the first wave of A-4Bs, enjoying almost complete surprise, had scored three direct hits and near-missed the *Fort Austin*. The inaccuracy of the IV and VI Air Brigade strikes which followed was in no way made irrelevant by the failure of V Air Brigade's bombs to explode, for the two LSLs were put out action for many critical days. The most significant failure was the obvious reluctance to attack the *Fearless*, large, immobile and very conspicuous at the head of San Carlos Water. The headquarters of the Amphibious Group and 3 Commando Brigade, she was a key target but offered such a fierce defence that the Argentine formations tended to split and go around her to take their chance with the Rapiers and lighter weapons beyond. After their first experience with Rapier on the previous day, the Argentine pilots believed that they could evade the Army missile, which appeared to them as a highly-visible 'flare with a long red tail', knowing that it had to score a direct hit to achieve a kill.[†] At least eight of the twelve aircraft admitted to have flown down San Carlos Water returned to base with varying degrees of damage inflicted by gunfire and missiles.

The Daggers had again suffered unacceptable losses and again the Sea Harriers were entirely responsible. The overall Argentine loss rate could not be sustained for long by any small air force, but the Daggers, with an overall loss rate now of ten out of the twenty-seven sorties which had got anywhere near San Carlos, were a particularly fast-wasting asset. The actual situation was even worse, for some of the aircraft which did return were 'write-offs' and it is doubtful whether VI Air Brigade could have mounted another eight-aircraft operation before the end of the month.

---

* Ethell & Price, op. cit., pp. 139–140; Romero Briasco & Mafe Huertas, op. cit., p. 223. The latter also claim that twenty-four combat sorties were flown over 'the target area' on 24 May, but only the sixteen described above are mentioned. This author is puzzled that although V and VI Air Brigades managed to put up two formations each for this important effort, the only one of the day, IV Air Brigade could field only one section of three aircraft. This Brigade had not been as heavily involved in the 21 May operations as the other two and had not reached the AOA since. If, as is possible, the two sides' accounts of the individual losses are accurate, then a second section of A-4Cs *was* involved. Some substance for this hypothesis is given by British reports that the 10.05am attack was a 'multiple Mirage/A-4' strike. The claims made by the *Sir Bedivere*'s Blowpipe section would thus tally with the loss of Bono's Skyhawk.

† *Aerospacio,* Nov/Dec, 1983.

The ships in San Carlos Water had had their worst moments, but that was not at all apparent at 2.25pm on 24 May. The *Sir Galahad* was beached and on fire, while the *Sir Lancelot* was anchored and on fire. Their Chinese hands were evacuated, leaving the officers and remaining crew members to fight the fires, assisted by teams from other ships. The fires were soon extinguished and the job began of looking for the bombs, which had burrowed deep into the ships' interiors. *Sir Galahad*'s was not found until 2.50pm, rolling around in the battery store among broken batteries and spilt acid. FCDT3 had only arrived that day aboard the *Sir Bedivere* and while the Commanding Officer, Lieutenant N. A. Bruen, dealt with the *Sir Galahad*'s bomb, Fleet Chief Petty Officer G. M. Trotter went after a bomb in the *Sir Lancelot*'s film store and an RAF team, led by Chief Technician Hankinson, rendered first aid to that ship's second bomb, until the naval team could deal with it in the long term. Not until 7 June would the *Sir Lancelot* complete temporary repairs, but in the meantime she acted as an accommodation ship and helicopter refuelling station. A total of 3,342 helicopter landings were recorded on this one ship during Operation 'Corporate'.

The knowledge that a proportion of Argentine bombs were failing to explode ought to have been kept a closely-guarded secret, but the media got wind of it after the *Glasgow* incident and there were Press reports before the landings. On 23 May the BBC World Service trumpeted the news that ships at San Carlos had unexploded bombs on board. This provoked Admiral Woodward's wrath and brought to an end all reference to the phenomenon outside official circles. It did not, however, bring to an end the BBC's policy of 'Broadcast and be Damned' which, though admired abroad for its relentless presentation of the truth, reduced the security of the sailors and troops in the immediate firing line.

The weather deteriorated from midday, haze, mist and low cloud giving the ships in the AOA their first natural cover since the landings. By the end of the day seven days' combat supplies for the Brigade had been put ashore. The *Sir Galahad* was refloated in mid-afternoon and anchored off Ajax Bay again; her bomb was removed and lowered over the side during the night and the ship was patched up to make her seaworthy for the passage to the 'Logistics and Loitering Area' (the 'LOLA'). *Sir Lancelot*'s bombs could not be removed without considerable difficulty and she remained, manned by her European personnel, until FCDT3, assisted by engineers from the *Fearless* and *Intrepid*, could cut them free and hoist them out. Her Chinese personnel left aboard other RFAs and the survivors of HMS *Antelope* were transferred to the *Norland*.

To guard against the possibility of a dusk strike on the Carrier Battle Group, the carriers launched additional aircraft on CAP at about 4.45pm and two 800 Squadron SHARs lofted 1,000lb bombs at Port Stanley to deter any ideas that the Argentine Air Force may have had about refuelling at the airfield. At 5.00pm, out of her fourteen Sea Harriers, the *Hermes* had eight airborne on CAP station or returning, two coming back from the attack on the airfield and two more manned and at three minutes' readiness on deck. The Sea Harriers' record of serviceability was most impressive: seldom was more than one aircraft 'down' at the beginning of each day's operations, or as many as four by the end of the day. By normal standards the two squadrons were under-manned; no maintainers had accompanied the eight extra aircraft of 809 Squadron and only eighteen 'key' NCOs had accompanied the RAF GR3s, so that 800 Squadron was, in effect, looking after nineteen aircraft with personnel for twelve. The contribution made by the British Aerospace and Ferranti representatives, working alongside the squadrons' technicians, was out of all proportion to their numbers.

DAY FIVE – 'VEINTECINCO DE MAYO'

During the evening of 24 May the *Plymouth* escorted RFA *Tidepool*, the *Norland*, *Sir Bedivere* and *Sir Tristram* out of the Falkland Sound and past the Eddystone Rock, fifteen miles to the north, where they were taken in charge by the *Ambuscade* for the passage out of the TEZ.

Everyone was very conscious that the Argentine forces would probably make a major effort on 25 May, the country's National Day, and although it was expected that the Air Force would be the major menace, all personnel were on the alert for any form of attack. Thus, when, at about 2.00am, first the *Resource* and then the *Fort Austin* reported hearing external noises, precautions were taken against an attack by 'frogmen'. Scare charges were dropped around the San Carlos anchorage and the members of the two Fleet Clearance Diving Teams who could be spared from bomb disposal duties carried out underwater searches of the hulls of the *Resource*, *Fort Austin* and *Stromness*. All ships had been checked by dawn, the warships' own divers looking at their ships' bottoms, and nothing had been found. The three big RFAs were moved and re-anchored, this time on the eastern side of the Water, where they were joined by the *Sir Percivale*, *Sir Geraint* and the two damaged LSLs. The ships were now further from where their cargoes were wanted, but the disposition would give better cover from air attack, for aircraft approaching from the south-east would have to run the gauntlet of the San Carlos Settlement Rapier sections, Blowpipes and machine-guns, and would have greater difficulty in lining up for their attacks than had been the case when their run-in had been over water all the way.

The Carrier Battle Group moved closer to the islands than it had been since 4 May and at dawn the *Hermes* was only eighty miles to the east of Port Stanley. As the SHARs now needed only twenty minutes to reach the AOA CAP stations, and could spend correspondingly longer on patrol, the carriers were able to retain more aircraft on deck, for the Group's protection or to thicken up the CAPs, and also to employ the fighters on other tasks. One of these missions was a search by four 800 Squadron aircraft for the *25 de Mayo*, to ensure that she had not managed to slip through the submarine screen unnoticed. The last long-range Nimrod sortie had seen no sign of warship movements, but the aircraft flying the 25 May mission had had to return to base before reaching the latitude of Argentina. The long-range Hercules had also been busy during the preceding days and one of them dropped stores to the *Cardiff* just outside the TEZ on this day.

A semi-official Argentine account of the events of 25 May denies that any special effort was made 'as a homage of blood as an act of national commemoration'.* After the losses of the previous days, such an effort was beyond the Argentine Air Force: sixty-three sorties had been planned for 21 May, forty-six on 23 May and sixteen/twenty had been achieved on the 24th. Only twenty-two were planned for National Day, with a maximum of six aircraft in any individual strike. Nevertheless, the pilots did manage to obtain their most spectacular single success of the war and one which removed a particular thorn from their sides.

The defences of San Carlos were disposed much as they had been on the previous day, with the two LPDs at the ends of the 'loch' and four frigates in support. Outside the Sound, off Pebble Island, but with a little more sea-room than before, the 'Missile Trap' was again provided by the *Coventry* and *Broadsword*, controlling the CAP over Pebble Island. The southerly approach was still inadequately covered by radar, but the defenders were now aware of the threat and the lookouts on the Sussex Mountains were alert.

The first raid was detected at about 8.30am, orbiting to the west of West Falkland. The *Coventry* kept the CAP in hand while the *Broadsword* tracked the aircraft as they came inbound over the island, the Type 22's computers 'talking' to the Type 42's Sea Dart system by means of a data link. At 8.37am the *Coventry*'s Type 909 guidance radar saw the target for itself and the Sea Dart was fired. Seconds later there was the characteristic 'bloom' on the radar which characterised a hit. The victim was *Capitan* H. A. V. Palaver, who had been leading a formation of A-4Bs of V Air Brigade. His wingmen withdrew without attempting to close San Carlos.

The next strike was picked up by the *Coventry* at 10.50am at long range. The CAP was vectored out to meet this formation, which may have been of Daggers, but hers was not the only radar about and *VYCA 2* was eavesdropping on the naval fighter control radio channels. The Argentine pilots were warned that the SHARs were on their way and they broke off their approach and returned to base. This was the first obvious instance

* *Aeroespacio*, November/December, 1983.

of this warning system being used and, although it proved to be very successful, denying the fighters any chance of closing within Sidewinder range for another two weeks, it also meant that the raids failed to reach San Carlos Water.

The third raid was successful in that it escaped detection until it was seen from the Sussex Mountains, entering the valley to the south-east of the Water just before 11.30am. The *Yarmouth* reacted immediately and her Seacat brought down one A-4C before it got as far as the *Fearless*. *Teniente* Ricardo Lucero was (by Argentine admission) the twelfth Air Force Skyhawk pilot to be shot down, but he was the first to survive the

25 May: *Teniente* Ricardo Lucero floats down (left, against the sky line) to land near the *Fearless* while his Skyhawk throws up a large plume of spray as it crashes near Red House Point, on the western shore of the Water. The wreck of the aircraft, shot down by a Seacat fired by the *Yarmouth*, was the only one found by the minehunter *Ledbury* during an exhaustive search of the bottom of San Carlos Water shortly after the end of hostilities *(MoD)*

Left 25 May: the splash of yet another non-exploding bomb which fell a long way off the damaged frigate *Argonaut's* starboard quarter *(MoD)*

experience (seven out of the thirteen Mirage and Dagger pilots had lived to tell the tale) and he was the first Argentine pilot to be taken prisoner, picked out of the water by one of the *Fearless*'s landing craft. Another three Skyhawks were claimed by the Rapiers, but three of the four aircraft which had got past the *Fearless* made it all the way past the *Plymouth* and *Arrow* at the other end. No ship was even near-missed by their bombs, the redisposition on the east side of the Water proving entirely successful.

The Skyhawks (and Daggers) had so far enjoyed almost complete freedom from attack after getting out of San Carlos Water. The *Coventry* had fired a hopeful missile after the retreating IV Air Brigade strike on the 24th, but otherwise the only fighter-bombers to be caught after they had attacked were the three naval A-4Qs on 21 May. The *Broadsword* now picked up the three surviving A-4Cs as they came away from the Water and handed over the track to the *Coventry*. The Type 42's Type 909 radar

The *Coventry* on Missile Trap patrol off Pebble Island during the afternoon of 25 May, seen from behind her goalkeeper *Broadsword*'s forward Sea Wolf launcher. This is believed to be the last photograph taken of this most successful destroyer before the Argentine Air Force attacks *(MoD)*

acquired a target as soon as the raid came out of the Falkland Sound and one Sea Dart was fired at 11.33am and was seen to score a hit. The victim, *Capitan* J. O. Garcia, leading the mission, was killed. *Alferez* G. G. Isaac's Skyhawk had been damaged during his run over San Carlos and, like Vazquez on the 24th, he had to be 'towed' home by a KC-130 tanker, pumping in fuel almost as fast as it ran out of the little delta's holed tanks.

The trap off Pebble Island was functioning as intended and had been responsible for the destruction of five aircraft in the past twenty-four hours – the three Daggers shot down by the CAP under the *Coventry*'s control on the 24th and now two Skyhawks. The *Comando Fuerza Aerea Sur* was aware of its activities, not only from returning aircraft but also from reports radioed by the Pebble Island garrison, which could see the Sea Dart firings. Six A-4Bs of V Air Brigade, led by *Capitan* Carballo, took off from Rio Gallegos at about 1.00pm and rendezvoused with a KC-130 just outside the TEZ. Two aircraft were obliged to drop out and return to base, but the others pressed on and were still at medium level when they were detected over 100 miles to the south-west of the AOA shortly before 2.00pm. The formation split into two pairs, led by Carballo and *Primer Teniente* Velasco, as they came up to the south coast of West Falkland, and as the Grantham Sound CAP headed out to meet them the Skyhawks, possibly advised by the Port Stanley radar, dived under the SHARs.

The raid had been tracking to the east and it was assessed that this was probably another strike bound for the valley down from the Sussex Mountains, an impression that was strengthened when the contacts faded from the radar near Fox Bay, still heading eastwards. The ships in San Carlos Water stood by for their second attack of the day, but when the raid was re-detected the first pair was pulling up to cross the 450-foot ridge on the east coast of West Falkland, opposite the North West Islands, heading *inland* towards Pebble Island. The 800 CAP from the northerly station was well placed to intercept, approaching from the northern entrance to the Falkland Sound narrows and the two pilots, Lieutenant-Commanders Thomas and Blissett, who already had a low-level kill each, had sighted the Argentine aircraft. The second pair of Skyhawks had not yet been re-detected by the *Broadsword*, which was again feeding the *Coventry*'s missile system. On the face of things the leading pair was doomed. Even if the Sidewinders missed, which from previous experience seemed to be an unlikely eventuality, they faced Sea Dart, fresh from two successful engagements in the past few hours, and then the *Broadsword*'s Sea Wolf under conditions ideal for the missile.

Unfortunately the Sea Harriers would not reach a firing position until just before reaching the limit of Sea Dart engagement range and, confident in the efficiency of his system and concerned for the safety of the friendly interceptors, Captain Hart-Dyke of the *Coventry* ordered Thomas and Blissett to haul off, much to the disappointment of the pilots. From that moment things began to go awry. The *Coventry*'s system, although prompted by the *Broadsword*, failed to pick up the A-4Bs as they hugged the water behind Pebble Island and then shot out into the open water through the gap between the island and Pebble Islet, just to the west. From there the Skyhawks had less than a minute's flying time to the two ships and still the Sea Dart system had not acquired, although they were harassed by the destroyer's 4.5in gun. The *Broadsword*'s Sea Wolf radar tracked the targets in, but just as the system should have fired automatically it became confused, possibly by the echoes of the explosions of the *Coventry*'s shells, and, as had happened in the *Brilliant* off Port Stanley, the two missile launchers slewed back to their fore-and-aft positions, leaving insufficient time for a re-engagement. Opposed only by the de-

Top Carballo and Rinke bore in on the *Broadsword*, the Leader bracketed by 40mm tracers, with two bursts visible, one above him and the other to the left of the No2 *(MoD)*

A bomb dropped by the first pair of Skyhawks bounced off the sea and upwards through the thin side plating, exited via the centre of the flight deck and then demolished the nose section of the *Brilliant* Flight Lynx on loan to the *Broadsword*. The impact of the bomb so far aft was caused by the pilots' inexperience in attacking large moving targets *(MoD)*

stroyer's and frigate's guns, Carballo and his wingman (*Teniente* Rinke) closed in, changing target from the Type 42 to the Type 22 as the ships, at high speed, moved across his track faster than he had anticipated. Although damaged by the gunfire, both aircraft pressed their attacks and released two 1,000lb bombs apiece. Three missed but the fourth fell short and ricocheted off the sea, up through the *Broadsword*'s side and then the flight deck, wrecked a Lynx* in its way and then fell into the sea without exploding. The other Lynx on board was slightly damaged.

Velasco and *Alferez* Barrionuevo came out from behind Pebble Island as Carballo and his No 2 pulled away from the ships. The CAP was in pursuit, but again the SHARs had to be warned off as they would not reach a firing position before they came within the Sea Dart envelope. Such faith in the latter merited better fortune, but again the Sea Dart fire control radar did not acquire and the *Coventry* was reduced to firing an unguided missile down the bearing of the attack, a gesture of defiance which was noticed by the Argentine pilots but which passed 300 yards from them. As the Skyhawks came closer, from the starboard bow, the *Coventry* altered course to port slightly, to bring the targets round to the beam and give the *Broadsword* a clearer shot. In the Type 22's Operations Room the Missile Directors followed the Skyhawks through the TV aiming displays as the Sea Wolf system tracked them automatically and with no signs of developing problems. At the critical moment, to the watchers' horror, the *Coventry* appeared in the screens, moving across the launchers' line of sight and preventing an engagement. Although it appeared at the time that the destroyer had turned to starboard, in fact the frigate had followed her alteration of course and, not noticing her steady up, had actually turned further to port, bringing the *Coventry* from dead ahead to broad on the starboard bow. The A-4B pilots delivered a better attack than the leading pair, managing to track the luckless destroyer and put three of their four bombs into her. Although they had been released at very low level and therefore should not have had time to

* To the annoyance of the *Brilliant*, whose aircraft this was. Her other helicopter had also been lost aboard the *Broadsword*, strafed while visiting on 21 May.

arm, at least two, and probably all three, exploded properly, in the ship's machinery spaces. The Skyhawks got away with minor damage.

The second attack was delivered at about 2.19pm. The *Coventry*'s port side was opened and she began to heel at once. The steepening angle and the smoke, which spread rapidly until the ventilation failed, made escape difficult, but thanks to their excellent discipline and knowledge of the ship, casualties were surprisingly light. There could be no question of fighting to save the ship; within fifteen minutes she was on her beam ends and shortly afterwards she rolled over completely. Even before this the first help was arriving from the AOA, Sea King 4s of 846 and 5s of 826 winching survivors off the exposed starboard side while the *Broadsword*'s boats and Wessex 5s of 845 Squadron picked men out of the water. Only nineteen men were lost with the ship, 263 unwounded survivors were flown to San Carlos and put on board the *Fort Austin*, which was to leave that night, four badly-burned men were taken to the hospital ship *Uganda*, well to the north of the Falkland Sound, in the 'Red Cross Box', and sixteen minor cases went to Ajax Bay for treatment.

Primer Teniente Mariano Velasco's bombs go off deep inside the *Coventry*, passing through from starboard to port to explode near the ship's side, under the bridge and in the forward engine room: one path of the blast was back to starboard, marked by the lightest-coloured smoke and the flying debris. The out-of-focus pattern framing the stricken destroyer is one of the *Broadsword*'s bridge windscreen wipers *(MoD)*

Below As evening approaches, the destroyer rolls on to her beam ends, exposing her stabilisers, and the Sea King 4s of 846 Squadron arrive from San Carlos to join rescue operations *(MoD)*

Four successful V Air Brigade pilots – (left to right) *Primer Teniente* Carlos Cachon, *Alferez* Nelson Barrionuevo, *Teniente* Carlos Rinke and *Primer Teniente* Mariano Velasco *(FAA via J.C. D'Odorico)*

The Battle of Clapp's Trap was over. Although it had ended so tragically for the Royal Navy, the British forces had scored a major victory in a grim campaign of attrition. Three modern ships had been sunk and two older warships had been seriously damaged by bombs; the *Brilliant*'s weapons systems had been put out of action by strafing and the *Broadsword* had been hit by shells and a bomb, but both Type 22s were ready for more action by the late afternoon of 25 May.

The same could not be said of the Argentine Air Force's three fighter-bomber brigades. Their losses and the accumulation of damage had reduced effectiveness to the point at which only by husbanding their resources would they be able to make a major effort from time to time and certainly not on a daily basis. Pilot morale was said to be still high and certainly those formations which had got through pressed home attacks, V Air Brigade's effort and determination being particularly impressive. But there were two areas in which there should have been cause for concern on the part of the Air Force command – the number of aircraft aborting missions and the number which claimed to have reached the targets but did not. Out of 167 sorties despatched during the five days, sixty-one turned back before reaching the islands and, according to figures from Argentina,* the other 106 attacked 'their assigned targets'. A correlation of the known Argentine Air Force missions and those reported by British forces reveals that not more than eighty aircraft engaged or were engaged by the defences (and that sixteen of these did not get as far as the Falkland Sound). Thus, only half the effort made by the fighter-bombers was at all effective and although the material state of the Skyhawks was blamed for

* *Aeroespacio*, November/December, 1983.

The *Yarmouth* alongside the *Ardent*, taking off the latter's men (clad in orange survival suits). The intense fire in the Type 21's canteen spaces is giving off dense black smoke, but the light colour of the smoke in the area of the hangar suggests that this fire is virtually under control *(MoD)*

The *Intrepid*'s landing craft (in this instance an LCVP) were distinguishable by their drab camouflage, those of her sister ship being adorned with 'Arctic' stripes *(MoD)*

The *Coventry* seen as the *Broadsword* passes up her port side, less than a minute after the explosion of the bombs. Personnel in the bridge-wing look down on the smoke escaping from the internal fires: externally, there is little sign of damage and the ship is still on an even keel *(MoD)*

Replenishment by every means available. RFA *Blue Rover* refuels the destroyer *Exeter*, loads one of *Intrepid*'s LCUs and 'vertreps' drummed petrol ashore, slung under a Sea King 5 of 826 Squadron *(MoD)*

many of the aborted sorties, this was not the whole story. It is doubtful whether the truth of the 'missing' twenty-six sorties will ever be known.

Even when the aircraft got through, they were not employed in a manner which could have achieved a favourable decision. On 21 and 23 May the Daggers and Skyhawks concentrated entirely on the warships, when absolute priority should have been given to the amphibious shipping. By the time that the *CdoFAS* got around to looking at the map and devising a way of getting into San Carlos Water without running the gauntlet of the frigates at the Falkland Sound entrance, the vital military stores were mostly ashore, so that the damage to the two LSLs would affect only the later resupply shipping capability. There was no obvious plan of attack once the aircraft were in the AOA, pilots going for the nearest, and often the easiest, targets instead of seeking out and concentrating on high-value targets such as the *Fearless* and *Intrepid*. The inability to co-ordinate attacks by more than one Brigade at a time over the target meant that defence suppression – attacks on the frigates or Rapier sections to reduce the volume of fire directed at aircraft attacking the amphibious shipping – could not be attempted. Although the Argentine pilots strafed targets of opportunity on their way in and out, there was no briefed method or pattern and thus no lasting effect from such random attacks.

What could not be realized by either side was that the Argentine Air Force successes were being obtained by a small band of leaders and that V Air Brigade was inflicting the majority of the damage. *Capitan* Pablo Carballo had led three strikes. On 21 May he had near-missed the *Ardent* and bent her radar antenna; on 23 May he and his No 3 had scored the two fatal hits on the *Antelope* and on the 25th he had hit the *Broadsword*. *Primer Teniente* Mariano Velasco had hit the *Argonaut* and sunk the *Coventry*. More was to come from this pair and from *Major* Carlos Martinez, who had led the first VI Brigade attack on the AOA and had scored the bomb hit on the *Antrim*. Apart from these three, only *Vice-Comodoro* Meriel of V Brigade and *Capitan* Horacio Gonzalez of VI Brigade had led formations which had scored bomb hits, on the LSLs on 24 May. IV Air Brigade had taken a beating, with five aircraft shot down and two severely damaged out of the eleven which had engaged, or been engaged by, the defences during the five days, without any compensating success.*

Very few of the British naval and military personnel in 'Bomb Alley', as the Water was predictably nicknamed by the media, had ever been under fire before or had experienced air attacks. All were remarkably steady but the Merchant Navy crew of the *Norland* drew particular admiration for the determination with which they worked their almost defenceless ship even through the 'Red' warnings. The coxswains and crews of the landing craft and Mexeflotes were particularly exposed, their craft being

* Romero Briasco & Mafe Huertas, op. cit. and Ethell & Price, op. cit. for Argentine details

too slow to reach any kind of cover if caught in mid-Water when the alarm of imminent attack was given. Although unlikely targets for 1,000lb bombs, they were frequently loaded with explosive or inflammable cargoes which would readily have 'brewed up' if hit by cannon shells. The helicopters could usually find some cover when an attack developed but occasionally had to dodge approaching aircraft.

By the afternoon of 25 May the beachhead was in good order and the Royal Marines and Paras were getting ready to march out. Their advance over the rugged and almost trackless terrain would be supported by the transport helicopters, particularly the half-dozen Wessexes of 848 Squadron and the four Chinooks of No 18 Squadron RAF. The aircraft, together with the rest of the gear needed to set up the Sea Harrier/Harrier forward operating strip at Port San Carlos, would arrive that night in the *Atlantic Conveyor*.

Chapter Three

The Loss of the
Atlantic Conveyor

The Carrier Battle Group had been 150 miles from San Carlos at the beginning of the day. As usual the TPS-43 radar at Port Stanley was tracking the Sea Harriers but on this day the conditions were particularly good and by 8.00am *VYCA 2* was able to pass a position to Rio Grande that was only five miles from the *Hermes'* actual position. The waiting Super Etendard pilots were alerted and briefed and were ready to start up by 10.00am, but the Air Force KC-130 tankers were at that stage committed to the Skyhawk strikes and the Navy pilots had to wait a further three and a half hours before they could take off.

Capitan de Corbeta R. Curilovic and *Teniente de Navio* J. Barraza were obliged to fly a circuitous route which took them 450 miles to the northeast to rendezvous with the tanker in a position 240 miles north of the Falklands. They then headed east for a few minutes before turning on to a southerly course to approach the Battle Group from an unexpected direction, descending to low level when 150 miles from the estimated position of the target. At about 3.30pm the Super Etendard pilots detected radar trransmissions to port and turned to the south-east.

The carriers were unusually far to the west – only about sixty miles to the north-east of Port Stanley – covering the *Atlantic Conveyor*'s passage to San Carlos and providing a reinforced CAP over the *Coventry* rescue operations off Pebble Island. Going in the other direction were the *Canberra*, *Norland* and *Antrim*, which had been detached to meet the *Queen Elizabeth II* at South Georgia. HMS *Leeds Castle*, which was on the north-west sector of the Battle Group's screen, was ordered to follow and left her station shortly after 3.00pm. Only one picket was available, the *Exeter*, which was stationed twenty-five miles to the west, upthreat from the carriers and the *Atlantic Conveyor*, which was five miles ahead of the *Invincible*. Admiral Woodward was short of escorts and besides the *Brilliant* and *Alacrity*, 'goalkeeping' for the *Hermes* and *Invincible* respectively, he had only the *Glamorgan* and the *Ambuscade*, which was screening the *Atlantic Conveyor*. Also in the immediate area were the LSLs *Sir Bedivere* and *Sir Tristram*.

The two Super Etendards popped up for their targeting radar sweep at 3.36pm, when they were just under forty miles from the *Hermes*. The

Agave radar transmissions were promptly detected and correctly identified by the *Exeter* and the *Ambuscade*, who warned the rest of the Group.
The *Ambuscade* and *Brilliant* then picked up the two aircraft on radar and
tracked them as they headed towards the former frigate. Curilovic and
Barraza, relying entirely on their radar screens for target identification,
saw only three contacts, one small and two large – the *Ambuscade, Sir Tristram* and *Atlantic Conveyor*, and, as in the *Sheffield* action, both aimed at
the same ship.* The two Exocets were launched at 3.38pm, twenty-two
miles from the *Ambuscade* and twenty-six miles from the big aircraft transport. The two Super Etendards broke away to port and escaped at low
level and high speed, evading the CAP which was vectored after them.

The missile launch was detected and all the warships went through the
appropriate drills, firing chaff patterns and turning to bring their
weapons to bear or to present the smallest radar target, depending upon
their AA capabilities. The *Brilliant*'s Sea Wolf system tracked the Exocets
as they approached and were observed to veer to the left and pass under
the *Ambuscade*'s chaff pattern. Unfortunately, as one of the missiles
emerged, baffled, from the cloud of reflective foil, the *Atlantic Conveyor*
appeared in its seeker radar's field of view and it began a fresh attack,
clearly visible from the *Hermes* and the *Brilliant* although outside the
range of the latter's Sea Wolf weapons. The new target, lacking chaff, had
no means of distracting or diverting the Exocet as it homed on her and at
3.41pm the merchant ship was hit on the port quarter, the missile
penetrating to the vehicle decks but failing to explode. Huge fires broke
out at once and the after section of the ship filled with the acrid smoke
noticed when the *Sheffield* was hit.

The warships were looking out for a possible follow-up attack and
shortly after the *Atlantic Conveyor* was hit the *Invincible* picked up a pair of
what appeared to be solid contacts twenty miles from herself and
heading for the *Hermes*, five miles to the north. The carrier's Sea Dart
system also 'saw' the contacts and six missiles were fired in rapid succession. These caused some consternation, the first two to one of the
carrier's own Sea Kings on the anti-submarine screen, the next pair to the
Brilliant's Sea Wolf system, which would have fired automatically at what
it saw to be a threat to its own ship had it not been manually over-ridden,
and the last to the *Hermes*, whose people were convinced that the *Invincible* was firing at their chaff pattern, the Sea Darts passing too close, in
their opinion, for comfort. The *Brilliant*'s radar had not detected any
further contacts approaching the Battle Group and it is likely that the *Invincible* had fired at a convincing 'spurious echo'.

Assistance was already on its way to the burning *Atlantic Conveyor*, the
Alacrity being preceded by the Sea Kings of 826 Squadron, but it was
apparent from an early stage that there was little chance of bringing the

---

* Villarino, *Exocet*.

fires under control, the open, end-to-end main cargo decks having no form of sub-division to check the spread of fire through the vehicles, stores and ordnance. The machinery spaces had to be abandoned due to the smoke and heat and by 3.50pm the ship was dead in the water, with no firemain pressure, leaving the Merchant and Royal Navy firefighting teams with only the auxiliary pumps to provide water for their hoses. These were unable to check the forward spread of the fires and, after the one-shot carbon dioxide 'drenching' system had been used as a last resort, at about 4.15pm, without success, the Master, Captain Ian North, and Senior Naval Officer, Captain Mike Layard RN, agreed that the ship should be abandoned as the fire was rapidly approaching an ordnance stowage containing 75 tons of cluster-bombs. The majority of the personnel on board were in the after section of the ship and they climbed down rope ladders into the sea and then into large inflatable liferafts. The flight deck party and a small team of fire-fighters were cut off by the fire and were lifted off by one of *Hermes'* Sea Kings.

The thirteen men rescued by helicopter were fortunate. Those in the water found that they were unable to get away from the ship's side without great difficulty or assistance and that once in the liferafts they could not paddle away, due to the suction caused by the heave of the rounded hull, which was now glowing red hot in places. The *Alacrity*

The *Atlantic Conveyor* derelict and on fire, on the day after the Exocet attack. So far, the damage is largely restricted to the after section of the ship, but not long after this photograph was taken the fire reached the ammunition stowage and her bows were blown off *(MoD)*

saved them from their very real danger by firing gun lines across the rafts and thus hauling them clear. Most of those in the liferafts were rescued by the *Alacrity*, but some were picked up by the *Brilliant* and a few by the *Invincible*'s helicopters. All of the 150 men rescued were picked up by 5.00pm. Twelve men were lost, among them the doughty Master, who perished between leaving the foot of the ladder and the liferaft.

The *Atlantic Conveyor* remained afloat for several days, but nothing could be salvaged from her. Hers was without question the most serious loss experienced throughout the campaign, that of the *Sir Galahad* not excepted. Although the loss of life was relatively slight, the destruction of three Chinooks and six Wessex 5s deprived 3 Commando Brigade of the reserve of helicopters needed to make it an air-portable, as opposed to air-supported, force. Not only would the Marines and Paras have to march, but the artillery, ammunition, fuel and rations would compete for scarce helicopter assets, delaying the build-up in the forward areas. Every day's extension of the conflict had a real cost in casualties and the midwinter weather brought a further toll of sickness and exposure. The four complete tented camps, with their accompanying field kitchens, laundry and sanitary facilities, capable of supporting 4,500 men in relative comfort, were a further serious loss, to be felt as much by the Argentinians as the British in the event. The aviation deficiencies were further exacerbated, for the runway tracking for the Port San Carlos STOVL* airstrip, a portable fuelling system and six 10-ton fuel tanks, as well as a large number of air-portable 'dough-nut' fuel tanks and large quantities of helicopter spares were left on board the ill-fated ship. One Wessex 5 of 848 Squadron had already been flown ashore and Chinook 'BN' was recovered to the *Hermes* and both helicopters were to play distinguished parts subsequently, although the Chinook lacked even the most necessary servicing tools.

Although they had inflicted no damage within the AOA, the Argentine Air Forces had marked the *Veintecinco de Mayo* anniversary in style, sinking the last of the original batch of Type 42s to arrive in the TEZ and also one of the most valuable of the stores ships, at no direct cost to the attacking aircraft. Replacements for the *Coventry* would join in twenty-four hours and improvisation would alleviate the effects of the loss of *Atlantic Conveyor*'s cargo, although the loss of the helicopters could not be compensated. Admiral Woodward was still not aware that the Super Etendards had been refuelled by the KC-130s and believed that Task Group 317.8 had been struck at the extremity of the aircraft's radius. The carriers were accordingly moved to the east, to remain beyond 460 miles from the nearest mainland airfields, but as the Super Etendards' refuelled radius was at least 750 miles this was of little practical value. It did, of course, complicate precise targeting by *VYCA 2*, but by far the most im-

* Short Take-Off, Vertical Landing.

portant factor which limited future operations by the 2nd Naval Fighter-Attack Squadron was the lack of AM-39 Exocets. Only one missile remained and no more could be obtained, in spite of strenuous efforts throughout the world.

Two bombardments were carried out after dark on 25 May. The *Glamorgan* was detached from the Battle Group and returned, for the first time since the night before the invasion, to her old firing line off Port Stanley. One hundred and forty-six rounds of 4.5in were concentrated on the airfield dispersal areas, just in case one or both of the Super Etendards had landed there after the attack. The *Plymouth*, which had used her main armament only against aircraft since the recapture of South Georgia, left San Carlos and went down the Fox Bay to shell the Argentine garrison. An SBS party took the Army spotters inshore but as the Pacific Searider inflatable was returning after a successful shoot the propeller was knocked off on an underwater obstruction close inshore. While the frigate's Gemini was on its way to the rescue, and to cover the tow back to the ship, the Forward Observation Officer called down more supporting fire to distract the enemy's attention from the two small craft. Altogether, the *Plymouth* fired 174 4.5in shells up to 3.00am, by which time the Gemini and the disabled Searider were out of danger.

In the midst of this activity off the south coasts, the *Fearless* quietly left San Carlos Water for the first time and, after refuelling from the *Tidepool* to the north of the Falkland Sound, headed along the north coast of East Falkland towards Port Salvador. This narrow and hazardous inlet gave access to San Salvador Water, a deep-water harbour whose many long arms reached close to the anticipated battleground in the Mount Kent area. One of these arms, Teal Inlet, had been selected as the Commando Brigade's forward base and shortly after midnight the *Fearless* launched SBS reconnaissance teams in Rigid Raiding Craft to survey Teal Inlet for suitable unobstructed beaches and to report on the whereabouts of Argentine forces. As soon as the Raiders were away, the LPD began the passage back to the AOA, where she anchored well before first light.

May 22: a Rapier 'fire unit' on the White Rincon, 1,000 yards north-east of San Carlos Settlement, ideally sited to cover the transport anchorage and the military build-up around the Settlement *(MoD)*

PART V

The Break-Out

26 MAY

Brigadier Thompson gave his orders for the land advance from the beach-head on 26 May. Two units, 45 Commando and 3 Para, would march overland to secure the shores of Teal Inlet, the Marines 'yomping' to Douglas Settlement and the paras 'tabbing' to Teal Inlet Settlement, carrying over 120lb (55kg) per man. So stretched were the transport resources, air and surface, that even the mortars, Milan anti-tank missiles and Blowpipe launchers had to be humped. While these troops marched to the east, 2 Para would move south to the Darwin Isthmus to screen or attack the Argentine garrison at Darwin and Goose Green, the main enemy position outside the Port Stanley area, other than those in West Falkland. Sea Kings would lift a half-battery of 105mm Light Guns forward and keep them supplied with ammunition, but once action was joined 2 Para would depend upon the Scouts of 3 Commando Brigade Air Squadron for small-arms and mortar ammunition. The 'Black Shoe Commando' – 40 – was to remain to defend the San Carlos area, much to the chagrin of its Marines, who were neither tasked nor equipped for mountain and arctic warfare. 42 Commando was held in reserve, to support any of the early leavers or to exploit any offensive opportunities which might present themselves. Special Forces patrols were out in numbers, probing for weakness and slackness, and the SAS was indeed to find the opportunity for which 42 Commando had been held back.

The Carrier Battle Group moved back to the eastern sector of the TEZ during the night of the 25th/26th and found itself in indifferent weather once again, in contrast to conditions in the AOA, where the day dawned clear. The two fresh Type 21s, HMS *Avenger* and *Active*, joined at about midnight, followed in the early hours by the *Bristol* and, shortly before noon, by the Type 42 *Cardiff*. Three more frigates joined before midnight, the *Minerva* and *Penelope*, armed like the *Argonaut* with Exocet and Seacat, and the *Andromeda*, a particularly welcome arrival as she was armed with Sea Wolf and thus provided a spare 'goalkeeper' for the carriers or other 'high-value units'. In spite of the losses and damage of the preceding four weeks, the force in the South Atlantic was now stronger than it had ever been, particularly as it had acquired experience as well as reinforcements.

The Battle Group spent most of the day replenishing with fuel and stores from the RFAs which were brought clear of the Amphibious Area by the *Ambuscade*. This ship was also detached to inspect the derelict *Atlantic Conveyor*, which was still on fire but otherwise in one piece. Admiral Woodward called forward the tug *Irishman* from the 'Logistics and Loitering Area' to attempt to salvage the damaged ship. In spite of the poor weather, the *Hermes* flew off several GR3 missions but only three of the nine aircraft delivered attacks, one lofting a pair of 1,000lb bombs at Port Stanley airfield and the other two destroying a Puma found at the Argentine forward base near Mount Kent, where the Harrier pilots had to dodge an 'unfriendly' Blowpipe.

On the 25th the *Hermes* and *Invincible* had achieved their highest daily total of SHAR sorties – sixty-three by the twenty-four aircraft embarked in the two ships, and on this day it fell only slightly, to fifty-seven, all of which were CAP missions. Unfortunately, although several patrols were vectored out after raids, none managed to close to near firing range, due to the introduction of revised tactics by the Argentine Air Force. The latter began to send out 'spoof' raids, diversions provided by Mirage IIIs, requisitioned civilian Learjets and strike aircraft, to draw off the SHARs from the real raids, which continued to come in 'under the radar'. *VYCA 2* at Port Stanley controlled the 'spoofers', turning them away as soon as it was clear that the CAP was fully committed. At the radii at which the carrier fighters were operating over the islands, they had sufficient fuel for only one combat or chase and so every time that the Argentine baiting tactics worked (as they had to do, for the naval fighter controllers could not afford to let any raid pass unchallenged) a pair of SHARs was eliminated from the top cover. The Argentine air defence organization at Port Stanley also advised the Dagger and Skyhawk strikes of the approach of the CAP, but this tended to work to the advantage of the defenders of San Carlos, for a strike thus warned seldom made a second approach.

In spite of the disappointment of not getting the *Atlantic Conveyor* in, there was considerable relief at San Carlos that five RFAs had got out in convoy during the night, the *Arrow* taking the *Fort Austin*, *Stromness*, *Resource*, *Tidepool* and *Sir Percivale* out through the North Falkland Sound to meet the *Ambuscade*. Apart from the two LPDs, the only amphibious shipping left in San Carlos Water at dawn on 26 May were the LSLs *Sir Geraint*, *Sir Lancelot* and *Sir Galahad* and the STUFT *Europic Ferry*. The unexploded bomb in the *Sir Galahad*'s battery room was removed at the beginning of the day, but that in *Sir Lancelot*'s film store was proving more difficult and it was fortunate that FCDT3 was able to finish the task in her sister-ship so quickly. The *Argonaut* still had a bomb lodged in her Seacat magazine and FCDT1 was still engaged in cutting and clearance five days after the bombing.

The work of unloading the *Europic Ferry* and ferrying the Marines and Paras to their starting points was undisturbed by enemy air action until early afternoon. At about 1.15pm a CAP section was vectored out after a raid picked up forty miles to the west and two minutes later a small formation of Skyhawks swept into the valley to the south-east of San Carlos Water. They were not prepared to close the ships, however, and dropped their bombs harmlessly behind the 2 Para positions on the Sussex Mountains. As these aircraft made off, pursued by another CAP section, a Dagger raid was detected fifty miles away. These aircraft also managed to evade the SHARs but although they arrived in the general area of San Carlos they did not attempt to attack any defended positions or the ships. A more successful mission was that flown by three Argentine Navy pilots, who brought their Macchi MB339s to Port Stanley undetected, to bring the number of these potentially useful armed jet trainers up to five on the eve of the British land offensive.

As darkness began to fall, 2 Para, accompanied by attached specialists such as a Royal Marines Blowpipe Air Defence Troop, an Artillery observation team and an RAF Forward Air Control section, led by a vastly-experienced veteran Squadron leader, set out on a 12-mile night march, the first stage of their advance on Darwin.

Seven hundred miles to the east the five minesweeping trawlers of the 11th Mine Counter Measures Squadron arrived at Grytviken, where they would await the call for their services. The Cable Ship/despatch vessel *Iris* had arrived on the previous day, bringing with her Lieutenant Keith Mills DSC and his detachment of *Endurance*'s Marines. The *Iris*, assisted by parties from the *Endurance*, began to load steel plate from Stromness and angle-iron girders and oxy-acetelene cutting gas from Leith. Although doubts had been expressed as to whether the Argentine 'scrap-metal dealers' had been on a genuine mission, they had come equipped for the task and had made some progress. Once the materials had been loaded, the *Iris* left for the Logistics and Loitering Area ('Lola', soon to become 'Trala') and transferred the steel and gas to the *Stena Seaspread*. A second Forward Repair Ship had now been taken up: so amenable had the *Stena Seaspread* proved to be to conversion that her sister, *Stena Inspector*, was chartered and converted under a commercial contract at the nearest suitable port, which happened to be Charleston, South Carolina. Special equipment, communications gear and the Naval Party had to be brought out from Britain and, although the work was completed in less than two weeks, the ship had not got further than Ascension by the end of the fighting.

27 MAY

The *Sir Geraint* and *Europic Ferry* left San Carlos during the night and were picked up when clear by the *Active*. There were no inbound sailings and San Carlos Water was left almost empty by comparison with the activity of a week before. The 'Amphibious Phase' was now officially complete and the Brigade was virtually self-sufficient ashore. The ships' main contribution was the provision of helicopters and their support facilities. COMAW's staff was coordinating the tasking of the Sea King and Wessex units, the latter now operating ashore at Port San Carlos with the single Chinook, while 846 Squadron's seven 'daylight' Sea Kings flew from San Carlos and the *Fearless* and the four passive night viewing device-equipped helicopters flew by night from the *Intrepid*. The Scouts and Gazelles of the Brigade Air Squadron were based ashore but made frequent calls on the ships' decks for refuelling, full use being made of the two damaged LSLs for this purpose. The frigates' Wasps and Lynxes were employed for load-lifting, but they were tasked primarily with patrols and searches along the eastern shoreline of the Falkland Sound, and as far north as Cape Dolphin, for signs of Argentine activity or incursions.

It fell to B Company, 40 Commando, to detect the first Argentine presence within the beachhead area. A patrol was fired on in the Verde Mountains overlooking the Water and they winkled out a very dirty Argentine *Capitan de Corbeta* of the Argentine Marine Corps' special forces from a well concealed hide. Ensconced in this vantage point, he had for several days radioed reports of the activity around San Carlos Water and, presumably, the lack of success by his own side in preventing the build-up.

27 May: a 40 Commando patrol brings in an Argentine Marine Corps 'special forces' officer who had been winkled-out while observing the British activities in San Carlos from an eyrie above San Carlos Settlement *(MoD)*

45 Commando and 3 Para set out on their epic hike for Teal Inlet on the 27th. 2 Para had reached the vicinity of Camilla Creek House, less than five miles from Darwin, before dawn and lay up in dead ground, out of sight of the enemy, throughout the day. The Argentinians remained completely unaware of the proximity of the battalion and its artillery troop, but that evening the BBC World Service announced the impending attack on Goose Green, to the fury of all the British commanders. The Argentine defences had already been reinforced since the San Carlos invasion and during the night of 27/28 May more troops were flown in by helicopter from Port Stanley.*

A pair of GR3s distracted the Argentine garrison at 1.00pm. Dropping cluster bombs on troop positions, they then ignored the oft-relearned lesson that re-attacks are invariably hazardous and came back for strafing runs. On his fourth pass Squadron Leader G. R. Iveson RAF was hit by 20mm AA fire and was forced to abandon his burning Harrier to the west of Goose Green. Finding shelter and food in a deserted house, he lay up until after the fall of Goose Green and was eventually retrieved by a naval

---

* It has not been established that the reinforcement was a result of the broadcast.

helicopter on 30 May. The other GR3 was also hit but, although the Argentine Air Force gunners believed that it had probably been destroyed, it managed to return undamaged to the *Hermes*. Another attack on Goose Green that day suffered no damage, the only weapons fired at the GR3s being two Russian-built SA-7 Strela shoulder-launched heat-seeking missiles; a consignment of Strelas, supplied to Argentina by the Peruvian government, had arrived in the islands in mid-May and had been distributed to supplement the existing AA batteries and to provide protection for areas outside the guns' envelopes of fire.

No air attacks threatened the San Carlos area until after noon. This was as well, for at 10.40am the cutting operations in the *Argonaut* led to a substantial fire which was not brought under control until 12.10pm and was extinguished ten minutes later, the frigate's firefighters having been assisted by teams and equipment from the two LPDs. For part of the time the *Argonaut*'s Operations Room had to be evacuated, depriving the anchorage of the only long-range air-warning radar at its disposal.

The expected air raids began in the gloom of the late afternoon, a pair of A-4Bs attacking from the south-east valley with little warning at 3.35pm. For the first time they deliberately attacked targets on shore (possibly as the result of the recently unearthed observer's report that there were no loaded transports present), selecting the Brigade Maintenance Area and the Ajax Bay refrigeration plant for their parachute-retarded bombs. Fortunately, those which hit the building failed to go off, thus sparing the Field Hospital. Unfortunately those which landed in the open supply dump did explode, killing five men and injuring twenty others of the Commando Logistics Regiment and starting major fires among the stacks of ordnance.

The strike had been led by *Primer Teniente* Velasco, who already had the *Argonaut* and the *Coventry* to his credit. This was his last success of the campaign, however, for his Skyhawk was hit and set on fire by the *Fearless*'s 40mm guns and he only got halfway across West Falkland before he was obliged to eject – only the second Air Force A-4 pilot to do so. (Velasco did not meet up with Argentine forces until five days later but was evacuated from the islands before the end of the fighting, aboard the *Bahia Paraiso*.)* *Teniente* Osses, his No 2, was also hit but returned to Rio Gallegos.

A second wave attacked fifteen minutes later. Again two Skyhawks came down the valley and these dropped their bombs on the opposite side of the water on the San Carlos Settlement positions. Two members of 40 Commando were killed and six others wounded, but little material damage was inflicted. Once more the aircraft were accurately engaged by the old Bofors guns, as well as by Rapiers and small arms fire, and one at least was seen to take hits. As had happened a few minutes previously,

---

* Romero Briasco & Mafe Huertas, op. cit.

the subsequent R/T conversation between the pilot of the badly damaged aircraft and his companion was intercepted by the *Fearless*. The tale of mounting problems culminated in an ejection over the sea twenty minutes after pulling away from the target area, an event which was reported by the surviving Skyhawk. The name and fate of the downed pilot is not known, for this loss has not been acknowledged by the Argentine authorities.*

All the casualties from Ajax Bay and San Carlos Settlement were evacuated to the *Intrepid* by 4.05pm. The 'Red and Green Life Machine', with one bomb wedged unexploded inside the building and another in the roof structure, was evacuated of all patients who were fit to be moved, until RAF bomb disposal personnel could examine the bombs in daylight. Flight Lieutenant A. Swan RAF slept beside the bomb inside the hospital as reassurance for the patients and staff who had to remain.

The task of fighting the fire in the nearby Maintenance Area was made more difficult by the strong wind and by the explosions of mortar bombs and Milan warheads. It was far from being under control when the next pair of Argentine aircraft arrived over the Falkland Sound at 4.15pm, shortly after sunset. These, and another section which followed about thirty minutes later, were unable to find San Carlos Water in the gathering darkness, the Ajax Bay fires being concealed behind the high ground of the Sussex Mountains, and after milling around at low level until 4.55pm they returned to their bases without having approached within ten miles of the anchorage.

This was the last low-level attack to be delivered against the British forces in San Carlos Water and the only one to concentrate on the land forces. The stores in the dump had been dispersed as much as was possible within the limited space to minimize losses from air attack, but the bombs from one aircraft had destroyed a large quantity of mortar ammunition and all of 45 Commando's Milan missile launchers and rockets. The Argentine Air Force, had it concentrated earlier on the military build-up, could have seriously disrupted the plans for the re-occupation of East Falkland, but its chance was now gone.

The Battle Group had continued to be affected by fog, low cloud and rain which prevented the carriers from operating their fighters until an hour after dawn. With sufficient escorts now in company, Admiral Woodward was able to detach the *Penelope* and *Avenger* to form an anti-surface screen well to the west of the main body. They also covered the approach of the *Irishman* to the *Atlantic Conveyor*, whose ordnance had by now exploded, blowing the bows off the ship and permitting flooding which gave her a 15° list to starboard. The tug had her in tow by 6.00pm, making to the east at about six knots.

The tow parted after half-an-hour and the two men who had pre-

* For details of this incident, and so many others during the conflict, I am grateful for the use I have been allowed to make of the personal notes kept by participants.

viously boarded the still-smoking *Atlantic Conveyor*, Able Seamen D. P. Betts and G. Bales,* went across again to reconnect a line from the *Irishman*. The tug once again took up the strain but fog had reduced visibility to less than the length of the tow-line and when the derelict ship suddenly plunged late that night there was no warning before the strain on the gear suddenly increased and the line parted. Captain W. Allen took the *Irishman* back and swept through the area but was able to find only three large containers afloat. He reported the loss and the position and made his way back to the Loitering Area.

Only thirty-four CAP sorties were flown, thanks to the weather and lack of Argentine air activity until late afternoon, but the *Hermes* flew off two long-range surface search missions, there having been no long-range Nimrod support for three days. A Nimrod from Ascension was, however, airborne and flew a surveillance mission in the Bahia Blanca area, 780 miles north of the Falklands, on this day. The Argentine 707 had also been active, flying along the main approach route from Ascension and investigating the ships in the 'LOLA'. It was reported by the *Glasgow*, which was receiving attention from the *Stena Seaspread*, but it refused to come within range of the destroyer's Sea Dart. The *Glasgow* left for Ascension and repairs in the United Kingdom on 27 May, running on one Olympus and one Tyne, the repair ship's engineers having jury-rigged plywood intake trunking for the latter engine. On the following day the remaining Olympus gave up but by then the second Tyne was available, although in manual control, and the remainder of her passage was uneventful.

Two GR3s attacked Port Stanley airfield at noon, lofting six delayed-action 1,000lb bombs at the runway and the dispersals, the intention being to make the occupants thoroughly uneasy and to disrupt the supply flights by explosions during the night.

The Royal Navy also had a supply mission that night. The last run into San Carlos had been the *Europic Ferry*'s, on 24 May, and now it was the turn of the *Elk*, which was laden with some 2,500 tons of ammunition as well as stores. The *Elk* was to unload as much as she could during the hours of darkness, but was to be sailed in time to be well clear of the islands by dawn, so as not to be exposed to the risk of air attack. Escorted by the *Ambuscade* and accompanied by the *Tidepool*, which was to replenish the ships in the AOA, she parted company with the Battle Group at 1.00pm and arrived in San Carlos Water about six hours later, escorted during the last stage by the *Plymouth*.

The Argentine Army had more to worry about during the night of 27/28 May than the arrival of two supply ships. The biggest bombardment programme so far had been organized to divert the occupiers' attention from the 2 Para attack on Darwin–Goose Green and to support the attack itself,

---

* Both of whom were awarded the British Empire Medal for their efforts.

five ships firing over 700 rounds of 4.5in (17½ tons of shells) between them. The *Glamorgan, Avenger* and *Alacrity* detached from the Battle Group at sunset and took up stations to the south of the peninsula on which Port Stanley stands. Captain Barrow took the *Glamorgan* back to a familiar target, the airfield. Only fifty rounds of 4.5in were fired to disturb the defenders and deter any air transport movements, but the destroyer introduced a new bombardment weapon. The Seaslug missile in the surface-to-surface mode weighed as much as a 15in shell and arrived almost as fast; effective against targets with 'vertical extent', such as the airfield buildings, it would appear that at least one did score a direct hit.

It is possible that both sides used missiles during the night. The Argentine Navy had improvised a trailer-mounted MM-38 Exocet coast defence battery, flying in the launch canisters landed from the Type A.69 corvettes. Targeting was provided by the ubiquitous TPS-43 radar and the missiles could be fired from anywhere along the hard road between Port Stanley and the airfield. The *Avenger* was to the south of Harriet Cove, between firing runs, when a large projectile hurtled noisily across her flight deck at a height of about five feet. The frigate was well out of range of the Argentine field guns and surface-to-air missiles and Captain H. M. White and his ship's company were convinced that they had been the target of the first shore-based Exocet firing.

One of the successful examples of Argentine Navy improvisation was the deployment of trailers mounting Exocet launchers taken from the A-69 corvettes. The trailers and their towing vehicles could not be used off the limited length of tarmac road in the Port Stanley area, which restricted their siting for firing at the bombarding ships. During the day the trailers were parked in the town, which was regarded as a sanctuary area by both sides *(MoD)*

Despite the interruption, the *Avenger* fired 100 rounds at Sapper Hill and defensive positions around Harriet Cove and the *Alacrity* distributed 109 rounds among the regiments holding the hills overlooking the town – Wireless Ridge, Mount Harriet and Tumbledown.

While the three ships from the Battle Group were harassing the enemy around Port Stanley between 10.30pm and 1.15am, one of the Amphibious Group frigates, the *Yarmouth*, was delivering even more shells to distract the enemy in the Port Howard area. The *Yarmouth* had been with the force since its arrival in the TEZ on 1 May and had helped to beat off the attacks on the AOA, but this was her first bombardment serial. A Royal Artillery Forward Observation Team spotted the fall of 300 rounds of 4.5in without any of the unwelcome excitement which had attended the *Plymouth*'s shelling of Fox Bay a few nights previously.

Opposite Port Howard, close up against the southern shore of Grantham Sound, Commander Bootherstone had taken the *Arrow* into almost the same position that the *Ardent* had occupied only a week before in order to support 2 Para's attack. At 10.35pm she opened fire with star-shell to illuminate Darwin, following up with high-explosive air bursts, initially on known positions and then as called for by the spotting teams. A gun defect caused a break in the support for a while, but this was rectified and the accurate, controlled fire resumed.

SOUTH GEORGIA, 27–30 MAY

As 3 Commando Brigade was opening its first battle of the campaign, 5 Infantry Brigade was nearing the combat area. At 9.30am (Falklands time) on the 27th the *Antrim* rendezvoused with the *Queen Elizabeth II* to the north-east of South Georgia and embarked the Commander, Land Forces, Falkland Islands (CLFFI), Major General Jeremy J. Moore OBE MC. As Major-General, RM Commando Forces and Admiral Fieldhouse's Land Forces Deputy, he had been involved in all the planning stages up to 20 May, when he left Northwood to fly to Ascension to join the *QE2*. He took with him to *Antrim* the commander of 5 Infantry Brigade, Brigadier M. J. A. Wilson OBE MC, and the destroyer set out to rejoin the Battle Group, where the two senior military officers would confer with the naval commanders, Admiral Woodward and Commodore Clapp, and then transfer to the *Fearless* for the last stage of the journey to East Falkland.

The *Fearless* sailed from San Carlos Water at 6.10pm, about an hour before the *QE2* anchored in Cumberland Bay, off Grytviken. The latter had been preceded to South Georgia by the *Canberra* and *Norland*, which had been led in by HMS *Endurance* at 11.00am, and the arrangements for the transfer of the men and stores had already been made. Although the infantry had not expected to move until the following morning, Captain

Barker, the naval commander in South Georgia, and Captain C. P. O. Burne, the *Canberra*'s Senior Naval Officer, insisted that the transfer should commence without delay. Not only were the battalions urgently required in the Falklands, there was a definite risk of air attack on South Georgia – the BBC World Service had announced that the Cunard liner was approaching the combat area – and the heaviest AA weapon in the area was the *Leeds Castle*'s single Bofors. Within an hour of the *QE2* anchoring, the tug RMAS *Typhoon* was alongside to begin embarking men of the two Guards' battalions and their weapons and stores. She was followed by the trawlers *Pict, Cordella* and *Farnella*, which plied between the two liners, and *Junella* and *Northella*, which, assisted by the *Typhoon*, took the Gurkhas to the *Norland*.

The cross-decking continued throughout the night and the next day, in the usual extremes of South Georgia weather – 'gin-clear, flat calm to 100 yards visibility in a 60-knot blizzard faster than you can shake a stick'. The new arrival had brought two Sea King 2s of 825 Squadron and these, with the *Endurance*'s two Wasps, flew continuously during daylight. It had been hoped to use the *Leeds Castle* as a ferry, but she was unable to berth under the *Queen Elizabeth II*'s flared hull and so she was used as a fuelling station between the liners, permitting the helicopters to fly maximum load-minimum fuel sorties. No less that 250 tons of stores of all kinds were ferried to the *Canberra* and *Norland* by the helicopters and small ships, with the captured orange LCVP also involved. Over 3,000 men of all three Services left the *QE2*. As well as the three battalions of riflemen and guardsmen, there were the personnel of 4 Field Regiment RA, 656 Squadron Army Air Corps and No 63 Squadron RAF Regiment (whose guns, helicopters and Rapier systems were embarked in the *Baltic Ferry*

RFA *Stromness* loads 5 Infantry Brigade stores from the *Farnella* off Leith, South Georgia *(MoD)*

The Guards battalions of 5 Infantry Brigade transfer from the QE2 to the rusting 'Great White Whale', using the two 825 Squadron Sea King 2s, the minesweeping trawlers and the *Canberra*'s boats *(MoD)*

and *Nordic Ferry*, bound direct for San Carlos Water), 16 Field Hospital, Royal Engineers of two Squadrons, the Brigade Signalling Staff and the naval personnel of 825 Squadron, whose two Sea Kings transferred to the *Canberra* at dusk on 28 May. Shortly before 9.00pm the *Canberra* and *Norland* weighed anchor and began their passage back to the Falklands TEZ.

Before they departed, the number of ships in the bays of South Georgia had been further increased – there were already more than were present at San Carlos during these days – by the arrival of RFAs *Stromness* and *Resource* from the TEZ and of the STUFT ammunition ship *Lycaon*, carrying thousands of rounds of 4.5in ammunition, naval missiles and other ordnance and dry stores, some of which had been picked up at Ascension. The *Stromness* transferred ammunition from the *Lycaon* and various stores from the QE2 while the *Resource* began an epic transfer from the refrigerator ship *Saxonia*, embarking frozen and fresh food and clothing with the aid of the 'Ellas' and with the opposition of the South Georgia weather, which did its worst during the next five days. The process was further complicated by an unconfirmed report of high-level air activity over Cumberland Bay on the 29th, obliging Captain Barker to disperse ships which were not actually transferring stores. The *Queen Elizabeth II* sailed at sunset, bound for the United Kingdom with the survivors of the *Ardent*, *Antelope* and *Coventry*. The luxury of their surroundings was in marked contrast to those in the tankers *British Esk* and *British Tay*, ferrying the uninjured survivors of the *Sheffield* and the *Atlantic Conveyor*, respectively, to Ascension. The *Leeds Castle* sailed at about the same time as the big liner and, like her, was routed to the east to remain beyond the considerable reach of the Argentine Air Force.

The *Stromness* left South Georgia, having visited Stromness Bay (named, like the ship, after a headland in the Orkney Islands), on the day after the QE2 and returned to the TEZ to transfer the ammunition to the

warships and the stores to the LSLs, which were consolidating in preparation for the establishment of a Forward Maintenance Area.

28 MAY

The *Arrow* fired twenty-two rounds of starshell and 135 rounds of high-explosive shell during the first five hours of 2 Para's advance. The 55lb HE projectiles had a devastating effect on the Argentine defenders, arriving with great accuracy from a range of over ten miles and, in the opinion of 3 Commando Brigade staff officers, were the decisive factor in the speed of the paras' advance through Darwin and up the narrow isthmus to the main Argentine defence line in front of Goose Green. As this line was reached, about two hours before dawn, the *Arrow* came to the end of her programmed contribution and she left her station, following her orders that she was to be back in San Carlos Water by dawn. That she had to withdraw as 2 Para was about to meet the stiffest opposition was unfortunate, but was dictated by experience. The *Ardent* had been lost after a bombardment operation in the same area and the *Arrow*'s weapons were still needed for the defence of the ships and stores in the San Carlos area.

Whether or not the Argentine Air Force was capable of mounting strikes, the weather was unsuitable at the mainland bases and there was extensive low cloud over the Falklands, with very patchy visibility beneath. It had been intended that 2 Para should have had close air support from No 1 Squadron's GR3s from dawn, but the carriers were shrouded in thick fog which did not lift until about 10.00am, preventing all jet flying. The advance on Goose Green was therefore supported only by the three 105mm Light Guns back at Camilla Creek House, firing as fast as 846's Sea Kings could bring up the ammunition from Ajax Bay, while the paratroops were opposed by the same number of Argentine howitzers and also the automatic AA cannon, which could lay down a withering fire on exposed positions. The paras' momentum was checked while they probed for weaknesses in the enemy line, and it was during this phase that Lieutenant-Colonel H. Jones, the Commanding Officer of the battalion, made the single-handed charge in which he was mortally wounded and for which he was awarded, posthumously, the Victoria Cross.

From soon after dawn the Pucaras based at Goose Green attempted to take a hand in the battle, at least two pairs taking off armed with rockets and napalm. The latter came as a particularly unpleasant surprise but the Argentine pilots released the tanks of jellied petroleum inaccurately and no casualties were suffered from this cause. The Pucaras, operating under the low overcast, against which they were clearly silhouetted, were engaged by machine-guns and rifles and also by the Marine Blow-pipe operators, one of whom picked off *Teniente* Cruzado's aircraft as it got airborne from the airstrip. Cruzado ejected and survived. *Teniente* H. Argonaraz was also hit by a Blowpipe as he pulled out of a napalm run and he too ejected safely, at very low level. Other Pucaras were hit by ground-fire but they could absorb such minor damage and the impact of an explosive projectile was needed to knock them down.

The *Hermes* flew off two Harrier missions, at 10.00am and noon, but neither was able to get into the battle area due to the poor weather. One pair, armed with rockets, was diverted to reconnoitre the Douglas Settlement area, ahead of 45 Commando, and the other dropped its bombs on Argentine positions in the vicinity of Mount Kent. The Argentine units based at Port Stanley were similarly frustrated in their attempts to reach the battlefield. Soon after dawn a pair of naval Macchi 339s took off but as they were approaching the target area the Argentine Air Force controller informed them that the visiblity was too bad and ordered them to return to base.

The Macchis were not ready for a second sortie until mid-afternoon but in the meantime Pucaras from Port Stanley managed to reach the Darwin area at about 11.00am, approaching up the long arm of Choiseul Sound. As they did so, two of 3 Commando Brigade Air Squadron's Scouts were sighted, flying towards Darwin. The Marine helicopters had been active since dawn, taking ammunition forward and ferrying casualties back to Camilla Creek House, where they were transferred to the artillery supply Sea Kings for delivery to the Ajax Bay Hospital. Captain J. P. Niblett RM and Lieutenant R. J. Nunn RM had been called up on this occasion to collect Major C. P. B. Keeble, second-in-command of 2 Para, from the Battalion Command Post and take him forward to the Tactical HQ, whence they were to evacuate the mortally-wounded Lieutenant-Colonel Jones and other casualties. The two Pucaras attacked the two Scouts, which managed to evade the first pass. The Argentine aircraft then ganged up on Lieutenant Nunn, making a co-ordinated attack with guns and rockets which scored hits, killing the pilot and seriously wounding the crewman, Sergeant A. R. Belcher. Captain Niblett and his crewman (Sergeant J. W. Glaze) were subjected to three further attacks, each of which was skilfully avoided by changes of speed and direction which prevented the Pucara pilots from getting a clear shot at the helicopter. The Pucaras broke off and the Scout went on with its mission on the battlefield.* The Argentine aircraft, once again, did not get away without loss, although on this occasion it was an accident that cost the life of *Teniente* M. A. Gimenez, who became separated from his wingman in cloud during the return to Port Stanley and whose wrecked aircraft was not discovered until 1986.

The naval Macchis were ready to take off again by 2.30pm but were prevented by a crosswind which did not moderate sufficiently for them to get airborne safely for another hour and a half. The *Hermes* had no such problem – a stiff breeze was positively helpful and she simply turned into it to fly off three GR3s to take advantage of the improvement in visibility which was brought by the same wind which kept the Port Stanley aircraft on the ground. Led by Squadron Leader P. Harris RAF, the Harriers flew down the strip of water that led from Grantham Sound and, at the request of 2 Para, attacked the AA gun sites which were firing over open sights at the troops. Two aircraft reduced the fire of the four Argentine Air Force 20mm guns still in action and silenced the two Army 35mm guns with a curtain of cluster bombs, the third following up from the north with the contents of two 36-round rocket pods, delivered into the general area from which the Argentine supporting fire was coming.

This attack was quite decisive. The defensive fire slackened appreciably and from 3.35pm, when it was delivered, the Paras began to make inroads on the Argentine positions, outflanking and driving back the defenders to the edge of the airstrip. (The Argentine Air Force claimed that their 20mm guns ran out of ammunition at about 4.30pm, but sufficient remained to supply the captured guns when the Royal Navy appropriated them for its own uses.) The Macchis' attack, delivered about half an hour after No 1 Squadron's intervention, had no effect on the renewed momentum of the advance and again it cost an aircraft, *Teniente de Corbeta* D. E. Miguel losing his life when his little jet was hit by yet another Blowpipe fired by the Marine Air Defence Troop.

More Marines were on their way. As dusk fell 'Juliet' Company, 42 Commando, was flown in to Darwin to reinforce 2 Para. This was a rather special company, for it was composed mainly of the members of Naval Party 8901 who had defended Port Stanley eight weeks before and had been re-equipped and sent out again. Helicopters also brought forward more ammunition and rations for 2 Para, the light aircraft flown by the Marines of 3 CBAS and the soldiers of No 656 Squadron AAC continuing

---

* Both Scout pilots were awarded the Distinguished Flying Cross (Lieutenant Nunn posthumously), although they were Royal Marine officers engaged in strictly military operations at the time and might have been expected to receive the Military Cross.

until well after nightfall, when the guns began to fall silent.

Events outside the Darwin–Goose Green area were much less dramatic, although the removal of the bomb from HMS *Argonaut*'s Seacat magazine marked the end of a week's nerve-racking endeavour by FCDT 1. The frigate was capable of steaming but required more extensive repairs than were at present available at San Carlos to make her fully seaworthy for the long passage home. The AOA was comparatively quiet, for with the departure of the *Fearless* and the quick turn-around of the *Elk* and RFA *Tidepool* it was emptier than ever, although activity ashore remained undiminished.

The *Fearless* met and passed through the Carrier Battle Group shortly before dawn on the 28th, 100 miles to the east of Port Stanley. Three hours later she was clear of the TEZ and enjoying a much-needed rest as she headed for a rendezvous with the *Antrim*. The weather, fog in the morning and a rising wind and sea in the afternoon, limited the carriers' flying programme to the three GR3 missions already described and just eighteen SHAR CAP sorties, the lowest number for a fortnight. Four of the Sea Harriers of 801 Squadron lofted a 1,000lb bomb apiece at Port Stanley airfield at the beginning of their patrols. Although the Argentine accounts do not mention the attacks, they may have been the reason for the lengthy turn-around needed for the two Macchis and the small scale of Pucara activity.

There was no mainland strike mission, but the presence of shadowers in the Logistics and Loitering Area led to the detachment of HMS *Bristol* as 'Lola Manager', to defend and manage the RFAs and STUFT, ensuring that ships bound for the Battle Group or the AOA were available, had the appropriate instructions and were ready to leave on time.

The *Elk* remained with the Battle Group throughout the 28th, in readiness for another in-and-out run to San Carlos, but the heavy head seas forced the abandonment of the operation. For the same reason there was no bombardment programme during the night.

Shortly before midnight the first Argentine night air raid was detected approaching from the north-west. The two Canberras of II Air Brigade did not overfly the San Carlos area and dropped their bombs blind through the cloud, some ten miles to the east of the anchorage. No British units were in the area. 45 Commando had reached Douglas Settlement late in the afternoon and 3 Para were even further to the east, resting before entering Teal Inlet Settlement the next day.

29 MAY

Major Chris Keeble began negotiations with the defenders of Goose Green before dawn on 29 May. With the arrival of Juliet Company, 42 Commando, he was stronger in riflemen than he had been at the beginning of the previous day. The Sea Kings had flown in another three 105mm Light Guns and enough ammunition, for another battle was on its way; if necessary, three GR3s could be called up. It was not necessary. The two Army Regiments, the 250 Air Force personnel and an infantry company which had been flown in to the south during the night, marching into Goose Green after dawn, surrendered to 2 Para at about 9.00am. Fewer than 700 British troops had taken a strong position occupied by about 1,100 Argentine personnel who had been able to call upon more firepower than the attackers could muster. British losses, mostly in 2 Para, were sixteen killed and thirty-four wounded. The Argentinians lost forty-seven dead and over 100 seriously wounded. The latter, like the British wounded, were flown back to Ajax Bay and treated in the 'Red and Green Life Machine'. For them, as for the dejected prisoners at Goose Green, the annual 'Army Day' holiday would be memorable for the wrong reasons.

Elsewhere the advance on Port Stanley was going to plan and an opportunity had presented itself to accelerate the pace. 3 Para reached Teal and 45 Commando, after a night's rest at Douglas, set out for the same place. An SAS patrol had been watching the Argentine mobile reserve on Mount Kent for several days and, as soon as the last company was flown out to Lafonia on the night of 28/29 May, the Special Forces troopers moved in to take over the position, which was the key to the outer gate of Port Stanley, just eleven miles to the east. That the Argentine Army should have left it even briefly unoccupied was surprising, that they failed to repossess it was incomprehensible. The opportunity was what 42 Commando had been held in reserve for, but the Sea Kings attempting to lift 'Kilo' Company forward were driven back by low cloud, fog and snow storms and the SAS had to fend for themselves (which they were well able to do) during the day.

RFA *Sir Percivale* returned to San Carlos early on the 29th, escorted to the AOA by HMS *Minerva*, which was back with the Battle Group by 4.00am. The LSL 'back-loaded' stores in preparation for opening up Teal Inlet as 3 Commando Brigade's forward maintenance area for the final drive on Port Stanley. At 6.00am Fleet Chief Petty Officer Trotter's FCDT 3 working party at last managed to drop *Sir Lancelot*'s bomb over the side and for the first time since early on 'D'-Day there was no unexploded bomb in any ship at San Carlos.

The usual bustle at San Carlos was briefly halted at 11.35am, when the Argentine Air Force made its first full-daylight entry to the Water since 25 May. A pair of aircraft, identified as 'a Mirage and a Skyhawk', an ill-matched pair if true, was engaged by the Rapiers as they passed between Fanning Head and Chancho Point and the Dagger flown by *Teniente* J. D. Bernhardt was shot down by a missile fired from the Port San Carlos foreshore.

It is likely that this intrusion was a reconnaissance mission, a peep under the weather to see what was happening, but there was no doubt about the offensive intent of the aircraft which found the southbound STUFT tanker *British Wye* 780 miles east-north-east of San Carlos just a few minutes before Bernhardt's Dagger was splashed. The Argentine Air Force 707s were still tracking British shipping as it moved up and down the 'Motorway' between Ascension and the operational areas, but since 'TC–92''s narrow escape from *Cardiff*'s Sea Dart on 22 May they had remained at high altitude and at a respectful distance from the surface contacts. Visual identification was obviously desirable and it appears that from 29 May, if not earlier, an armed low-level probe was used for investigation of some radar contacts.

At 11.15am (Falklands time), *British Wye* was 400 miles north of South Georgia and 1,000 miles from the nearest Argentine airfield when she was subjected to a number of low-level bombing runs, to which she was unable to reply. The aircraft, an Argentine Air Force C-130 Hercules, dropped eight bombs in all but only one hit and that bounced off the ship's forecastle into the sea. At the time it was reported that the bombs had been pushed out of the open rear cargo door but the Argentinians have since said that the aircraft had been fitted with multiple bomb racks normally used on Pucaras.

The Argentine Air Force was short of C-130s. Only nine aircraft of the type were on strength, of which two were permanently reserved for flight refuelling duties and the others might have been expected to be held back for the dangerous Port Stanley resupply run. But the Argentine Air Force had correctly identified the most fragile link in the British operation – the long supply line. No ship came south without urgently required stores of some kind, needed to keep ships, aircraft and men in action, and the loss of any one of the tankers or stores ships would have had an impact on the campaign. Warships could not be spared to escort individual supply ships and the need for swift delivery did not allow of any delay, so that convoys were not formed. After the capture of the submarine *Santa Fe*, the Royal Navy took a calculated risk, relying upon the nuclear submarines, backed up by the long-range Nimrod sorties (the most recent had been on 27 May), to give warning of a possible surface 'raider' force and routeing the STUFT and RFAs beyond the radius of action of the mainland-based Canberras, which were the Argentine Air Force's only purpose-built long-range bombers. The C-130 could reach 400 miles further than the Canberra – it was known to have reached South Georgia – but its use as a direct attack aircraft appears to have come as an understandable surprise to the Royal Navy.

To counter further such raids, ships between the operational areas and Ascension were ordered to use tracks further to the east. Besides the *Fort Grange* and the *British Wye*, the only other southbound ship was the *Atlantic Causeway*, ferrying twenty-eight assault helicopters and the Rapiers of 63 Squadron RAF Regiment. Northbound were three tankers, the *British*

Tamar, the *British Tay* (with the *Atlantic Conveyor*'s 133 fit survivors on board) and the *British Avon*, which had left the Logistics Area on 25 May. The concentration of shipping at South Georgia could only be warned to remain alert until a guardship, with longer-range radar and weapons than HMS *Endurance*, could be provided.

HMS *Fearless* met the *Antrim* in the early hours of the 29th, 100 miles from the eastern edge of the TEZ, and at dawn began to transfer Major-General Moore, Brigadier Wilson and their staffs, using the one 845 Squadron Wessex 5 which she had brought from San Carlos. Once the embarkation was complete, the LPD headed for the Carrier Battle Group, accompanied by the *Antrim*, which would replenish with fuel, stores and provisions before proceeding to South Georgia to assume responsibility for local air defence. Thanks to the efforts of her crew and assistance from other ships, the destroyer now had one 'barrel' of her Seaslug launcher operational and the Wessex was again serviceable.

The carriers operated in a full gale and a rough sea all day. The nineteen CAP missions found no 'trade', but the heaviest strike programme since the opening day was flown by the SHARs, 800 Squadron making two attacks on each of Port Stanley and Pebble Island, where renewed activity on the ground had been observed, and 801 Squadron delivering one strike by a pair of 'bombers' and a couple of bombs by a CAP mission, all at Port Stanley airfield. The pilots regarded it as rather unusual, but nonetheless welcome, that there should be no warning radar detections or anti-aircraft fire at either airfield. The bombing was accurate, putting one of the Pebble Island strips out of action (for the expenditure of twelve 1,000lb bombs), while at least fourteen of the twenty bombs lofted at Port Stanley fell in the runway area. The third strike on Port Stanley coincided with the only GR3 mission of the day, an attack on Argentine positions in the Mount Kent area, in support of the SAS patrol. The intervention appears to have been successful, for the troopers continued in possession of the vital feature.

In mid-afternoon the *Invincible* lost a Sea Harrier to a freakish accident. Lieutenant-Commander M. Broadwater's aircraft was lined up for take-off for a CAP sortie as the ship turned into wind for the launch. As it did so, the combined effects of a heavy sea and the wind caused his aircraft to pivot and slide until one of the outriggers went over the deck-edge and the whole aircraft toppled over the ship's side. Mike Broadwater escaped by using his rocket-powered ejection seat and was quickly picked up from the water by a Sea King, having suffered only superficial injury.

The *Fearless* and *Antrim*, which had been screened from the edge of the TEZ by the frigate *Active*, had by now met up with the Battle Group and General Moore and Commodore Clapp had flown across to the *Hermes* at 2.00pm to confer with Admiral Woodward. They remained on board until 3.45pm, discussing the roles all three commanders would play during the remainder of the land campaign. The *Fearless*, meanwhile, was 'vertrepping' stores for herself and the units at San Carlos and embarking personnel, including the Surgical Support Team from the *Hermes* and the crew of the *Sir Lancelot*. Bad weather brought a halt to helicopter transfers an hour after sunset and at 6.40pm the LPD detached to return to the AOA, escorted by the *Minerva* and the *Penelope*.

Two other groups had previously left for inshore waters. The *Elk* and *Tidepool* had left as early as 11.30am, escorted by the *Andromeda* and *Alacrity* and taking advantage of the bad weather which would screen them from detection and attack. At 2.40pm the *Glamorgan* and *Ambuscade* detached with the *Avenger*, the last-named to insert a Special Forces patrol in East Falkland and the other two ships to continue the harassment of the Port Stanley area.

The warship traffic was two-way, making this one of the busiest nights of the campaign. The *Intrepid* and *Plymouth* sailed after dark, to rest and replenish with the Battle Group, and the *Arrow* went down the Falkland Sound to shell Fox Bay, last visited four days before. As the *Yarmouth* was also at sea, to shepherd in the *Elk* and *Tidepool*, San Carlos Water, with only the *Argonaut* and three LSLs, was for a while almost empty.

Completely unknown to the British, the Argentine Air Force was involved in a very courageous mission around sunset on that day. A light twin-engined STOL transport (a De Havilland Twin Otter), escorted as far as the Jasons by a Fokker F.27 transport, managed to land on the only strip useable at Pebble Island. It had been intended that it should pick up its passengers without stopping its engines, but the dusk SHAR CAP had been seen in the area and take-off was delayed for an hour and a half, until 4.55pm, by which time it was completely dark. The Twin Otter crew had expected to collect two Dagger pilots – *Major* Puga and *Capitan* Diaz, shot down on the 24th – but they were asked to evacuate three naval pilots, a sick naval rating and the body of *Teniente* H. Volponi, recovered from the wreckage of the Dagger shot down by Lieutenant Hale on 23 May. Six hundred pounds (75 gallons) of fuel had to be pumped out of the aircraft to enable it to take off from the 550-yard rough strip of soggy grass, surrounded by bomb craters and the wreckage of the aircraft blown up in the SAS raid. Only a minimum of lighting could be used, but the Twin Otter pilot took off safely, turned immediately to avoid the 900-foot hill less than two miles from the end of the runway and flew back to Puerto Deseado at low level picking up the F.27 escort which had been orbiting off the Jasons at low level for over two hours. The two unarmed aircraft landed safely and their passengers were transferred to hospital.*

---

* *Aeroespacio*, September/October, 1984.

30 MAY

Apart from the *Penelope* being obliged to return prematurely to the Carrier Battle Group due to mechanical problems, the night's movements went as planned. The *Elk* and *Tidepool* remained in San Carlos Water, unloading ammunition and refuelling the guardships respectively, for about four hours. As they left the Sound to rejoin the *Andromeda* – left to patrol off the Eddystone for six hours – they passed the inbound *Uganda*, her white upperworks and red crosses brightly illuminated. The hospital ship, which had been stationed about thirty miles to the north of the Falkland Sound since D-Day, was moving in to anchor in Grantham Sound, to be in smoother water for surgical operations and to reduce the distance which the casualty evacuation helicopters had to fly from the Ajax Bay Dressing Station. Even after the *Fearless* had brought in the surgical team from the *Hermes*, the staff at Ajax Bay were unable to deal as quickly as desirable with the wounded from Goose Green and the availability of the properly equipped hospital ship, with full intensive-care facilities, close at hand (but removed from all combat or support areas) probably saved many lives, Argentinian as well as British.

The *Arrow* fired 100 rounds at targets in the Fox Bay area, starting several fires. The *Glamorgan* and *Ambuscade* had to bombard the Port Stanley area without the benefit of spotters, the weather being unsuitable for helicopter observation, but between them they fired 190 rounds of 4.5in, plus another Seaslug from the destroyer, to keep the garrison awake and deter any C-130 flights which might attempt to sneak in. The Argentine Army artillery batteries replied with a heavier fire than had yet been experienced and showed that they were learning the rudiments of firing at moving ships, pitching shells within fifty yards on occasion. The shoot finished at 1.00am and the two ships rejoined the Battle Group an hour after dawn, followed shortly afterwards by the *Avenger*, which had carried out her unobtrusive mission without interruption, and, at 10.00am, by the *Plymouth* and *Intrepid*.

The carriers were still operating in heavy seas on the 30th, although the wind had decreased and visibility improved during the day. CAP missions began before dawn, as usual, but the first strike was not flown off until 11.00am, when all four GR3s were launched. One pair was carrying a new weapon which had only recently been delivered to the *Hermes*, the 1,000lb laser-guided bomb. The GR3s, each of which was carrying one of the 'smart' bombs under one wing and a 'dumb' bomb under the other, were fitted with laser range-finding equipment and this mission was intended to be a trial, to see if the range-finder could act as the target 'illuminator' required by the bombs' laser homing device. In the event the attack, on Port Stanley airfield, proved that the GR3's laser and the homing system were not compatible and another fortnight elapsed before the bomb, a proper illuminator and a suitable target could be brought together.

The other section of GR3s was armed with 2in rocket pods and was after Argentine Army helicopters. Failing to find these, which spent the daylight hours camouflaged among the houses at Port Stanley, they attacked troops and an artillery battery. As the two aircraft joined up for their return to the *Hermes*, the No 2 noticed that his Leader, Squadron Leader J. Pook RAF, was losing fuel, the result of small-arms fire from the troops attacked. Steadily 'bleeding to death', the Harrier flew on for 100 miles before Squadron Leader Pook ejected as his fuel gauges reached zero; the *Hermes* was only thirty-one miles away and one of the screening helicopters rescued the downed pilot within a few minutes.

The GR3s also flew two armed reconnaissance missions, one in the morning to see how the SAS were faring on Mount Kent and the other in the early afternoon to look for targets of opportunity to the north of Port Stanley. Only one of the first pair attacked Argentine positions, due to the continuing cloud and low visibility among the hills, but the other pair bombed two 'suspected radar stations'.

The Argentine Air Force made no attempt to attack the AOA during the day. There was thus no interference with the preparation of stores to be moved to Teal Inlet and for the reception of 5 Infantry Brigade. The provision for the accommodation of the unwounded prisoners from Goose Green was inadequate – the loss of the tented camp with the *Atlantic Conveyor* was thus felt as much by the Argentinians as by the British – and 300 men were transferred from the sheep pens where they were being held to *Sir Percivale*, as a temporary measure of relief. The 'Ambulance Ship' HMS *Herald* was ordered into San Carlos Water from the Red Cross Box to pick up convalescent patients from Ajax Bay but this was subsequently rescinded as her arrival in a defended area might have been misconstrued by the Argentine authorities. The *Uganda* weighed anchor and left Grantham Sound in time to be clear of the North Falkland Sound before last light.

The *Antrim* detached from the Battle Group before dawn and proceeded to South Georgia. During the afternoon she received an airdrop of stores for herself and the ships at South Georgia, courtesy of one of the indefatigable Hercules of No 47 Squadron RAF, making another of their regular 25-hour trips to the edge of the TEZ. The *Elk* and *Tidepool* set out for the AOA, escorted by the *Brilliant* and *Ambuscade*, as early as 11.10am. They were to have been joined by the *Atlantic Causeway* and the *Europic Ferry* but the heavy seas so delayed their passage from the Loitering Area that the latter pair was ordered to return.

As the small inbound convoy was starting out, an Argentine strike was taxying for take-off from Rio Grande. Two Super Etendards, the leading one armed with the last AM.39 Exocet, were accompanied by four Skyhawks of IV Air Brigade, each armed with three 500lb bombs. Although the A-4s of the 3rd Naval Attack Squadron would have been the logical partners for the Super Etendards, and the A-4Bs of V Air Brigade had been achieving a great deal of success against shipping, the A-4Cs were preferred as they had a greater oxygen capacity, enabling their pilots to fly a 4-hour mission without difficulty, and all were fitted with the accurate Omega long-range navigation aid. The Skyhawks would trail the missile aircraft and follow the Exocet, striking whatever ship it hit. It does not appear to have occurred to the Argentinians that the missile might be aimed at any target other than a carrier. The six aircraft took off together and rendezvoused with both of the KC-130 tankers at about 12.15pm, 380 miles to the south-east of Rio Grande (250 miles south of Port Stanley). The eight aircraft then tracked to the east for about 180 miles, tanking at the beginning and end of this leg so that when they finally left the KC-130s they were fully topped-up. After a short jink to the north-east, during which the Skyhawks took station behind the Super Etendards, the strike aircraft turned to the north-north-west, 300 miles to the south-east of Port Stanley and heading for the Carrier Battle Group, believed to be 200 miles distant. Once on track, the six aircraft descended to remain below the radar lobe.

The approach had not been detected, thanks to the circuitous route and the pilots' strict adherence to radio silence, and Admiral Woodward had already begun to detach ships for the round of nocturnal activities. The two Type 42s, *Cardiff* and *Exeter*, were twenty miles from the centre of the Battle Group, acting as pickets against attacks from the west. Ten miles to the south of the *Exeter* (and seventeen miles south-west of HMS *Invincible*), the *Avenger* was heading for East Falkland. She was taking advantage of the apparent quiet period to reposition her 20mm Oerlikons and the port gun was actually being carried down to its new position aft when the *Exeter* reported the interception of the Super Etendard's Agave radar at 1.31pm.

The weather in the area was favourable to both sides, with visibility of about ten miles below the overcast, except in scattered heavy showers. The Super Etendards popped up when the pilots estimated that they were within Exocet range, but the echoes of the ships could not be distinguished from those of the showers and they descended once again to close the range. At this point the *Avenger* was about thirty miles dead ahead and the *Invincible* was 30 degrees to starboard of the Super Etendards' track, at a distance of about forty-five miles. On receipt of the warning of this first quick burst of radar, the *Cardiff*, *Exeter* and *Avenger* all turned to meet the threat from the south and when, about three minutes later, the Super Etendards popped up for a second look they were immediately detected by both the Type 42s, thirty-two miles from the *Exeter*, which lost no time in locking her Sea Dart system on to the three contacts which she held.

Capitan de Corbeta A. Francisco fired the Exocet at a firm contact at a range of twenty-one miles (39km), which corresponded to neither the

Avenger nor the *Exeter*, being almost exactly half way between them. Whatever it was – ship, helicopter, shower or chaff – it was not, nor was it anywhere near, the *Invincible*. Leaving the Skyhawks to pursue the missile, the two Super Etendards broke away to port and headed to the south-west to find the tankers. Two SHARs were vectored out after them but, although the Blue Fox radar transmissions thoroughly alarmed the Argentine pilots, the latter had a head start and were not in serious danger.

The Skyhawks, on the other hand, were. They watched the Exocet accelerate away, out of sight, and followed its track, tightening up their formation. A ship was sighted at a range of eight miles. To the Argentine pilots, looking through salt-streaked windscreens at low level, it appeared to be the *Invincible*, with smoke pouring from both sides of her island, seen from 30 degrees on the quarter. No anti-aircraft fire could be seen. In fact, they were looking at the *Avenger* from about 30 degrees on her starboard bow, with the dense exhaust smoke associated with the Olympus main engines, and the frigate was firing back with her 4.5in gun. Ten miles beyond her, the *Exeter* had already fired two Sea Darts and a third was about to be launched.

The first Sea Dart salvo narrowly missed a patrolling Lynx, roared over the *Avenger* and, five miles beyond the frigate, took out *Primer Teniente* J. D. Vazquez' Skyhawk in a huge explosion. The three shaken survivors, who had not seen the missiles coming, pressed on to attack the frigate, which could bring only the 4.5in and two LMGs on the bridge to bear fine on the starboard bow. As the Skyhawks flew through the shell bursts and machine-gun fire, the right-hand aircraft, flown by *Primer Teniente* O. J. Castillo, was seen to be hit and it crashed close off the starboard beam. The bombs of the remaining two aircraft fell around the *Avenger* but missed her. The Argentine aircraft broke away to port and turned to the south-east to make their getaway.

The Exocet was detected by both the *Exeter*, whose third Sea Dart had been fired at it, and the *Avenger*, which claimed to have destroyed it with her opening 4.5in rounds, but it was not seen by either ship and may have been decoyed to the west of its intended track by the frigate's chaff.

The returning Skyhawk pilots gave a graphic description of how they had attacked the *Invincible*, scoring hits on the carrier, set on fire by an Exocet. Lurid artists' impressions and retouched photographs depicted the burning *Invincible* and appeared in the Argentine Press as 'proof' of the success of the strike. At the tactical level *VYCA 2*, monitoring the carrier fighters' movements, detected fewer sorties and this was taken as strong evidence by the Argentine Air Force. In fact the *Invincible* flew forty-four SHAR sorties on 31 May and 1 June (more than on the two preceding days). When the carrier returned to Portsmouth, the Argentine commentators were at a loss to explain her ostensibly undamaged state (although they tried hard) and could point only to part of her starboard

The *Sir Percivale* refuels from the *Tidespring* on return from her first trip to Teal Inlet *(MoD)*

Clearing up *Glamorgan*'s hangar after the Exocet hit, with lighting provided by two emergency lights. The hole made by the explosion of the missile's warhead is at bottom right. *(MoD)*

The *Ambuscade* at anchor in Port William with, beyond, the *Canberra*, three of the LSLs and the RMAS tug *Typhoon* (MoD)

Late Arrivals: the minehunters HMS *Brecon* and *Ledbury* formate on their STUFT 'mother-ship', the *St Helena*, the only merchant ship to be allocated its own Wasp helicopter (MoD)

side which had been 'suspiciously recently painted'.*

The Argentine Navy had now expended all its air-launched Exocets and in spite of exhaustive shopping around the world it was unable to obtain more missiles at any price. The Super Etendard pilots had scored two hits and two major successes, psychological in the case of the *Sheffield* and material in the sinking of the *Atlantic Conveyor*, but they had failed in all three strikes to attack the ships that they had been sent out to get – the carriers. On 4, 25 and 30 May, they had fired their precious missiles at the first target to appear when they turned their radars on and on each occasion it had been an escort – the *Sheffield*, the *Ambuscade* and lastly the *Avenger*. No attempt was made to ensure that a high-value target had been selected, but on each occasion it was assumed that the missiles had been fired at a carrier. Whether the pilots of the 2nd Naval Fighter-Attack Squadron were being cautious to preserve surprise or to conserve their aircraft, they did not have the decisive effect which could have been achieved by the incapacitation of a carrier and which would have amply compensated for the loss of one or more of these aircraft. From 31 May, the Super Etendard squadron began to train for conventional bombing attacks but even with the experienced pilots available the unit was not operational in this role before the end of hostilities.

The Battle Group's radar screens were clear of Argentine aircraft by 1.40pm and the preparations for the night's activity continued. The *Intrepid* and *Minerva* left for the AOA, where they were to be joined by the *Avenger* after the latter completed her night's task. The *Alacrity* headed for the Fitzroy area to provide gunfire support in the Mount Kent area and the *Glamorgan* detached to the east, to relieve the *Bristol* as the Logistics and Loitering Area manager.

It was still not fully appreciated that the Super Etendards were using in-flight refuelling to reach the Battle Group and shortly after the Exocet attack a pair of 800 Squadron SHARs was launched to loft six 1,000lb bombs at Port Stanley airfield's dispersal area, just in case the Argentine jets were refuelling there. Another such strike was delivered before dusk and at 3.45pm the *Cardiff* was ordered to station herself some twenty miles to the east of Port Stanley as a missile trap, to engage aircraft attempting to land or take off.

The SAS on Mount Kent called for and got a GR3 close-support mission at about 2.30pm, the two Harriers firing 144 2in rockets into Argentine positions. More help was on its way and at dusk the PNG Sea Kings of 846 Squadron began flying in Kilo Company of 42 Commando, followed by their mortars and Blowpipe section and ammunition for three 105mm Light Guns which were brought up as a single load by the Chinook of No 18 Squadron RAF. The SAS were actually engaged in a brisk 'fire-fight'

---

* *Aeroespacio*, March/April, 1983, pp. 19–32. This article gives an interesting account of the approach and tactics used in this, the only co-ordinated strike to be delivered by the Argentine Air Forces.

with the Argentinians as the reinforcements were flying in, but the only damage sustained by any of the helicopters was to the Chinook, which flew into a lake while leaving the area in a snowstorm and was fortunate to be able to pull away and return to Port San Carlos with remarkably little damage. The *Alacrity* stood by until after midnight to provide covering fire if required, but her assistance was not needed.

The *Avenger* operated off the north-east corner of East Falkland, shelling observation posts on Mount Brisbane and McBride Head to cover the insertion of an SBS patrol in Volunteer Bay. The diversion and the landing were accomplished without any enemy reaction and after firing 125 rounds of 4.5in the frigate went on to enter Falkland Sound for the first time.

The *Elk* made another overnight unloading visit, escorted in and out by the *Yarmouth*, but the *Tidepool* remained in San Carlos Water on this occasion. The *Argonaut* had at last sailed, with the RFAs *Sir Galahad* and *Sir Lancelot*, so that the only ship which had been present for the entire ten days and remained undamaged, the *Yarmouth*, became the undisputed 'oldest inhabitant'. The *Argonaut*'s role as air-defence co-ordinator was passed on to the *Minerva*, which anchored up the Water.

31 MAY

The TPS-43 radar of *VYCA 2* was recognized by the British command to be one of the major obstacles to the gaining of absolute air superiority over the Falklands. Not only was it alerting the AA defences of the Port Stanley area and assisting inbound supply missions, it was keeping mainland strike aircraft out of reach of the SHARs and was believed to be targeting the Exocet attacks (as indeed it was). The radar site, on the edge of the 'built-up area' of Port Stanley, could not be bombed or shelled owing to the risk from stray ordnance injuring the Falkland Islanders and a precision weapon was therefore required. There was no such weapon in the Carrier Battle Group until such time as a laser target illuminator could be brought within range of Port Stanley, but during May an RAF Vulcan was fitted to carry four Shrike anti-radar missiles, first used by the US Navy during the Vietnam War. The first strike took off from Ascension on 28 May but had to be aborted when one of the supporting Victor tankers developed a defect during the outbound flight.

The second attempt was more successful, the Vulcan taking off late on the 30th and reaching the Port Stanley area at about 4.00am. At 3.20am a Sea Harrier took off from the *Invincible*, armed with three 1,000lb bombs which it delivered in separate attacks on the airfield area. A second SHAR of 801 Squadron followed, taking off at 4.10am and going through the same routine, but using different attack headings. The *VYCA 2* operators recognized these tactics for what they indeed were, teasing to ensure that all the defensive radars were switched on, to provide homing sources for the Vulcan's Shrikes,* and gave orders that all other radars should be shut down. The TPS-43's power was gradually reduced, to lead the British electronic eavesdroppers closer to the transmitter and the AA guns and Roland missile site. The Vulcan's crew was well aware of its position in relation to these and the two teams shadow-boxed for over half-an-hour, the big bomber orbiting so slowly that the Argentinian radar operators believed that they were dealing with a helicopter. Finally, having closed to within five miles, the Vulcan fired two of its Shrikes at the radar and then had to begin its return to Ascension at 4.40am.

The results were regarded by the British authorities as 'unquantifiable', although the Vulcan electronics specialist, Flight-Lieutenant R. Trevaskus RAF, believed that the target radar had ceased transmitting at the time that the missile was due to impact. He was quite correct, for the first Shrike detonated between ten and fifteen yards from the TPS-43 antenna, inflicting repairable damage but causing the set to be shut down; the second missile missed by eighty yards. Although the main radar was fully operational again within twenty-four hours, the crew was not prepared to risk the effects of a hit on their operations trailers by another such attack and these were surrounded with a wall of soil-filled fuel drums and given overhead protection, covering metallic runway planking with a layer of soil, so that only the antenna was exposed, though surrounded by a blast wall.

The *Hermes'* aircraft found the Port Stanley AA defences as active as formerly when they returned just after dawn on the 31st, three GR3s delivering the first strike. A report that a CAP aircraft had seen what appeared to be swept-wing aircraft on the dispersal resulted in a joint 800 Squadron/ No 1 Squadron attack which took off at 10.54am, the SHARs lofting airburst bombs to keep the gunners heads down while the GR3s rocketed the Argentine aircraft. No Super Etendards were there, but two Macchis, parked on triangular pads which from high altitude distorted the plan view, were damaged. Both GR3s were damaged by flak and so the third and last strike of the day was carried out by three 800 Squadron aircraft two hours later.

About two hours after the Vulcan's attack, as the bomber was 1,000 miles out on its return to Ascension, it passed over the area in which the RFA *Fort Grange* was heading in the opposite direction. Half an hour earlier, shortly after daybreak, a turboprop aircraft had been heard to pass directly overhead, above the low cloud. It was realized that in this position it could only be an Argentine aircraft. At 6.50am (Falklands time)

* *Aeroespacio*, May–June, 1983, p. 28: '. . . *puesto que nuestros operadores estaban advertidos de que podrian ser el blanco elegido por los agresores.*' (. . . because our operators had been warned that they might be the selected target by the attackers.) It will be recalled that on the 29th, when the first Shrike attack had been programmed, the British pilots observed that for the first time there were no fire-control radar signals. The Argentine statement of fore-knowledge of an ARM attack on the 31st, taken with the AA defences' passivity on the 29th, is of interest.

a C-130 was sighted to the north-west at low level, making an approach from the port quarter, and the big (22,700 tons, 600 feet) RFA prepared to defend herself with her one machine gun and some rifles. It is probable, however, that her appearance – large and grey, with a conspicuous flight deck and hangar – was her best defence against the lumbering Hercules, for the aircraft sheered off as it approached a range of 2,000 yards and made off in the direction from which it had come. Both sides were undoubtedly relieved – the RFA that an attack had not been pressed, the Argentine aircrew that they had not made the mistake of attacking a very large warship.

The *Uganda* entered the Falkland Sound in daylight and proceeded to her Grantham Sound anchorage to operate and to embark wounded from Ajax Bay. The latter process proved to be more time-consuming than had been expected, due mainly to the need to clear the stretcher cases from each helicopter off the flight deck before the next load was landed. Although the hospital ship had been programmed to pass out of the Falkland Sound before dusk, her departure was delayed and she did not return to the 'Red Cross Box' until midnight, five hours later than had been intended.

The first Argentine hospital ship, the *Bahia Paraiso*, was now inside the TEZ. Her route and intentions had been correctly signalled, via the International Commission for the Red Cross, and, just as correctly, Commo-

31 May: the transport *Bahia Paraiso* heaves-to south of the Falkland Sound to permit *Minerva* Flight to land an inspection team. The Argentine Navy operated Lynxes and was acquainted with Royal Navy flight-deck procedures and the reception committee includes a surcoated Flight Deck Officer and a pair of 'firesuitmen' in the hangar entrance *(Lt Cdr Graeme R. Moodie RN via Captain S.H.G. Johnston RN)*

dore Clapp exercised his right of search. The *Bahia Paraiso*, whose role as an assault transport at Grytviken had not been forgotten, was found by the Lynxes of the *Arrow* and *Minerva* at 10.40am, sixty-five miles south of West Falkland, and shortly afterwards a Wessex took off from San Carlos with an inspection party. The helicopter returned at 1.10pm to report that the cursory search for 'contraband' (weapons, cypher material and stores intended for purposes other than relief) had found nothing and that the reception had been friendly, particularly on the part of the Executive Officer, who had done specialist training with the Royal Navy! The *Bahia Paraiso* was bound for Fox Bay to embark wounded from West Falkland and was then proceeding to Port Stanley to land medical stores and pick up more wounded, after which, it was agreed, she would meet the *Uganda* in the Red Cross Box to collect all the Argentine wounded for repatriation. The Puma lost at South Georgia had been replaced by another helicopter of the same type, painted white with red crosses, and she had a smaller Bell 47 on board as well.

The unloading of the ammunition from the *Elk* continued throughout the day, uninterrupted by any Argentine air activity, and the *Tidepool* transferred aviation fuel ashore for the Forward Operating Bases at Port San Carlos, where the naval Wessex and the single RAF Chinook were located, and San Carlos Settlement, to which the Sea King 4s of 846 Squadron had been moved. The assault helicopters were busy throughout the 31st, taking the headquarters of 3 Commando Brigade up to Teal Inlet and supplying the Marines and Paras on the northern flank where, so far, only two LCU loads (about 240 tons of ammunition and stores) had arrived by sea. The tracked Volvo 'Bandwagons' of the Commando Logistics Regiment and the seven light armoured vehicles of the Blues and Royals brought up much material from the beachead area, but the nature of the 80-odd mile journey across the difficult ground was not such that they could be used for routine resupply.

One 846 Squadron mission was spared from the transport shuttle to secure the flank of the advance. On the previous day a covert Royal Marines observation post had watched seventeen Argentine troops – a patrol from *No 602 Comando*, parachuted under cover of night and bad weather – approach and occupy Top Malo House farm, five miles south of Teal Inlet Settlement. A dawn attack was planned for the 31st, but, due to other tasks, it was not until after noon that a Sea King took off with nineteen Marines of the Mountain and Arctic Warfare Cadre embarked, approached unseen and unheard at very low level and dropped the assault party within a mile of their objective. Captain R. Bell and his eighteen NCOs moved up, surprised the Argentinians in the house and drove them out to surrender after a brisk short-range gun-battle in the open. These were elite Argentine troops, but their incredible lack of elementary vigilance put them at a disadvantage which cost them five dead and five wounded, who, like the seven unwounded men, were taken prisoner.

This was the Royal Marines' only daylight engagement of the war and the MAW Cadre lost three of its sergeants badly wounded.

The Argentine Air Force, which had not been detected near the AOA at low level for several days, appeared at dusk. The last CAP of the day had left shortly before, but the intruders remained in the Falkland Sound and did not approach closer than six miles to San Carlos Water. The night's traffic began as soon as the radar screens were clear, the *Elk* and *Tidepool* leaving to return to the edge of the TEZ and the *Intrepid* to make another round trip to Port Salvador. The convoy inbound from the Carrier Battle Group – the *Baltic Ferry*, *Atlantic Causeway* and RFA *Blue Rover*,* escorted by the *Brilliant* – had begun its passage shortly before noon and was followed by the *Norland*. Carrying the 1st Battalion, 7th Duke of Edinburgh's Own Gurkha Rifles (who were to be the first infantrymen of 5 Brigade to land on the Falklands), the *Norland* had been delayed while she embarked a contingent from HMS *Hermes*, consisting of the carrier's Royal Marines detachment and sailors of her 'Blue Beret Platoon', who were to be employed as prisoner-of-war guards afloat. She left the carrier group at 4.15pm, escorted by the *Active*, who handed over to the local escort to the north of East Falkland.

The *Alacrity* and *Ambuscade* detached from the Carrier Battle Group during the afternoon, as did the *Exeter*, the Type 21s to carry out separate bombardment missions while the Type 42 was to provide the missile trap off Port Stanley. Like the *Cardiff* on the previous night, she was to find no trade.

The Royal Navy had now been off the Falklands for a full month of full-scale combat operations. Early demonstrations of anti-surface and anti-air superiority had persuaded the Argentine Navy to keep its Fleet in harbour and the Air Force to hold back its strike force until the British invasion was launched. The Achilles Heel of the Carrier Battle Group's air defences was, however, its lack of early warning of the approach of low-flying aircraft and this had been exploited at an early stage by the Argentine naval air arm in its attack on the *Sheffield*. It also limited the effectiveness of the air, gun and missile defences of the Amphibious Operating Area when the assault was carried out, but despite this such losses were inflicted on the Argentine air forces on the first day that they were unable to mount sustained pressure thereafter. Although they sank three warships and damaged four more, as well as two landing ships, in four days of determined attacks, the Argentinians were obliged to concede defeat in the battle of attrition.

* The *Blue Rover* was loaded with a part-cargo of fuel for the land forces' vehicles, the majority of which, like the Rapier system generators, required petrol ('MoGas'), a highly volatile fuel which is universally loathed by the crews of ships required to carry it in bulk. Not for over twenty years had the Royal Navy needed high-octane fuel in large quantities, but the cargo capacity, with the special stowage and transfer arrangements, had had to be retained in RFAs because the military had not switched completely to safer diesel fuel.

By the end of May, therefore, the Navy's traditional projectile had been successfully discharged and was well on its way to the main target, having already scored a remarkable 'hit' at Goose Green. Up to the time that the break-out began, the ships and aircraft had been the main participants. Now that the Marines and Paratroops were closing in on the main Argentine positions, the Navy's was a supporting role. The ships, naval, auxiliary and merchant, would ensure that reinforcements and material reached the land battle and they would protect the troops from outside attack and support their offensives, while denying the enemy such aid. But complete victory could only be won by the men on the ground.

The logistic effort was ever-growing. Rations, stores and ammunition were needed in increasing quantities as more ships and men arrived 'down South' and reached the front line. Thanks to the efforts of the RFA tankers and the nine chartered merchant tankers which had so far pumped over to them, as well as refuelling escorts on occasion, fuel oil was not a source of concern. During the first fortnight in June only two more freighting tankers, the RFA *Bayleaf* and Shell's *Eburna*, would be needed in the 'Tug, Repair and Logistics Area', as the 'LOLA' was redesignated. During the same period four of the first BP 'Rivers' left, or prepared to leave, on their second voyages south, *British Esk, Avon* and *Tay* from Portsmouth and *British Tamar* from Gibraltar. The much larger *Alvega* had arrived at Ascension on 21 May to serve as the local 'station tanker' – a floating bunker to refuel warships – and the *Scottish Eagle* was on her way to fulfil the same function at South Georgia.

Another ship heading for South Georgia was the anchor-handling tug *Wimpey Seahorse*, recently built to serve the offshore oil industry, towing rigs, laying out moorings in deep water and carrying bulky cargoes. She was to lay moorings off Leith, Stromness and Grytviken, where the deep water and bad weather was already making anchoring a nightmarish experience for some ships. The *Wimpey Seahorse* left Devonport on 16 May with 600 tons of chain, cable and anchors, as well as other stores, took on another 100 tons of mixed stores at Ascension, which she left on 29 May, and finally reached South Georgia on 8 June, after encountering storms and icebergs.

The dry-stores ships *Resource, Regent* and *Stromness* dispensed over 12,000 pallets up to the cease-fire, by ship-to-ship jackstay transfer and helicopter. In May the RN helicopters flew no less than 2,000 'Vertrep' sorties, usually lifting more than one load per sortie, not only between the ships out in the TEZ, but also offloading the RFAs and STUFT transports in San Carlos Water. Though there were few Wessex 5s with the Task Force, compared with the other types, they provided over 1,100 of these sorties.

The Wessex 5, some of which were almost as old as their pilots, also supplied nearly a quarter of the assault lift effort, but the honours in this role went to 846 Squadron, whose Sea King 4s flew day and night, in all weathers, for a total of over 800 hours. But for sheer time spent in the air, there was no one to touch the anti-submarine Sea King squadrons. Operating from the two carriers, RFA *Fort Austin* (which was also issuing large quantities of stores) and the tankers *Olmeda* and *Olna*, between them the three squadrons (820, 824 and 826) maintained the equivalent of four aircraft continuously airborne throughout the month on anti-submarine and surface search sorties. Only at the beginning of the month had a handful of crews had the real satisfaction of contact with the enemy on the surface or underwater, although the 826 Squadron detachment in the AOA had had some of its patrols enlivened by Daggers and Sky-hawks roaring past. The long, empty anti-submarine patrols were an essential part of the naval operations and the crews had to remain alert, however slight the possibility of the presence of Argentine submarines.

The aircrew could, at least, get away from their ships for a while, so some wry humorists put it. The majority of those afloat had not been ashore for eight weeks, while the carriers and some of their RFAs had not sighted land for six (and still had more than three weeks to go!). Life on board, in mid-winter, was hardly comfortable and all hands had to make their way about the ships festooned with anti-gas respirators, 'once-only' survival suits, inflatable lifejackets and the new Emergency Life Support Apparatus ('Elsa'), thousands of which had been bought and sent out to provide protection against the smoke and toxic fumes which had been such a feature of the *Sheffield* and *Atlantic Conveyor* incidents. Progress through the ships at Defence Stations, awkward enough with only the small manhole hatches open, was further impeded by the smoke curtains rigged in passageways. As the month wore on and the ships became entirely dependent upon the provisions supplied by the RFAs, meals became more basic and although no one went hungry, staples such as potatoes began to run short. Far more serious, as far as almost everyone was concerned, was the shortage of 'nutty' – sweets and chocolate, which were supplied by the NAAFI canteens. This was not resupplied in the same volume as victuals and, in spite of rationing, it ran out altogether in some ships before the end of May.

The discomfort and minor privations were accepted philosophically. 'Jack' inevitably grumbled (there would have been more cause for concern if he hadn't) but this was a thoroughly professional Task Force and because information about events was shared, so that everyone knew what his part was, there was never any question of confidence in morale. For the civilian crews of the merchant ships and the RFAs, the same was true. Less well-informed and in some cases facing dangers for which they'd never signed on, they remained efficient and willing and met every challenge which their new role presented. Only one group was to be found wanting, but even then the majority of its members worked perfectly normally: signs of concern had been noticed among the Chinese crews of the LSLs as soon as the Bofors guns were fitted at Ascension and in some of these, and at least two other RFAs, this developed into a sort of passive fatalism which gave their officers little confidence in their crews' likely reactions in the event of the ships being damaged. In the event, only two LSLs had been seriously damaged, but their crews had to be evacuated and one declined to return to operations. The other crew followed its officers, went back to sea and then, most unluckily, suffered even worse damage and serious casualties.

The presence of the repair ship *Stena Seaspread* was of nearly as much moral support as material, for she provided first-aid which would only have been otherwise available no nearer than Gibraltar. She had patched up the *Glasgow* sufficiently to give confidence in the destroyer's machinery for the long solo passage home. The *Brilliant*'s weapons systems had then been restored (although certain limitations remained) during the days between the last two air-launched Exocet attacks. The *Argonaut* was now in company, with Naval Party 1810, led by Captain P. Badcock CBE RN, pumping out flooded mess-decks and restoring them to habitability and putting the finishing touches to the frigate's boiler-room repairs. Her next customer was to be the *Arrow*, undamaged by the enemy but much restricted by her cracked decks and in need of hull strengthening. The repair ship possessed versatility beyond the range of repairs achieved, thanks to her automatic station-keeping equipment and the remarkable array of five propellers and 'thrusters', which permitted her to be moved sideways as easily as ahead or astern. Her Master, Captain N. Williams, was adept at taking full advantage of this manoeuvrability to transfer heavy gear to and from the *Stena Seaspread*'s customers, but one of the tricks which most impressed naval onlookers was his refuelling of the *Glasgow*. Stationing his ship across the bows of the destroyer and passing the line across by the port-side midships crane, over the receiver's forecastle, he steamed sideways, ahead of the *Glasgow*, to maintain the latter's steerage way.

Thus assured of logistics, material and medical support, the warships of Admiral Woodward's TG317.8 and Commodore Clapp's TG317.0 were as ready to provide offshore cover and assistance to the troops of General Moore's TG317.1 as they had been to win the local naval and air superiority needed to put the Brigades ashore.

The one Task Group to which no reference has been made, the submarines, was still making sure that the major units of the Argentine Navy did not leave the twelve-mile inshore strip, while keeping track of merchant ship movements and those of radar-equipped aircraft. Four nuclear-powered submarines were on station at the end of the month and at 8.00pm on the 31st the diesel-electric *Onyx* arrived in San Carlos Water, escorted by the *Avenger* and *Arrow*. The newest arrival would be used for patrols within the TEZ, making brief visits to the 'Transport Area', as the

Amphibious Operating Area became from midnight on 31 May/1 June, during darkness. Ideally suited to clandestine operations, she was able to insert and extract SBS patrols with less chance of detection than the frigates which had been tasked with such landings hitherto.

PART VI

Chapter One

The Siege of Stanley

1 JUNE

At about midnight on 31 May/1 June the *Intrepid* arrived off Port Salvador and docked down to float out an LCU and two LCVPs. The two smaller craft were fitted with a lightweight minesweeping gear developed by the underwater warfare establishment at Portland and were to carry out a check sweep to discover whether the Argentine Navy had attempted to close off the large and sheltered Salvador Water anchorage. Preceded by the LCU, laden with 100 tons of 3 Commando Brigade stores but still drawing insufficient water to be endangered by mines, the LCVPs swept a channel deep enough for a loaded LSL all the way to Teal Inlet, where they lay up for the day. No mines were swept, nor were any present. The passage of the small flotilla was covered by the *Ambuscade*, which distracted attention by firing fifty-six rounds of 4.5in at an Argentine observation post on Salvador Hill, five miles to the east of Port Salvador. On completion of their tasks, the *Ambuscade* and the *Intrepid* returned to the Battle Group and the newly-renamed Transport Area respectively.

As mentioned earlier, there had been a large number of arrivals in San Carlos Water during the night. Unwanted extras were a quartet of Argentine Air Force Canberras, detected approaching by the *Minerva* at 3.55am. Lieutenant A. N. McHarg of 800 Squadron was scrambled from the *Hermes*, 210 miles to the east, but by the time that the SHAR reached the target area the last bomber was already outbound. Several bombs had fallen around the 846 Squadron operating base at San Carlos Settlement, inflicting very little damage and no serious casualties. McHarg was vectored after the last bomber by the *Minerva*, while the Canberra crew, warned by *VYCA 2* and their own radar receiver that the fighter was closing, used violent evasive manoeuvres, supplemented by chaff and infra-red decoys, to hold the SHAR off. McHarg managed to close to within five miles before his critical fuel state obliged him to break off at about 4.35am to return to the *Hermes*, 300 miles away. This was the night bombers' closest approach to a successful raid and the night-fighters' closest approach to the bombers.

The *Atlantic Causeway*, which had flown off four Sea Kings of 825 Squadron to Port San Carlos during the previous afternoon, began to offload her cargo of military stores and provisions before dawn, transferring vehicles ashore via the Mexeflotes and her stern ramp. After dawn the rest of her helicopters, four Sea King 2s and twenty Wessex 5s of 847 Squadron, were also flown off, a disembarkation complicated by a shortage of pilots. The *Atlantic Causeway* had not been able to accommodate all the squadrons' personnel and the balance were still en route, in the *Canberra* and *Engadine*, which were also bringing two more Sea Kings and four more Wessex 5s. Until the two squadrons could be brought up to full complement, a dozen of their helicopters were 'stored' in gullies near the airstrip, along the San Carlos River.

The big Aircraft Ferry landed airfield matting and more Harrier VTOL pads, which were used by the Royal Engineers to provide the STOVL strip with 'hardstandings' for aircraft standing-by on the ground for interception or close air support calls. The 280-yard runway was actually completed on 1 June, but fighter operations were delayed to permit the addition of the pads and the tracks, which would add greatly to its usefulness.

The RAF Regiment Rapier Squadron which came ashore from the *Atlantic Causeway* with its ninety vehicles was smaller than the Royal Artillery Rapier Battery, with eight fire units instead of twelve, but they were equipped with 'Blindfire' fire-control radar for night and bad-weather engagements. The new arrivals took over the static air defence of the two San Carlos air base areas, freeing two sections of 'T' Battery to prepare to move up to Teal Inlet and Fitzroy.

While the Gurkhas went ashore at Ajax Bay from the *Norland*, more of 5 Infantry Brigade's material was landed from the *Baltic Ferry*, which included among her cargo three more Scout helicopters of 656 Squadron, Army Air Corps, and a battery of 4th Field Regiment RA's Light Guns.

The hard-working P&O North Sea ferry *Norland* at anchor in San Carlos Water on 2 June, during her third (and least disturbed) landing operation *(MoD)*

Off San Carlos Settlement – (left to right), the *Blue Rover, Norland,* the bows of *Sir Lancelot, Atlantic Causeway* and the brightly-coloured *Nordic Ferry*, during the unloading of 5 Infantry Brigade's stores *(MoD)*

Most of the 1,800 tons had to be unloaded by water transport as the helicopters were fully committed to flying in support of 3 Commando Brigade, ferrying the guns and ammunition of 29 Commando Regiment RA and 42 Commando's rations to the Mount Kent positions and taking stores and personnel forward to Teal Inlet. 3 Para had now left the latter and were making for Estancia House, four miles to the north-west of Mount Kent, where the Commando Brigade would soon have its headquarters for the forthcoming battles for the mountains.

During the night the *Alacrity* had bombarded enemy positions to the west of Port Stanley, between Moody Brook and Two Sisters ridge, firing 134 shells which were spotted by her own Lynx and a 42 Commando OP. A second Company ('Lima') of this Commando was flown in during the day, together with much-needed rations and bivouac material for 'Kilo' Company, who had passed thirty-six hungry and exposed hours since their first insertion on 30 May. The Marines' positions on Mount Kent and Mount Challenger were now quite secure, for the Argentine Army units facing them were apparently content to sit tight, strictly on the defensive, holding a line based on (from north to south) Mount Longdon, Two Sisters and Mount Harriet, three features which provided strong natural defences.

Argentine Air Force long-range reconnaissance aircraft were out and about during the morning. At South Georgia the *Antrim* tracked a Boeing 707 from 6.00am until 8.15am, as it closed from 200 miles to eighty miles and then opened again. At San Carlos the *Minerva*, which had seen only the successive CAPs since the Canberra faded at 4.45am, saw two or three 'paints' forty-five miles to the north at 9.50am. The fighter controller informed the Pebble Island CAP section, which, although it was already starting to climb out to the east, low on fuel, went to investigate. Descending below the cloud to low level, Lieutenant-Commander Ward of 801 picked up the target on his radar and began a tail-chase after the

Argentine aircraft. It was a C-130 engaged on reconnaissance and had popped up briefly for a quick radar sweep, only to be detected by the alert *Minerva*. Possibly warned by *VYCA 2*, the C-130 made off at high speed and low level but was caught by the much faster SHAR. Lieutenant-Commander Ward, needing a quick 'kill' because his fuel was already marginal for a safe return to the *Invincible*, fired his first Sidewinder out of range but hit with the second and then, unable to wait to see if the missile was sufficient against such a big target, emptied his 30mm cannon into the Hercules. The victim crashed on fire into the sea eight minutes after it had been detected and all three officers and four non-commissioned officers were lost. The CO of 801 and his No 2, Lieutenant Thomas, had barely 45 gallons of fuel apiece to fly the 180 miles back to their ship. Before 'Corporate' such a trip would not have been considered practical. With the previous month's experience of fuel management, it became marginal and both pilots reached the ship, though with nothing to spare for a baulked landing.

One consequence of the first interception during the morning of 1 June was the rapid modification of the *Fearless*'s and *Intrepid*'s helicopter fuelling systems to deal with Sea Harriers and the devising of flight deck drills for recovery. Both had been improvised by 9.45am but 801 Squadron's action took place too soon afterwards for the word to have got around of the availability of this facility.

The Carrier Battle Group in the eastern sector of the TEZ acted once more as a forward area receipt and despatch unit, sending the almost-empty *Elk* back to the 'Trala'. The *Canberra* joined from South Georgia at noon and remained in company until she detached with the *Tidepool*, escorted by the *Broadsword*, for the afternoon convoy to the Transport Area.

There were two more unconventional arrivals during the day. The first was a pair of Harriers of No 1 Squadron which had flown direct from Ascension, refuelling from eight Victor tankers during the eight-and-a-

On 1 June, two Harrier GR3s were flown direct from Ascension to join the *Hermes* in the TEZ. In-flight refuelling was provided, as ever, by the Victors (a No 57 Squadron aircraft is illustrated) and a Nimrod provided Search and Rescue support *(MoD)*

half-hour flight. A Hercules of No 47 Squadron RAF was also airborne for search-and-rescue support; the RFA *Engadine* was 1,400 miles to the north-east of the TEZ and there was a second Hercules further to the south on a supply mission. The long trip went without incident, however, and the two GR3s were met by a pair of SHARs 200 miles from the *Hermes* and escorted to uneventful landings. One of the pilots, Flight-Lieutenant M. Macleod RAF, was no stranger to carrier operations. Four years earlier, at the end of a loan tour with 892 Squadron, he had flown the last Phantom to be catapulted by HMS *Ark Royal*. The two GR3s, which landed on at 12.55pm, brought No 1 Squadron's strength up to five aircraft, a very welcome reinforcement on the eve of the main land offensive.

Late in the afternoon the *Penelope* met the transport Hercules on the north-east edge of the TEZ. This was the 21st programmed air-drop mission and it brought, as well as the usual urgent stores, a number of Army personnel who were also parachuted – to naval eyes an unusual joining procedure. Among the new arrivals, who were quickly retrieved, was Lieutenant-Colonel D. R. Chaundler, who was to command 2 Para, led since Lieutenant-Colonel Jones's death by Major Keeble.

There was, meanwhile, another man in the water and he was to remain there for considerably longer. At about 2.00pm Flight-Lieutenant I. Mortimer RAF, 801 Squadron's Air Warfare Instructor, was returning from CAP alone and decided to carry out a distant visual inspection of Port Stanley airfield, skirting the Roland missile's 'envelope'. Unfortunately this was greater than had been believed and the SHAR was hit at 13,000 feet, seven miles south of the airfield. Mortimer ejected safely and got into his life raft, from which he broadcast a short 'Mayday' call on the distress frequency. This was picked up by another aircraft and relayed to the *Invincible* but nothing could be done to rescue Mortimer for some hours. An Argentine Air Force Chinook, covered by a Pucara, searched for the British pilot for a couple of hours, giving up when *VYCA 2* warned of the approach of a SHAR section.*

The *Active* and *Ambuscade* parted company with the Battle Group at about the time that the Sea Harrier was shot down and with the *Exeter* headed for the Port Stanley area, the first two for the usual nocturnal bombardment and the last to provide the missile trap off the airfield. Their departure coincided with the receipt of a disturbing report of helicopter movements at Pebble Island which tied in with indications that Exocets were to be based in the Falklands. The helicopters, identified as Sea Kings, had been seen to land during the afternoon of 31 May but had not departed. As the Sea King could be modified to fire Exocet (as the Iraqis had demonstrated), this was a serious threat, affecting not only the

---

* *Aeroespacio*, Jan/Feb, 1984. The Argentine helicopter's failure to find the downed pilot was probably due to its search area being too far out to sea, left to fifteen miles south of the airfield.

convoys to and from the TA but also the Battle Group, which could be reached if it approached within 180 miles of the helicopters' base. The use of the Sea King made matters even more complicated, for there was now the risk of the enemy making use of an aircraft common to both sides to penetrate the outer defences. An elaborate 'delousing' drill was devised to sort out Royal Navy Sea Kings from possible Argentine 'cuckoos' before the latter could get within missile range.

Unfortunately for the Royal Navy, the report from Pebble Island gave only half of the story. Two Sea Kings of the Argentine Navy's 2nd Helicopter Squadron had flown from Rio Gallegos to 'BAN Borbon' during the afternoon of 31 May. Stripped of sonar gear and even the cabin seats, they had each carried five drums of fuel from which the aircraft's tanks were replenished to enable them to reach Pebble Island in safety. The two Sea Kings landed at 4.35pm, as the twilight faded and shortly after the attention of the British forces around San Carlos had been distracted by aircraft in the Falkland Sound. The arrival was remarked by a reconnaissance patrol somewhere in the Saunders Island area. What the patrol did not know was that the helicopters had been sent to evacuate the remaining naval aviation personnel, a pilot and nine maintenance ratings, and that, after refuelling from the Pebble Island fuel dump, the Sea Kings took off again at 5.15pm, when it was completely dark, and took a different route when withdrawing. Three hours and forty minutes later, they were back at Rio Grande after an epic mission. A week was to elapse before the British forces could be certain that there were no operational helicopters at Pebble Island, the return of bad weather from 2 June making air reconnaissance impossible. During that week the Battle Group had to remain at arm's length, by night and day and in low visibility. While the San Carlos convoys could not be halted, their escort over the last leg, from the Eddystone Rock, was reinforced by ships from the TA. The Royal Navy Sea King crews, in the TA and with the carriers, were meanwhile obliged to put up with being regarded as inherently suspicious and, on occasion, held off from their own 'mother', covered by her machine guns, while their *bona fides* were established.

Two SHARs of 800 Squadron were sent to look at Pebble Island at sunset on the 1st, and an hour later, at 5.40pm, a pair of 801's aircraft carried out a further reconnaissance, using Lepus flares to illuminate the area of the airstrip. This activity was complicated by the appearance of a low-level contact to the north of the island. The CAP spent twenty minutes chasing the Argentine aircraft but was unable to achieve an interception.

The garrison of Pebble Island was given little rest, for, after the Lepus display, the *Avenger* laid down the heaviest bombardment yet fired by a Type 21 in a single night – 273 rounds of high-explosive and twenty star-shell rounds. Her Lynx, spotting with the help of the star-shell, was fired on by a heavy machine gun. This bombardment covered the early exits from the TA, the *Intrepid* to pick up her LCVPs from Port Salvador and the *Sir Percivale* to become the first transport to make the run through the swept channel to Teal Inlet. The LSL remained to land 3 Commando Brigade stores while the *Intrepid* continued to the 'Trala' to consolidate in preparation for the deployment of 5 Infantry Brigade.

The two frigates shelling Port Stanley airfield and the Argentine installations to the south and west of the town were screened by Sea Kings of HMS *Invincible*'s 820 Squadron whose crews were keeping their eyes open for Flight-Lieutenant Mortimer. At 10.50pm the latter heard a helicopter and switched on his emergency light. The helicopter crew, who had 'extended their sector' in the hope of sighting the pilot, saw the light and made the rescue without difficulty. Mortimer's Sea Harrier was the sixth and last naval fighter to be lost but only the second to be a victim of Argentine action. The *Invincible* was back to the number with which she had sailed but the *Hermes* was still two up, so that the Battle Group had twenty-two SHARs, of which twenty could be relied upon to be fully serviceable at the beginning of every day.

2 JUNE

The *Exeter*, *Active* and *Ambuscade* withdrew from their positions around Port Stanley from 2.00am on the 2nd to be back on the Battle Group's screen before dawn. The *Avenger*, after completing her Pebble Island bombardment and before returning to the Battle Group, covered the inbound and outbound convoys which exchanged close escorts, the *Broadsword* taking back the oiler *Blue Rover*, while the *Yarmouth* escorted the *Canberra* and *Tidepool* over the last stage of their incident-free approach to the Transport Area. The liner anchored deep in San Carlos Water, off Ajax Bay, an hour before dawn.

To the relief of all who had been in the *Canberra* on 21 May, the day dawned with a fog which would protect the anchorage from air attack without greatly interfering with offloading the two Guards battalions and the stores. The first LCU arrived alongside at 6.30am, thirteen minutes after the ship anchored, and so anxious was the ship's merchant and naval company to clear the soldiery that four of her own boats were lowered to assist the landing craft. To many of those afloat and ashore who had seen the earlier disembarkations, the Guards' was rather leisurely. Admittedly, this was an 'administrative landing', not an assault, but under the circumstances it might have been better if the guardsmen had unloaded their own kitbags and suitcases, particularly as the fog cleared during the early afternoon. Volunteers from the P&O crew, the Marine bandsmen (when they weren't receiving Argentine casualties from Ajax Bay), the naval personnel and a small contingent of guardsmen were left to shift the personal luggage as well as the military and naval

stores. Not surprisingly, unloading was not completed by the time that the liner was due to depart and she had to remain overnight, with the prospect of another nervous day under threat of air attack.

The early fog hampered a dawn reconnaissance of Pebble Island by the first 800 Squadron CAP and, half an hour later, a look by the only GR3 mission of the day. The later improvement in the weather within the TA was a local phenomenon, for from 9.00am thick fog began to develop in the eastern sector of the TEZ, bringing all Sea Harrier and Harrier operations to a halt after just eight CAP missions and the one GR3 recce. The Argentine Air Force inactivity was thus providential. The Sea Kings flew on.

The northern approach to Port Stanley was by now properly established with the opening of Teal Inlet to LSLs and a bold move by 2 Para, still commanded by Major Keeble, brought the leading unit of 5 Infantry Brigade thirty miles along the south coast. The three Army Air Corps Scouts had flown down to Goose Green on disembarking from the *Baltic Ferry* and were promptly used to take a dozen Paras to seize a house overlooking Swan Inlet. From the house Major J. Crosland made the famous telephone call to Fitzroy Settlement to enquire whether the Argentinians were still in occupation. On learning that they were not, he informed the headquarters of 2 Para, where it was decided that Fitzroy should be secured by a *coup de main*. The first stage was to seize the Chinook, which had appeared at Goose Green with a load of stores, load it with no fewer than eighty-one Paras and their weapons and then conduct an overload flying trial en route to Fitzroy, where two of the Scouts had already selected a landing zone and conducted a clearance search without sighting any enemy. The gallant Chinook landed safely with its Paras and then returned for another seventy-five who were disgorged at the end of the afternoon. With most of two companies installed by nightfall, another important base area had been secured, complete with a land-locked deep-water anchorage.

2 June: the *Canberra* lies at anchor off Fanning Island as she unloads the guardsmen of 5 Infantry Brigade during her second, less harassed, visit to San Carlos Water. RFA *Sir Bedivere*, in the foreground, heads for an anchorage off Ajax Bay (MoD)

The next stage, resupplying the new forward area and bringing up reinforcements and the stores to support a second front, was not quite so straightforward. The arrival of the *Atlantic Causeway* had eased the helicopter shortage but until the extra dozen crews could arrive there were still only barely sufficient to build up the 3 Commando Brigade Forward Maintenance Area and the stocks of artillery ammunition as the 105mm Light Gun batteries moved east to the mountains. The LSLs, which would be needed for bringing up the bulk of the provisions and stores, had been reduced in carrying capacity by the damage to *Sir Lancelot* and *Sir Galahad* and had only just begun the Teal Inlet build-up, *Sir Percivale* unloading the first 300 tons that day. The vital LCUs, too, were needed for the time being at Teal and San Carlos Water, where they were engaged in unloading the 5 Infantry Brigade material. The three Royal Marine Commandos and their supporting arms were intended to be maintained in the field by the Commando Logistics Regiment. The latter had become 'mother' to five Army battalions, none of which had prior experience of the special problems of amphibious warfare or a water-supplied campaign and who lacked this specialized administrative back-up.

The *Baltic Ferry* and *Atlantic Causeway* finished unloading at San Carlos on 2 June, while the *Sir Galahad* and *Sir Bedivere* back-loaded stores and ammunition for Teal Inlet. The ships sailed at 9.00pm, escorted by the *Minerva* and the *Yarmouth*; the former would turn back once the convoy was past the Pebble Island danger zone, but the *Yarmouth* was to continue to the 'Trala' for a maintenance period in company with the *Stena Seaspread*. The inbound convoy from the Battle Group, the *Stromness*, *Nordic Ferry*, *Blue Rover* and *Sir Tristram*, detached earlier than usual, at 1.30pm, thanks to the cover provided by the thick fog. The *Brilliant* and *Avenger* escorted them, the latter going all the way through to San Carlos.

Although the *Active* and *Ambuscade* proceeded inshore for a harassing bombardment, the poor visibility prevented the necessary visual spotting and they had to restrict themselves to a surface sweep. It was the *Cardiff*'s turn on the missile trap station off Port Stanley, where she was due at 7.00pm, and it was hoped that the bad weather would encourage the Argentine Air Force to send its C-130s on resupply flights. The hope was not misplaced and as the destroyer arrived she detected an aircraft approaching along the south coast of East Falkland at low level. A Sea Dart was fired at extreme range but, warned by the radar station of the destroyer's presence and its own radar detection of the missile launch, the C-130 was able to take timely avoiding action and landed safely but shaken at Port Stanley. Twenty minutes later, when it took off again, it was treated to another Sea Dart, to speed it on its way. The *Cardiff* remained until 3.00am on the 3rd, but no further aircraft movements were observed.

The *Arrow* was also out. A repair team from the *Stena Seaspread* had arrived in the TA during the night of 31 May/1 June aboard the *Elk*, to reinforce the roving repair parties so far provided by the *Fearless* and *Intrepid*. The new arrivals' first task was the application of a 20-foot girder to the side of the *Arrow*, as a makeshift repair to restore the longitudinal strength lost due to the cracks caused by weather damage. Fit once again for the open sea, the *Arrow* took Fox Bay under fire, 101 rounds of 4.5in high-explosive shell being spotted by her Lynx. Argentine anti-aircraft guns engaged the helicopter without success.

Other Argentine soldiers were spending a more peaceful and comfortable night than they had enjoyed for a while. Just over half of the prisoners from Goose Green were now accommodated in the *Norland*, where they were to remain, guarded by 160 Royal Marines and sailors, until they could be shipped home. Negotiations were already under way, via the Red Cross and the Uruguayan Government, to use the good offices of the latter to enable the men to be returned via Montevideo.

3 JUNE

The *Cardiff* and *Active* rejoined the Carrier Battle Group at about 4.00am. Visibility in the East Falkland area and in the eastern sector of the TEZ was less than half a mile and the cloudbase was 200 feet at most. It had been intended that Sea Harriers should repeat their baiting tactics to support another Ascension-based Vulcan anti-radar attack but the weather ruled this out and the bomber attracted all the defences' attention. Unfortunately, *VYCA 2*, after the fortunate escape early on 31 May, shut down the TPS-43, which was the most important radar, but the Argentine Army obliged by using their Skyguard fire-control radars to lay the 35mm AA guns. One of the two Shrike missiles fired by the Vulcan destroyed a radar and injured the crew.

The Vulcan withdrew and headed north-east for its single refuelling rendezvous on the flight home. There the flight-refuelling probe broke, leaving the Vulcan with barely sufficient fuel to reach Rio de Janeiro, 700 miles to the west of the direct Falklands–Ascension track. The Brazilian authorities acted with great correctness, impounding the aircraft, and a Shrike which had stubbornly refused to be jettisoned, until an agreement had been reached whereby the Vulcan was released on condition that it was not again used in the campaign. Only five of the aircraft had been modified for 'Corporate' operations. It is not known whether this aircraft (XM597) was the only one fitted for Shrike launching, or whether it was significant that no further anti-radar missions were flown.

The poor weather continued throughout 3 and 4 June and prevented any fighter operations by the carriers. Mist and low cloud over East Falkland also slowed the air-transported build-up but before dawn six Sea King 5s were flown in to the TA to assist with the unloading of transports and the back-loading of the LSLs intended for Teal Inlet and Fitzroy. These helicopters were provided by 824 Squadron's *Olmeda* Flight and the 826 detachment from the RFA *Fort Austin*. This ship, the longest-serving in the South Atlantic with the exception of HMS *Endurance*, was about to be relieved by her sister-ship, the *Fort Grange*, which joined the Battle Group during the morning with air stores, ordnance and provisions, coming in from the 'Trala' with the *Elk* and *Tidepool*.

Information of the Exocet firing from the Port Stanley area reached the naval commanders early on the 3rd and advantage was taken of the weather, which effectively prevented any Argentine air strikes on ships, to search for the launching site. The *Minerva* was despatched from the TA and by dawn was between Fitzroy and Seal Point, with her Lynx inshore making a visual reconnaissance along the coast. At 7.45am the helicopter crew were startled by a Roland missile which hurtled out of the gloom and missed by about twenty feet, followed by a second which missed by a wider margin as the pilot took violent evasive action.

The only other encounter with Argentine forces, apart from the troops' patrol activities, was by the *Engadine*, which was overflown by a Boeing 707 1,000 miles to the north-east of the Falklands. After their debut in the maritime strike role a few days earlier, the C-130s were being 'rested', probably because the bad weather in the TEZ was allowing the Argentine air transport units to step up their resupply effort. The small helicopter training carrier was relatively well-armed, for she sported fourteen GPMGs and LMGs and could field a team of twenty riflemen as an effective deterrent battery.

The unloading of the *Canberra* was completed at San Carlos, with over 100 helicopter loads flown from her two pads during the day and a continuous shuttle of LCUs carrying stores ashore. The Fleet Clearance Divers, having disposed of all the unexploded bombs in ships, turned their attention to the wreck of the *Antelope*, to salvage secret material and any items which could be set to work. One such find was the frigate's starboard 20mm gun and mounting (which had shared in the destruction of a Skyhawk on 23 May). This was transferred to the *Avenger* and installed in the port bridge wing position, which had been the original location for the Type 21s Oerlikon.* The gun's shield was suitably embellished – 'ANTELOPE's AVENGER'.

The *Fearless*'s engineers went down to Darwin and were taken to the *Monsunnen* to survey her damage and restore her to operations. She was not much harmed, for when she had run aground on 23 May the thick kelp had absorbed the impact, and the main task was restoration after neglect and tidying up the mess which the liberators had now come to expect. The state of most enclosed spaces (and many open ones) indicated an exotic approach to sanitary practice which the British found quite revolting. The coaster was operational by the end of the day and,

* See p. 255.

HMS *Avenger*, with the *Intrepid* in the background, off Doctor's Head, at the northern end of San Carlos Water *(MoD)*

manned by a small 'prize crew', it was put into service to carry 5 Infantry Brigade stores to Fitzroy.

On the southern 'front' the Gurkhas had lost no time in getting forward, marching to Darwin on the day after their arrival, while 2 Para occupied the area around Bluff Cove Settlement. In the north RFA *Sir Percivale* completed unloading at Teal Inlet, using a Mexeflote which she had brought, an LCU which the *Intrepid* had sent in earlier and a detachment of Sea Kings of 846 Squadron which used the LSL as a refuelling platform. These helicopters also moved 45 Commando up from Teal to the lower slopes of the hills which were the British front line, a distance of about twelve miles, but the low cloud reduced the resupply of the troops on the high ground and the build-up of ammunition dumps.

The *Canberra*, *Stromness* and *Blue Rover* sailed from San Carlos Water at 6.00pm, escorted by the *Plymouth* and *Minerva*, the former accompanying the convoy past Pebble Island, which was still regarded with suspicion. The *Minerva* went all the way back to the Battle Group, her place being taken by the *Penelope*, which brought in the *Intrepid*, *Elk* and *Sir Galahad*, the latter detaching to make her way to Teal Inlet independently.

The *Fearless* was also on her way to Teal, or, rather, to despatch an LCU from the mouth of Port Salvador. Escorted by the *Avenger*, she left San Carlos an hour after the transport convoy and arrived off the entrance to Port Salvador at a quarter to midnight as the *Sir Percivale* came out. The two ships, maintaining radar silence, passed close in poor visibility, somewhat to the *Fearless'* alarm. The LCU was sent off at 12.10am and the LPD and LSL returned in company, escorted by the *Avenger*, to anchor off Ajax Bay five and a half hours later.

The *Plymouth*, returning from her escort duties, had meanwhile continued south past the TA and awakened the Port Howard garrison with 150 4.5in shells. A week had elapsed since the last such visit, by the *Yarmouth*, although Fox Bay had been bombarded twice in the interval.

The first three minesweeping trawlers left South Georgia on 3 June. They had been intended for use in the clearance of the approaches to Port Stanley when the town was captured, but the Argentine shore-based Exocet launcher was apparently sited to cover the sector hitherto used by ships bombarding the Port Stanley area. The 'sweepers were now required to clear waters where a gunline could be established outside the missiles' reach.

Far to the north RFA *Plumleaf* had been brought to a stop by a defect in her diesel machinery cooling system. The tanker had left Ascension on 7 May with the Amphibious Group but had been dropped off on the 16th to act as a 'Motorway Station' for ships proceeding to and from the South Atlantic. For the next two weeks she operated in an area to the north of South Georgia, well within the range of the 707s, supplying individual ships or groups. The *Bristol* Group replenishment took thirty-two hours, with the *Plumleaf* connected to one or other warship for twenty-two of those hours and most of her deck crew continuously on duty throughout. The attack on the *British Wye* demonstrated the long reach of the Argentine Air Force and the *Plumleaf* had accordingly been moved north, to a smaller area just 1,100 miles south-west of Ascension. Here her breakdown was not quite such a risky occurrence and she was able to repair it unthreatened by the enemy.

4 JUNE

The inbound convoy did not anchor in San Carlos Water until dawn, well after the return of the *Fearless*, and the *Sir Galahad* did not begin her entry through the Salvador narrows until it was fully light. There was, however, little risk of air attack for the low cloud and mist had still not cleared and the mainland airfields were also 'weathered-in'. Unloading went on undisturbed throughout the daylight hours but was slower than desirable, due mainly to unfamiliarity with the new Brigade's loading scheme. The *Sir Percivale* spent the day back-loading 3 Commando Brigade material for Teal Inlet, while the *Sir Tristram* loaded ammunition and stores for Fitzroy. The team from the *Stena Seaspread*, assisted by engineers from the two LPDs, was working on the *Sir Lancelot*, to repair her sufficiently to resume supply operations.

The weather again limited helicopter employment, with the southern front also badly affected, to the extent that only one 105mm gun could be lifted into Bluff Cove during the day. The *Monsunnen* made her first trip though, taking two companies of Gurkhas from Darwin to Bluff Cove, the remaining company being left for the time being to garrison Darwin and Goose Green and to patrol Lafonia, where they picked up Argentine stragglers from time to time.

The Carrier Battle Group also had a fairly quiet day. The *Argonaut*, patched up with steel plating, shoring and concrete for her passage home, transferred all the ammunition and stores which she could spare to other ships in the Group and left at midday, when she was formally released from Operation 'Corporate'. The *Glasgow*, three days' steaming south of Ascension, was released at the same time.

The *Queen Elizabeth II* was already in the Ascension area, after an undisturbed run from South Georgia. She rendezvoused with HMS *Dumbarton Castle* fifty miles south-west of the island and, with the aid of a Sea King of No 202 Squadron RAF, transferred stores which had been discovered since leaving South Georgia and personnel who required to be flown back to the United Kingdom. The helicopter was unable to land on the 'Castle' to refuel but an in-flight refuelling rig had been improvised, with the ship's fuel hose being picked up by the rescue winch (as described earlier on p. 122). Although a routine exercise for naval helicopters, it was believed that this was the first occasion on which it had been conducted with an RAF Sea King.

The *Bahia Paraiso* arrived in the Red Cross Box during the day and transferred Argentine wounded from the *Uganda*. Her Captain stated his intention of entering the Falkland Sound to pick up wounded from Port Howard and Fox Bay – an indication that the recent bombardments had been on target. This request led to the cancellation of another bombardment planned for Port Howard that evening by the *Plymouth*, but in the event the Argentine hospital ship returned direct to the mainland, so that the enemy troops enjoyed a rather undeserved respite.

The Battle Group had suspended its bombardments of the Port Stanley area until the Exocet threat had been more clearly examined. As a first step, the *Exeter* was detached at 2.00pm to operate outside MM-38 range, to the south of the airfield. To cover the destroyer, and also to give the Argentinians something to worry about, the *Invincible* and *Brilliant* followed forty minutes later, shortly before the inbound TA convoy – *Sir Geraint* and *Blue Rover*, escorted by HMS *Andromeda* – started off. Somewhat unusually there was no outbound convoy from San Carlos to the Battle Group or 'Trala'.

The first activity came from the Argentine Air Force. Probably advised by the radar controllers of *VYCA 2* that there had been no Sea Harrier flying for over forty-eight hours, a high-level raid appeared in daylight for the first time since 1 May. Four aircraft were detected at 3.00pm and were observed with interest as they tracked in from the south-west, passed ten miles to the south of Ajax Bay and continued on to the Port Salvador area, where they turned to the south-east and, at 3.25pm, dropped three bombs near Green Patch Settlement at the head of Berkeley Sound. The formation then departed, disappearing from the radars about twenty minutes later. From the direction of their approach and their speed, it was believed that the bombers were Daggers and this has been confirmed by Argentine sources.

Two hours later, at 5.10pm, another formation of four aircraft appeared, again from the south-west. These also passed to the south of the Transport Area and then, splitting into two pairs and possibly descending to a lower altitude, attacked the Mount Kent area, where ten bombs were seen to explode about 500 yards to the east of the Commandos' front line. Again there was some doubt as to the identity of the raiders. Although it was probable that these were Canberras, there was a possibility that they were Skyhawks, for radio conversations indicating flight refuelling activity were overheard.

Whatever the Argentine aircraft may have been, the incursions were extremely frustrating for the Royal Navy. The *Invincible*, to the south-east of Port Stanley, had still not found a clear patch of weather for operating her SHARs, and the *Exeter*, though closer to East Falkland, was not yet close enough to engage with Sea Dart. Within the TA the only long-range AA systems were the four frigates' 4.5in guns. Ineffective against low-level targets at short range, they would have been a powerful deterrent against bombers flying steady (and therefore predictable) courses at medium altitude.

The *Exeter* arrived on her station at about 7.00pm and flew off her Lynx. Carrying a large, home-made radar reflector, the helicopter flew slowly to the 'gun line' area to the south of Port Stanley and pretended to be a bombarding ship, in the hopes of attracting an Exocet. Either the Argentine Navy was not expecting a bombardment that night or the operators were not so easily deceived. In any case, no missile was fired. After recovering the Lynx, the *Exeter* continued to the south-west, having been ordered to proceed to San Carlos Water to reinforce the air defences. Her pre-dawn arrival was not noticed by the Argentinians.

The *Invincible* and *Brilliant* reached the position in which it was hoped to begin flying at 9.30pm, only to find themselves still in fog. They pressed on to the west and by 11.00pm the visibility had improved sufficiently to launch the first SHAR mission since the morning of 2 June. Taking off to the south of the Falkland Sound, the fighters patrolled out to the maximum radius of the ship's high level radar cover, where they could be seen heading westwards by the Argentine radars at Port Stanley, Rio Gallegos and Rio Grande. As this first probe turned back and a second was launched, the carrier and her 'goalkeeper' reversed course, in order to be to the east of Port Stanley well before dawn but still be ready to take action against any reaction which the probes into the fringe of Argentina's continental air defence zone may have provoked.

5 JUNE

The *Invincible* recovered her SHARs safely and then kept a pair of fighters manned on deck. At 4.40am one of these, flown by Lieutenant C. Cantan, was scrambled to investigate a contact held by the *Exeter* and approaching from the west. The Argentine aircraft turned back as the SHAR closed in and made no attempt to return again. The carrier had meanwhile entered a thick fog bank, so that when Lieutenant Cantan arrived over the port quarter at the end of a radar-controlled 'talk-down' he was unable to see the ship, although he was less than fifty yards away. A second approach was made, also radar-controlled, but with the aircraft moving very slowly ahead (relative to the ship), following a line of flame-floats in the wake over the last few hundred yards. When he at last found the ship and landed, Charles Cantan had less than twenty gallons of fuel remaining.

The patchy fog continued in the Battle Group's sector throughout the day, but visibility improved sufficiently to resume fighter operations. The first CAP of the day, flown off before dawn from the *Hermes*, landed at the Port San Carlos strip, christened 'HMS *Sheathbill*' (following the naval practice of naming air stations after birds). Two GR3s also flew in, to be on call for close air support missions for the troops. The strip, which had four readiness hardstandings, extended the endurance of the Sea Harriers, so that the carriers could operate farther to the east while the aircraft spent longer on CAP station, but the advantage for the RAF Harriers was that their reaction time to a call for assistance from the troops was much reduced. Only fuel was available; as yet there was no provision for reloading ordnance.

General view, looking east up Port San Carlos, with the runway of HMS *Sheathbill* in the right foreground and the settlement, where the Wessex helicopters were based, beyond and to the left *(MoD)*

Careful briefing of the pilots and all air defence positions minimized the risk of the fighters being engaged by the San Carlos weapons, but the first arrivals still caused alarms, even though the SHARs came through the Fanning Head narrows at slow speed, with their wheels down and landing lights burning bright. 800 Squadron sent another CAP section into the strip later in the day, but this was the full extent of the first day's usage. The two GR3s remained until 11.30am, when they took off to rocket Argentine troop positions on Two Sisters.

The improvement in the weather over East Falkland allowed Commodore Clapp and Major-General Moore to make the best use of the forty helicopters which were now available. Two complete artillery batteries were moved into forward positions. A Rapier Troop was lifted to Teal Inlet and considerable quantities of ammunition, fuel and rations were supplied to the front-line units.

Certain elements of the Teal Rapier troop were ferried in the *Sir Percivale*, which sailed from San Carlos, with the *Plymouth* as escort as far as the Eddystone Rock, at 1.30am. The LSL entered Port Salvador at about dawn and, as the *Sir Galahad* had not completed off-loading, acted as a helicopter fuelling base until she could move closer inshore and begin to transfer her cargo to the Mexeflote. The *Sir Percivale* refuelled nearly fifty Sea Kings and Wessex on the 5th, a rate of one helicopter every ten minutes, and she took all the *Sir Galahad*'s remaining aviation fuel before the latter left that night to return to San Carlos.

The *Nordic Ferry* and *Elk*, whose off-load for 5 Infantry Brigade was progressing relatively slowly due to lack of transport shipping, were still in

5 June: the *Sir Galahad*, on her first task after sustaining damage on 24 May, offloads 3 Commando Brigade stores in Teal Inlet, assisted by a pair of 825 Squadron's Sea Kings. Included in her load was a Rapier troop of 12 Air Defence Regt., whose four 'fire units' were particularly welcome in such an open location *('Soldier' Magazine)*

San Carlos Water. The *Sir Tristram* had already loaded for Fitzroy but the *Sir Geraint* devised a new method to speed up transfers from the *Elk*, positioning herself so that a Mexeflote could bridge the gap between the STUFT and herself, permitting pre-loaded transport or fork-lift trucks to run between the ramps of the two ships and in and out of their cargo decks. Not only material was being loaded. The 2nd Battalion Scots Guards was now ready to be moved up and embarked in the *Intrepid* during the forenoon of the 5th. The 1st Battalion, Welsh Guards, began to march to Darwin but was obliged to turn back after covering five miles as the transport carrying the equipment was delayed.

NIGHT OF 5/6 JUNE

Somewhat unusually, there were no inbound or outbound convoys in the Transport Area during the night of 5/6 June. There was, however, considerable inshore activity by the warships of TG 317.0. The *Intrepid* sailed from San Carlos Water at 2030 with the 2nd Battalion, the Scots Guards, embarked for passage to the southern (5 Infantry Brigade) area. For the passage down the Falkland Sound the LPD had HMS *Plymouth* as close escort. The *Exeter*, *Avenger* and *Arrow* had left San Carlos shortly before, the last-named to take up the 'picket' station at the northern entrance to the Falkland Sound and the Type 42 to patrol in the Grantham Sound area, to bring the entire length of the Falkland Sound within range of her Sea Dart system. The *Avenger* preceded the *Intrepid* and *Plymouth* until she reached the level of Fox Bay, where she detached to carry out a bombardment to harass the garrison and divert the attention of any coast-watchers from the LPD. 133 4.5in shells were fired before the frigate headed for the southern extremity of West Falkland to fly off her Lynx to look for any sign of Argentine occupation.

Three ships of TG317.8 were also in, or approaching, coastal waters, having detached from the Carrier Battle Group in mid-afternoon. The *Cardiff* and *Yarmouth* were to operate in the Port Fitzroy area, the frigate bombarding targets on Mount William, Tumbledown and around Moody Brook, while the destroyer would combine bombardment of Argentine positions on Wireless Ridge and Sapper Hill with a missile trap patrol, to interdict any air supply missions into Port Stanley airfield. The *Active*, which had no Naval Gunfire Support observation party embarked, took up station off Volunteer Point, to the north of Port Stanley, to stand by to support Special Forces if the latter called for assistance. Both gunlines were outside the estimated arcs of fire of the Argentine Navy's shore-based Exocet and the beat off Port Fitzroy gave the *Cardiff* better coverage of the south-west approaches to Port Stanley than the usual position off Cape Pembroke.

The *Plymouth* left the *Intrepid* as the latter passed round Lafonia and returned up the Sound at high speed to relieve the *Arrow* as the San Carlos 'sentry', the latter being already outbound to the north of East Falkland, to collect the LSL *Sir Galahad*, which was to leave Teal Inlet at about 0400 to return to the 'TA'.

Unbeknown to the *Arrow*, LCU *F.4*, which had been left at Port Salvador by the *Fearless* several nights previously, had also been ordered to make its way back independently to San Carlos, where the shortage of landing craft was becoming acute. At 0310 the *Arrow* detected this unexpected 'intruder' off the coast and illuminated *F.4* with starshell, preparatory to engaging with 4.5in. The Coxswain, Colour Sergeant Johnston RM, and his crew undoubtedly received a fright before they managed to satisfy the frigate, but this was only their first of the night and they were not to be alone in the experience.

Meanwhile the *Intrepid* had reached a position in the shelter of Lively Island and undocked her four LCUs, in which the 560 men of the Scots Guards were embarked. It was expected that the 35-mile passage to Bluff Cove, off Port Fitzroy, would take about five hours. The LPD left the LCUs at 0200 and headed back to the TA in a rising sea, to be back inside the cover of San Carlos Water by dawn.

HMS *Cardiff* and *Yarmouth* arrived off Port Fitzroy as the LCUs set off and began their bombardment serials. At about 0400 the Type 42 detected a slow-moving contact approaching overland from the west, tracking towards Port Stanley over ground not occupied by British forces. Three Sea Darts were fired as the aircraft, assessed as being a helicopter, approached and the second gave indications of a hit, at about 0410, at a range of some eleven miles. Tragically, the victim was an Army Gazelle of No 656 Squadron AAC, which had taken off from Goose Green with an urgently required radio relay station and was within two miles of its destination on Mount Pleasant Peak when it was hit. All four occupants, the two crew and two Signals specialists, were killed. Not until some while afterwards were the coincidences of the times of loss and the *Cardiff*'s claim correlated, and the probability recognized that an 'own goal' had been scored.

The *Cardiff*'s alarms were not yet over. Some while after the missile engagement, she detected a group of surface contacts to the south-west, heading towards her. Four starshell rounds were fired to illuminate the vessels, which were immediately recognized as LCUs. *Intrepid*'s 'skips' were making heavy weather in the gale which had now blown up and they and their cargo of soaked and seasick guardsmen were encouraged on their way, which was to end at Bluff Cove after seven miserable hours.

The *Active* was not required by the forces in her area and she left shortly after 0400. The *Yarmouth* and *Cardiff* completed their bombardment tasks at 0600, after firing a combined total of 438 4.5in shells, and returned to the Carrier Battle Group without any further unscheduled activity.

As the bombarding ships left, *F.4*, on the other side of East Falkland, was facing her second encounter of the night. At 0610, as the LCU entered the North Falkland Sound, she was challenged by the *Plymouth* which, like the *Arrow* earlier, had not been informed of the movement and kept her 4.5in turret trained on the craft until Colour Sergeant Johnston had made the correct reply. The same welcome awaited the *Sir Galahad* two and a half hours later, when she aroused suspicion by failing to respond promptly to the frigate's first challenge. The *Intrepid* and *Avenger* returned to San Carlos Water without incident before dawn, when the *Exeter* entered after what had been, for her, an uneventful night.

The unexpected meetings experienced during this one night by the *Arrow*, *Cardiff* and *Plymouth* were remarkable in that they provided virtually all of the Royal Navy's inshore encounters of this nature during 'Corporate'. Hitherto remarkably close co-ordination of the various forces' movements had been achieved and it was to be re-enforced thereafter. The 'Blue-on-Blue' missile engagement was the only one of its kind during the campaign – an even more remarkable achievement – and was almost certainly due to the 'fog of war', confused by the multiplicity of command authorities and units within a relatively small and complicated combat theatre.*

6 JUNE

The weather, after its brief improvement on the 5th, 'clamped' again, reducing the helicopters' contribution to the build-up on both Brigades' fronts. Only the first CAP of the day and one pair of GR3s were able to use the Port San Carlos strip before strong cross-winds forced the suspension of fixed-wing operations. The carriers were in a foggy, but calm, area on the edge of the TEZ, 200 miles to the east. No Argentine aircraft appeared during the day and again unloading proceeded undisturbed in the Transport Area, the *Nordic Ferry* being emptied of her Army stores at last.

---

* This night's operations provide a good example of the complexity of planning and co-ordinating sea–land activities. *Cardiff* and *Yarmouth*, under CTG 317.8's command, were co-operating with 3 RM Commando Brigade, under CTG 317.1 (Commander, Land Forces, Falkland Islands), but their station was off, and they were firing over, the sector of another TG 317.1 unit, 5 Infantry Brigade. *Intrepid* and her LCUs, which were to pass through the bombardment area, were TG 317.0 (Commodore, Amphibious Warfare) units, co-operating with 5 Infantry Brigade. Transport helicopter movements were controlled by TG 317.0, but the two Brigades tasked their own light helicopters and the bombarding units enjoyed completely autonomous control of their Flights for tactical purposes. *Exeter* was the Air Warfare Coordinator for the Transport Area, but the *Cardiff* was ordered to interdict the approaches to Port Stanley airfield, which lay far outside the TA. Such a combination of threads could only be woven into a fully coherent pattern if good communications could be maintained unbroken over the entire theatre. This was not always possible in the Falklands, where terrain, weather and notoriously difficult atmospheric conditions combined, albeit rarely, to leave a hole in the fabric.

Another ship to be emptied was the *Blue Rover*, which dispensed the last of her Dieso and aviation fuel to various ships and to the two forward air bases, but was unable to replenish the LPDs with aviation fuel due to the bad weather. The *Sir Geraint* continued to back-load 3 Commando Brigade stores for Teal Inlet, but the *Sir Tristram* completed her cargo for Fitzroy Cove and hoisted in a Mexeflote for use in off-loading in the forward anchorage.

Also bound for the southern beachhead were the Welsh Guards, who embarked aboard the *Fearless* at noon. The LPD had only two of her own LCUs, the others being at Teal Inlet, and she would therefore rendezvous with *Intrepid*'s north of Lively Island, where the soldiers would be transferred. The *Fearless*, escorted by the *Avenger* and *Penelope*, sailed from San Carlos at dusk.

The *Exeter*, as on the previous night, patrolled in the Falkland Sound, covering the *Fearless* and the *Sir Tristram*, which sailed independently some hours later, as well as the night's convoys to and from the Battle Group – the *Blue Rover* and *Nordic Ferry* outbound with HMS *Arrow* and the inbound *Baltic Ferry* and *Norland*, escorted as far as the Eddystone Rock by HMS *Andromeda*.

The Battle Group had had another quiet day, which had begun with a major RAS for the big ships. The *Fort Austin* had begun transferring all her remaining stores to the *Fort Grange* during the previous day and the process was completed on the 6th. She also passed the 826 Squadron detachment's equipment to the *Atlantic Causeway*, which was to serve as the relief Sea King carrier after her departure. The helicopters themselves were still inshore at the San Carlos Settlement base. When this was completed, Commodore Dunlop took his splendid, hard-working auxiliary out of the TEZ to the 'Trala' for the last time, before heading for South Georgia and home.

RFA *Fort Grange* transfers stores from the *Fort Austin* (nearer camera) prior to the latter's departure for home *(MoD)*

The *Active* and *Ambuscade* detached for the usual bombardments and the *Invincible* and *Brilliant* headed for a position to the south of the Falkland Sound to wait for Canberras or any C-130s which might be reported over the Falklands.

The *Hydra* arrived at Montevideo on the first of the ambulance visits. Negotiations to secure the good offices of the Uruguayan Government had been complicated by the tortuous diplomatic chain, whereby the British Government communicated with Buenos Aires via Berne and the Junta replied via Rio de Janeiro. The Argentine rulers' dark suspicions of the International Committee of the Red Cross led to a long delay before that respectable organization was allowed to play its proper role. However, by 6 June Argentine agreement to the use of Montevideo as a trans-shipment port for wounded, from unarmed ambulance ferries to RAF transports, was obtained and the first fifty-one men were landed that morning.

The 'Ambulance Ferries' HMS *Herald* (nearer) and *Hydra* alongside at Montevideo, where a fleet of police ambulances waits to take the wounded to the airport to be flown home by RAF VC-10 *(MoD)*

7 JUNE

The *Fearless* and her two frigates reached the rendezvous off Lively Island before midnight and awaited the arrival of the LCUs from Bluff Cove. In fact they had not sailed and the LPD, unaware of this, waited until the last possible moment before returning to San Carlos. Before she did so, she despatched her own two LCUs with two companies of guardsmen. The weather was still rough, so that the *Fearless* could not refuel the *Avenger*, as had been planned, and again the soldiers had a very unpleasant trip inshore, although they were spared the extra excitement of sudden illumination.

The *Avenger* conducted a brief bombardment of Sea Lion Island during the return passage but the main concern of the small group was to reach the shelter of San Carlos Water as soon as possible. It was already growing light as they passed Grantham Sound (where the *Uganda* was again at anchor to perform surgical operations in calm water) and the *Fearless* did not anchor in the Water until after the day had dawned bright and clear.

The *Active* and *Ambuscade* between them fired only 100 shells at the Argentine positions on Mount Harriet and immediately to the west of Port Stanley. The two Commandos and 3 Para on the 3 Commando Brigade front were conducting deep reconnaissance patrols to establish the limits of the defensive minefields around Two Sisters and Mount Longdon and would call for fire only in case of necessity.

The improvement in the weather was welcomed by all. The thirty-six transport helicopters began flying at dawn and continued until nightfall, when 846 Squadron's four PNG Sea Kings began their 'day's work'. The crews snatched refreshment when the opportunity offered, usually aboard the ships, some of which went to great length to ensure that hot food and drink was always available for the boats' crews and aircrew. In the two forward anchorages the *Sir Percivale* and *Sir Tristram* acted as re-fuelling platforms for the stream of Sea Kings and Wessex. Close control over the helicopters was maintained by COMAW's staff, to ensure that the overall task met the demands of the commander and the campaign and not the individual units which, given half a chance, would have appropriated passing aircraft for their own use.

The *Hermes* had withdrawn from the TEZ early on 7 June. Her steam turbine machinery, which had by now driven her over 20,000 miles – the equivalent of once around the Earth (for 20,000 nautical miles are the equivalent of 23,000 statute miles) – was in urgent need of overhaul and there was much remedial work to be carried out in the boiler rooms. One at a time, her boilers were shut down and cleaned, a task never before attempted at sea in a war zone, and the corresponding pumps, pipes and burners were cleaned, repaired or replaced when possible. In spite of her extra distance from Port San Carlos, she was still able to contribute air cover, thanks to the availability of 'HMS *Sheathbill*'. Three pairs of 800 Squadron SHARs flew double CAPs, one patrol on the way to Port San Carlos and one on the way back, alternating with 801 Squadron's fighters, which were not, as yet, using the strip. The GR3s do not appear to have used Port San Carlos during the day but made two attacks on what were believed to be 155mm gun positions.

The Argentine Air Force also welcomed the clear skies. None of their aircraft had seen the San Carlos area in daylight since 25 May and, presumably lulled into a false sense of security by the lack of reaction to the high-level night raids and the success of *VYCA 2* in giving ample warning of the activities of the CAP, a formation of unarmed Learjets was

The *Plymouth* passes *Intrepid* at the entrance to San Carlos Water. The Type 42 *Exeter*, at right, arrived early on 5 June to assume responsibility for air defence co-ordination in the Transport Area *(MoD)*

despatched on a high-level photographic reconnaissance mission. The *Exeter*, back in San Carlos Water after her night patrol, detected the aircraft at long range at 7.59am. The CAP, far below the Argentine aircraft, which were flying at about 40,000 feet, was held off by the *Exeter*, which delayed 'system acquisition' until the targets were well within range. By the time that the destroyer fired a salvo of Sea Darts, all eyes in the anchorage were watching the approach of the two contrails, flying a few miles apart. The *Exeter* fired at 8.10am: one missile went 'rogue' but the other worked pefectly and one minute later hit and destroyed the Learjet flown by *Vicecomodoro* R. M. de la Colina, the most senior Argentine Air Force officer to lose his life in the conflict. The wreckage fell in the vicinity of Pebble Island, none of the five members of the crew surviving. The other Learjet was deliberately not re-engaged and was allowed to return with the news that the San Carlos area was as unpleasant as ever.

The Argentine Air Force did not return during that day and the activity at San Carlos continued undisturbed. The *Norland*, which had had 520 prisoners on board for several days, had come back for the balance of those held in the Ajax Bay compounds: 496 were embarked by landing craft on the 7th and the ship was able to proceed at 5.50pm, in company with the *Elk* and escorted out by the *Penelope*. Also embarking personnel from midday was the *Sir Galahad*, which was to take a Rapier Troop, a Field Ambulance and vehicles to Fitzroy Cove, and now had the 350 Welsh Guards of the rifle company and the support company which had not been landed the previous night. Embarkation went slowly and the ship sailed late, at 10.00pm, with 470 Army personnel and a Sea King of 825 Squadron embarked to begin the off-load at first light. She was not directly escorted, but there was assistance on call at short notice from warships and aircraft operating to the south of East Falkland.

The lack of enemy air activity gave the carriers a relatively quiet day, in spite of the excellent weather. The *Alacrity* became the first 'routine' warship departure for home. Commander Christopher Craig and his ship's company had served with distinction from the first day of operations in the TEZ and were now returning only because the 4.5in gun barrel had exceeded its life. The ship had signalled 'Propose to go on until it drops off', but Admiral Woodward did not concur and, after the usual transfer of stores needed in the ships remaining, the *Alacrity* left. Other ships joined: the *Junella*, *Cordella* and *Pict* from South Georgia and the *Engadine* from the north. These four joined the RFA *Olna* and *Atlantic Causeway* and set off for the TA escorted by the *Ambuscade*, rather later than was customary, at 3.00pm.

The *Cardiff* and *Yarmouth* had already left for the southern gunline when this convoy detached and the *Arrow* went off to support Special Forces' operations in the north-east corner of East Falkland. The *Invincible* and *Brilliant*, which had drawn a complete blank during the previous night, repeated their patrol to the south of the Falkland Sound, hoping to catch either Canberras or C-130s. With the *Andromeda* away on the north-eastern edge of the TEZ, awaiting an RAF Hercules and its consignment of six tons of stores and ten paratrooping passengers, the Battle Group was reduced to three frigates (*Broadsword*, *Active* and *Minerva*) screening the *Hermes* and a few RFAs.

All the warships in the TA were also on the move as well. The *Fearless* left San Carlos Water at about 7.00pm to bring back two LCUs from Teal Inlet. The *Sir Percivale* began the return journey at about the same time. The other LPD, *Intrepid*, set off with the *Plymouth* to pick up her four LCUs in Low Bay, Lafonia, whence they had made their own way from Bluff Cove. The *Sir Galahad* was to have gone with the *Intrepid* but, as recounted earlier, her departure was delayed. The *Exeter* alone remained in the TA proper, taking up her station in Grantham Sound for the night.

The Argentine air transport units by now knew that the pattern of Royal Navy activity gave them two periods when the Air Force C-130s and the Navy Electras could approach and depart in comparative safety. From 4.00pm until 7.00pm no British warship would be in the open sea along the south coasts of the islands or close to Port Stanley and the bombarding units would leave at least three hours before dawn. With no ships to detect the blockade-runners and no airborne early warning to control CAPs, SHAR patrols would be unproductive and not even a deterrent to the determined and skilful Argentine 'Truckies'. The only means of stopping the movements was a permanent dusk to dawn missile trap patrol. Two ships had been hit by air attack while on patrol in daylight (the *Glasgow* and *Coventry*) and, although the Argentine Air Force's most recent attack, on 30 May, had been a total failure, Admiral Woodward, who had only two Type 42 destroyers left and no prospect of early replacements in the event of their being put out of action, respected his adversary and was not prepared to risk any ships in daylight close to the islands. On the evening of 7 May the *Cardiff* had been about ninety miles to the east of Port Stanley when darkness fell and she arrived within missile range of the airfield shortly before 7.00pm. On the hour an aircraft was detected to the south-west of Port Stanley and a Sea Dart was fired two minutes later. The missile malfunctioned, exploding two or three miles ahead of the target, which was observed to accelerate and to turn away abruptly and make no attempt to reach the airfield. The destroyer vectored a Sea Harrier from the *Invincible* towards the 'bogey' but the latter managed to avoid interception.

The *Avenger* had spent the day in the splendid scenery of Albemarle Harbour, undisturbed by friend or enemy. At dusk she emerged, patrolled the south coast of West Falkland and then conducted a search to the west of the tangle of islets and inlets around Weddell Island. No signs of the enemy were seen or detected and the frigate returned to San Carlos Water before dawn on the 8th.

8 JUNE

Tuesday 8 June, 1982, will be remembered by the man in the street as the day of the 'Disaster at Bluff Cove'. But to those in the Battle Group, the San Carlos area, in the front line on the hills and even in the headquarters in the United Kingdom, the air attack on the LSLs was just one of several incidents in an 'action-packed' day, albeit the most serious in terms of the logistic support of the campaign since the loss of the *Atlantic Conveyor*.

The *Cardiff* and *Yarmouth*, after the attempted missile engagement, skirted the suspected Exocet danger area and took up their bombardment line to the south-east of Bluff Cove. The *Yarmouth* delivered 187 shells on Moody Brook, Wireless Ridge, Sapper Hill and Mount Harriet, but the *Cardiff* suffered a further disappointment when her Mark 8 gun malfunctioned after firing only eleven rounds. The Argentine 155mm guns, sited around Sapper Hill, replied quite accurately, indicating that they were being spotted from ashore. It is likely that the night movements of the LSLs *Sir Tristram* and *Sir Galahad* into Port Pleasant (the inlet to Fitzroy Cove) were also observed with the assistance of the Argentine Army's modern night-viewing devices. The *Sir Galahad* had a trouble-free passage and anchored in Port Pleasant at 6.50am. By this time the *Intrepid* and *Plymouth* were back in San Carlos Water, with the LCUs on board, and the *Invincible* and *Brilliant* had returned to the Battle Group, on the edge of the TEZ, after another very quiet night.

Matters did not proceed quite so smoothly to the north of East Falkland, only the *Sir Percivale*'s return from Teal Inlet going without a hitch. The inbound convoy, already delayed by its late start, was being further held back by the slow minesweeping trawlers and RFA *Engadine*. Commodore Clapp accordingly ordered these four vessels and the *Ambuscade* to turn back towards the Carrier Battle Group, while the *Penelope* went eastward to pick up the *Olna* and *Atlantic Causeway*. The *Fearless* reached the RFA and aircraft transport first, at 2.15am, to the north-east of Port Salvador, and remained in company for two hours, refuelling. She detached just in time to make a fast passage to be in San Carlos Water by dawn.

The two parts of the convoy had not reached any safe haven by first light. The slow portion, which had turned back, remained to the west of the Battle Group for most of the day, reinforced by the *Minerva* and with a CAP on call, if not overhead. The two ships which pressed on had rounded Cape Dolphin by first light, when the escorting *Penelope* picked up what appeared to be an Exocet radar transmitter in the direction of Pebble Island at 7.20am. The frigate immediately launched chaff and placed herself between the threat and the two big ships. The *Exeter*'s Lynx joined as a radar decoy and the *Penelope*'s was launched for a visual reconnaissance of Pebble Island, where it was greeted by accurate automatic AA fire which prevented a close inspection. The ships reached the safety of the Fanning Head narrows at about 7.40am, by which time it had been assessed that the warning was spurious but that the *Penelope*'s response had been appropriate.

COMAW's staff believed that two Argentine observation posts were reporting the comings and goings of the convoys and ordered steps to be taken to eliminate them. The first to be dealt with was at Cape Dolphin and at 9.10am Marines of Bravo Company, 40 Commando, were lifted for a daylight assault on the position, the Sea Kings of 846 Squadron being supported by the 848 Squadron Wessex 'gunship'. The position was found to be unoccupied, in the event, and the only Argentine equipment consisted of a number of empty one-man liferafts, presumably left by Dagger pilots shot down on 23 and 24 May. The other OP was in Argentine-occupied West Falkland – the 1,400-foot Mount Rosalie, which was regarded as being a particular nuisance but which had so far not been attacked directly. The *Plymouth* was ordered at midday to bombard the position. The Argentine Air Force was on the offensive even earlier. At about 6.00am the Liberian-registered tanker *Hercules* was some 300 miles north-east of the TEZ, heading northbound in ballast, when she was approached by an aircraft which first circled her and then attacked with bombs, possibly scoring one hit. The outraged Master radioed his agents in New York with a description of his attacker which made it clear that the ship had been bombed by its flying namesake. The British did not hear of the incident for some hours but, in the meantime, HMS *Alacrity* reported that she had been approached by a shadower at 9.00am.

The good weather in the islands allowed the build-up ashore to be progressed to the point where the delays caused by the earlier 'clamp' had almost been made good. The *Sir Geraint* completed loading for the next trip to Teal Inlet and the *Sir Lancelot*, repairs almost finished, began consolidating her load from the Ajax Bay BMA and the *Atlantic Causeway*. At Port Pleasant the Sea King brought by *Sir Galahad* off-loaded the Rapier troop and other helicopters of 825 Squadron and the Wessex of 847 Squadron transferred loads from this ship and the *Sir Tristram* to the various 5 Infantry Brigade dumps and artillery positions.

Sir Galahad's arrival off Fitzroy had been unexpected, due to communications difficulties, so that only one LCU and one Mexeflote were on hand. Both were already loaded with ammunition from the *Sir Tristram*. The two Welsh Guards companies were offered whatever room could be found on them, to land at Fitzroy. The guardsmen, however, had been ordered to join their battalion at Bluff Cove, which they believed to be some sixteen miles' march (they were unaware that 2 Para's engineers had repaired the bridge at the head of Port Fitzroy, reducing the trek to about six miles) and preferred to wait until LCUs could be made available to ferry them there. First to go ashore, however, were most of the elements of the 16 Field Ambulance, which were landed at Fitzroy, but at 12.30pm the LCU came back to the LSL to begin moving the Welsh Guards to Bluff Cove.

Unfortunately, the LCU's ramp was defective and loading had to be carried out over the LSL's side, using rope ladders. This cumbersome process was further aggravated by the restricted access aboard the *Sir Galahad* caused by the previous bomb damage. Disembarkation and offloading was so slowed that three-quarters of an hour later the Guards personnel were still aboard the LSL.

The carriers had provided CAPs over San Carlos and Fitzroy since first light, under the control of the *Exeter*, back in her daylight anchorage in San Carlos Water. The *Hermes* was still boiler-cleaning, far outside the TEZ and 250 miles from Port Stanley, but the availability of 'HMS *Sheathbill*' meant that 800 Squadron could still remain on patrol longer than if the SHARs had been flying only from the ship on her usual station inside the TEZ. *Invincible*'s 801 Squadron was still not yet using the Port San Carlos strip but had 140 miles less to fly on a round trip, giving its SHARs an extra twenty minutes on CAP.

The GR3s went ashore early in the forenoon, a pair standing by for close air support. Unfortunately, at 10.50am, just after the second 800 CAP section of the day had taken off, a GR3 suffered a major loss of power when taking off and crashed on the aluminium planking of the strip. The pilot escaped with only superficial injuries. The damage to the runway was also superficial but the lack of spare sections meant that the damaged area had to be taken up and relaid, a task that would take an estimated three hours. For this period the *Hermes*' SHARs would be severely handicapped, with a time on patrol of about fifteen minutes over East Falkland. If a combat occurred then the aircraft would probably have to make a vertical landing and take-off from either the LPDs or from the

VTOL pad at Port San Carlos. In the meantime the *Hermes* made her way to the west in order to reduce the distance her aircraft had to fly.

The Argentine Air Force had still made no appearance in the TEZ when, at 12.50pm, the *Hermes* recovered a pair of GR3s which had flown down from Ascension with the assistance of the Victor tankers. No 1 Squadron RAF was back to the number of aircraft which it had had embarked on 21 May.

The GR3s' long haul had been supported by a Hercules of No 47 Squadron RAF which was carrying survival gear and acting as a communications relay between the fighters and Ascension. At about 12.00 noon (Falklands time) a radio call was overheard on the distress frequency – 'Hercules, Hercules, this is Argentine Air Force, you must stop'. Understandably the RAF crew drew the wrong conclusion and took their unarmed transport into the nearest cloud. At much the same time a wireless call on the international distress frequency was intercepted by the *Hydra*, returning after transferring her casualties at Montevideo, and also the *Herald*, northbound with the next consignment. This message, which reputedly came from Ushuaia, ordered the tanker *Hercules* to make for the nearest Argentine port. The two ambulance ships could not pass on this information, operating as they were under the Red Cross international conventions. Thus, the first that was known to Admiral Woodward was an indignant report from the neutral tanker that she had again been attacked and now had two unexploded bombs lodged in her empty tanks. From her description of the attack, she had been circled by two aircraft while a third actually carried out the bombing run. A definite possibility exists that the shadowers were C-130s, which had been attempting to divert the *Hercules* towards Argentina and that the bomber was a Canberra from Trelew, 600 miles to the west, and which was rather carried away by over-enthusiasm. The tanker pressed on doggedly and finally anchored off Rio de Janeiro. No one had been hurt and this was the only incident in which an innocent 'outsider' became directly involved in the war.

The situation over the Falklands just before 5.00pm was that there was one pair of SHARs on CAP over the Fitzroy area and another over the Falkland Sound. The STOVL strip was still unusable and the *Plymouth* was in the open water of the Sound, preparing to open fire on Mount Rosalie. At the time the Royal Navy was convinced that the first daylight sortie outside the San Carlos Water AA 'umbrella' by a frigate, the non-availability of the airstrip and the reappearance, after a two-week break, of enemy strike aircraft were definitely connected. It is, however, clear from the Argentine account* that the renewed activity was coincidental and not a deliberate exploitation of brief weakness.

The Argentine Air Force briefings had begun at about 9.00am (Falk-

* *Aeroespacio*, January/February, 1983.

lands time), the first wave of the day being a 'maximum effort' against the Port Pleasant area by the Rio Grande Daggers and the Rio Gallegos Skyhawks, providing six and eight aircraft respectively. Supporting roles were to be played by a KC-130 tanker from Comodoro Rivadavia, a *Fenix* Squadron Learjet 35 to lead the Dagger formation to the Falklands and a pair of VIII Air Brigade Mirages which would fly a high-level top-cover/ diversionary sweep to draw off the Sea Harriers from the fourteen strike aircraft.

Leading the V Air Brigade Skyhawks was *Capitan* Pablo Carballo, who had already damaged three ships in previous strikes. The rest of 'Dogo' division was made of *Primer Teniente* Cachon, *Teniente* Rinke and *Alferez* Carmona. The other Skyhawk division – 'Mastin' – was led by *Primer Teniente* Filippini, who had taken part in the successful attack on the *Argonaut*, as had his No 3, *Teniente* Autiero; the two wingmen were *Teniente* Galvez and *Alferez* Gomez. The VI Air Brigade Daggers also had a successful leader in *Major* Carlos Martinez, who had hit the *Antrim*, but the remainder of 'Perro' and 'Gato' divisions – *Capitaus* Rohde and Cimatti, *Primer Tenientes* Ratti and Antonietti and *Teniente* Gabari – had so far been less fortunate. The Skyhawks took off at 10.50am for their rendezvous with the tanker, followed an hour and ten minutes later by the faster Daggers, which had less distance to cover to their target. Antonietti's windscreen cracked soon after take-off and he turned back, leaving five Daggers.

The first Skyhawk to drop out was Filippini's with fluctuating oil pressure, but at the rendezvous two more had to turn back, Carballo and Autiero experienced frozen refuelling probes which prevented their taking on the necessary additional fuel. The remaining section leader, *Primer Teniente* Cachon, who does not as yet appear to have taken part in an actual attack, was thus left with four relatively inexperienced wingmen, all of whom had delivered attacks, and the words of Carballo ringing in his ears – 'Take charge of the formation and lead it to glory!'*

The five A-4Bs began their descent about sixty miles to the west of West Falkland and were detected by the *Exeter* as they did so, before they disappeared below the coverage of her radar. The *Plymouth* was warned, but with twenty minutes in hand before an attack might be expected, Captain Pentreath held on, to begin the bombardment of Mount Rosalie. At 12.58pm, as he was about to open fire, a look-out sighted five aircraft approaching from about two miles away.

The Daggers had overtaken the Skyhawks and were not detected as they approached at sea level from the south-west. From his own account† it is clear that *Major* Martinez, like Columbus, although not necessarily

* Romero Briasco & Mafe Huertas, op. cit. This relies, in turn, on the account in *Aeroespacio*, January/February, 1983.

† Ethell & Price, op. cit.; copy of interview given by Martinez (origin unknown) and held in HMS *Plymouth*.

lost, was not entirely sure where he was or, when he returned, had been. He was certainly never near his briefed target in the Fitzroy area. It must have been with some relief that the Dagger formation caught sight of the isolated *Plymouth* off Chancho Point. They approached at high speed and very low level, firing their cannon before they released their bombs and pulled up to avoid the frigate. The *Plymouth* returned the fire with the Seacat, the port Oerlikon and machine guns. There was no doubt in the minds of any of those on board, and several witnesses ashore firmly believed, that one Dagger was brought down short of the ship by a Seacat missile. Four bombs struck the ship and there was a scattering of 30mm shells and, as the Daggers flew over the ship and away, the starboard Oerlikon opened fire, claiming hits on the exposed belly of an aircraft which was again witnessed from the ship and ashore to crash into the sea.

Four gun-camera views of the attack on the *Plymouth* as she turns hard to port off Chancho Point. The large splash off the frigate's starboard bow in the first shot becomes a cloud of spray and is subsiding by the third and not evident in the last: this isolated (and relatively distant) splash gave

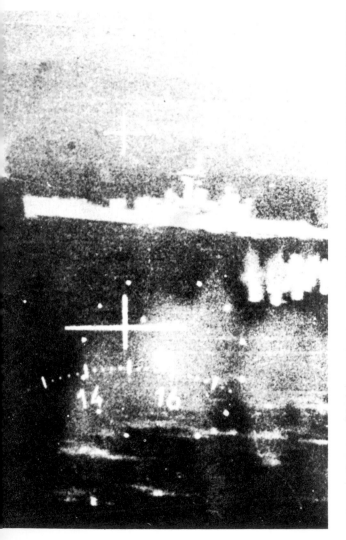

Not one of the bombs exploded. One went through the funnel, leaving a smallish hole on the port side and tearing away plating on the starboard side as it emerged. Two hit in the vicinity of the anti-submarine mortar, forcing the three barrels completely out of alignment and damaging the mortar hoist and handling gear before leaving the ship by the starboard side. The fourth bomb landed on a helicopter depth-charge stowed on the starboard side of the flight deck. The bomb went into the water but the depth-charge exploded. A thin-cased weapon, intended for under-water shock effect, it did not throw off heavy fragments and vented most of its force outwards. It did, however, blow in a three-foot-square hole immediately below the point of impact and this started a fire in the Petty Officers' Mess and the Dining Halls. Two men were seriously injured and three others slightly, but the only 'fatality' was the Chief Yeoman's bicycle. He had bought this at Gibraltar for his wife (!) and stowed it

rise to the confident British claim that one aircraft had been shot down. The last frame also clearly shows the hole in the funnel caused by one of the Leader's bombs and was probably taken by the aircraft which hit the depth-charge on the *Plymouth's* flight deck *(FAA via J. C. D'Odorico)*

behind the plating of the foremast, where it was written off by a 30mm cannon shell. The 4.5in turret had also been hit by gunfire and was temporarily out of action until holed hydraulic and electrical lines could be repaired.

The *Plymouth*'s machinery and watertight integrity were intact and the only assistance she required as she returned to the shelter of San Carlos Water to fight her fire at anchor was a supply of additional breathing apparatus and oxygen bottles, which were delivered by a helicopter in exchange for the wounded, who were whisked off to Ajax Bay. By 1.10pm the fire was under control and it was extinguished by 1.40pm.

The 801 Squadron CAP over Fitzroy was sent in pursuit of the Daggers by the *Exeter*, but the enemy aircraft were warned by *VYCA 2* that the SHARs were on their way down and, with a head start, out-ran the slower interceptors with ease. The Argentine Air Force claims that all five aircraft returned to base, the only damage being a gashed drop-tank. Of all the discrepancies between British claims and Argentine admissions, this is the most difficult to reconcile. Overclaiming by the defences usually originates from several units claiming one victim, but in the *Plymouth*'s case she was the only unit and her claims were corroborated by 'outsiders' who were not shooting.

The *Plymouth* was the first ship to be attacked on 8 June, caught in open water under Fanning Head by five Daggers. On fire aft and pouring smoke from her damaged funnel, the frigate turns to run for the shelter of San Carlos Water *(MoD)*

The damage to *Plymouth*'s funnel was impressive, but superficial [inset left]; far more serious was the fire started by the explosion of a depth-charge on the starboard edge of the flight deck [inset right]; while a bomb which passed through the mortar handling room could have had catastrophic effects had it exploded. Note the spare Seacat missiles forward of the launcher, on the roof of the hangar (MoD)

As the Daggers were running out to the west, convinced that, as they had hit their target, it followed that she had been sunk, the five Skyhawks were approaching the southern point of West Falkland, passing through showers from time to time. At very low level, and undetected since shortly after beginning their let-down, they skirted Lafonia and the southern coast of East Falkland, looking into the many openings. When they looked into Port Pleasant, where they had been briefed to expect British ships, they could see nothing, the LSLs being hidden around a bend in the inlet. *Teniente* Cachon took his formation a little further, to examine Port Fitzroy, the next opening, on which lay Bluff Cove, but seeing nothing there either he decided to turn to starboard, away from the land, and return to base. The two aircraft on his starboard side moved across (to the upper side of the turn, as is usual in low-level formation manoeuvres), climbing slightly as they did so. The extra height was sufficient to give one pilot a glimpse of the upper masts of the two LSLs off Fitzroy Cove. He informed the leader, who climbed to look for himself and then led the five aircraft round to run up Port Pleasant from seaward, still at wave-top height, instructing the two remaining 'Mastin' aircraft to attack the further ship while he and 'Dogo' took the closer one – the *Sir Galahad*.

The two LSLs had too little warning of the attack even to open fire with their Bofors and they barely had time to warn the crews and passengers to take cover. At 1.15pm Cachon and Rinke hit the *Sir Galahad* with two, possibly three, 500lb bombs, not all of which exploded. Carmona's bombs hung up but he scored hits with his 20mm cannon. Galvez and Gomez, following closely behind, attacked the *Sir Tristram*, 600 yards to the west, and scored two direct hits on her after section as well as one near-miss under her stern. The two bombs which hit failed to explode, but the near-miss certainly went off, tearing off the LSL's stern ramp.

Both ships caught fire immediately, the *Sir Galahad* so seriously that her Master, Captain P. J. G. Roberts RFA, ordered her immediate abandonment. It was also apparent that the casualties were heavy, particularly among the Guardsmen, caught by the first explosion or the resulting fires and the secondary explosions caused by their own ammunition and ordnance. Fortunately four Sea Kings and at least one Wessex were on hand, as were the LCU and the Mexeflote, while the *Sir Tristram* could spare sufficient hands from her own firefighting efforts to send two of her lifeboats. With the *Sir Galahad*'s own lifeboats and emergency liferafts, these were able to complete the evacuation of all the able-bodied survivors and walking wounded within thirty-five minutes. Of the ship's company, only the officers remained on board with Royal Army Medical Corps personnel attending to the seriously burned and wounded men, who were being winched off the forecastle by the helicopters. Eventually, at 2.15pm, an hour after the attack, Captain Roberts was lifted off, the last to leave the LSL, which was burning furiously, with continual explosions.

The *Sir Tristram*'s crew fought her fires as best they could but eventually had to concede defeat and abandon her. The accommodation spaces abaft the bridge were burned out and much of her electrical wiring was destroyed, but her machinery remained intact and the fires did not reach what was left on board of her cargo of ammunition.

The final casualty toll from the raid came to fifty men killed or missing and fifty-seven wounded, most of the latter being badly burned. The Welsh Guards took the brunt of the casualties, with other units losing only four killed and eighteen wounded of the Army total of forty-three killed and forty-six wounded. Two of *Sir Tristram*'s ship's company were killed, while the *Sir Galahad* lost five dead and eleven men injured. One of those who died aboard the latter was Second Engineer Officer Paul A. Henry RFA, who was awarded the George Medal posthumously for giving the only available breathing apparatus in the smoke-filled Engine Room to a Junior Engineer Officer to enable him to escape. Third Officer Andrew Gudgeon RFA was awarded a Queen's Gallantry Medal for twice entering the accommodation area to search among the smoke for trapped survivors.

That the casualties were not more numerous was undoubtedly due in large measure to the helicopter crews, first by their swift reaction and afterwards by their skill and persistence, whether in hovering over the burning ships amid the debris of intermittent explosions or amid the thick smoke astern of the *Sir Galahad*, lifting survivors from the water or

8 June: An 825 Squadron Sea King 2 evacuates burned and wounded personnel from the *Sir Galahad*; four of the squadron's aircraft were engaged in this duty and many of those whom they rescued owed their subsequent survival to the helicopters, which flew them back to the Ajax Bay hospital *(MoD)*

using their rotor downdraught to blow liferafts away from the burning ship. After the LSLs had been evacuated, the task began of lifting the injured to Ajax Bay and the LPDs for further attention. The Commanding Officer of 825 Squadron and two of his pilots were decorated for their part in the afternoon's work, Lieutenant Commander H. S. Clark's Distinguished Service Cross citation specifically drawing attention to his conduct, while the Queen's Gallantry Medals awarded to Lieutenants J. K. Boughton and P. J. Sheldon were in recognition of their 'professionalism and bravery' on this occasion.

The Argentine Air Force had not yet finished its day's work. The third element in this first wave, the pair of Mirage IIIs, went unnoticed in the wake of the attacks on the Falkland Sound and Port Pleasant, as did an attack claimed by the Argentine Navy by a pair of its A-4Q Skyhawks on Broken Island,* but the next wave was obvious enough. The first for-

---

* As this island lies between Pebble Island and West Falkland it seems an unlikely target for a strike, unless the Argentine garrison believed that a British Special Forces patrol had been located.

mation to appear, at about 3.35pm, was a divison of four A-4Cs of IV Air Brigade. No long-range warning of their approach was given but when they attacked troop positions in the Bluff Cove area they were given a warm reception by the Scots Guards and 2 Para, running the gauntlet of machine-gun and rifle fire, as well as Blowpipe and Rapier missiles. No damage was caused by the aircraft and the troops claimed to have destroyed one of the Skyhawks; the Argentine Air Force admits that two were seriously damaged but claims that all four returned to base.

Next to arrive were four A-4Bs of V Air Brigade. These were detected at about 3.40pm, as one of two formations. The only available CAP was vectored after the other, which proved to be a Mirage III section at high altitude, and the Skyhawks slipped through while their 'top cover' declined combat and withdrew. The strike aircraft, like their predecessors, followed the coast of Lafonia at low level and found a target in the entrance to Choiseul Sound. Unknown to the Argentine pilots, a SHAR CAP had just arrived above the same position and was actually looking down at the same ship. From 10,000 feet the camouflaged Skyhawks were almost invisible in the gathering dusk.

The vessel in Choiseul Sound was the much-travelled LCU *F4*. During the previous night it had been sent from Bluff Cove to Darwin to collect the Headquarters vehicles of 5 Infantry Brigade and was now returning fully laden, with sixteen men of her crew and the drivers of the vehicles. Her only armament was a single machine gun. In the attack at least one bomb hit was scored but although it killed three Marines and two naval ratings of her crew, including the gallant Colour Sergeant Brian Johnston,* it is unlikely that it exploded, for the 75-ton landing craft remained afloat for some hours.

The splashes in the water alerted the Sea Harrier pilots, who then saw one or two of the Skyhawks. The two pilots, Flight Lieutenant D. H. S. Morgan RAF and Lieutenant D. A. Smith of 800 Squadron, were on a training sortie, the main purpose of which was dusk deck-landing practice, but they had been sent inshore to 'thicken up' the CAP, pending the arrival of an 801 Squadron section. Diving after the Skyhawks, Flight-Lieutenant Morgan swiftly caught up with the No 4, whom he suspected as being an escort as he had watched it overfly the LCU without releasing bombs, and despatched it with a Sidewinder. His second victim had seen the first explosion and attempted to out-manoeuvre the next Sidewinder unavailingly. Lieutenant Smith could see two aircraft ahead of him, one of which was his Leader, and was unwilling to fire until he had some positive identification. This was provided by Morgan hopefully firing his cannon at the Argentine aircraft from long range. Smith saw the splashes around the enemy and fired his first Sidewinder, which again worked

---

* Subsequently awarded a posthumous Queen's Gallantry Medal for his part in the rescue of the *Antelope*'s ship's company on 23 May.

perfectly. By this time he had lost sight of the leading Skyhawk, which escaped into the gloom.

Most of the combat had been witnessed from above by Lieutenant-Commander Ward of 801, who confirmed that a *fourth* Argentine aircraft had been shot down. From his account, however, it would seem that this was Lieutenant Smith's victim, which crashed on the beach at Hammond Point. Flight-Lieutenant Morgan identified the formation as being made up of 'Mirages'. As none of the V Air Brigade pilots shot down – *Primer Teniente* D. R. Bolzan, *Teniente* J. J. Arraras and *Alferez* A. J. A. Vazquez – survived to be taken prisoner, the misapprehension lingered for months. Not that misapprehension was limited to one side. The sole survivor, *Teniente* H. Sanchez, reported that an LSL had been hit and the Argentine Air Force added 'Sir Belvedere' to its list of probables.

The CAP which had been sent after the high-level decoy made a dusk landing at HMS *Sheathbill*, while the victorious Morgan and Smith returned to the *Hermes* for their deck-landing practice session. The 801 CAP which had seen the combat in Choiseul Sound was in turn vectored after what turned out to be a third Mirage III mission, covering a raid by six Daggers, probably from Rio Grande. This raid was detected at about 3.55pm but it turned back before reaching the Falkland Sound, apparently due to shortage of fuel. One Argentine account refers to the loss of a Dagger, the pilot ejecting to safety, and it may be that this aircraft was one of this last formation.

The Argentine Air Force, which many naval personnel outside the staffs of the commanders had begun to believe was a spent force, had rallied to despatch five strikes, four of which had reached a target and three of which had inflicted substantial damage, but none of which had tilted the scales in favour of the Argentine cause or detracted greatly from the forces at General Moore's disposal. The British land commander still had seven major infantry units and two-thirds of the Welsh Guards battalion. His artillery was intact and the ammunition supply was building up satisfactorily, if rather more slowly than he wished.

From the naval point of view the loss of the two LSLs for further operations was serious, but the three which were still immediately available (*Sir Geraint*, *Percivale* and *Lancelot*) could meet the short-term needs of the campaign, particularly as the build-up in the north had proceeded without hindrance. The *Plymouth*, too, was repairable with the aid of the *Stena Seaspread* and would be able to return to gunnery support duties in the near future.

In human terms, and for the Welsh Guards as a regiment, the attack on the LSLs at Port Pleasant *was* a disaster. But it was exaggerated beyond its true scale by the media, in particular the television coverage, which left a visual impression which, for many, is the abiding image of the Falklands campaign. For the most part the Press representatives were unfamiliar with the realities of war, but at last they had witnessed an incident at first hand (they had not been on the scene when the *Sheffield*, *Ardent*, *Coventry* and *Atlantic Conveyor* had been hit) and even if they were not quite clear where it had happened it had all the horror, heroism and hint of dreadful blunder of which banner headlines are made. Coming so close to the end of the fighting, it was to overshadow the clinical professional achievement of the Marines and the Paras in their battles for the hills above Stanley.

Unnoticed by the Press, LCU *F4* was also lost. Damaged and drifting after the Skyhawk attack, she was found by Sea Kings which winched off the eleven survivors. The *Monsunnen*, manned by Naval Party 2160, was then directed to the landing craft, which was taken in tow. Unfortunately *F4* was taking water which could not be pumped out and the coaster had to cast her off at 11.00pm, shortly before she sank.

9 JUNE

There were no movements out of San Carlos Water during the night of 8/9 June apart from the *Exeter*'s anti-aircraft patrol in the Falkland Sound. The *Minerva* brought in the *Engadine* and the three minesweeping trawlers after a day spent in a rather exposed position to the north-east of Port Stanley. Another arrival was the *Andromeda*, which came straight from the air drop to land her stores and passengers and leave in time to be back with the Battle Group by dawn. This was to be her only visit to San Carlos before the end of the fighting.

The *Yarmouth* shelled the Moody Brook area before midnight, firing 124 rounds, some in a duel with the 155mm battery, which managed to land some shells quite close to the frigate. At 12.45am, as she was withdrawing, the *Yarmouth* was called to the aid of the *Monsunnen*, on her way to Port Pleasant with stores from Darwin. The coaster had a rope wrapped around her screw and required the assistance of divers to remove the snag. By 2.30am the two ships were once again on their way, the *Monsunnen* to Fitzroy Cove and the *Yarmouth* to the Battle Group, which she did not reach until two hours after first light.

Apart from two Air Raid Warnings Red, in the forenoon and evening, unloading at San Carlos went on undisturbed. Now that the *Engadine* had at last arrived with her four helicopters and, more important, air and ground crews, the full potential of COMAW's helicopter transport force began to be realized. For day operations there were sixteen Sea King 2s and 4s of 825 and 846 Squadrons, twenty-three Wessex 5s of 845 (five), 847 (sixteen) and 848 (two) Squadrons, as well as the solitary hardworking Chinook of No 18 Squadron RAF. The four PNG Sea Kings of 846 Squadron made up the night lift force, although most of the other

A 3 Commando Brigade Air Squadron Scout refuels at the Teal Inlet FOB; the 'box' projecting above the left-hand seat is the stabilised sight for aiming SS.11 missiles (MoD)

experienced pilots could and did operate from the ships and from the main shore operating bases by night. Supplementing the naval squadrons, each Brigade had six Scouts and six Gazelles under direct control and these, too, were used for light transport tasks. A Forward Operating Base had been established at Teal Inlet on the 8th and four of 847 Squadron's Wessex were allocated, together with 845 and 848 Squadrons. Goose Green supported the Fitzroy area for the time being, with the remainder of 847 and 825 Squadron's Sea Kings assisting in the 5 Brigade build-up. The main loads continued to be 105mm artillery ammunition and mortar shells, delivered direct from the maintenance areas to the batteries, but provisions were also taken to the troops in the front lines and, sadly, there was always a small but steady stream of casualties, wounded and sick, to be brought back to the Field Hospital at Fitzroy, the Dressing Station at Teal or all the way back to Ajax Bay.

The unwounded survivors of the two Welsh Guards companies were flown back to San Carlos from Fitzroy and accommodated in the *Intrepid* until they could be kitted out and rearmed again from the resources at Ajax Bay. The casualties from the *Sir Galahad* had been given first aid aboard the two LPDs, the *Atlantic Causeway* and, of course, by the 'Red and Green Life Machine', but the many serious burns cases needed the specialist attention of the *Uganda*'s burns unit and the hospital ship was again ordered into Grantham Sound to collect the wounded from San Carlos. This provoked a protest from the Junta, who alleged that the *Uganda* was bringing in military stores. That this was not the case would be witnessed by the Red Cross team from Geneva who would soon arrive from Montevideo in the *Norland*. Included was the hospital ship adviser, M. Philip Eberlin, formerly an officer in the French Navy.

The STOVL strip at Port San Carlos was used from dawn, with 801 Squadron landing for the first time. The *Hermes* was back out at 250 miles again and sending in the GR3s to be tasked at San Carlos. Four pairs arrived during the day and departed to rocket the Argentine artillery batteries which, despite the Royal Artillery's counter-battery fire, were inflicting casualties and hindering movement along the British line. The CAP was vectored out by the *Exeter* twice during the day, to investigate contacts to the south-west and north-west, but the enemy retreated and was not seen on either occasion.

The Battle Group replenished during the morning. The *Ambuscade*'s engines were in need of attention and she was detached to the 'Trala' to seek assistance from the *Stena Seaspread*. She was followed out by the *Andromeda*, which was to collect stores dropped to the *Glamorgan* by yet another long-range Hercules mission. Another detachment was the *Brilliant*, to escort the *Europic Ferry* north for a rendezvous with the third Aircraft Transport, the *Contender Bezant*; this ship had left Devonport on 20 May in company with the Sealink ferry *St Edmund* and had four more Chinooks and two Wasps as her original load. Four Harriers and three more helicopters joined at Ascension.

There was, inevitably, traffic in the other direction. The *Yarmouth* spent only six hours with the Battle Group, refuelling and ammunitioning, before setting off once again on her 25-knot, 180-mile dash to the gunline off Port Pleasant, where she arrived before midnight. The *Active* took the *Fort Grange* out of the formation and met the *Nordic Ferry* for a run into San Carlos Water. The RFA, which had been dispensing 'nutty' to sweet-starved ships, exchanged one of her three Sea King 2s of 824 Squadron for the *Tidespring*'s two Wessex 5s, which were to be transferred ashore to increase the transport force.

The *Intrepid* and *Avenger* left San Carlos in the early evening for a supply run to support 5 Infantry Brigade, but most of the traffic leaving the TA went northabout. At 6.00pm the *Plymouth* escorted the *Atlantic Causeway* and *Olna* out of the Falkland Sound, followed by the *Sir Geraint*, *Cordella* and *Pict*. The frigate was to take the two big ships all the way back to the 'Trala', where she too would be patched up by the *Stena Seaspread*. The trawlers accompanied the LSL to Port Salvador, where they would lie up in preparation for their first minesweeping task. The *Exeter* took up her customary anti-aircraft patrol in Grantham Sound, from which the *Uganda* had sailed before sunset.

10 JUNE

The *Yarmouth*'s bombardment was particularly effective. Two Sisters, Mounts Harriet and William, Sapper Hill and Moody Brook were all pounded, causing explosions in ammunition dumps and setting vehicles on fire at the last-named, which was 18,000 yards from the frigate. She ceased fire at 1.00am and ran out to the south, to remain clear of the suspected Exocets' coverage. After a few minutes a radar contact was picked up but, instead of illuminating it with starshell, Commander Morton sent out his Wasp to investigate. The unknown turned out to be the *Monsunnen*, making another of her nightly runs from Darwin.

The *Invincible*, screened by the *Andromeda* (back from her brief visit to the 'Trala' to collect stores from the *Glamorgan*), made a two-hour trip to the west to fly off two Sea King 5s of 820 Squadron to the San Carlos Settlement helicopter base. With three full crews and a maintenance party, they would fly night searches and patrols off West Falkland until the very end of hostilities.

Another bright but cold day was used to progress the stores and ammunition build-up. A helicopter forward operating base was established at Fitzroy and four Wessex of 847 moved in. Each of the two advanced bases now had a 9,000-Imperial gallon fuel depot and the Chinook was tasked almost exclusively to keep these topped up, bringing four of the air-portable rubber tanks on each trip. 846 Squadron had brought a dozen with them and these had been supplemented by as many more which had been found after the capture of Goose Green. Other liberated material included a number of 20mm AA guns and machine guns which were supplied to the ships to supplement their AA defences. The *Fearless* mounted one of the Rheinmetall guns on her quarterdeck and others were fitted on the LSLs allocated to the Teal Inlet run.

The *Sir Geraint* off-loaded at Teal and three LCUs were launched by the *Intrepid* off Lively Island during the night. With a cargo capacity of 100 tons each, the LCUs were able to deliver almost the equivalent of an LSL assault load direct to the beach where it was required. The disadvantage for the force was that these craft, and those loading for the next night's insertion, were not available for the unloading of stores ships in San Carlos Water, or for the back-loading of LSLs for Teal. The *Fort Grange*'s provisions RAS of the ships at San Carlos was therefore relatively slow, even with the two loaned 845 Wessex 5's help. That some ships were in urgent need of her supplies is clear from the *Sir Percivale*'s state, with only two days' balanced rations remaining on the 10th.

Fuel was also needed, for the ships and also to top up the Port San Carlos main aviation fuel dump. The *Blue Rover* had been pumping over in the 'Trala', where the requisitioned tankers *Eburna*, *Anco Charger* and *British Wye* were topping up the RFAs, and she joined the Battle Group during the day, escorted by the *Ambuscade*, whose defects had been sorted out by the *Stena Seaspread*'s versatile staff.

The Argentine Air Force was in action early. In an attempt to reduce the volume of British artillery fire, which was sapping morale as well as strength, the Argentine Army and Air Force co-operated in a dawn strike. The 155mm battery fired smoke shells to indicate the positions of the guns around Mount Kent and four Pucaras attacked out of the rising sun, achieving surprise, but although the Argentinians claimed complete success the rockets inflicted no damage and the guns continued to fire.

No 1 Squadron RAF's GR3s flew five missions during the day. Four aircraft from HMS *Sheathbill* dropped cluster bombs on the enemy artillery to the west of Port Stanley and in the afternoon two Harriers from the *Hermes* followed up an earlier low-level tactical reconnaissance with a strike on the forward Argentine positions on Mount Longdon. A laser-guided 'Paveway' bombing mission had to be aborted for tactical reasons.

Forty-four CAP sorties were flown by the two carriers' SHARs during the day, many of 800 Squadron's being doubled by the use of the Port San Carlos strip. The mainland Air Force did not show up until early afternoon, the first indication, at 1.15pm, being a Mirage III radar transmission. Thus alerted, the *Exeter* promptly picked up a formation eighty miles to the west and scrambled the pair of Sea Harriers at the strip, vectoring out the CAP already airborne on station over the Falkland Sound. The fighters saw the Argentine aircraft as the latter closed to within thirty miles of the TA but once again *VYCA 2* was 'on the ball' and the Mirages turned away, ten miles to the west of the frustrated SHAR pilots.

Within five minutes the *Exeter* had detected another inbound formation, followed by a third, trailing thirty miles behind. The nearer was at forty miles by 1.45pm, when the CAP was committed. The destroyer was saving the raid at seventy miles for her Sea Dart but had two more CAP sections in hand, to defend the ditch before the last. Once again the radar station at Port Stanley spoiled a promising set-up. As the 800 Squadron CAP bored in, the leading formation turned tail and the second faded from the *Exeter*'s radar, possibly as it descended to sea level. All areas were warned to stand by for a low-level attack and the carriers launched more fighters, so that by 2.10pm there were ten SHARs, in five CAP sections, on call over Teal, Fitzroy and the Falkland Sound. No attack materialized and it was surmised that the Argentine activity was a diversion for a supply-dropping mission in West Falkland. Whether this was the case, or a genuine attack had been foiled, the ability of the Carrier Battle Group to put up sixteen aircraft over the Falklands during an hour cannot have escaped the attention of the Argentine Air Force radar watchers.

The day ended with no further Argentine air activity and the various Groups prepared for another full night's work. The *Ambuscade* and *Blue Rover* had begun their inbound passage in the early afternoon but, as usual, the ships in San Carlos Water did not begin to leave until dusk. The *Fort Grange, Baltic Ferry, Olna* and *Atlantic Causeway* left the TA outbound for the Battle Group and the *Intrepid* sailed for another Fitzroy LCU insertion, covered by the *Avenger*, who was to spend the night lurking off Fox Bay to catch the *Bahia Buen Suceso*, which had been lying there, with no obvious sign of damage, since the Sea Harrier strike on 16 May.

The *Yarmouth*, after three consecutive nights' bombardments, was rested and the *Active* and *Arrow* went inshore to the southern gunline. Although all the targets indicated by the spotters ashore could be reached, the frigates' movements were circumscribed by the Exocet threat and to open an alternative station which would be safe from the missiles the minesweepers HMS *Cordella* and *Pict* sailed from Port Salvador to carry out a clearance sweep of Berkeley Sound, to the north of Port Stanley.

The third trawler, the *Junella*, remained at San Carlos as a maid-of-all-work, including among her tasks the landing and retrieval of Special Forces teams. Although relatively small, the trawlers were of deeper draught than was generally believed and needed almost as much water as a frigate, so that they were not as suitable for close inshore work as had been expected.

The *Exeter*, on AA patrol, was diverted to the Port Howard area to support the rescue of a compromised SAS team. Captain G. J. Hamilton, who had taken part in all of the major Special Forces 'occasions' – the Fortuna Glacier débâcle, the capture of Grytviken, the Pebble Island raid and the Darwin diversion, as well as the seizing of Mount Kent – was killed while covering his signaller's escape during the forenoon of 10 June,* but the three survivors got away to be picked up after dark, under the cover of the *Exeter*'s shelling.

In the front line ashore, above Bluff Cove, Alfa and Charlie Companies of 40 Commando settled in for the night as part of the Welsh Guards. The Marines had been flown forward during the day to reinforce the battalion until its own depleted companies had been refitted.

11 JUNE

All the convoy and insertion movements went much as planned and with no sign of Argentine interest. The *Avenger* waited in vain for the naval transport to emerge from Fox Bay. Her two sister-ships, *Active* and *Arrow*, enjoyed a satisfactory shoot, firing 189 rounds on direct fire and harassment. The *Active* engaged enemy defences facing 42 Commando and had the satisfaction of causing a major ammunition explosion on Mount Harriet, while the *Arrow* fired on the one hard metalled road from the outskirts of Port Stanley to Moody Brook.

HMS *Cordella* and *Pict* entered Berkeley Sound unobserved and proceeded with their sweep of a lane five miles long and half a mile wide. The *Pict*'s acoustic sweep gear, with an inappropriate choice of timing, went 'on the blink' but Lieutenant-Commander D. G. Garwood, realizing that it was essential that the intended gunline was fully swept, turned on all the trawler's auxiliary machinery and, with his ship's company on the upper deck, made a noisy trip down the lane. This, like the magnetic sweep and the 'old-fashioned' wire sweep, turned up no mines, but the *Pict*'s sacrificial run earned her commanding officer a well-merited

---

* *London Gazette Supplement*, 8 October, 1982.

Mention in Despatches. The trawlers were back in Port Salvador well before daybreak.

Any intention that the Argentine Air Force may have had of repeating their dawn Pucara strike against the British Artillery was dispelled by 800 Squadron's Sea Harriers. Four of them, led by Lieutenant-Commander Auld, ran in from the east at 7.00am to loft air-burst thousand-pounders at the dispersal areas. There was no question of surprise, for every gun around the airfield opened fire when the strike was still eight miles out over the sea. Deeply impressed by the welcome, the SHAR pilots pulled up to toss their bombs, eleven of which fell in the intended area, starting fires, and then broke away to return, undamaged, to the *Hermes*. This strike was the last to be delivered against Port Stanley airfield, which had been attacked by 123 Sea Harriers and RAF Harriers, releasing eighty-six tons of bombs. Considerable damage had been inflicted on buildings, store dumps and parked aircraft, as well as many personnel casualties, but not one of the fighter-bombers had been shot down, although seven had been hit by gunfire. By a coincidence, *Comodoro* Hector Destri, commanding *La Base Aerea Militar Malvinas*, claimed that his defences had destroyed five and damaged two jets. The total was correct, but the claims were over-optimistic.

Port Stanley itself came under direct attack as 800 Squadron pulled away from the airfield. The police station had been identified as being used by the Argentine military staff as a headquarters and, at the request of General Moore's staff, Commodore Clapp provided the only weapons combination which could deliver an accurate attack on a target within the closely-guarded built-up area. Lieutenant P. C. Manley RN, with Petty Officer Aircrewman J. A. Balls BEM as his aimer, took off from the Teal Inlet Forward Air Base at 7.15am, flying an 848 Squadron Wessex 5 armed with AS.12 missiles. In support was a Wessex 'gun-ship' of 845 Squadron, ready to come to the assistance of the strike helicopter if necessary. Peter Manley, an experienced Helicopter Weapons Instructor and himself a trained missile aimer, brought the Wessex in from the north, pulling up two miles from the Stanley waterfront to fire the first missile over the top of the Navy Point ridge. The AS.12 malfunctioned and, straying from the intended course, crashed into the water 200 yards from the hospital ship *Bahia Paraiso*. The Argentine AA gunners awoke but few had any idea where the Wessex was and thus their fire was ineffective. It became more accurate when PO Balls fired the second AS.12. This flew truly and he steered it right into the upper storey of the police station, where the Argentine military command's Intelligence Section officers were still abed and suffered very heavy casualties.

Lieutenant Manley, by now under accurate fire, broke away and escaped at low level up the Murrell River, unseen by the covering Wessex, which, concerned by the volume of AA fire, closed towards Port Stanley and was horrified to see a helicopter hit and spiral down on fire, to crash near the town. This incident was witnessed by other watching British eyes, to whom it was obvious that the Argentinians had scored an 'own goal' against one of their own Bell 212 or UH-1H helicopters. This was not apparent to the naval pilot, who attempted to close to see if he could effect a rescue but was driven back by the AA. He returned sadly to Teal to find Manley and Balls enjoying a cup of coffee.

The Argentine authorities in Buenos Aires made a formal (and understandable) complaint about the near-miss AS.12 going too close to the *Bahia Paraiso*, but it was garbled in its transmission since the message left Port Stanley, so that the Red Cross passed it on to the British as a complaint about a Harrier rocket attack. The GR3s had not used 2in rockets since 9 June and did not use them thereafter and the allegation caused some mystification to the authorities in London for some time, until details of the Wessex attack became known.

At first light 801 Squadron's first CAP went out to look for signs of supply dropping in West Falkland but found nothing. The weather was again clear under continuous cloud cover, conditions which had previously been favoured by the Super Etendards for Exocet attack. Although those in the Battle Group were almost certain that the Argentine Navy had expended all of its original air-launched Exocets, no chances were taken and some ships remained at Action Stations throughout the day. In the event, no Argentine air activity whatsoever was detected. The SHARs passed the milestone of 1,200 take-offs from the carriers (since entering the TEZ) during the afternoon, but the CAPs flown from the ships and *Sheathbill* were all uneventful.

The GR3s, on the other hand, had a busy day. Four two-plane missions took off from the airstrip, three to drop cluster bombs on the Argentine positions on Two Sisters, Mount Harriet and Mount Longdon – the objectives for the land assault due that night – and the other to bomb the Moody Brook barracks and Mount Tumbledown. Both of the last pair had fortunate escapes: Flight-Lieutenant M. Hare RAF was chased off Tumbledown by a pair of Blowpipes and Wing-Commander P. Squire's cockpit was traversed by a single small-calibre bullet. Two more GR3s armed with cluster bomb units took off from the *Hermes* but in the light wind left the end of the ski-jump ramp with insufficient speed for safety and had to jettison their ordnance. They continued with their mission, strafed targets of opportunity to the west of Stanley and returned direct to the carrier.

For the first time since the landings, there were no Air Raid Warnings Red in the San Carlos area. The *Sir Percivale* loaded with material for Teal Inlet, the *Blue Rover* replenished ships and topped up the shore fuel dumps and at Teal the *Sir Geraint* completed her off-load, then remained to act as an additional helicopter fuelling pad. With the good flying weather, the helicopters were able to improve on previous days' efforts and between dawn and dusk 825 and 847 Squadrons flew 150 hours,

The Royal Navy's Wessex 5, here seen unloading mortar ammunition in dead ground behind the front-line, proved to be as reliable a work-horse in its last campaign as it had been in Borneo and Aden. Although available in appreciable numbers only during the last fortnight of fighting, it flew more sorties than any other type of helicopter, other than the carriers' Sea King 5 *(MoD)*

some crews spending up to eight hours in their aircraft and actually shutting down their engines only two or three times during the day. Not a single load was lost in feeding the insatiable appetites of the 105mm guns, thirty of which were now maintaining a steady fire on the unfortunate Argentine troops. One 847 Squadron Wessex was damaged when, taking supplies forward to the Scots Guards near Bluff Cove, it came under accurate mortar fire and sustained several splinter hits.

The Pucaras, which could have severely disrupted the vital helicopter shuttle services, remained on the ground until dusk, when again a co-ordinated artillery/air strike was attempted against the 3 Commando Brigade batteries in the Mount Kent sector, with no more success than on the morning of the previous day, neither damage nor casualties being inflicted. This was the last known Pucara mission. The aircraft had achieved much less than had been expected by either side, its one real success being the destruction of the Royal Marine Scout on 28 May. By the time that the Argentine Air Force got around to using the aircraft imaginatively it was too late to have any pronounced effect on the ground fighting. The twenty-odd Pucaras found wrecked on their airfields, at Pebble Island, Goose Green and Port Stanley, were symbols of missed opportunity.

The day was largely dedicated to preparing for the Commando Brigade's assault on the first line of the Argentine defences, in which 42 and 45 Commandos and 3 Para would attack Mount Harriet, Two Sisters and Mount Longdon respectively. During the preceding days all three units had scouted the enemy positions facing them and had taped routes through defensive minefields, routes which had all been found at the cost of casualties, through clashes with Argentine patrols or locating mines by accident. A six-gun Royal Artillery battery would be available to support each assault, as would a frigate or destroyer. The other two batteries and a fourth ship would be on call for counter-battery or harassing fire on rear areas or to bring additional firepower down on areas of stiff opposition. Eight Wessex, four each at Teal and Fitzroy, were allocated to be ready for casualty evacuation at first light. 847 Squadron received some last-minute practice in this role during the afternoon of the 11th. A 40 Commando patrol came across half-a-dozen sick and frost-bitten Argentine soldiers to the north of Port San Carlos, the remnants of the Fanning Head garrison, and these poor men were flown to Ajax Bay for much-needed medical attention.

The *Uganda* was now entering Grantham Sound daily to embark casualties, anchoring after dawn and departing before sunset. The *Hecla* also came in on this day, to collect another group of convalescents for passage to Montevideo. As before, the ships bearing the red cross remained outside San Carlos Water, so that there could be no doubt that their mission was other than exclusively humanitarian. The *Bahia Paraiso* had returned from Santa Cruz and, after 'making her number' in the Red Cross Box, she continued to Port Stanley with an International Red Cross representative embarked.

The unwounded survivors of the two LSLs damaged at Bluff Cove had been given passage out of the TA by the *Atlantic Causeway* and the men from *Sir Galahad* were transferred to the *British Test*. The *British Trent*, which was pumping over the remainder of her cargo to the *Olna*, later took the *Sir Tristram*'s crew. The *Sheffield*'s survivors, who had gone north to Ascension in the *British Avon* and then flown home, had returned on 27 May. The largest single contingent – the ships' companies of the *Ardent*, *Antelope* and *Coventry* – received a spectacular welcome on the 11th, as the *Queen Elizabeth II* steamed into the Solent, greeted by a gun salute fired by HMS *Lowestoft* and honoured by the presence of HM Queen Elizabeth the Queen Mother in the Royal Yacht *Britannia*.

The *Glamorgan*, which had been managing affairs in the 'Trala' since the beginning of June, was called forward, her place being taken by the *Plymouth*, and joined the Battle Group during the forenoon. There she was briefed for the night's tasks and at 1.00pm she led the *Yarmouth* and *Arrow* away for the night's bombardments. Two hours later the *Andromeda* took the *Elk* and *Sir Bedivere* in charge and set off for the TA.

Movements out of San Carlos Water began at sunset. There was no outbound convoy, but the *Sir Percivale* left for Teal Inlet at 5.30pm, escorted by the *Exeter*, which brought back the *Sir Geraint*. The *Cordella* and *Pict* made their own way home to San Carlos Water. The *Intrepid*, escorted by the *Minerva*, went round to Lively Island for the third night in succession to launch three LCUs for the Fitzroy area. As before, cover as she left the Falkland Sound was provided by the *Avenger*, again hopefully lying in wait off Fox Bay. The *Bahia Buen Suceso* did not sail but an *Invincible* CAP, skirting the northern edge of the Port Stanley AA defences at dusk, reported that the hospital ship *Bahia Paraiso* was underway and heading out of Port William to the north. The *Avenger* waited as long as she could and then set off to the east, to join the southern gunline. By 8.00pm she, the *Glamorgan* and the *Yarmouth* were awaiting the first call for fire. On the Berkeley Sound gunline the *Arrow* had already been on station for about an hour.

Chapter Two

Battles in the Mountains

The Marines and Paras crossed their start lines at 10.00pm on 11 June. 42 Commando, led by Lieutenant-Colonel N. F. Vaux, carried out his plan almost to perfection. Advancing round the southern side of the Mount Harriet ridge, the Marines took the enemy from the flank and in rear, from the east, and were so successful in obtaining surprise that not until they were among the Argentinians on the rocky crest did the latter react. Resistance was fierce but relatively brief before the 200 defenders surrendered, with all their heavy machine-guns and mortars. The Commando, which had lost one Marine killed and a dozen wounded, 'went firm' long before dawn on the 12th, facing the next hilltop on the road to Port Stanley. This, Mount Tumbledown, had been subjected to the main weight of the artillery fire and naval bombardment, HMS *Yarmouth*, the allocated frigate, firing 261 rounds up to 2.30am.

3 Para (Lieutenant-Colonel H. W. R. Pike MBE), on the other flank, was supported by the *Avenger*, whose task was to interdict the Argentine supply and reinforcement route to Mount Longdon and shell the supporting positions on Wireless Ridge. The Paras took the first lines of defence on Mount Longdon to plan but then encountered very strong resistance which was not subdued until after the daybreak. The 105mm guns of 29th Commando Regiment and the *Avenger*'s 4.5in helped to break down the enemy but the latter had to curtail her bombardment unexpectedly at 2.40am, after firing 156 rounds, and the artillery could not reach the Argentine batteries in front of Port Stanley, which gave good support to the defenders. 3 Para sustained the heaviest casualties suffered in any land attack, with eighteen killed and thirty-nine wounded, the dead including Sergeant Ian Mackay, who was awarded a posthumous Victoria Cross for his selfless leadership and courage.

45 Commando, who faced a frontal attack on the ridge and twin peaks of Two Sisters, did not begin to move forward, under Lieutenant-Colonel A. F. Whitehead, until midnight, by which time the battle on the northern flank, for Mount Longdon, had thoroughly awakened 45's immediate opponents. Nevertheless the Marines made a 'silent' approach and it was not until they were within 500 yards of the nearer, southern peak

that they were detected. The defenders opened a heavy and accurate mortar and machine-gun fire and called down an artillery barrage. Caught in the open, one company lost three dead and a number of others wounded, but the momentum of the attack was maintained, the Commando going forward under the cover of its own Carl Gustavs, '66s', Milans and machine-guns, while the artillery and naval bombardment provided a heavy weight of fire. The 105mm Light Guns were at one stage engaging bunkers only fifty yards ahead of the Marines, while the *Glamorgan* and, when she could be spared from her 3 Para commitments, the *Avenger*, fired on more distant targets (200 yards ahead). The naval gunfire support spotting officer was wounded during the early stages of the attack, but his assistant, Bombardier E. M. Holt, took over and continued to give swift and accurate directions to the ships and was subsequently awarded the Military Medal. By 4.40am the craggy peaks of Two Sisters were secure, at a cost to the attackers of only two fatal casualties and eleven wounded. The Argentine defenders fought hard but were defeated by 45 Commando's aggression and skilful use of controlled fire-power. With their escape route open, the surviving Argentinians were able to get away to the east, leaving behind their dead and thirty-two prisoners and most of their heavy weapons.

The *Glamorgan* and *Yarmouth*, which had between them fired 428 HE shells at Two Sisters, Mount Harriet and Tumbledown, began their withdrawal at about 2.15am, leaving the *Avenger* on the gunline to support 3 Para's dour fight for Mount Longdon. Captain Hugo White, with less distance to return to his safe haven at San Carlos, and with the further option of Albemarle Sound if need be, expected to be able to remain for at least another hour. At 2.35am, when she was about seventeen miles south-west of Port Stanley, the *Glamorgan* detected an approaching radar contact. It resembled, in the size of the echo and its speed, one of the howitzer shells which had been tracked on many previous occasions and no radar emissions were detected to suggest that this was other than another shell, fired well out of range. Thus it was that not until it continued beyond gunfire range and was actually sighted by the *Avenger*, ten miles north of the *Glamorgan*, was it recognized as an Exocet, fired from the metalled road behind Port Harriet. The destroyer held her fire until the missile was within a mile and then launched a Seacat. Never intended as an anti-missile weapon, the Seacat was nevertheless guided so close that, in passing, it deflected the Exocet upwards and exploded a short distance behind, as seen from the *Avenger*. The deflection was insufficient to cause the incoming missile to fly over the *Glamorgan* and at 2.37am it struck the port upper deck edge, slid diagonally across the deck into the hangar and exploded.

The hangar area was devastated and with it the Wessex 3, whose burning fuel spilled down through a hole in the deck caused by the explosion of the Exocet warhead. The near-miss Seacat had been the port

launcher's last, for this too was destroyed. The galley area was burning fiercely and a fireball had entered the gas turbine gear room down the engine exhaust trunking. The fire in the machinery space was rapidly subdued by steam drenching, minimizing damage so that the ship's speed never fell below 10 knots, but the galley and hangar fires were not to be brought under control so readily.

The explosion had been seen from many points in the Falklands, by the Marines and Paras still fighting on their hills, as a glow on the horizon from San Carlos Water and, of course, by the *Yarmouth* and *Avenger*, both of which hastened to the *Glamorgan's* assistance. Although he was offered the alternative of proceeding to Fitzroy to anchor under the protection of the Rapier troop and the CAP, Captain Barrow preferred to make his way back to the Battle Group. Forty minutes after the hit the damaged ship was making 18 knots to the east, still ablaze but with the fires contained. She had an 8° list due to the flooding caused by the fire-fighting but she was seaworthy and her radar, gun turret, Exocets, starboard Seacat and Oerlikons were operational. The galley and hangar fires were brought under control at 4.40am (coinciding with 45 Commando's securing of Two Sisters) but another two hours were to elapse before they were completely extinguished. Nine men had died, another four were missing and fourteen others had been injured, one of them very seriously. Most of the casualties had been suffered by the chefs and the helicopter maintenance crew. The *Glamorgan* and her escort rejoined the Battle Group at 11.00am, covered by CAP from long before dawn.

The *Arrow* returned to the Carrier Battle Group before dawn, having enjoyed a busy and profitable night on the Berkeley Sound gunline, firing 238 rounds into the Sapper Hill, racecourse and airfield areas. The main

Good damage control and the dedication of the fire-fighting teams contained the damage caused by the Exocet to the area of *Glamorgan's* hangar and its immediate vicinity. No spare Wessex 3 was available and a Wessex 5 was transferred from RFA *Tidepool* on 14 June *(MoD)*

attack on the airfield was delivered at 4.45am (just after the securing of Two Sisters and *Glamorgan*'s fires had been brought under control) by the fifth and last Ascension-based Vulcan raid. The twenty-one 1,000lb bombs were intended to damage installations and aircraft on the ground, not the runway, but from the subsequent photographs and an Argentine plot of the bombs,* it would appear that half-a-dozen of the bombs failed to explode and that the long stick fell some distance to the north-west of the main dispersal area.

As an exercise in the art of the possible, the 'Black Buck' raids had been an unqualified success, demonstrating the flexibility conferred by a large air-to-air refuelling force and the professionalism and skill of the five bomber and sixty tanker crews involved. The delivery of ordnance as the purpose of the missions caught the imagination of the public and politicians far more than the unsung delivery of air-dropped supplies, which had become a daily event by the beginning of June.

It has been claimed that the demonstration of long-range strike capability, with its implicit threat of attack on the Argentine mainland, reduced the pressure on the Carrier Battle Group by drawing off the Mirage interceptors to defend the mainland cities. If this was the case, then the achievement was counter-productive, for one of Admiral Woodward's main objectives was the reduction of Argentine air strength by air combat attrition, which could not be completely achieved if the enemy removed his top-cover fighters. In fact, it was the loss of three such fighters to Sea Harriers on the first day of combat which led to the FAA's refusal to accept air combat thereafter. Contrary to the claims, Mirages *did* remain in the south and *did* operate over the TEZ after the first Vulcan raids but they never again allowed the carrier interceptors to come within even long Sidewinder range.

The 3 Commando Brigade units were all secure on their objectives by 8.00am, the Marines and Paras settling in under continuous harassing artillery and mortar fire. 3 Para, who had killed forty and captured thirty-nine of the tough regiment which had been forced off Mount Longdon, came in for particular attention and sustained further casualties during the day. The Brigade Air Squadron and naval 'Casevac' helicopters flew out the wounded with a minimum of delay, often working among the forward positions. That a wounded man could be in a forward dressing station within twenty minutes of being hit was a great moral reassurance to the troops and was the key to the remarkably low ratio of fatal casualties during the campaign.

The helicopters resumed the ammunition supply shuttle at first light, while the Sea King 4s of 846 Squadron lifted 29 Commando Regiment's eighteen guns to new sites on the captured ground. The Regiment had

---

* *Aeroespacio*, July/August 1983, pp. 52–53.

fired some 3,000 105mm rounds during the Brigade's advance and over 100 lifts were needed to replenish the stocks, over and above the number needed to move the guns and the ammunition left over from the battle. It was fortunate that the weather remained generally clear, though distinctly wintry, with snow showers and the unceasing wind which effectively reduced the temperature still further.

General Moore had intended that the next phase of the offensive should be mounted that night, 12/13 June, by 5 Infantry Brigade, to keep up the momentum. It was decided that more time was required for reconnaissance of Mount Tumbledown, which the Scots Guards were to attack, as well as to replenish stocks of ammunition and stores, and the operation was therefore postponed by twenty-four hours.

The *Sir Percivale* unloaded rapidly at Teal Inlet, while the *Sir Geraint*, alongside the *Elk* in San Carlos Water, reloaded equally quickly for her next run with 3 Brigade stores. The *Blue Rover*'s aviation fuel cargo was drained for the second time, being taken ashore to Port San Carlos by 'dracone' and pumped into the *Sir Geraint*'s tanks for delivery to Teal Inlet.

The *Norland* arrived off the River Plate at dawn and entered Montevideo to land her 1,016 Argentine passengers. The Uruguayan authorities held the Press at arm's length and the transfer of the men to a pair of Buenos Aires ferries was carried out under the eyes of a Red Cross inspection team. The British ferry then put to sea once again to return to the Falklands. The *Hecla* set out from Grantham Sound with another load of wounded for passage home at about the same time.

Thanks to the good offices of the ICRC, agreement had been reached with the Uruguayan and Argentine Governments to permit the three ambulance ships, HMS *Hydra*, *Herald* and *Hecla*, to enter Montevideo by way of the Plate main channel without seeking separate permission for every visit. On the islands general agreement had been negotiated for the establishment of a 'Red Cross Zone' in Port Stanley, although details required to be finalized. In practice, the British forces had not at any stage deliberately fired upon the built-up area of the small town – a restraint which the occupiers traded upon, dispersing not only the TPS-43 radar, vehicles and helicopters among the buildings but also ammunition stocks. There was to be one deliberate (and very accurate) departure from this policy and, regrettably, one accidental infringement, in which two islanders were to be killed by a naval shell.

The *Exeter* had been in the Transport Area for nearly two weeks and it was decided that she should be replaced by the *Cardiff*. The latter started inbound for San Carlos with the *Olna* and HMS *Andromeda*, while the former sailed from the TA with the *Blue Rover* and *Sir Geraint* at 5.30pm. The LSL parted company after passing the Eddystone Rock and made for Teal Inlet, passing the departing *Sir Percivale* in the Port Salvador narrows at 10.00pm. The *Minerva* brought the hard-working 'Sir Percy' back to San

Carlos Water after midnight.

Only the *Penelope* was left in the Falkland Sound/San Carlos area while the convoys were at sea and there were thus no LPD movements to drop off LCUs. The *Avenger*, which had expected to be back in the TA, was still with the Battle Group and was not particularly enjoying the experience. Four frigates were detailed for a night bombardment programme and left the carriers' screen, but the *Yarmouth* and *Ambuscade* were recalled when they reported mechanical defects. It was more important that these should be rectified to permit the maximum number of gun ships to be available for the next brigade attack than they should be used only for harassing the Argentinians.

13 JUNE

The *Active* and *Arrow* used the Berkeley Sound gunline to harass positions on Sapper Hill and along the Moody Brook. This was to be HMS *Arrow*'s last shoot during 'Corporate' and it brought her total of rounds fired to 902 in bombardments since entering the TEZ as one of the original group. With the *Yarmouth*, she was the only undamaged survivor of that first batch of escorts still in the operational area, but she had possibly had a very close escape from the *San Luis*'s torpedo and she had had to be patched up to make good the ravages of the weather on her cracking hull. The *Arrow* delivered 103 4.5in shells on her targets and the *Active* fired eighty-three, of which twenty-five were starshell, giving the enemy a feeling of nakedness as well as helplessness under the bombardment.

The two Type 21s returned to the Battle Group an hour after sunrise on yet another clear day, the seventh in a row. The overnight convoy had already arrived and the *Andromeda* had been despatched for another stores drop recovery. This proved to be a rather exciting duty, for some of the eight containers parted company from their parachutes and fell ballistically. So accurate was the Hercules' aiming that these very narrowly missed the ship. Happily, the twenty-two passengers who jumped out of the aircraft had no such problems and were picked up without incident.

In the 'Trala' the *Stena Seaspread* finished repairs to the *Plymouth*, plating over the holes, tidying up the damaged dining halls and messdecks and setting the 4.5in turret to work. The mortar would have to await dockyard assistance, as would the battered funnel casing. The frigate's ship's company lined the side and cheered Naval Party 1910 as the *Plymouth* pulled away to rejoin the Battle Group, her place being taken immediately by the *Glamorgan*.

The only Argentine air activity detected on 12 June had been a diversionary probe which had not come within 100 miles of the TA. There was at least one overnight transport sortie to Port Stanley, the aircraft being seen by 3 Commando Brigade spotters who called down 105mm fire on the airfield. This missed and the CAP was unable to detect the aircraft when it left shortly afterwards for the mainland.

The weather overland was not as good as in the eastern half of the TEZ, frequent snow showers reducing visibility and bringing down the cloud-base. The helicopters, which had flown so many sorties during the previous two days, managed only about two-thirds of the hours on the 13th. Nevertheless, all the forward troops were supplied, casualties and prisoners of war were flown back and the 105mm batteries had over 400 rounds per gun by nightfall.

The Sea Harriers provided the usual dawn-to-dusk CAP, using *Sheath-bill*. Nothing was reported until about 10.40am, when an 801 Squadron section over Choiseul Sound reported sighting an Argentine patrol craft near Becher Island. Although it was thought to be the *Rio Iguazu*, driven aground on 22 May by 800 Squadron's attacks, it wasn't where it had been left and the SHARs received permission to strafe it before they returned to the *Invincible*.

Twenty minutes after the attack the *Cardiff* detected a raid approaching fifty miles to the south-west of San Carlos Water. The CAP over the Falkland Sound was vectored out but the contact then faded and the SHAR pilots could find nothing. All areas were warned that a raid was probably imminent, but nothing was seen or heard by the naval fighter controllers between 11.10am and 11.21am, when there was a report from Teal Inlet that a gaggle of Skyhawks had overflown the area. The Fitzroy CAP was sent in hot pursuit, too late to have any chance of catching the departing enemy.

The raid had consisted of seven A-4Bs of V Air Brigade (eight had taken off but one had dropped out en route) which had paralleled the south coast of East Falkland at very low level and had turned to coast in to the east of Fitzroy and then attacked Mount Kent from the south-east. Whether by chance or, as is possible, given Argentine claims that their radio intelligence sections intercepted much British military signals traffic, by intent, the strike made for the 3 Commando Brigade Tactical HQ at the time when Brigadier Thompson had gathered his unit commanders for an 'Operations Group' briefing, at which Major-General Moore was also present. The Brigade helicopter operating base, 500 yards away, attracted one division but the bombs dropped by the others landed too close for the assembled commanders' comfort. Few of the 500lb parachute-retarded bombs exploded and no casualties were inflicted, but a Scout and a Gazelle were damaged, the former seriously. Three of the Skyhawks were damaged by ground-fire.

As they withdrew, they encountered naval helicopters on the Teal–Mount Kent shuttle, but only two of the vulnerable transports were attacked. An 847 Squadron Wessex on a casevac mission was 'bombed' by an A-4B which jettisoned its external fuel tanks at it, but Lieutenant-Commander S. C. Thornewill, the Commanding Officer of 846 Squadron, was singled out by four A-4Bs. Attacked initially from astern, he evaded the first pass and, with the able assistance of his co-pilot and air-crewman, repeated attacks by the Skyhawks. The enemy's fire was nevertheless sufficiently accurate to put a 20mm shell through one of the Sea King's main rotor blades. Lieutenant-Commander Thornewill landed and waited until another of his aircraft brought up a spare blade and the mechanics; he was back on task within an hour.

Another helicopter was having a much narrower escape at much the same time. The *Cardiff*'s Lynx had been launched to carry out the routine forenoon surface clearance search to the south of the Falkland Sound, a routine sweep which covered about 7,500 square miles by radar, to ensure that no blockade-runners were approaching or departing. As Lieutenant C. H. Clayton was returning at 1,000 feet, fifty miles south of Lafonia, he and his crewman heard a rapid series of explosions and were surprised to see a Dagger flash past fifty yards away. It had approached from astern, in the Lynx's wide blind arc, and missed its sitting target with the contents of two rocket pods. The helicopter crew then saw a second fighter and Clayton broke towards it as he dived to sea level. The enemy aircraft made a firing pass from the beam but was unable to track the tight-turning Lynx and his rockets came no closer than 100 yards. A third Dagger was countered by turning into its attack. Forced to fire head-on, it missed. The fighters then broke off and returned to base. The lone Lynx must have been a tempting target, but the Argentine pilots had been irresponsible to attack it when their ordnance was needed much more urgently in the battlefield area. Fortunately for the helicopter crew, the leader's aim had been as poor as his tactical sense and the naval pilot did not give his wingmen the opportunity for a simple shot.

So ended the last daylight raid on British forces. By this stage it was almost predictable that its should have been the old A-4Bs of V Air Brigade that got through to deliver their attack on the intended target. Well-led and individually courageous, they had been responsible for most of the damage inflicted by the Argentine Air Force, destroying the *Coventry*, *Antelope*, *Sir Galahad* and LCU *F4*, as well as damaging the *Argonaut*, two more LSLs, the *Glasgow*, the *Broadsword* and the Ajax Bay ammunition dump. Sixteen missions, totalling about fifty individual sorties, appear to have reached the target areas and these cost the Brigade ten aircraft and nine pilots. It was as well for the Royal Navy (and the troops ashore) that only the brigade from San Luis, 360 miles from the sea, showed such an aptitude for shipping strike.

While 3 Commando Brigade moved its TacHQ to a new location and the land forces commanders resumed their interrupted briefing, a pair of GR3s flew direct from the *Hermes* to deliver a laser-guided bomb attack on the Argentine artillery in the Moody Brook area, ten minutes after the Skyhawks' departure. One 'Paveway' bomb scored a direct hit on a 155mm gun.

The number of such guns in the line was reduced only temporarily, for a fourth '155' and eighty rounds of ammunition had been flown in during the previous night by a C-130 and was brought up and emplaced after nightfall on the 13th.

Another arrival at Port Stanley, during daylight on 13 June, was the hospital ship *Almirante Irizar*. She brought with her a team from the ICRC, whose members had already inspected the British hospital and prisoner of war arrangements. A 'Red Cross Zone' around the Cathedral was suggested and both sides agreed to respect it as a weapons-free sanctuary area for civilians and casualties. The *Irizar* remained, embarking wounded.

The Finnish-built icebreaker *Almirante Irizar* in Port William after the surrender. Although declared as a hospital ship by June, she had visited the Falklands in the assault transport role, for the April invasion *(MoD)*

The Argentine military command was well aware that another major assault was imminent and of its likely targets. The Mount Tumbledown–Mount William high ground to the south-west of Port Stanley and Wireless Ridge to the north-west commanded the peninsula and were the last credible line of defence. The Tumbledown area was entrusted to the 5th Marine Infantry Battalion, which had a lower proportion of conscripts than any of the Army units, and the Wireless Ridge to the Army's 7th Mechanized Infantry Regiment, both units being at full strength. About twenty-four 105mm howitzers were available, most of them dug in in bunkers, to provide defensive fire and, although these were out-ranged by the British Light Gun, all the likely targets were well within their 11,000-yard reach.

General Menendez still had over 9,000 soldiers facing General Moore's 6,000 Marines, Paras, Guardsmen, Gurkhas and Gunners. The great majority of the Argentinians were in fighting units. The lack of a proper support 'tail' was a grave handicap, felt mainly by the conscript soldiers who, unless their NCOs knew where to forage and had the sense to look after their men's well-being, went hungry and were ill-clothed. Such men, and they were very many of the 75% of the occupation force who were conscripts, were unlikely to fight well for their sleek, selfish and often incompetent NCOs. At the other extreme, represented by the marine battalion, professional officers and NCOs looked after and led men who fought hard and well to the end.

Argentine aircraft activity continued after the attacks on Mount Kent and the *Cardiff*'s Lynx. Shortly before noon a raid, thought to be four Skyhawks, approached West Falkland but did not close after the CAP was vectored out. At 1.15pm the Chinook, ferrying in prisoners, made a heavy landing on the Port San Carlos STOVL strip and tore up some of the planking. A pair of 800 Squadron Sea Harriers was approaching the end of their CAP and, with insufficient fuel to return to their carrier, they were obliged to land on the LPDs' flight decks, Lieutenant S. Hargreaves on the *Intrepid* at 1.24 and Lieutenant-Commander N. W. Thomas on the *Fearless* three minutes later. Although the RAF versions of the Harrier had landed aboard an LPD, this was the first SHAR use of their decks.

The fighters refuelled (although they could not take their normal load, for which a rolling take-off and the ski-jump were needed) and remained at alert on the LPDs. When an Argentine formation was detected at 2.50pm, seventy miles to the south-west, the standing CAP over the Falkland Sound was sent out to intercept. Although this raid turned away as had been half-expected, the CAP had been drawn to the south when a second formation was picked up on radar at low level to the north of the Falkland Sound. The two SHARs on deck were scrambled at 2.57pm and went to look for the intruders but failed to find them. Their quarry was a

13 June: two 800 Squadron SHARs, unable to land on the damaged *Sheathbill* strip and with insufficient fuel to return to the *Hermes*, were recovered by the *Intrepid* and *Fearless*. Here, Lt-Cdr Neil Thomas's aircraft is refuelled by the *Fearless'* flight deck party; war has clearly relaxed the rules, for in normal peacetime circumstances men would not have been allowed to congregate in front of live missiles (M.C. Cudmore)

pair of Argentine Navy A-4Qs, briefed to attack Darwin, and this pair, keeping a good look-out, saw the SHARs coming and 'ducked' into the overcast. Prudently deciding that the enemy was alert and out in strength, the Skyhawk pilots abandoned their mission and returned to Rio Grande. Neil Thomas and his No 2, the last SHAR pilots to have had any chance of a kill, returned to the *Hermes*.

The abandoned *Rio Iguazu* was again strafed by an 801 Squadron CAP and before dusk the *Penelope*'s Lynx hit it with a Sea Skua. The frigate herself sailed east with the *Nordic Ferry*, to be handed over to the *Arrow* to the north-east of East Falkland in exchange for the inbound *Baltic Ferry* and *Lycaon*. The *Cardiff*, on her first night as anti-aircraft guardship, also sailed to the north out of the Falkland Sound, to cover the convoys and the bombardment groups which were to be in Berkeley Sound that night. The gunfire support ships sailed in two pairs, the *Avenger* and *Yarmouth* leaving the Battle Group at noon and the *Active* and *Ambuscade* three and a half hours later.

The *Intrepid* and *Minerva* set off on another run to deliver and collect Fitzroy LCUs. By 9.20pm the two ships were off the southernmost point of Lafonia, some fifty miles south-west of Fitzroy. The *Penelope* was with the *Nordic Ferry*, forty-five miles on the other side of Fitzroy, with the *Cardiff* about fifteen miles to the west-north-west of her. Almost simultaneously the two frigates and the guided missile destroyer detected the first of a stream of aircraft which came in from the west towards the *Intrepid* and then turned to fly along or parallel to the southern coast of East Falkland. One does not seem to have followed this path. Watched with considerable attention by the *Penelope*, an airborne radar transmitter betrayed its approach from over Pebble Island, across the San Carlos area, south of Teal Inlet and over the front lines until it faded overhead Port Stanley. As this aircraft disappeared at 9.34, another, believed to be a Mirage III, overflew the *Intrepid* and *Minerva*, which had taken cover in a nearby snowstorm.

The *Cardiff* was tracking the contact which rather worried the two ships off Lafonia and watched as it, another to the north and at least one more to the west, flew on towards Fitzroy and Port Stanley. By 9.44 the leading contact was well within Sea Dart range, over land to the north of Port Stanley, and the *Cardiff* opened fire with a single missile as the aircraft began to turn away to the south. *Capitan* R. Pastran claimed that he had just bombed Mount Kent when his Canberra was hit and went into a spin. Although he ejected and came down close to the coast, his navigator, *Capitan* F. Casado, failed to escape. The end of the bomber was seen by all the ships, including the *Fearless*, the only warship left in San Carlos Water, as well as by the troops ashore, the British waiting to begin their attack and the Argentinians waiting to receive it and already under intense bombardment.

The 'flame like a falling leaf', as Captain Larken described it, must also have been seen by the other Argentine aircrew, but two at least kept coming. At 9.47 flashes were seen over the Fitzroy area by the *Fearless*, *Minerva* and *Penelope*. To the last they appeared as a bright glow and a trail, coming straight at her and the ferry. Commander Peter Rickard took evasive action, fired chaff to screen himself and the *Nordic Ferry* and opened fire with Seacat and his Bofors as the missile closed at low level. It finally ditched, or possibly exploded above the water, about 1,000 yards between the frigate and her charge. The two aircraft in the Fitzroy area turned away as the missile arrived and headed for base, one going sufficiently close to the *Intrepid* and *Minerva* to cause them serious worry. By 10.00pm the radar screens were again clear, apart from an aircraft passing far to the south of the islands, westbound.

Considerable mystery surrounds this last raid, not the least being where Pastran's alleged bombs fell. His aircraft was twelve miles to the east of Mount Kent when the *Cardiff* launched her 'bird' and had not passed within five miles and, furthermore, no bombs were noted by any British troops, including the advanced reconnaissance screens to north and south of Stanley. The Canberra span in almost vertically, as observed by eyewitnesses, yet the *Cardiff*, tracking a contact to the south from the point of impact of the Sea Dart, believed that the bomber had crashed at least twenty-five miles to the south. To further complicate any analysis, the destroyer claimed a 'Mirage', on the strength of the unmistakable 'noise' of a figher-type radar on the target's bearing. This had also been intercepted by the *Minerva*, coming from the aircraft which had flown over her ten minutes before the shoot-down, and was again detected fifteen minutes afterwards. The absence of such a radar from the Argen-

The last successful missile engagement by a warship was the *Cardiff*'s destruction of a Canberra bomber late on 13 June. The Type 42 is seen in San Carlos water after the end of the fighting, receiving assistance from the *Stena Seaspread* (MoD)

tine Canberras' electronics fit leads one to deduce that either a Mirage was at low level (and therefore undetectable) below the bomber and it climbed out when the latter was hit, or that the two were in very tight formation, so that the *Cardiff*'s radar could not discriminate between the two aircraft.

The attack on the *Penelope* also requires some explanation. Only an educated guess can be made without the Argentine account and this has not been forthcoming. There can be little doubt that she was fired at, although her claims were regarded at the time with some disbelief. The *Fearless* and *Minerva* both reported 'flashes' or 'explosions' in the sky at the time that the *Penelope*'s lookout saw the 'glow', and the bearings cor-

The last intended victim of a missile was the frigate *Penelope*, attacked minutes after she had watched the *Cardiff*'s Sea Dart strike and the Canberra's spiral descent. Alongside the frigate as she lies off Yorke Bay is the captured patrol boat *Islas Malvinas* (*Lt-Cdr L.E. May RN*)

HMS *Minerva* lies at anchor in San Carlos Water on the last day of the war. The visitor – a Sea King 2 of 825 Squadron – is remarkable and is believed to be a 'first', no other 'Leander'-class frigate having previously landed (or, at least, having admitted to having landed) such a large helicopter on its small flight deck (*via Captain S.H.G. Johnston RN*)

respond to a position about five miles south-west of Fitzroy Settlement, where the Rapier troop reported hearing explosions overhead. The lack of any interception of a missile radar homing head was rightly taken to mean that an Exocet had not been fired. But Exocet is not the only air-launched anti-shipping missile, nor is active radar the only form of homing. Low-light television, optical radio-command, anti-radar and infra-red are examples of techniques which require no radar transmissions from either the launch aircraft or the missile. A Canberra, pointed towards a suitable target by a radar-equipped companion, could carry such a guided or homing missile, to be released when the operator or the electronics saw the target. There is, however, a limited number of missiles capable of the range at which the *Penelope* was attacked and there was, at the time of the war, an even more limited range of potential suppliers. There were persistent rumours, which were consistently denied in Tel Aviv, that Israel was continuing to supply weapons to Argentina. A few months after the end of hostilities the existence of an air-launched version of the successful Gabriel anti-shipping missile was announced. With a range of about fifty miles, it can be launched by Mirage and Skyhawk aircraft, among others. Although this version is offered with active radar homing, earlier models have used radio-command and TV guidance as well as radar.

The bombers were not the only Argentine aircraft active over the Falklands. A C-130 arrived with 155mm artillery ammunition after nightfall, and at about 1.00am on 14 June a naval Lockheed Electra transport made the last landing on 'BAM Malvinas', watched by the soldiers on the hills and the artillery spotting officers. The *Ambuscade*'s gunfire was diverted to this target, happily to no effect, and the aircraft took off with the last load of wounded to return in freedom to Argentina. The gallant and courageous transport pilots had had some very close calls, but they had survived not only the natural hazards but also all the British attempts to catch or thwart them.

As soon as the Electra was safely outbound, the Commanding Officer of *VYCA 2* rendered the TPS-43 radar unserviceable by pouring acid in the cooling system, cross-wiring circuits and removing three essential printed circuit cards. The radar station personnel had also carried out their task in a manner in which they could take pride.

Chapter Three

The Last Battle

At approximately 10.00pm the British launched the expected infantry attacks, preceded by an artillery and mortar barrage and accompanied by bombardments by two frigates in support of each element of the assault. 2 Para, the unit which had not been involved in the attack two nights previously, now moved forward to take the western half of Wireless Ridge and the Scots Guards advanced on Mount Tumbledown. Once the latter was secured, the Gurkhas would take Mount William, while the composite Welsh Guards/40 Commando 'battalion' would exploit any opportunity for a rapid follow-up.

Supported by the *Yarmouth* and *Ambuscade*, 2 Para drove the enemy from the northern part of Wireless Ridge before midnight and were secure on their original intended objectives by 1.50am. Not satisfied with that, they sought and obtained General Moore's sanction to exploit ahead, to meet up with a force of SAS troopers who had turned a diversionary raid across the Murrell River on to the easterly peninsula which ended in Navy Point into a full-scale assault. This had been detected by the defenders, an AA battery, who had called for supporting fire and illumination – the latter was provided by a searchlight on the *Irizar*. The SAS force withdrew, only to land again to the west of the original objective and be joined by the advanced elements of 2 Para before 5.00am. The light tanks of the Blues and Royals moved up, providing close support for the Paras' advance and came within range of the main Argentine positions. The troops were now on ground which was within the range and line of sight of the Argentine 35mm AA guns on Port Stanley racecourse and these had to be dealt with by the *Avenger* and *Yarmouth*.

The *Active* fired in support of the attack on Mount Tumbledown, providing eight starshell and 220 high-explosive rounds. The Argentine marines defending the long rocky feature actually outnumbered the attackers and fought tenaciously and well from prepared positions. These brought the Scots Guards to a virtual halt for nearly three hours, from 1.00 to 4.00am, while the Royal Artillery, the infantry's mortars and HMS *Active* and *Avenger* poured in an impressive weight of fire on the ridge and the Argentine artillery, to give the troops cover while they probed for weaknesses in the defences.

The frigates had left Berkeley Sound long before dawn, the *Ambuscade* after firing 228 rounds, the *Yarmouth* 244 and the *Avenger* 156, taking the last named's total to over 1,000 4.5in shells fired during coastal bombardments. Captain White was returning to San Carlos Water but on this occasion he was unable to leave later than the other frigates, although he had less distance to go, for on entering the Sound at the beginning of the gunnery serial, one of the *Avenger's* propellers had apparently struck an underwater obstruction and had certainly shed a blade. The resulting vibration reduced the Type 21's speed to a maximum of 16 knots.

The Argentine artillery fire increased in volume and accuracy after the departure of the ships, being a particular nuisance to 2 Para on Wireless Ridge, where the forward Company was having to beat off counter-attacks from Moody Brook. The helicopters of 3 Commando Brigade Air Squadron and the attached flight of 656 Squadron AAC had been active during the attack, bringing up ammunition and ferrying out casualties. The Paras and SAS had lost two dead and a dozen wounded. In the dawn twilight a mixed Royal Marine/Army Scout formation, led by Captain J. G. Greenhalgh of 656 Squadron, rendezvoused behind Wireless Ridge before striking at the enemy artillery lines. Each of the three light helicopters was armed with four SS.11 wire-guided missiles, smaller, earlier members of the same family as the AS.12 which had already seen useful service. Captain Greenhalgh made an initial reconnaissance, firing one of his missiles at a group of soldiers, and then led all three aircraft over the crest of the ridge to fire at bunkers. Two such 'passes' were made and of the five missiles fired (one hung up) three scored direct hits on 105mm gun pits. The weather intervened, one of the snowstorms which were sweeping across the battlefield reducing visibility to less than 800 yards, and when the Scouts came back for a third attack they were more easily seen in the growing daylight and were driven off by accurate and effective mortar fire.

With the coming of day, the Argentine marines holding Mount Tumbledown finally broke as the Gurkhas came around their flank to take Mount William. The Scots Guards had by now occupied two-thirds of the Tumbledown ridge and had lost a score of men (one of whom was killed) in the battle. With the high ground in British hands, the Argentine positions to the west of the town were virtually untenable. Attempted counter-attacks by infantry and a sortie by the dozen armoured cars were broken up by British field artillery before the Argentinians could engage. The Argentine artillery suffered further losses when GR3s from the *Hermes* delivered a laser-guided bomb strike on a battery covering the marines' pull-back from Tumbledown and soon after most of the surviving guns found themselves in the front line, with no way of extracting themselves to withdraw to more favourable positions. By 9.00am General Menendez could rely upon four infantry companies and remnants of the five regiments which had been committed to the battle and two further companies garrisoning the airfield. Less than a dozen 105mm howitzers remained and there was no ammunition left for the 155mm guns. Fresh stocks had been flown in during the night but these, too, had been fired. The only eminence left in Argentine hands was Sapper Hill, only a little to the west of Port Stanley.

The naval transport helicopters had been very active since before dawn, supplying ammunition to the troops, the artillery and to the light tanks which had supported 2 Para so effectively. They were now concentrated to provide resources for a 'two-company lift' in which they flew forward Alfa and Charlie Companies of 40 Commando for the only opposed helicopter assault of the campaign, on Sapper Hill. The first Troop was dropped too close to the enemy and, although the helicopters were not hit, two Marines were wounded, the last casualties that the naval forces were to suffer from enemy action. For, almost as soon as the first lift had set down all its men, the men of 40 Commando were ordered to cease fire. The Argentine Army was negotiating for a cease-fire.

General Menendez and his staff had assessed that, although there were rations for a few more days, forty-eight hours would be needed to reorganize the broken and demoralized fragments which had streamed back into Port Stanley. Whether or not the thousands of conscripts who had decided that this was not their war could be motivated anew to fight on, little ammunition remained. The main dump was on the racecourse, now in British hands. The General, attempting to salvage something from the wreckage, radioed Buenos Aires to suggest that the Junta accept the UN Security Council Resolution 502 forthwith, in the faint hope that the British Government would agree to a mutual withdrawal. Otherwise, he would have no alternative to surrender. Shortly before 11.00am the reply came from Galtieri, the Commander in Chief of the Argentine Forces: the fight should go on as the British were probably as exhausted as the Argentinians in Port Stanley. The Junta was as out of touch with reality as ever.

Even as Menendez was being ordered to continue the defence, one of his staff, *Capitan de Navio* M. Hussey, had been contacted by General Moore's staff by means of the islanders' medical radio channel. This was not the first such contact, nor was it the first suggestion of a cease-fire, but by 11.05am on the 45th day General Menendez was ready to come to terms. Twenty-five minutes later British forces, who were by now in Port Stanley (2 Para) and overlooking it from Sapper Hill (40 Commando), were ordered to fire only in self-defence.

Admiral Woodward and the Battle Group learned of the cease-fire via one of the GR3 pilots. Set for another laser-guided bomb attack, Squadron Leader P. Harris RAF was instructed to hold off and was sent back to the *Hermes* at 11.50am with the news that white flags had been seen over Port Stanley. The San Carlos CAP was informed at about the same time

General Mario B. Menendez (lower right), the Military Governor, and General Oscar L. Joffre (centre), his Army commander, with their staffs in the Argentine 'Combat Information Centre' set up in a building at Port Stanley airport *(FAA via J.C. D'Odorico)*

by the *Cardiff*, back in the Transport Area after her night's success. In the 'Trala', aboard the *Canberra*, the buzz had been passed around even earlier, for Army personnel on board were listening in on the Artillery 'net' and heard the first mention of a surrender as early as 11.22am. The Admiral was aware that the negotiations which were being undertaken by General Moore's staff concerned only the Argentine forces on the islands, and he warned his ships accordingly. Describing the situation as 'very delicate', he went on, 'Our guard must not be reduced but we must not jeopardize results so far achieved.... ARG air threat (overland) remains and must be countered. The threat at sea has not changed.'

The SHARs had provided the usual CAP since dawn and continued to do so, although the *Sheathbill* strip was unusable due to ice during the morning. The fighters also flew radar surface searches to the west and north-west, to ensure that the Argentine Navy had not slipped past the three nuclear-powered submarines on patrol for a last desperate sortie 'for the honour of the flag'. The *Plymouth* and *Yarmouth* detached during the afternoon to proceed to Berkeley Sound, where they would remain on call to provide gunfire support in the event of the negotiations breaking down and the resumption of fighting. The only movement from the Battle Group to San Carlos was the *Andromeda*, carrying a large consignment of blankets and stretchers to accommodate the influx of wounded Argentine prisoners taken during the last battle. The anti-submarine helicopters aboard the two carriers and the *Atlantic Causeway* continued to patrol and the *Hermes* acted as a service station for a RAF Chinook which was en route to San Carlos from the *Contender Bezant*, just too late for the fighting but much needed for the aftermath.

Appropriately, it was one of the anti-submarine Sea Kings from the carriers which made what was, in effect, the last operational flight of the campaign. The arrangements for the surrender were not completed until after dark, by which time the weather had deteriorated to the point where the snowstorms were almost continuous, and so one of the 820 Squadron aircraft at San Carlos Settlement was chosen to take General Moore from the *Fearless* to Port Stanley. Flown by Lieutenant-Commander Keith Dudley, the General was delivered safely through the bad weather to Government House, where he arrived at about 6.00pm. Two hours later, at midnight Greenwich Mean Time, General Menendez and General Moore signed the formal Instrument of Surrender.

The following morning Juliet Company of 42 Commando (latterly Naval Party 8901) raised the Governor's flag, which had been brought back to Britain by the same Marines, on the flagstaff outside Government House. It had been down for seventy-four days.

Chapter Four

Aftermath

The end of the fighting was marked by a change for the worse in the weather. After a week of clear but cold conditions, interspersed with occasional snow showers, the snow fell steadily and the wind drove it hard. The *Plymouth* and *Yarmouth*, returning to the Battle Group after a quiet night in Berkeley Sound, reported the worst weather that they had experienced since leaving for the South Atlantic, with a Force 10 storm and confused seas which reduced their speed to 11 knots. In the early hours of 15 June the Battle Group had to abandon replenishment and then withdraw the Sea King 5s from the anti-submarine screen – the first time for over a month since this had been necessary.

The *Glamorgan* had 'borrowed' one of the *Tidespring*'s Wessex 5s and this aircraft was severely damaged on deck. The destroyer's hangar was open to the elements after the Exocet explosion. Outside the TEZ the RAF maintenance personnel of No 18 Squadron aboard the *Europic Ferry* were preparing the replacement Chinooks brought south by the *Contender Bezant*, stripping off the weatherproof covering and fitting rotor blades on board the aircraft transport before flying the big helicopters across to the ferry for final checks prior to sending them inshore, via the *Hermes*. The first such replacement had been despatched on 14 June, arriving in East Falkland a couple of hours after the ceasefire and a second Chinook landed on the *Europic Ferry* that evening. It was to remain for two days, 15 tons of topweight on the heavily-rolling North Sea ferry, whose officers more than once considered jettisoning it. The helicopter not only survived, it escaped damage and was flown off on 16th, by which time the weather had moderated.

The surrender of the Argentine forces in West Falkland was the main concern of Commodore Clapp's ships on the 15th. Captain White took the *Avenger* to Fox Bay, where she arrived shortly after midnight, but the *Cardiff* did not set off for Port Howard, escorting three of the *Intrepid*'s LCUs, until dawn. Another LCU went around to Pebble Island. Two intact regiments surrendered – 1,748 troops who had been engaged only by ships' gunfire and aircraft, as well as the 155 men of a marine company occupying Pebble Island. These prisoners were ferried to San Carlos

Water, where they were joined by General Menendez and the senior members of his staff, who were transferred to the *Fearless* by helicopter.

The British forces were now looking after 10,254 prisoners, over 8,000 of whom were moved from the Port Stanley area to the airport peninsula, where they had to improvise shelter from the elements. The state of the 6,000 conscript soldiers, the majority of whom were in poor physical condition due to the neglect of their officers and NCOs, greatly concerned General Moore, whose staff did their best to alleviate the misery by tracing and making available the Argentine stocks of food and clothing which their own quartermasters had been unable to devise means of distributing. The risk of mass deaths due to exposure or disease was very real but could not be averted until the Junta agreed to a plan for their evacuation.

A start had been made on processing the prisoners on the first day of full British control. The *Canberra* had returned to San Carlos Water at dawn and she embarked 1,121 Argentinians before dark. Each prisoner was properly documented as he came on board and then identified, using P&O baggage labels. The cabin accommodation on B Deck and below was allocated to them, while the 100 Welsh Guardsmen and RAF personnel detailed as guards lived on A Deck. Argentine wounded, mainly from the battle of the 13/14th, were transferred to the *Bahia Paraiso*, which joined the *Uganda* in the Falkland Sound during the day.

At 8.15am on 16 June the *Canberra* left San Carlos Water, escorted by the *Andromeda* and the *Cardiff*, and five hours later was off Port William. The position of the minefield laid in mid-April off Cape Pembroke had been given to the Royal Navy and was already being swept by the 'Ellas', but the *Canberra* was routed around it, preceded by the *Andromeda*, which was thus the first British ship to enter Port William. The liner anchored outside the Port Stanley narrows, protected by the Sea Wolf-fitted frigate and with a Sea Harrier CAP overhead. A company of 3 Para joined as additional guards and then the embarkation of prisoners from the airfield began, using the *Forrest* and three of the *Canberra*'s own motor boats on a shuttle service throughout the night.

Captain David Pentreath was ordered on the 15th to assume the duties of 'Queen's Harbour Master' at Port Stanley and it was appropriate that HMS *Plymouth* should be the first ship to enter the harbour, early on 17 June, followed by the hard-working RFA *Sir Percivale*, whose Master, Captain Pitt, promptly sent a signal to inform the Navy that the Blue Ensign was once again flying off Port Stanley. The LSL was a welcome arrival, for she was used as a Rest and Recreation vessel for the cold, tired and dirty Commandos and Paras, who were able to enjoy 'the indescribable bliss of a hot shower, followed by a meal prepared by someone else, and a few beers'.

Port William rapidly became very full. The *Canberra* and *Andromeda* were joined by the *Fearless, Minerva* and *Sir Bedivere* from San Carlos,

HMS *Active* passes STUFT in Port William after the surrender – the *Lycaon*, *Geestport* and *Astronomer*, with RFA *Olna* at extreme right *(MoD)*

while the *Brilliant* brought in the *Contender Bezant*, *Europic Ferry*, *Tor Caledonia* and *St Edmund* from outside the 'Trala'. The last two ships carried, respectively, the equipment and personnel of another Army Rapier battery and a mobile RAF radar station for the defence of Port Stanley. The naval helicopters were flying as hard as ever, even though the land fighting was over, ferrying men and material between the various base areas and the ships and to support them the *Atlantic Causeway* anchored in Port William. The *Nordic Ferry*, RFA *Resource* and *Fort Toronto* also came in from the 'Trala', the first two with stores and provisions and the last bringing her fresh water. The Port Stanley water supply had been interrupted by damage to the pumping station – even when this was patched up by the Royal Engineers it would be quite insufficient for the vastly-increased population. The much-travelled tug *Typhoon* made up the group.

Admiral Woodward's Battle Group maintained vigilance. Although it was believed that the Junta would not order an attack on the Port Stanley area as long as the prisoners were still present, there was no sign that the Argentinians accepted that the war was over. The SHARs and Sea Kings maintained their defensive patrols and the radar warning cover was extended to the west by stationing a frigate off West Falkland, the first such picket being HMS *Minerva*. A STOVL strip was laid on Stanley racecourse and No 1 Squadron's GR3s were disembarked, while up to four SHARs were sent ashore every day to spend daylight at readiness, occasionally scrambling when the picket ship detected Argentine aircraft probing the edge of the TEZ.

The *Canberra* completed loading prisoners on 17 June, by which time she had 4,167 on board. Thanks to the intercession of the Red Cross and the efforts of the Swiss and Brazilian Governments, the Junta agreed to the return of the Argentinians aboard the *Canberra*, which was given a safe-conduct to proceed unescorted to Puerto Madryn, 650 miles to the north-north-west of Port Stanley. The liner sailed from Port William during the morning of the 18th, as news of the resignation of General Galtieri as Commander-in-Chief and President of Argentina was received. The *Norland* reached Port William later on the same day and began to load another 2,047 prisoners. An Argentine oil rig support ship, the *Yehuin*, assisted in ferrying these men out. Found by the *Plymouth* alongside the Falkland Islands Company's jetty, she had been adopted as a suburb and renamed 'HMS *Oggie*'.* Another Argentine vessel, the Coastguard patrol vessel *Isla Malvinas*, was also found in seaworthy condition. This name was quite unacceptable and, manned by a party from HMS *Cardiff*, she became 'HMS *Tiger Bay*'. The other prize in Falklands waters was the *Bahia Buen Suceso*. Abandoned by her crew in Fox Bay, with minor hull damage but defective machinery, the *Avenger* discovered her aground, infested with rats and still loaded with a large quantity of ammunition and explosives.

The ex-Argentine oil-rig support vessel *Yehuin*, used for inter-island supply from an early stage of the occupation, escaped attack and, found intact at Port Stanley, was pressed into British service for harbour tasks *(MoD)*

The *Canberra* entered Argentine territorial waters at 10.00am on 19 June and was escorted to Puerto Madryn by the Type 42 *Santissima Trinidad* and the ex-American *Comodoro Py*. The *Canberra* secured alongside a long ore pier, on which a queue of lorries and buses was drawn up to transport the returning prisoners and the process of negotiating and then unloading began. Three hours after the first man stepped ashore, to be greeted by a VIP reception party, the liner slipped from the jetty and began a 24-knot run back to the Falklands.

The *Norland* brought the next contingent to Puerto Madryn two days later and the balance of the prisoners were carried home by the *Bahia Paraiso* and the *Almirante Irizar*. The use of the latter was appropriate as she had, on 2 April, brought some of the earliest unwanted arrivals.

* The west Country name, used universally in the Navy, for a Cornish Pasty.

While the British forces had been establishing themselves in Port Stanley and the Argentine prisoners were being taken home, the final steps to eject invaders from British territory were being taken. South Thule, 450 miles to the south-east of South Georgia, lay at the further end of the South Sandwich Islands, barely thirty miles north of the internationally-agreed demilitarized Antarctic, which began at 60° South. The Argentine Navy and Air Force had illegally established a weather reporting station on the island in 1976, manned by up to forty Servicemen. Diplomatic requests to remove them had had no effect and now they were to be taken away by force, if need be.

The *Yarmouth* and *Olmeda* were detached from the Battle Group during the forenoon of 15 June and proceeded to South Georgia, where two rifle troops of Mike Company, 42 Commando, were to be embarked as the assault force. The Reconnaissance Sections and a mortar crew went aboard the *Endurance*, which borrowed a Wessex 5 from the RFA *Regent*, which was storing from the provisions ships *Saxonia* and *Geestport* at Stromness. The frigate and tanker arrived at Grytviken on 17 June, shortly before the ice patrol ship and the tug *Salvageman* sailed, and ferried the eighty-one Royal Marines on board by helicopter, using the *Olmeda*'s Sea Kings. Captain Nick Barker's Task Unit was thus made up of representatives of all the main elements of the naval contribution to Operation 'Corporate' – a warship, an RFA, a merchant vessel, no fewer than six helicopters and Royal Marine commandos, plus his own HMS *Endurance*.

The *Endurance*'s Wasps landed ten Marines of the Recce Sections behind the weather station on 19 June. Realizing that this insertion could not have passed unnoticed, further flights were made to simulate landings here and there, to confuse the Argentinians as to the intentions and strength of the troops ashore. The *Yarmouth* and *Olmeda* joined the *Endurance* and *Salvageman* off South Thule at about midnight on the 19/20th and Commander Morton was ordered to proceed inshore to support a landing. At dawn on 20 June the Marines ashore were ordered to advance down towards the station, while the *Yarmouth* was to conduct a gunfire demonstration at 9.30am. The sight of the advancing Marines was sufficient for the Argentinians. They emerged from their huts to surrender six minutes before the *Yarmouth* was due to open fire.

Only ten men had been occupying the base, the rest having been taken away early in the campaign. The weapons had been dumped as soon as the first wireless invitation to surrender had been received, resistance by such a small and isolated group being clearly useless. The prisoners were flown off to the *Endurance*, which remained behind with the *Salvageman* after the departure of the frigate and tanker with the Marines, to tidy up the inevitable mess left by the Argentinians and to secure the building against the Antarctic weather. Captain Barker returned to South Georgia on 24 June.

Last Act: Royal Marines of 'M' Company, 42 Commando, prepare to raise the Union Jack and the White Ensign over South Thule on 20 June, after their unopposed repossession of the island *(MoD)*

The interim President of Argentina, General Bignone, was sufficiently secure in office by 21 June to be able to announce that the ceasefire of 14 June would be observed by the forces on the mainland, but that no full peace was possible until the Falklands had been 'restored' to Argentina. The British Government welcomed the acceptance of the ceasefire but decided that a force adequate to repel any further adventure should be retained in the area.

The *Glamorgan*, with her Seaslug system operational thanks to the attentions of the *Stena Seaspread* (by now established at San Carlos), and the *Plymouth* began their passage home on the 21st, the day that the

10 July: her starboard side showing no indication of the damage caused by the Exocet hit, the *Glamorgan* passes Haslar Creek on her way up Portsmouth Harbour *(MoD)*

Glasgow arrived to a warm welcome at Portsmouth. Four days later the *Alacrity* returned to Devonport and the *Canberra* sailed for the last time from Port William, carrying the Royal Marines of 3 Commando Brigade and their magnificent supporting Army formations. The *Norland* and *Europic Ferry* left on the same day with the two Parachute Regiment battalions, who would fly home from Ascension Island. Most of the 183 Marine and Army personnel wounded while serving with the brigade had already left, but sixty-eight officers and men were left buried at Ajax Bay, Teal Inlet and Darwin.

3,000 miles to the north-east of the Falklands the *Invincible* was conducting a self-maintenance period at sea, screened by the *Andromeda*. The two ships had detached from the Battle Group late on 18 June and reached 23° South latitude five days later. There she began a main engine change, a task which had never been attempted at sea before but which was accomplished with complete success in six days. On 1 July her ship's company went back once more to Defence Watches as she passed the latitude of the River Plate. The *Hermes* had carried the weight of air defence during the *Invincible*'s absence. With the return of the latter she could now be detached, to return on 21 July to Portsmouth.

The Task Force bade farewell to another of its stalwarts, and probably one of the best-known, on 25 June. The *Sir Galahad*, which had lain off Fitzroy Cove since she had been hit on 8 June, was towed out to sea and scuttled by a torpedo fired by HMS *Onyx*, to the south-west of Port Stanley. Not all the casualties of the attack had been recovered for burial ashore and, like the wrecks of all the ships of both sides sunk during the campaign, hers is a war grave. The *Sir Tristram* was refloated and towed from Fitzroy Cove to Port Stanley, where she was moored as an accommodation hulk, her tank deck providing shelter for men and stores. In 1984 she was brought back to Britain as deck cargo on a salvage barge and taken in hand for reconstruction.

The submarine *Santa Fe*, aground off King Edward Point, South Georgia, was raised to clear the jetty and beached out of the way. Not until early 1985 was it decided that she should be refloated for the last time, to be towed out to sea by tugs and scuttled in deep water off Cumberland Bay. A much earlier disposal was the *Bahia Buen Suceso*. She was

Opposite 14 July: a quiet reception for the *Intrepid* as she approaches the old fort guarding the entrance to Portsmouth on a misty morning – her great welcome had been on the previous day, when she had disembarked her Marines and landing craft at Plymouth *(MoD)*

16 May: the *Bahia Buen Suceso*, a naval auxiliary, which had landed the civilian workers at Leith Harbour, South Georgia, two months earlier, was strafed at Fox Bay by *Hermes'* Sea Harriers and left immobilised until the surrender *(MoD)*

towed from Fox Bay to San Carlos Water in late June and her cargo of ordnance was unloaded during the next few weeks. No further use being seen for her, she was towed to the south of the Falkland Sound and, on Trafalgar Day, 1982, was used as a target for every type of gun, given a *coup de grace* by the *Onyx* and depth-charged as she went down.

Admiral Woodward was relieved on 1 July by Rear Admiral Derek Reffell, who had transferred to HMS *Bristol* from the *Iris*, which had brought him out to the TEZ from Ascension. It had been intended that Port Stanley airfield would be ready to permit RAF Phantom fighters to assume the SHARs' air defence task from mid-July, but the necessary airfield matting, shipped in by the STUFT *Strathewe*, did not arrive until then. The *Invincible* therefore stayed on, sighting land for the first time in ninety-eight days (on 12 July), transiting the Falkland Sound (on 28th) and anchoring in Berkeley Sound for a celebratory dinner, as her predecessor had done in December, 1914. The TEZ had been reduced to a radius of 150 miles on 22 July and its title changed to 'Falkland Islands Protection Zone'.

On 27 August the new HMS *Illustrious* arrived. A near-identical sister of the *Invincible*, her completion had been advanced ahead of the original building programme by months, thanks to the efforts made by her builders, the Tyneside yard of Swan Hunters, and the Royal Dockyards. Her air group consisted of ten Sea Harriers of the re-formed 809 Squadron, eight Sea King anti-submarine helicopters of 824 Squadron and two Sea Kings modified to carry a Thorn-EMI Searchwater radar in a massive

The new *Illustrious* (furthest from the camera), completed months ahead of schedule, arrives on 27 August to relieve the *Invincible* as the carrier on station and to take over from the *Bristol*, flying the flag of Rear Admiral Derek Reffell, as flagship of the squadron off the Falklands *(MoD)*

pivoting hemisphere carried on the starboard side of the cabin. This combination, which had been developed in just eleven weeks, provided the much-needed Airborne Early Warning capability which had been so sorely missed during the campaign. For her own last-ditch self-defence against missiles such as Exocet, the *Illustrious* was armed with two Phalanx systems purchased from the United States Navy. Each mounting consisted of a six-barrelled 20mm Gatling-type gun, firing 4,000 high-density rounds per minute, with a computer adjusting the point of aim by comparing the relative positions of the target and the stream of shot.

The *Illustrious* left the area on 21 October, four days after the arrival of the first Phantoms at Port Stanley. All the warships which had seen service in the TEZ between 1 May and 14 June, with the exception of the *Onyx*, had returned to the United Kingdom and some were on their way out again for a second tour. Many of the merchant ships were still serving on charter in the South Atlantic, providing fuel, ferrying passengers and freight between the islands and Ascension or providing specialist services, like the *Stena Inspector*, which had taken over from the *Seaspread*. The last RFA to return from the invasion under her own power was the *Sir Bedivere*, which reached Marchwood in November, 1982, with her sad cargo of the bodies of those men whose relatives wished them to be interred at home.

28 July: the end of a successful deployment for HMS *Exeter* as she enters Portsmouth Harbour, escorted by naval and RMAS craft and, overhead, an RAF Phantom *(MoD)*

Opposite top 21 July: the *Hermes* comes home, her aircraft and ship's company lined up for the full 'Procedure Alfa' entry into harbour. In the foreground is the *Herald*, which had arrived earlier on the same day – the first of the 'Ambulance Ferries' to come home *(MoD)*

Opposite lower 17 September: the last ships come home – *Bristol*, with her escort of small craft in the foreground and 'yesterday's Navy' in the background, passes the Portsmouth Dockyard waterfront *(MoD)*

More festive had been the return of the other ships, the *Norland* to Hull – few merchant ships had been placed in greater danger or had seen more varied service – the *Stromness* to Portsmouth, to resume the run-down prior to sale to the US Government, and all the other auxiliaries to their home ports, few to any great fanfare other than by those who knew the ships, their men and what they had accomplished.

The warships, too, had their own special welcomes. HMS *Arrow* was greeted by the RAF's 'Red Arrows' formation team, trailing red, white and blue smoke, as she passed up Plymouth Sound on 7 July. At Rosyth, Chief Yeoman Ron Doakes, egged on by his mess-mates, had to repeat the story of his mangled bicycle to Radio Forth when the *Plymouth* returned on 14 July, her battered funnel casing bearing testimony to her narrow escape.

14 July: with her hull number repainted and once more wearing the black funnel-band which identifies her as the Leader of the 6th Frigate Squadron, the *Plymouth* passes North Queensferry on her way to a warm welcome at her base port, Rosyth *(MoD)*

The national experience, with live television coverage, was, however, reserved for the 'big three'. Few who watched the return of the *Canberra* to Southampton on 11 July will forget the moving experience as 'The Great White Whale', with rust streaks around almost every hatch and opening in her sides, came alongside the crowded quay, her decks thronged with the men of 3 Commando Brigade, while Naval Party 1710 lined the edge of the forward flight deck, where the Royal Marine Band was playing, inaudibly.

For the *Hermes*, returning on a weekday, there was again live TV cover, as there was for the *Invincible* when she reached Portsmouth with the *Bristol* on 17 September. With their homecoming, the man in the street felt that the war was indeed over.

What it was all about – the right of the people to
choose their own future *(MoD)*

And what it cost – the Type 21 Memorial on Campito
Hill, overlooking the last resting place of the *Antelope*
off Ajax Bay and, in the other direction, the *Ardent*,
off the North West Islands, in the Falkland Sound
(MoD)

STUFT

Ships Taken Up From Trade

9 May: the first elements of 5 Infantry Brigade sailed from Southampton aboard the 'TT' ferries *Baltic Ferry* (illustrated) and the identical *Nordic Ferry* – not for these ships the high-profile send-off which the *QE2* enjoyed three days later *(MoD)*

The brand-new offshore oilfield support vessel *Wimpey Seahorse* arrived at South Georgia on 8 June to lay moorings and buoys which she had ferried out from the United Kingdom. She performed the same service in the Falklands in July and was home early in September *(via MoD)*

United Towing's *Salvageman* was the largest of the three requisitioned salvage tugs and was the first to reach the operational area – she was also the last to leave, for she did not return to the UK until mid-1984 *(FotoFlite)*

The tug *Irishman* was one of the smallest vessels sent south but was given one of the largest tasks, attempting the salvage of the *Atlantic Conveyor* *(MoD)*

The *British Tamar*, seen here with RFA *Regent's* Wessex 5, was one of the two BP tankers which had carried out replenishment trials with the Royal Navy before the Falklands war. The only STUFT tanker to make two trips, refuelling at Gibraltar in between, she passed most of her first load to RFA *Plumleaf* in an epic RAS which took nearly 53 hours. On her second voyage she acted as the mid-way 'Motorway Oiler', replacing an RFA oiler *(Cadet S Talton RFA)*

British Wye was the only STUFT ship to be attacked deliberately, by an Argentine Air Force Hercules on 29 May: here she is seen a few days later, in company with the *Tidespring* in the 'TRALA' *(MoD)*

View from RFA *Bayleaf*'s bridge as she closes her 'civvie' sister-ship *Balder London* to pump over the STUFT's cargo. The *Balder London* exchanged her attractive colour scheme for the RFA's grey in 1984 when she became the *Orangeleaf* *(via MoD)*

The *Bayleaf*, identical to the *Brambleleaf* and *Appleleaf*, commissioned as a Royal Fleet Auxiliary on 25 March 1982 but her conversion was not complete when the conflict began and the final touches to her fitting-out were applied at Portland. Here she embarks fuel from the *Alvega* off Ascension *(MoD)*

The *Scottish Eagle* seen at speed, with a full load. Originally despatched to South Georgia as the 'station tanker', she moved on to Port Stanley where she served in the same role until September 1983 *(via MoD)*

The *Fort Toronto*
accompanied the Amphibious
Group, to supply fresh water
to whose distilling capacities
were not always adequate to
the needs of the embarked
troops. The Port Stanley water
supply, damaged during the
final stages of the conflict, was
unable to cater for the huge
increase in the population and
the *Fort Toronto* remained
until the spring of 1984 *(Lt
Cdr L. E. May RN)*

The *Avelona Star* loads
provisions for the South
Atlantic, her own array of
cranes being supplemented by
the big quayside and floating
cranes *(MoD)*

The refrigerator ship
Geestport returns to her
peacetime occupation,
repainted and with the
helicopter platform removed
(via MoD)

The Russian-built *Lycaon* carried a cargo of ammunition and AA missiles to South Georgia, whence the first instalment was collected by the *Stromness* at the end of May. *Lycaon* was in the TRALA during the last three days of the war, cutting the length of the supply line when ammunition expenditure was at its highest *(Skyfotos Ltd)*

South Georgia Sunset – the stores ship *Saxonia* lies at the moorings put down by the *Wimpey Seahorse (MoD)*

The Harrison Line container ship *Astronomer* was the last 'Aircraft Ferry' to be taken up, as a replacement for the *Atlantic Conveyor*; sailing from Devonport on 8 June, she did not reach the Falklands until the end of the month. She became RFA *Reliant* in 1983 and, after service off Lebanon in 1984, redeployed to the South Atlantic as a Helicopter Support Ship *(MoD)*

The centre-section of *Atlantic Causeway*, seen from an RFA approaching for a RAS, with six of their eight 825 Squadron Sea King 2s visible in the gap in the 'big boxes' lining the deck *(MoD)*

The *Contender Bezant*'s most important cargo was a flight of four Chinooks, embarked as reinforcements for the *Atlantic Conveyor*'s contingent – in the event, they were replacements but did not arrive until immediately after the Argentine surrender. Purchased by the Royal Navy in 1984, this ship was re-named *Argus*, extensively modified and commissioned as an RFA to replace the helicopter training ship *Engadine (MoD)*

British Telecom's cable-ship *Iris*, seen here at Plymouth on 30 April, ferried personnel and stores between Ascension, South Georgia and the TEZ; among her more notable transfers were the return of Lieutenant Keith Mills and his Marines to *Endurance* and the transport of metal plate and girders from Leith Harbour to the *Stena Seaspread (British Telecom)*

The South Atlantic weather would not allow Townsend Thoresen to preserve the anonymity which the *Europic Ferry* sought. Seen here during the south-bound passage, she has an Army Air Corps Scout helicopter tucked in close to the superstructure and on the after deck can be seen the six 105mm Light Guns of 29 Battery, 4th Field Regiment, Royal Artillery *(MoD)*

Tor Caledonia brought out stores for 5 Infantry Brigade and a mobile radar station, arriving in the TEZ shortly before the cease-fire *(via MoD)*

APPENDICES

Appendix I

RN SHIPS & WEAPONS

The Royal Navy deployed thirty-five of its ships to the South Atlantic during Operation 'Corporate', supported by fifteen Royal Fleet Auxiliary logistic supply vessels, six RFA-manned landing ships and a helicopter training ship. The warships were of fifteen different classes, some known by the lead-ship of the class, others by a Type number and others by a functional designation, and there were twelve types of RFA, some of them with names which, misleadingly, suggested uniformity of appearance. Even the five trawlers taken up from trade and commissioned as HM Ships were of three types. The helicopters, of which there were six types in RN and Royal Marines service, came in eight quite distinct variations, with two different Marks of Wessex and three Marks of Sea King.

The following details are provided as a basic guide to the types of ship. Fuller details are available in the many reference books published each year – highly recommended is the U.S. Naval Institute Press edition of *Combat Fleets of the World* by J. L. Couhat, translated by A. D. Baker III. Besides accurate and up-to-date descriptions and illustrations of warships and auxiliaries, it also lists naval aircraft, weapons and electronic equipment.

The abbreviated date following the name of each ship is that of completion for the Royal Navy; the decorations in square brackets following the names of the Commanding Officers are those awarded for service during the operations – Mentions-in-Despatches are abbreviated as 'M-i-D'.

AIRCRAFT CARRIERS

HERMES   Nov 59   Captain L. E. Middleton ADC [DSO]

Displacement (tons)
   23,900   Standard
   28,700   Full Load

Dimensions (feet [metres])
Hull	744× 90 [227.9×27.4]
Flight Deck	600×112 [182.9×34.1]

Machinery
   2 sets of geared steam turbines
   76,000shp = 26 knots (approx)

Armament
   2 Seacat systems (GWS 22)
   4 LCVP (Landing Craft, Vehicles & Personnel)

Aircraft
pre-'Corporate'	5 Sea Harriers
	9 Sea King 5
	9 Sea King 4
21 May 1982	15 Sea Harriers
	6 Harrier GR3
	6 Sea King 5
	2 Lynx, 1 Wessex 5

INVINCIBLE   1980   Captain J. J. Black MBE [DSO]

Displacement (tons)
   16,000   Standard
   19,500   Full Load

Dimensions (feet [metres])
Hull	678×90 [206.6×27.5]
Flight Deck	590×105 [180.0×31.9]

Machinery
   4 Rolls-Royce *Olympus* gas turbines
   112,000shp = 29+ knots

Armament
   1 Sea Dart system (GWS 30)
   (14 7.62mm GP machine-guns added)

Aircraft
pre-'Corporate'	5 Sea Harriers
	9 Sea King 5
21 May 1982	10 Sea Harriers
	9 Sea King 5
	1 Lynx

GUIDED MISSILE DESTROYERS

'County' Class

ANTRIM   Mar 71   Captain B. G. Young [DSO]
GLAMORGAN   Oct 66   Captain M. E. Barrow [DSO]

Displacement (tons)
   5,440   Standard
   6,200   Full Load

Dimensions (feet [metres])
   520×54 [158.5×16.5]

Machinery
   2 sets geared steam turbines, 2 G6 gas turbines
   30,000shp + 15,000shp = 32.5 knots

Armament
   2×4.5in (114mm) Mark 6 dual-purpose (surface/AA) guns
   2×20mm Oerlikon AA guns
   1 Seaslug 2 system (GWS 10)
   2 Seacat systems (GWS 22)
   4×MM.38 Exocet

Aircraft
   1 Wessex 3
   (both ships embarked, additionally, a Wessex 5 for special tasks and when the *Glamorgan*'s Wessex 3 was destroyed on 12 June, 1982, it was replaced by a Wessex 5)

Type 82

BRISTOL   Mar 73   Captain A. Grose

Displacement (tons)
   6,100   Standard
   7,100   Full Load

Dimensions (feet [metres])
    507×55 [154.6×16.8]

Machinery
    2 sets geared steam turbines, 2 R-R *Olympus* gas turbines
    30,000shp + 44,600shp = 28+ knots

Armament
    1 × 4.5in Mark 8 dual-purpose gun
    4 × 20mm AA guns
    1 × Sea Dart system (GWS 30)
    1 × Ikara ASW missile system
    1 × three-barrelled ASW Mortar Mark 10

Type 42

CARDIFF   Oct 79   Captain M. G. T. Harris
COVENTRY   Nov 78   Captain D. Hart-Dyke
EXETER   Sep 80   Captain H. M. Balfour LVO
GLASGOW   May 79   Captain A. P. Hoddinot OBE
SHEFFIELD   Feb 75   Captain J. F. T. G. Salt

Displacement (tons)
    3,150   Standard
    4,100   Full Load

Dimensions (feet [metres])
    410×47 [125×13.3]

Machinery
    2 R-R *Olympus* gas turbines
    54,400 shp = 30 knots
    2 R-R *Tyne* gas turbines
    8,200 shp = 18 knots (cruising)

Armament
    1 × 4.5in Mark 8 gun
    2 × 20mm AA guns
    1 × Sea Dart system (GWS 30)
    2 × triple ASW torpedo tubes (STWS)

Aircraft
    1 Lynx

FRIGATES

Type 12

PLYMOUTH   May 61   Captain D. Pentreath [DSO]
YARMOUTH   Mar 60   Commander A. Morton [DSC]

Displacement (tons)
    2,380   Standard
    2,800   Full Load

Dimensions (feet [metres])
    370×41 [112.8×12.5]

Machinery
    2 sets geared steam turbines
    30,000 shp = 28 knots

Armament
    2×4.5in Mark 6 guns
    2×20mm AA guns

1 × Seacat system (GWS 20)
1 × ASW Mortar Mark 10

Aircraft
    1 Wasp

'Batch II' 'Leander' Class

ARGONAUT   Aug 67   Captain C. H. Layman LVO
                     [DSO]
MINERVA   May 66   Commander S. H. G. Johnston
PENELOPE   Oct 63   Commander P. V. Rickard

Displacement (tons)
    2,650   Standard
    3,200   Full Load

Dimensions (feet [metres])
    372×41 [113.4×12.5]

Machinery
    2 sets geared steam turbines
    30,000 shp = 28 knots

Armament
    2 × 40mm Bofors AA guns
    3 × Seacat systems (GWS 22)
    4 × MM.38 Exocet
    2 × triple ASW torpedo tubes (STWS)

Aircraft
    1 Lynx

'Batch III' (Broad-Beam) 'Leander' Class

ANDROMEDA   Dec 68   Captain J. L. Weatherall

Displacement (tons)
    2,640   Standard
    3,100   Full Load

Dimensions (feet [metres])
    372×43 [113.4×13.1]

Machinery
    as batch II 'Leander'-class

Armament
    2 × 40mm AA guns
    1 × Sea Wolf system (GWS 25)
    4 × MM.38 Exocet
    2 × triple ASW torpedo tubes

Aircraft
    1 Lynx

Type 21

ACTIVE   Jun 77   Commander P. C. B. Canter
ALACRITY   Apr 77 Commander C. J. S.
                              Craig [DSC]
AMBUSCADE Sep 75   Commander P. J. Mosse
ANTELOPE   Jul 75   Commander N. J. Tobin [DSC]
ARDENT   Oct 77   Commander A. W. J. West [DSC]
ARROW   Jul 76   Commander P. J. Bootherstone
                              [DSC]
AVENGER   Apr 78   Captain H. M. White

Displacement (tons)
2,750   Standard
3,250   Full Load

Dimensions (feet [metres])
384×42 [117.0×12.8]

Machinery
2 × *Olympus* gas turbines
50,000 shp = 31+ knots
2 × *Tyne* gas turbines
8,500 shp = 18 knots (cruising)

Armament
1 × 4.5in Mark 8 gun
2 × 20mm AA guns (3 in *Avenger* from June)
1 × Seacat system (GWS 24)
4 × MM.38 Exocet (not in *Ambuscade, Antelope*)
2 × triple ASW torpedo tubes (STWS) (only in *Ambuscade, Antelope, Avenger*)

Aircraft
1 Lynx (except *Active* – 1 Wasp)

Type 22

BRILLIANT   Apr 81   Captain J. F. Coward [DSO]
BROADSWORD   May 79   Captain W. R. Canning [DSO]

Displacement (tons)
3,500   Standard
4,400   Full Load

Dimensions (feet [metres])
430×48.5 [131.2×14.8]

Machinery
as Type 42 destroyers
Olympus = 29+ knots
Tynes = 18 knots

Armament
2 × 40mm AA guns
2 × Sea Wolf systems (GWS 25)
4 × MM. 38 Exocet
2 × triple ASW torpedo tubes (STWS)

Aircraft
2 Lynx

PATROL SUBMARINE

ONYX   Nov 67   Lieutenant-Commander A. P. Johnson

Displacement (tons)
1,610   Standard
2,030   Full Load, Surface
2,400   Submerged

Dimensions (feet [metres])
295×26.5 [89.9×8.11]

Machinery
2 sets of diesel–electric motors
7,360 shp = 17.5 knots (surface)
6,000 shp = 15 knots (submerged)

Armament
6 × 21in (533mm) bow torpedo tubes

FLEET SUBMARINES

'Valiant' Class

CONQUEROR   Nov 71   Commander C. L. Wreford-
                          Brown [DSO]
COURAGEOUS   Oct 71   Commander R. T. N. Best
VALIANT   Jul 66   Commander T. M. le Mar-
                          chand [M-i-D]

Displacement (tons)
3,500   Standard
4,000   Full Load, Surface
4,900   Submerged

Dimensions (feet [metres])
285×33 (86.9×10.1)

Machinery
1 nuclear reactor + geared steam turbines
20,000 shp = approximately 25 knots submerged

Armament
6 × 21in bow torpedo tubes

'Swiftsure' Class

SPARTAN   Sep 79   Commander J. B. Taylor [M-i-D]
SPLENDID   Mar 81   Commander R. C. Lane-Nott
                        [M-i-D]

Displacement (tons)
4,200   Full Load, Surface
4,500   Submerged

Dimensions (feet [metres])
272×33 [82.9×10.1]

Machinery
As 'Valiant'-class

Armament
5×21in bow torpedo tubes

AMPHIBIOUS ASSAULT SHIPS

FEARLESS   Nov 65 Captain E. J. S. Larken [DSO]
INTREPID   Mar 67 Captain P. G. V. Dingemans [DSO]

Displacement (tons)
11,060   Standard
12,120   Full Load
16,950   Dock Flooded

Dimensions (feet [metres])
520×80 [158.5×24.4]

Machinery
2 sets geared steam turbines
22,000 shp = 21 knots

Armament
2 × 40mm AA guns
4 × Seacat systems (GWS 20)
2 × 20mm Rheinmetall RH202 AA guns (*Fearless* only in early June)

Aircraft
various combinations of helicopters up to 4 Sea King Mark 4 operated

Assault Force
1 RM Commando (650 men) + logistic elements
1 Commando Light Battery RA (6 × 105mm guns)
Vehicles
4 × Landing Craft, Utility
4 × Landing Craft, Vehicles & Personnel

Landing Craft (Utility) 1964–66

Displacement (tons)
75   Standard
176   Full Load

Dimensions (feet [metres])
84×21 (25.7×6.5)

Machinery
2 diesel engines
624 bhp = 9 knots

Armament
1 × 7.62mm GPMG

Assault Load
100 tons cargo or two tanks or 140 men

Landing Craft (Vehicles & Personnel)

Displacement (tons)
8.5 tons   Empty (fuelled)
13.5 tons   Full Load

Dimensions (feet [metres])
43×10 [13.1×3.1]

Machinery
2 diesel engines
200 bhp = 9 knots

Assault Load
5 tons of cargo or one vehicle or 35 men

OFFSHORE PATROL VESSELS

DUMBARTON CASTLE   Mar 82
Lieutenant-Commander N. D. Wood
LEEDS CASTLE   Dec 81
Lieutenant-Commander C. F. B. Hamilton

Displacement (tons)
1,250   Standard
1,450   Full Load

Dimensions (feet [metres])
266×38 (81×11.5)

Machinery
2 diesel engines
5,640 bhp = 20 knots

Armament
1 × 40mm AA gun
2 × 7.62mm GPMG

SURVEY VESSELS
(employed as Ambulance Vessels)

HECLA   Sep 65   Captain G. L. Hope
HERALD   Oct 74   Captain R. I. C. Halliday
HYDRA   May 66   Commander R. J. Campbell

Displacement (tons)
1,915   Standard   (*Herald* 2,125)
2,733   Full Load   (*Herald* 2,945)

Dimensions (feet [metres])
260×49 [79.25×14.94]

Machinery
3 diesel engines supplying 2 electric motors
2,000 hp = 14 knots

Aircraft
1 Wasp   (no ordnance carried)

ANTARCTIC PATROL VESSEL

ENDURANCE   1968   Captain N. J. Barker [CBE]
(ex-*ANITA DAN*, built 1956, purchased by Admiralty Feb 67)

Displacement (tons)
2,640   Gross Register
3,600   Full Load

Dimensions (feet [metres])
307×46 [93.58×14]

Machinery
1 diesel engine
3,220 bhp = 14.5 knots

Armament
2 × 20mm AA guns

Aircraft
2 × Wasps
(1 Wessex 5 embarked mid-June)

MINESWEEPING TRAWLERS

CORDELLA   1973   Lieutenant M. C. G. Holloway
ARNELLA   1972   Lieutenant R. J. Bishop
NORTHELLA   1973   Lieutenant J. P. S. Greenop
J. Marr & Son, Hull

Tonnage
1,238   Gross Reigster

Dimensions (feet [metres])
230×42 [70.2×12.7]

Machinery
1 diesel engine
3,250 bhp (2,780 bhp *Farnella*) = 16.5 knots

JUNELLA   1975   Lieutenant M. Rowledge
J. Marr & Son

Tonnage
1,615   Gross Register

Dimensions (feet [metres])
217×43 [66.3×13.1]

Machinery
1 diesel engine
3,180 bhp = 15.5 knots

PICT   (1973)   Lieutenant-Commander D. G. Garwood
[M-i-D]
British United Trawlers, Hull

Tonnage
1,478   Gross Register

Dimensions (feet [metres])
230×42 [70.1×12.9]

Machinery
1 diesel engine
3,246 bhp = 13.5 knots

GUNS

4.5in (114mm)
Mark 6 | twin-barrelled turret
55lb High-Explosive shell (AA/Surface)
16 rounds per minute per gun ('burst')
12 rpm/g sustained fire
17,500 yards (16km) max. range

Mark 8 | single-barrelled turret
55lb HE shell (AA/Surface)
25 rounds per minute (automatic)
22,000 yards (20km) max. range

40mm 60-cal. Bofors
Marks 7 & 9 | single-barrelled power-driven mounting
2.2lb (1kg) HE shell (AA)
100–120 rounds per minute
4,000 yards (3.6km) effective range

20mm 65-cal. Oerlikon
Mark 7 | single-barrelled, manually-operated mounting
4oz (120gm) HE/Incendiary/solid shot
470 rounds per minute ('burst')
1,200 yards (1.1km) effective range

SURFACE–AIR MISSILES

Seaslug 2 | (Hawker-Siddeley Dynamics)
Beam-riding radar guidance
Missile weight   1,980lb (900kg)
Length   19.5ft (5.9m)
Solid-fuel rocket (with rocket boosters)
Range   15 miles (27.6km)

Seacat | (Short Brothers & Harland)
Optical or radar command guidance
Missile weight   150lb (68kg)
Length   4.75ft (1.47m)
Solid-fuel rocket
Range   5,000yds (4.6km)

(variants) | GWS 20: Visually guided
GWS 22: Radar/visually guided
GWS 24: TV guided

Sea Dart | (Hawker-Siddeley Dynamics)
Semi-active radar homing
Missile weight   1,210lb (550kg)
Length   14.4ft (4.4m)
Ramjet motor (with rocket booster)
Range (achieved in action)
Low-level   11 miles (20km)
High-level   34 miles (63km)

Sea Wolf | (British Aerospace)
Radar or TV command guidance
Missile Weight   180lb (82kg)
Length   6.25ft (1.9m)
Solid-fuel rocket
Range   c. 2,700yds (2.5km)

ANTI-SHIP MISSILES

AS.12 | (Aerospatiale)
Helicopter-launched, wire-guided
Missile weight   165lb (75kg)
Length   6ft (1.87m)
Solid fuel rocket
Range (approx)   7,500yds (7km)

MM.38 Exocet | (Aerospatiale)
Ship-launched, inertial mid-course guidance, active radar terminal homing
Missile weight   1,540lb (700kg)
Length   17ft (5.2m)
Solid-fuel rocket (rocket booster)
Range   20+ miles (37+km)

Sea Skua | (British Aerospace)
Helicopter-launched, semi-active radar homing
Missile weight   460lb (210kg)
Length   9ft (2.8m)
Solid fuel rocket
Range   c. 5 miles (9km)

Appendix II

ROYAL FLEET AUXILIARIES

Note on Tonnage
The two measurements given for the RFAs and for the merchant vessels which follow are the 'Gross' and 'Deadweight' tonnages. The former is derived from the volume of enclosed revenue-earning capacity, being the cubic footage divided by 100. Deadweight tonnage is often a better indication of load-lifting capacity, being the weight of cargo, passengers, fuel, ship's stores and fuel when the ship is loaded to the maximum summer loadline.

FLEET OILERS

'O' Class

OLMEDA   Oct 65   Captain A. P. Overbury [OBE]
OLNA   Apr 66   Captain J. A. Bailey

Tonnage
    10,890 Light Displacement
    33,240 Full Load
    18,600 Gross Register
    22,350 Deadweight

Dimensions (feet [metres])
    648×84 [197.5 × 25.6]

Machinery
    2 sets geared steam turbines
    26,500 shp = 19 knots (service speed)

Armament
    Improvised – machine-guns and rifles

Aircraft
    2 Sea King Mark 2

'Tide' Class

TIDEPOOL   Jun 63   Captain J. W. Gaffrey
TIDESPRING Jan 63   Captain S. Redmond [OBE]

Tonnage
    8,530 Light Displacement
    25,930 Full Load
    14,130 Gross Register
    18,900 Deadweight

Dimensions (feet [metres])
    583×71 [177.6×21.6]

Machinery
    1 set geared steam turbines
    15,000 shp = 17 knots (service speed)

Armament
    Improvised

Aircraft
    2 Wessex Mark 5

'Rover' Class

BLUE ROVER   Jul 70   Captain J. D. Roddis

Tonnage
    4,700 Light Displacement
    11,520 Full Load
    7,510 Gross Register
    6,800 Deadweight

Dimensions (feet [metres])
    461×63 (140.5×19.2)

Machinery
    2 diesel engines (1 propeller)
    16,000 shp = 19 knots

Armament
    Improvised

Aircraft
    Helo Deck – no embarked aircraft

SUPPORT OILERS
(Modified Commercial Tankers chartered by RFA)

PEARLEAF   1960   Captain J. McCulloch

Tonnage
    12,353   Gross Register
    18,797   Deadweight

Dimensions (feet [metres])
    568×72 [173.1×22]

Machinery
    1 diesel engine
    8,000 bhp = 15 knots

PLUMLEAF   1960   Captain R. W. M. Wallace

Tonnage
    12,549   Gross Register
    19,200   Deadweight

Dimensions (feet [metres])
    560×72 [170.7×21.9]

Machinery
    1 diesel engine
    9,500 bhp = 15 knots

APPLELEAF   Nov 79   Captain G. P. A. MacDougall
BAYLEAF   Mar 82   Captain A. E. T. Hunter
BRAMBLELEAF   Mar 80   Captain M. S. J. Farley

Tonnage
    19,975   Gross Register
    33,750   Deadweight

Dimensions (feet [metres])
    560×85 [170.7×25.9]

Machinery
    2 diesel engines (1 propeller)
    14,000 bhp = 16 knots

FLEET REPLENISHMENT SHIPS

REGENT   Jun 67   Captain J. Logan
RESOURCE   May 67   Captain B. A. Seymour

Tonnage
	Light Displacement
23,000	Full Load
18,030	Gross Register
	Deadweight

Dimensions (feet [metres])
640×77 [195.1×23.5]

Machinery
1 set geared steam turbines
20,000 shp = 19 knots

Armament
Improvised

Aircraft
1 Wessex Mark 5

STROMNESS   Mar 67   Captain J. B. Dickinson [OBE]

Tonnage
9,010	Light Displacement
16,800	Full Load
12,360	Gross Register
7,780	Deadweight

Dimensions (feet [metres])
524×72 [159.8×22]

Machinery
1 diesel engine
11,520 bhp = 17 knots

Armament
Improvised

Aircraft
Helo Deck – no embarked Flight

'Fort' Class

FORT AUSTIN   May 79   Commodore S. C. Dunlop
                            CBE [DSO]

FORT GRANGE   Captain D. G. M. Averill CBE

Tonnage
15,300	Light Displacement
22,750	Full Load
16,000	Gross Register
8,300	Deadweight

Dimensions (feet [metres])
603×79 [183.8×24.1]

Machinery
1 diesel engine
23,200 bhp = 20 knots

Armament
Improvised

Aircraft
2 Sea Kings (designed)
3 helicopters of various
        types actually embarked

HELICOPTER SUPPORT SHIP

ENGADINE   Dec 67   Captain D. F. Freeman

Tonnage
3,640	Light Displacement
8,960	Full Load
6,380	Gross Register

Dimensions (feet [metres])
424×58 [129.3×17.9]

Machinery
1 diesel engine
5,500 bhp = 16 knots

Armament
Improvised – 14×7.62mm machine-guns

Aircraft
4×Wessex 5

LANDING SHIPS (LOGISTIC)

SIR BEDIVERE   May 67   Captain P. J. McCarthy [OBE]
SIR GALAHAD   Dec 66   Captain P. J. G. Roberts [DSO]
SIR GERAINT   Jul 67   Captain D. E. Lawrence [DSC]
SIR LANCELOT   Jan 64   Captain C. A. Purtcher-
                            Wydenbruck [OBE]
SIR PERCIVALE   Mar 68   Captain A. F. Pitt [DSC]
SIR TRISTRAM   Sep 67   Captain G. R. Green [DSC]

Tonnage
3,270	Light Displacement
5,674	Full Load
4,473	Gross Register
2,400	Deadweight

Sir Lancelot
3,370	Light Displacement
5,550	Full Load
4,400	Gross Register
2,180	Deadweight

Dimensions (feet [metres])
366×60 [126.5×17.7]

Machinery
2 diesel engines
9,400 bhp = 17 knots

Armament
2 × 40mm AA guns (only 1 installed in *Percivale* and
    Galahad)

Assault Load
   402 troops
   340 tons of stores/vehicles
   2 Mexeflote sections

Aircraft
   3 × Light helicopters (Gazelle or Scout)
   2 Helo decks (amidships and aft)

ROYAL MARITIME AUXILIARY SERVICE

TUG

TYPHOON   1960   Captain J. N. Morris

Displacement
   800   Standard
   1,380   Full Load

Dimensions (feet [metres])
   200 × 40 [60.5 × 12.3]

Machinery
   2 diesel engines (1 propeller)
   2,750 bhp = 17 knots

Mooring Vessel

Employed at Ascension from late May, 1982, in laying buoys and moorings.

GOOSANDER   1973   Captain A. MacGregor

Displacement
   750   Standard
   1,200   Full Load
   283   Deadweight

Dimensions (feet [metres])
   186 × 36.5 [55.4 × 12.2]

Machinery
   2 diesel engines
   550 bhp = 10 knots

Appendix III

SHIPS TAKEN UP FROM TRADE

Only those ships which sailed for the South Atlantic before 15 June, 1982, are listed; several others were taken up from trade before this date but did not deploy until the period of hostilities ended.

AUXILIARY FLEET SUPPORT

Hospital Ship

UGANDA   Passenger Liner   1952
P & O   Captain J. G. Clark
Naval Party 1830   Commander A. B. Gough RN
Senior Medical Officer   Surgeon Captain A. J. Rintoul RN

Tonnage
   16,907   Gross Register
   5,705   Deadweight

Dimensions (feet [metres])
   540×71 [164.6×21.8]

Machinery
   2 sets geared steam turbines
   12,300 shp = 17 knots

Helicopter Platform

Minesweeper Support Ship

ST HELENA   Passenger/Cargo Vessel   1963
United International Bank Ltd   Captain M. L. M. Smith
Naval Party 2100   Lieutenant-Commander D. N. Heelas RN
(Flight Commander)

Tonnage
   3,150   Gross Register
   2,264   Deadweight

Dimensions (feet [metres])
   329×48 [100.3×14.6]

Machinery
   1 diesel engine
   4,200 bhp = 15 knots

Armament
   2 × 20mm AA guns

Aircraft
   1 Wasp

Mooring Vessel

WIMPEY SEAHORSE   Offshore Support Vessel   1982
Wimpey Marine   Captain M. J. Slack [OBE]
Naval Party 2000   RMAS

Tonnage
   1,600   Gross Register
   2,085   Deadweight

Dimensions (feet [metres])
227×52 [69.3×16]

Machinery
4 diesel engines
bhp = 15.5 knots

Repair Ships

(Offshore Support Ships built in 1980)

STENA INSPECTOR
Stena (Caribbean)   Captain D. Ede
Naval Party 2010   Captain P. J. Stickland RN

STENA SEASPREAD
Stena (Atlantic)   Captain N. Williams
Naval Party 1810   Captain P. Badcock [CBE] RN

Tonnage
6,061   Gross Register
4,835   Deadweight

Dimensions (feet [metres])
367.5×90.5 [112.2×27.6]

Machinery
5 diesel engines, 4 electric motors
18,000 bhp = 16 knots

Helicopter Platform

Salvage Tugs

IRISHMAN   1978
United Towing   Captain W. Allen
Naval Party   RMAS

YORKSHIREMAN   1978
United Towing   Captain P. Rimmer
Naval Party   RMAS

Tonnage
686   Gross Register

Dimensions (feet [metres])
138×38 [42×11.6]

Machinery
2 diesel engines = 13 knots

SALVAGEMAN   1980
United Towing   Captain A. J. Stockwell
Naval Party   Captain B. W. Vere-Stevens RMAS

Tonnage
1,598   Gross Register

Dimensions (feet [metres])
227×49 [69.1×14.9]

Machinery
4 diesel engines (2 propellers) = 17.5 knots

LOGISTIC SUPPORT

Support Oilers

ANCO CHARGER   Motor Tanker   1973
P & O   Captain B. Hatton
Naval Party RFA

Tonnage
15,568   Gross Register
25,300   Deadweight

Dimensions (feet [metres])
541×82 [165.1×25]

Machinery
1 Diesel engine
12,000 bhp = 15.5 knots

BALDER LONDON   Motor Tanker   1979
Lloyds Leasing   Captain K. J. Wallace
Naval Party   RFA

Particulars as RFA *Appleleaf,* etc (chartered 1984 by RFA as *Orangeleaf)*

BRITISH AVON   1972
British Petroleum   Captain J. W. M. Guy
Naval Party   RFA

Tonnage
12,973   Gross Register
25,620   Deadweight

Dimensions (feet [metres])
562×82 [171.2×25.05]

Machinery
1 diesel engine
9,000 bhp = 15.5 knots

BRITISH DART   1972   Captain J. A. N. Taylor
Naval Party   RFA
BRITISH ESK   1973   Captain G. Barber
Naval Party   RFA
BRITISH TAMAR   1973   Captain W. H. Hare
Naval Party   RFA
BRITISH TAY   1973   Captain P. T. Morris
Naval Party   RFA
BRITISH TEST   1973   Captain T. A. Oliphant
Naval Party   RFA
BRITISH TRENT   1973   Captain P. R. Walker
Naval Party 1790   1st Officer Spencer RFA
BRITISH WYE   1974   Captain D. M. Rundell [OBE]
Naval Party   RFA

Tonnage
15,650   Gross Register
25–26,000   Deadweight

Dimensions (feet [metres])
562.5×82   [171.5×25]

Machinery
 1 diesel engine
 9,000 bhp = 15.5 knots (*Dart, Tamar*)
        14.75 knots (others)

EBURNA   1979
Shell (UK)   Captain J. C. Beaumont
Naval Party   RFA

Tonnage
 19,763   Gross Register
 31,375   Deadweight

Dimensions (feet [metres])
 558×85 [170×26]

Machinery
 1 diesel engine
 11,200 bhp = 14.5 knots

GA WALKER   Motor Tanker   1973
Canadian Pacific (Bermuda)   Captain E. C. Metham

Tonnage
 18,744   Gross Register
 30,607   Deadweight

Dimensions (feet [metres])
 560×85 [170.7×26]

Machinery
 1 diesel engine
 12,200 bhp = 15 knots

Employed on freighting in European waters until June 1982, when she sailed for the South Atlantic.

Base Storage Tankers
Ascension
ALVEGA   Motor Tanker   1977
Silver Line   Captain A. Lazenby

Tonnage
 33,329   Gross Register
 57,372   Deadweight

Dimensions (feet [metres])
 690×108 [210×32.9]

Machinery
 1 Diesel engine
 17,400 bhp = 16 knots

South Georgia (did not arrive until 18 June, 1982)
SCOTTISH EAGLE   Motor Tanker   1980
King Line   Captain A. Terras

Tonnage
 33,000   Gross Register
 56,490   Deadweight

Dimensions (feet [metres])
 689×106 [210×32.3]

Machinery
 1 diesel engine
 17,400 bhp = 16.5 knots

Fresh Water Tanker

FORT TORONTO   Motor Chemical Tanker   1981
Canadian Pacific (Bermuda)   Captain R. I. Kinnier
Naval Party   RFA

Tonnage
 19,982   Gross Register
 31,745   Deadweight

Dimensions (feet [metres])
 556×89 [169.6×27.2]

Machinery
 1 diesel engine
 11,200 bhp = 15 knots

STORES SHIPS

AVELONA STAR   General Cargo Vessel   1975
(Refrigerated Stores)
Blue Star Line   Captain H. Dyer
Naval Party   RNSTS

Tonnage
 9,784   Gross Register
 11,092   Deadweight

Dimensions (feet [metres])
 511×70.5 [155.8×21.5]

Machinery
 1 diesel engine
 17,400 bhp = 24 knots

Helicopter Platform

GEESTPORT   Refrigerated Cargo Vessel   1982
(Refrigerated Stores)
Geest Industries   Captain G. F. Foster
Naval Party   Mr R. A. Reeve RNSTS

Tonnage
 7,729   Gross Register
 9,970   Deadweight

Dimensions (feet [metres])
 522×70 [159×21.4]

Machinery
 1 diesel engine
 13,100 bhp = 19.5 knots

Helicopter Platform

LAERTES   General Cargo Vessel   1976
(Military Supplies)
China Mutual Steam Navigation   Captain H. T. Reid
Naval Party   RNSTS

LYCAON   as *Laertes*: both ships built in USSR
(Ammunition)
China Mutual   Captain H. R. Lawton
Naval Party 1900   Lieutenant-Commander D. J. Stiles RN

Tonnage
     11,804   Gross Register
     13,450   Deadweight

Dimensions (feet [metres])
     533×73 [162.5×22.3]

Machinery
     1 diesel
     10,600 bhp = 18 knots

Helicopter Platform

SAXONIA   Refrigerated Cargo Vessel   1972
(Naval Stores and Provisions)
Cunard   Captain H. Evans
Naval Party   RNSTS

Tonnage
     8,547   Gross Register
     12,182   Deadweight

Dimensions (feet [metres])
     533.5×75 [162.6×22.8]

Machinery
     1 diesel engine
     23,200 bhp = 23.5 knots

Helicopter Platform

TRANSPORTS

Aircraft Transports
(all Roll-on/Roll-off Container Ships)

ASTRONOMER   1977
Harrison Line   Captain H. S. Braden
Naval Party 2140   Lieutenant-Commander R. Gainsford RN

Tonnage
     27,870   Gross Register
     23,120   Deadweight

Dimensions (feet [metres])
     670×102 [204.2×31]

Machinery
     1 diesel engine
     26,100 bhp = 20 knots

Armament
     2×20mm AA guns

Aircraft Cargo
     6 Wessex 5
     4 Scout
     3 Chinook

ATLANTIC CAUSEWAY   1969
Cunard   Captain M. H. C. Twomey
Naval Party 1990   Commander R. P. Seymour RN

Tonnage
     14,950   Gross Register
     18,150   Deadweight

Dimensions (feet [metres])
     696×92 [212.1×28.1]

Machinery
     2 sets of geared steam turbines
     38,500 shp = 23 knots

Aircraft Cargo
     8 Sea King 2
     20 Wessex 5

ATLANTIC CONVEYOR   1970
Cunard   Captain I. North [DSC – posthumous]
Naval Party 1840   Captain M. G. Layard [CBE] RN

Particulars as *Atlantic Causeway*

Aircraft Cargo
     8 Sea Harrier
     8 Wessex 5
     6 Harrier GR3
     5 Chinook

CONTENDER BEZANT   1981
(Harland & Wolff)   Captain A. Mackinnon
Naval Party 2050   Lieutenant-Commander D. H. N. Yates
RN

Tonnage
     11,445   Gross Register
     17,993   Deadweight

Dimensions (feet [metres])
     568×100.5 [173×30.6]

Machinery
     2 diesel engines
     23,400 bhp = 19 knots

Aircraft Cargo
     1 Sea King 5
     2 Wasp
     4 Harrier GR3
     4 Chinook
     2 Gazelle

DESPATCH VESSELS
(see also HMS *Leeds Castle* and *Dumbarton Castle*)

BRITISH ENTERPRISE III   1965
Mother Ship for Submersibles
British Underwater Engineering   Captain D. Grant
Naval Party 2090   Lieutenant-Commander B. E. M. Reynell
RN

Tonnage
    1,595   Gross Register
    1,197   Deadweight

Dimensions (feet [metres])
    249×42 [75.9×12.9]

Machinery
    1 diesel engine
    2,140 bhp = 14 knots

Helicopter Platform

CS IRIS   Cable Vessel   1975
British Telecom   Captain G. Fulton [OBE]
Naval Party 1870   Lieutenant-Commander J. Bithell RN

Tonnage
    3,874   Gross Register
    2,150   Deadweight

Dimensions (feet [metres])
    319×49 [97.3×15]

Machinery
    2 diesel engines
    5,200 bhp = 15 knots

Helicopter Platform

PERSONNEL AND VEHICLE TRANSPORTS

BALTIC FERRY   Roll-on/Roll-off Ferry   1978
Stena Cargo Line   Captain E. Harrison
Naval Party 1960   Lieutenant-Commander G. B. Webb RN

Tonnage
    6,455   Gross Register
    8,704   Deadweight

Dimensions (feet [metres])
    495×71 [151×21.7]

Machinery
    2 diesel engines
    15,600 bhp = 17 knots

Aircraft Cargo (UK to San Carlos)
    3 × Scout (AAC)

CANBERRA   Passenger Liner   1961
P & O   Captain W. Scott-Masson [CBE]
Naval Party 1710   Captain C. P. O. Burne [CBE] RN

Tonnage
    44,807   Gross Register
    9,910   Deadweight

Dimensions (feet [metres])
    818.5×102.5 [249.5×31.3]

Machinery
    2 sets geared steam turbines
    88,200 shp = 27.5 knots

Aircraft
    1 Sea King 4   (Ascension–San Carlos)
    2 Sea King 2   (South Georgia–San Carlos)

ELK   Roll-on/Roll-off Cargo Vessel   1977
P & O   Captain J. P. Morton [CBE]
Naval party 2050   Commander A. S. Ritchie [OBE] RN

Tonnage
    5,463   Gross Register
    8,652   Deadweight

Dimensions (feet [metres])
    495×71 [151×21.3]

Machinery
    2 diesel engines
    15,600 bhp = 18.5 knots

Armament
    2 × 40mm AA guns

Aircraft Cargo (Ascension to TEZ)
    3 Sea King 4
    3 Scout (AAC)

EUROPIC FERRY   Roll-on/Roll-off Ferry   1975
Atlantic Steam Navigation   Captain C. J. C. Clark [OBE]
Naval Party 1720   Commander A. B. Gough RN

Tonnage
    4,190   Gross Register
    2,784   Deadweight

Dimensions (feet [metres])
    451×70 [137.6×21]

Machinery
    2 diesel engines
    13,360 bhp = 19.25 knots

Aircraft Cargo (UK–San Carlos)
    3 Scout (AAC)   (transferred to *Elk* for Ascension-TEZ 'leg')

NORDIC FERRY   Roll-on/Roll-off Ferry   1978
Stena Lines   Captain R. Jenkins
Naval Party 1950   Lieutenant Commander
M. St. J. D. A. Thorburn RN

Particulars as *Baltic Ferry*

Aircraft Cargo (UK–San Carlos)
    6 Gazelle (AAC)

NORLAND   Roll-on/Roll-off Ferry   1974
P & O   Captain M. Ellerby [CBE]
Naval Party 1850   Commander C. J. Esplin-Jones [OBE] RN

Tonnage
    12,998   Gross Register
    4,036   Deadweight

Dimensions (feet [metres])
    502×83 [153×25.2]

Machinery
    2 diesel engines
    18,000 bhp = 19 knots

Aircraft
    1 Sea King 4 (Ascension–San Carlos)
    2 Sea King 4 (21–23 May)

QUEEN ELIZABETH II   Passenger Liner   1969
Cunard   Captain P. Jackson
Naval Party 1980   Captain N. C. H. James RN

Tonnage
    67,140   Gross Register
    15,976   Deadweight

Dimensions (feet [metres])
    963×105 [293.5×32.1]

Machinery
    4 sets geared steam turbines
    110,000 shp = 28.5 knots

Aircraft
    2 Sea King 2 (UK–South Georgia)

ST EDMUND   Roll-on/Roll-off Ferry   1974
Passtruck Shipping   Captain M. J. Stockman
Naval Party 2060   Lieutenant-Commander A. M. Scott RN

Tonnage
    8,987   Gross Register
    1,830   Deadweight

Dimensions (feet [metres])
    427×74 [130×22.6]

Machinery
    2 sets of diesel engines
    20,400 bhp = 21 knots

Helicopter Platform

Purchased by UK Ministry of Defence in 1983 and renamed
Keren; employed as Ascension–Falklands personnel ferry
until completion of Mount Pleasant air terminal in 1985.

TOR CALEDONIA   Roll-on/Roll-off Ferry   1977
Whitwill, Cole & Co   Captain A. Scott
Naval Party 2020   Lieutenant-Commander J. G. Devine RN

Tonnage
    5,056   Gross Register
    9,882   Deadweight

Dimensions (feet [metres])
    534×69 [162.8×21]

Machinery
    2 diesel engines
    12,000 bhp = 18.5 knots

Helicopter Platform

FALKLAND ISLANDS MERCHANT VESSELS
(Seized by Argentine Forces at the time of the invasion)

FORREST   Motor Coaster   1967
Government of the Falkland Islands

Tonnage
    144   Gross Register
    140   Deadweight

Dimensions (feet [metres])
    86×23 [26.2×7]

Machinery
    1 diesel engine
    320 bhp = 10 knots (approximately)

MONSUNNEN   Motor Coaster   1957
Falkland Islands Company

Tonnage
    230   Gross Register
    240   Deadweight

Dimensions (feet [metres])
    139×21 [42.3×6.5]

Machinery
    1 diesel engine
    240 bhp = 8.5 knots

Appendix IV

ARGENTINE WARSHIPS & AUXILIARIES

AIRCRAFT CARRIER

VEINTECINCO (25) DE MAYO   1969
RN *Venerable* 1945
R Neth. N. *Karel Doorman* 1948

Displacement (tons)
   15,892   Standard
   19,896   Full Load

Dimensions (feet [metres])
   Hull   698×80 [212.7×24.5]
   Flight Deck   544×133 [165.8×40.7]

Machinery
   2 sets of geared steam turbines
   40,000 shp = 24.5 knots (designed)
                 less than 20 knots in practice

Armament
   9 × 40mm AA guns (70-cal)

Aircraft
   30 April 1982   8 A-4B Skyhawk
                       4 S-2E Tracker
                       3 SH-3D Sea King

CRUISER

GENERAL BELGRANO   1951; USN *Phoenix* 1938

Displacement (tons)
   10,800   Standard
   13,479   Full Load

Dimensions (feet [metres])
   608×61.5   [185.3×18.8]

Machinery
   4 sets geared steam turbine
   100,000 shp = approximately 25 knots

Armament
   15 × 6in (152mm) guns
   8 × 5in (127mm) dual-purpose guns
   20 × 40mm AA guns (60-cal)
   2 × 20mm AA guns
   2 × Seacat systems (GWS 22-equivalent)

Aircraft
   1 × Alouette III helicopter

Sister-ship *Nueve de Julio* (ex-USS *Boise* – 1938) was laid up,
non-operational)

DESTROYERS

Type 42

HERCULES   May 76
SANTISSIMA TRINIDAD   Jul 81
Details as Royal Navy T42s, except that they carried 4 MM.38
Exocet missiles without sacrificing any other weapons.

'Gearing' Class

COMODORO PY   1973; USN *Perkins* 1945

Displacement (tons)
   2,400   Standard
   3,600   Full Load

Dimensions (feet [metres])
   391×41   [119.2×12.5]

Machinery
   2 sets geared steam turbines
   60,000 shp = 36 knots (designed – less in 1982)

Armament
   4 × 5in dual-purpose guns
   4 × MM.38 Exocet
   2 × three-barrelled ASW torpedo tubes
   2 × 'Hedgehog' ASW spigot mortars

Aircraft
   provision for 1 helicopter, none carried

'Allen M Sumner' Class

HIPOLITO BOUCHARD   1972; USN *Borie* 1944
PIEDRA BUENA   1976; USN *Collett* 1944
SEGUI   1972; USN *Hank* 1944

Displacement (tons)
   2,200   Standard
   3,300   Full Load

Dimensions (feet [metres])
   376.5×41   [114.8×12.5]

Machinery
   As *Comodoro Py*

Armament
   As *Comodoro Py*

Aircraft
   As *Comodoro Py*, except *Segui* – nil

(All, plus *Comodoro Py* disposed of 1983–85)

SUBMARINES

'Balao' Class

SANTA FE   1971; USN *Catfish* 1944

Displacement (tons)
   1,517   Standard
   1,870   Full Load Surfaced
   2,340   Submerged

Dimensions (feet [metres])
   307×27.5 [93.6×8.4]

Machinery
   3 diesel engines, 2 electric motors
   4,875 bhp = 18 knots (surface)
   5,400 bhp = 14 knots (submerged)

Armament
   6 × 21in (533mm) torpedo tubes forward
   4 × 21in torpedo tubes aft

Sister-ship *Santiago del Estero* (ex-USS *Chivo* – 1945) was laid up, non-operational.

'Type 209' Class

SALTA   May 74
SAN LUIS   May 74

Displacement (tons)
   980   Standard
   1,105   Full Load Surfaced
   1,230   Submerged

Dimensions (feet [metres])
   180×21.6 [55×6.6]

Machinery
   4 diesel engines, 1 electric motor
   3,600 bhp = 12 knots (snorting)
              = 21 knots (5-minute submerged 'dash')

Armament
   8 × 21in torpedo tubes forward

CORVETTES

'A.69' Class

DRUMMOND   Oct 78
GRANVILLE   Jun 81
GUERRICO   Oct 78

Displacement (tons)
   1,170   Standard
   1,320   Full Load

Dimensions (feet [metres])
   262.5×34 [80×10.3]

Machinery
   2 diesel engines
   11,000 bhp = 24 knots

Armament
   1 × 3.9in (100mm) dual-purpose gun
   1 × 40mm AA gun (70-cal)
   2 × 20mm AA guns
   4 × MM.38 Exocet (landed in May 1982)
   2 × three-barrelled ASW torpedo tubes

PATROL CRAFT

'Sotoyomo' Class (ex-US Navy Ocean Tugs)

ALFEREZ SOBRAL   1972; USN *Catawba* 1945
COMODORO SOMERELLA   1972; USN *Salish* 1945

Displacement (tons)
   689   Standard
   800   Full Load

Dimensions (feet [metres])
   143×34 [43.6×10.4]

Machinery
   1 set diesel-electric motors
   1,800 bhp = 12 knots

Armament
   2 × 20mm AA guns

Sobral disposed of in 1984, *Somerella* in 1985

'LLE' Class (*Prefectura Naval* [Coast Guard])

ISLAS MALVINAS   1981
MADRYN   1981
RIO IGUAZU   1979

Displacement (tons)
   81   Full Load

Dimensions (feet [metres])
   91 × 17 [27.7×5.3]

Machinery
   2 diesel engines
   2,100 bhp = 22 knots

Armament
   1 × 20mm AA gun
   2 × 7.62mm machine-guns

LANDING SHIP (TANK)

CABO SAN ANTONIO   Nov 78

Displacement (tons)
   4,300   Standard
   8,000   Full Load

Dimensions (feet [metres])
   443×62 [135×18.8]

Machinery
   6 diesel engines (2 propellers)
   13,700 bhp = 16 knots

Armament
   12 × 40mm AA guns (60-cal)
   2 × 20mm AA guns

Assault Cargo
   4 LCVP
   700 men
   23 tanks or LVTs
   460 tons of military stores

Helicopter Platform

OILER

PUNTA MEDANOS   Oct 50

Tonnage
        16,331   Full Load Displacement
        8,250   Deadweight

Dimensions (feet [metres])
        502×62 [153×18.9]

Machinery
        2 sets geared steam turbines
        9,500 shp = 18 knots

NAVAL TRANSPORTS

BAHIA BUEN SUCESO   Jun 50

Displacement (tons)
        3,100   Standard
        5,255   Full Load

Dimensions (feet [metres])
        335×47 [95.1×14.3]

Machinery
        2 diesel engines
        3,750 bhp = 15 knots

BAHIA PARAISO   Dec 81

Displacement (tons)
        5,270   Gross Register
        9,200   Deadweight

Dimensions (feet [metres])
        429×64 [130.7×19.5]

Machinery
        2 diesel engines
        15,000 bhp = 18 knots

Armament
        nil

Aircraft
        2 helicopters (1 Puma, 1 Alouette in April, 1982)

Up to 250 troops can be carried.

ALMIRANTE IRIZAR   Ice Breaker   Dec 78

Displacement (tons)
        11,811   Standard
        14,900   Full Load

Dimensions (feet [metres])
        391×82 [119.3×25]

Machinery
        4 diesel engines, 2 electric motors
        16,200 bhp = 16.5 knots

Armament
        2 × 40mm AA guns

Aircraft
        2 helicopters (1 Puma in April 1982)

ISLA DE LOS ESTADOS   Motor Coaster   1975

Tonnage
        834   Gross Register
        1,761   Deadweight

Dimensions (feet [metres])
        267×44 [81.3×13.4]

Machinery
        1 diesel engine
        2,940 bhp = 14 knots

Armament
        not known

MERCHANT TRANSPORTS

FORMOSA   General Cargo Vessel   1978
Empresa Lineas Maritimas Argentinas (ELMA)

Tonnage
        12,762   Gross Register
        20,704   Deadweight

Dimensions (feet [metres])
        522×75 [159×22.8]

Machinery
        1 diesel engine
        9,900 bhp = 15.5 knots

RIO CARCARANA   General Cargo Vessel   1962
ELMA

Tonnage
        8,482   Gross Register
        10,430   Deadweight

Dimensions (feet [metres])
        516×67 [157.4×20.4]

Machinery
        1 diesel engine
        10,300 bhp = 16 knots (approximately)

YEHUIN   Offshore Support Vessel   1967
Geomatter

Tonnage
        495   Gross Register
        756   Deadweight

Dimensions (feet [metres])
        175.5×37 [53.5×11.3]

Machinery
        2 diesel engines
        1,900 bhp = 12.5 knots

'SPY TRAWLER'

NARWAL   Freezer Trawler   1962
Compania Sudamerica de Pesca y Exportacion SA

Tonnage
    1,398   Gross Register
    1,199   Deadweight

Dimensions (feet [metres])
    231×38 [70.5×11.6]

Machinery
    1 diesel engine
    2,330 bhp = 14 knots (approximately)

Two other fishing vessels were identified as also being
engaged in reconnaissance operations but neither appears to
have been encountered by British forces.

Equivalent Ranks

Argentine		British	
Navy	**Air Force**	**Navy**	**Air Force**
(Note – only the more junior ranks relevant to the text are given)			
Capitan de Fragata	Vice-Comodoro	Commander	Wing Commander
Capitan de Corbeta	Mayor	Lieutenant-Commander	Squadron Leader
Teniente de Navio	Capitan	Lieutenant	Flight Lieutenant
–	Primer Teniente	–	–
Teniente de Fragata	Teniente	Sub-Lieutenant	Flying Officer
Teniente de Corbeta	Alferez	Acting Sub-Lieutenant	Pilot Officer

Sources

Many individuals have allowed me to use their private notes, diaries and correspondence written during the campaign; others have spent hours in conversation; inevitably, much of a personal nature – opinions and feelings – emerged but could not be disclosed, even though this would have given depth to an often dry narrative. A number of contributors wished to remain anonymous and I have therefore decided that none should be named, trusting that any disappointment that this may cause will be eased by the rather fuller accounts of their ships' and squadrons' activities which their assistance made possible.

Published Sources

Many published sources were consulted in the preparation of the book and are acknowledged in footnotes. Those which follow were considered to be the most accurate and informed.

Periodicals

Aerospacio   bi-monthly (Buenos Aires)
Air International   monthly (London)
Air Pictorial   monthly (Windsor)
Air Sonic   monthly (Madrid)
Armas y Geostrategia   quarterly (Buenos Aires)
Defence   monthly (London)
Globe and Laurel   the quarterly Journal of the Royal Marines.
International Defence Review   quarterly (Geneva)
Royal United Services Institution Journal   quarterly (London)
US Naval Institute Proceedings   monthly (Annapolis)

Books

Buxton, C. & Price A., *Survival South Atlantic* (Granada, London, 1983)
Ethell, J. & Price, A. *Air War South Atlantic* (Sidgwick & Jackson, London, 1983)
Frost, J., *2 Para at War* (Buchan & Enright, London, 1983)
Kon, D., *Los Chicos de la Guerra* (New English Library, London, 1983)
Lockett, A. (Ed.), *HMS Endurance 1981–82 Deployment* (Lockett, Gosport, 1984)
Moro, R. O., *La Guerra Inaudita* (Editorial Pleamar, Buenos Aires, 1986)
Muxworth, J. L., *CANBERRA – the Great White Whale goes to War* (P&O, London, 1982)
Planchar, R., *La Guerre de Bout du Monde – Iles Falkland 1982* (Denel, Paris, 1985)
Romero Briasco, J. & Mafe Huertas, S., *Falklands, Witness of Battles* (Domenech, Valencia, 1985)
Southby-Tailyour, E., *Falkland Islands Shores* (Conway Maritime Press, Greenwich, 1985)
Thompson, J. H. A., *No Picnic – 3 Commando Brigade in the South Atlantic 1982* (Leo Cooper, London, 1985)
Villar, R., *Merchant Ships at War – the Falklands Experience* (Conway Maritime Press, 1984)
Villarino, E., *Exocet* (Siete Dias, Buenos Aires, 1983)

British Government Publications

The Falklands Campaign – the Lessons: Secretary of State for Defence, 1982 (Cd. 8753)
Falklands Review: Franks Committee Report, 1983 (Cd. 8787) 1
Admiral Sir John Fieldhouse's Despatch: Supplement to the *London Gazette*, 13 December, 1982

Index

Page numbers in italic refer to illustrations

UNITS